9/04

DEAR JOSÉ (IF I MAY):

I HOPE THAT THIS COPY
WILL AT LEAST BEGIN TO MAKE
UP FOR THE FACT THAT I HAVE
MANAGED TO STAY OUT OF TOUCH
SINCE THE YEAR 2000 (OR SO).

APOLOGIES, AND BEST
WISHES,

DAVID GRAIZBORD

D1711612

Souls in Dispute

JEWISH CULTURE AND CONTEXTS

Published in association with the Center for Advanced Judaic Studies of the
University of Pennsylvania

David B. Ruderman, Series Editor

Advisory Board
Richard I. Cohen
Moshe Idel
Deborah Dash Moore
Ada Rapoport-Albert
David Stern

A complete list of books in the series is available from the publisher.

Souls in Dispute

Converso Identities in Iberia and the
Jewish Diaspora, 1580–1700

David L. Graizbord

PENN

University of Pennsylvania Press
Philadelphia

Publication of this volume was assisted by a grant from the Program for Cultural Cooperation between Spain's Ministry of Education, Culture and Sports and United States Universities.

Copyright © 2004 University of Pennsylvania Press
All rights reserved
Printed in the United States of America on acid-free paper

10   9   8   7   6   5   4   3   2   1

Published by
University of Pennsylvania Press
Philadelphia, Pennsylvania 19104-4011

Library of Congress Cataloging-in-Publication Data
Graizbord, David L.
    Souls in dispute : converso identities in Iberia and the Jewish diaspora, 1580–1700 / David L. Graizbord.
        p. cm.—(Jewish culture and contexts)
    Includes bibliographical references (p.) and index.
    ISBN 0-8122-3749-8 (cloth : alk. paper)
    1. Marranos—Spain. 2. Jews—Spain—History—17th century. 3. Jews—Spain—History—18th century. 4. Jews—Spain—Identity. 5. Spain—Ethnic relations. 6. Social integration—Spain—History—17th century. 7. Social integration—Spain—History—18th century. I. Title. II. Series.

DS135.S7G73 2003
946'.004924—dc22

                                                                    2003065755

Contents

1   Introduction   1

2   Conversos: The Iberian Context   19

3   Exile and Return   64

4   Interrogation, Confession, and Reversion to Christianity   105

5   The Conversion and Reconversion of
     Antonio Rodríguez de Amézquita   143

6   Conclusion: On the Historical Significance of
     Renegades' Self-Subjugation   171

     Appendix   179

     Notes   191

     Glossary   235

     Selected Bibliography   237

     Index   251

     Acknowledgments   263

Chapter 1
Introduction

On August 18, 1661, Cristobal Méndez Silveira, a thirty-eight-year-old merchant, deposed in Madrid before three officers of the Spanish Inquisition. He revealed that he was a Judeoconverso, or "New Christian"—namely a baptized Christian of Jewish ancestry—and a native of Seville who had been fully educated in the Roman Catholic faith. On the eve of his deposition, Méndez had been living and trading in Madrid for nearly a year. During the prior eleven years, however, he had resided in the Netherlands as a member of Amsterdam's *Jewish* community. Throughout that time, he had traveled extensively in the western Jewish Diaspora, socializing and worshipping among Jews in such places as Venice, Livorno, Bourdeaux, and Bayonne. He had since returned to Spain, where Judaism had been banned for centuries. In the remainder of his deposition, Méndez provided damning information regarding 105 of his fellow conversos, several of whom were prosecuted as a result of his testimony. By the end of his depositions, Méndez had renounced Judaism and had once again embraced Catholicism.[1]

Méndez was only one of hundreds of Judeoconversos who returned to Iberian territory throughout the 1600s despite the fact that they had flagrantly abandoned Christianity and were therefore in danger of being persecuted by Inquisitorial authorities in Spain and Portugal. This book is an attempt to explain the behavior of these returnees and explore their mentality on historical grounds. To begin that exploration, it is necessary to become acquainted with the cultural and historical situation of early modern Judeoconversos.

Central Dilemmas of Converso Existence

Iberian history and Jewish history intersect at various points. One fateful intersection occurs in the Early Modern Period,[2] when thousands of Judeoconversos[3]—the Christian descendants of Jews who had converted to Christianity during the fourteenth and fifteenth centuries—negotiated their individual and social identities amid fierce debates concerning the true and proper loyalties of New Christians. Among so-called Old Christians in Spain and Portugal, opinions varied as to the moral, religious, and social character of Judeoconversos, yet suspicions that New Christians were in fact nefarious Judaizers (secret Jews) were extremely widespread. Fear and antipathy toward conversos informed Iberian concepts of social danger from the fifteenth through the eighteenth centuries. Expressed in the allied (though not always concordant) ideologies of honor, purity of blood (*pureza de sangre*), and purity of faith (*pureza de fe*), a virulent phobia motivated attempts to stigmatize and isolate conversos throughout the very period during which many of the latter struggled to blend into the Ibero-Christian mainstream.

For many Judeoconversos who escaped to the Sephardi Diaspora, the question of their legitimate place in the world was ostensibly solved once they opted to become absorbed into Jewish milieux. Yet even when they chose to adopt the faith of their ancestors, Sephardim of converso origin developed unique responses to fellow Jews and to normative Judaism that revealed the difficulty of harmonizing a newfound Judaic heritage with an intimate knowledge of and affinity toward Iberian culture. Compounding that difficulty was the lingering question: Were Judeoconversos who stayed in the Iberian Peninsula as practicing Christians, or returned to it as penitent Christians, really Jewish? Clear halakhic dicta notwithstanding, this conundrum was never solved definitively within Sephardi *kehillot*. For instance, it does not appear that rabbinical authorities in the Sephardi strongholds of the Netherlands, Italy, and Northern Africa applied the talmudic principle "although he sins, he is a Jew" with systematic consistency.[4] It is also doubtful that any consensus on this question developed at the unofficial level of popular Jewish perception, where a myriad of opinions included the diverse views of the Iberian refugees themselves. In the end, the problematic status of Judeoconversos did not disappear until the latter half of the nineteenth century. By that period, intermarriage and acculturation had rendered conversos largely (if not totally) indistinct from the Christian and Sephardi communities that surrounded them.

The central predicament of early modern Judeoconversos both inside and outside the Iberian Peninsula lay in the fact that they inhabited a cultural threshold. This threshold was at once a boundary and a crossroads between the Christian and Jewish worlds. Collectively, New Christians were neither full insiders nor full outsiders of either world, but were simultaneously part of both. Because normative views of religion construed the boundaries of the Christian and Jewish camps as rigid and impermeable, the very existence of

Judeoconversos confounded traditional meanings of religious community and religious identity. Notably, the anomalous condition of Judeoconversos—I will call it cultural liminality—was socially and historically determined; it was neither inherent in physical descent from Jews, nor always dependent on the conversos' religious beliefs and intentions.

As titular Christians, conversos partook of an Ibero-Christian culture that many of them internalized as their own. One may say that conversos actually formed an integral part of Spanish and Portuguese life. In the main, however, Old Christians denied conversos complete, unqualified membership in Ibero-Christian society. The imaginary association of New Christians with Jews and Judaism tainted even the most Hispanicized and Christianized of Judeoconversos. It also sustained such peculiar mechanisms of persecution and social exclusion as the Holy Office and the statutes of purity of blood. These mechanisms institutionalized and magnified the attritional force of popular prejudice, itself rooted in Judeophobia. As a result, conversos—believing Christians, ambivalent ones, and crypto-Jews alike—had little choice but to remain outside the social mainstream, even when they participated fully in many of its facets.[5]

If Old Christian society was largely unwilling to accept conversos as "true" Christians, diasporic *kehillot* welcomed converso refugees only if the latter submitted to a public self-transformation. This entailed a process of reeducation, sometimes accompanied by penitential purification.[6] To be sure, not all of the returnees were prepared to adapt to Jewish life even after experiencing their formal incorporation into Judaism. The same was true of several of the immigrants' immediate descendants. Although a majority of the escapees underwent a successful cultural transition, an important minority abandoned mainstream, rabbinic Judaism for a variety of mystical-messianic, rationalistic, or wholly equivocal alternatives. Some refugees remained within the Christian fold throughout their exile. Others, as we shall see in the chapters that follow, returned to Iberia, where they became penitent Catholics.

The options of heterodoxy and full-fledged dissidence proved similarly appealing to Judeoconversos who lingered in the Iberian Peninsula. While most conversos chose to blend into Christendom as quietly as possible, several notorious ones were influenced by messianic, illuminist, and Erasmian currents.[7] Still others actualized their sense of difference through a gamut of secret, eclectic practices with real or imagined origins in Jewish ideas, rituals, and folklore.[8]

It is important to note, however, that the religious status of Judeoconversos was not the only factor that shaped their cultural profile. A key determinant of the social position of the *cristianos nuevos* (*cristãos-novos* in Portuguese) was political and economic in nature. Like their forbears in the Iberian *juderías* conversos constituted a predominantly urban minority. Its members were chiefly engaged in commercial, professional, scholarly, artisanal, and other nonagricultural occupations.[9] From the 1580's through the second half of the seventeenth century, an influential stratum of Judeoconversos and Sephardi grandees built and operated vast mercantile networks from entrepots such as Amsterdam, Istanbul, Curaçao, and Venice.[10] When it did not derive from connections to these networks, the power of converso notables in Spain and Portugal was usually the product of alliances with Old Christian elites. Such alliances often entailed service to the crown, the church, and the Old Christian nobility, and were frequently built through the painstaking circumvention of social barriers. For example, several Judeoconversos improved their lot by securing bogus certificates of *pureza*, by marrying their children into the Old Christian nobility, or simply by purchasing forbidden offices and titles from corrupt officials.[11] Yet, the basic social and political situation of these ambitious individuals remained fundamentally akin to that of the vast majority of conversos in the Iberian Peninsula and elsewhere: Usually the social climbers were not *labradores* (unskilled manual laborers). Neither did they belong to the traditional ruling classes, especially the hereditary nobility. Indeed, Judeoconversos comprised a middle class in the simplest and most immediate sense of the term. For rich and poor conversos alike (particularly for those in the peninsula) economic and political "in-between-ness" went hand in hand with religious liminality.

New Christians reacted to the condition of liminality in a variety of ways. I have already alluded to some of the least studied of converso behaviors. Again, these included maintaining a heartfelt Christian identity in exile, and returning to the Iberian Peninsula—and to Catholicism—after professing Judaism in the Diaspora. A third reaction, perhaps the most sinister, was the choice to cooperate willfully with the Inquisition. Conversos who pursued the latter strategy usually served as semiprofessional informers after undertaking formal penance for their own actual or alleged Judaizing.

The phenomena of return to Iberia, reversion to Catholicism, and the corollary incidence of voluntary denunciation have remained largely unexplored; this despite the fact that even cursory surveys of inquisitorial history reveal the existence of what one may call religious "wafflers," habitual returnees, spontaneous self-incriminators, and enthusiastic informers of converso origin. The relative paucity of studies on such ostensibly unconventional types is doubly puzzling given the enormous energies that scholars have expended in reconstructing the institutional history of the Spanish and Portuguese Inquisitions.

To be sure, experts on Iberian Jewry have devoted articles, book chapters, and footnotes to the problem of converso "deviants" or "renegades." A number of scholars have written about the most notorious of *medieval* Jewish apostates (as distinct from informers), including anti-Jewish polemicists such as Abner of Burgos, Gerónimo de Santa Fe, and the ultra-Judeophobe Alonso de Espina, whose status as a converso remains uncertain. A few scholars have contributed articles on the incidence of slander among Spanish Jews of the thirteenth and fourteenth centuries.[12] For their part, students of early modern Europe have been diligent in scrutinizing the personalities and intellectual careers of Uriel da Costa, Baruch (or Bento or Benedict) Spinoza, and a handful of other arch-dissidents of converso origin. However, to my knowledge no investigator has ever placed the phenomena of return to the Iberian Peninsula, reversion to Christianity, and voluntary collaboration with the Inquisition at the center of an extensive analytical venture.[13] Aside from Yosef Kaplan, no scholar has attempted to explain these phenomena or sufficiently analyzed the fact that that their "peaks" occurred in the late sixteenth and seventeenth centuries. That period saw the intensification of inquisitorial persecution in Portugal, the flight of thousands of Portuguese New Christians into Spain, the concomitant resurgence of the Spanish Holy Office, the massive emigration of Judeoconversos from the Iberian Peninsula, and finally, the integration of hundreds if not thousands of converso refugees into the Jewish Diaspora.

My own interest in the phenomena abbreviated by the labels "dissident" and "renegade" behavior centers on five clusters of questions that existing scholarship has tended to underanalyze or neglect altogether.

First and foremost, why did converso "renegades" exist at all? Why did many conversos choose to return to Iberia? Why did many of them return to Christianity? Why did some of the returnees opt to denounce themselves and their fellows without any apparent or direct pressure from the Inquisition?[14]

Second, were the returnees and spontaneous informers simply idiosyncratic individuals prone to "strange" behavior? Were they mere opportunists? Were they following their religious conscience(s)?

Third, were there specific historical forces or circumstances to which the dissidents' behavior served as a response or strategy of adaptation? If so, what were these factors?

Fourth, how typical or atypical were the so-called renegades?

Fifth, and most importantly, what did it mean to the renegades to be

Jewish? What did it mean to them to be Christian? What did it mean to them to shift from one identity to the other?

The present study focuses on otherwise ordinary converso "renegades" of the late sixteenth and seventeenth centuries in order to answer these questions. Here I deal primarily with a group of highly mobile Judeoconversos of Portuguese origin who traveled throughout the Iberian Peninsula but resided at least temporarily within the poorer corners of the Sephardi Diaspora, chiefly in southwestern France, as well as within the jurisdiction of the Toledan tribunal of the Spanish Inquisition. (The judicial district of Toledo encompassed all of New Castile, including the towns of Alcalá, Guadalajara, Talavera, Guadalupe, Ciudad Real, Toledo, and the most populous of all Spanish cities, Madrid.) A plurality of the individuals I have studied were small- to mid-scale merchants who at one time or another had resided in southwestern France but were subsequently captured by the Inquisition while trading in Madrid, either as temporary or permanent residents of the city.

By focusing on this population I test a hypothesis that seemingly aberrant converso behaviors, chief among them returning to Iberia and reconverting to Catholicism, were not simple matters of opportunism, idiosyncratic preference, or fear of persecution, but were nonexceptional and quite logical strategies by which conversos adapted to an especially difficult historical environment. My conclusion is that, given that environment, the options of return to Iberia, reversion to Christianity, and voluntary collaboration with the Inquisition were earnest and practical choices, ones as "normal" as the option of "returning" to the ancestral culture via crypto-Judaism or by unequivocal resettlement in the Sephardi Diaspora.

Underpinning this interpretation is a recognition that the social and historical context of identity construction was pivotal in the development of renegade behaviors. One of my chief findings in this regard is that cultural border crossers were invariably confronted with the collective expectations—indeed, the vehement demands—of their host communities. A central challenge of this study, then, has been to show how renegades coped with those demands, and ultimately, how and why these individuals accommodated and at the same time failed to accommodate to the self-image, values, and social conventions of their neighbors.

My exposition follows the following outline. In the second chapter I depict the general historical conditions within which the processes of successful and unsuccessful accommodation took place. Specifically, I portray Spain's era of economic and political crisis—the end of the Habsburgian

Golden Age. Here I emphasize the profound contradiction that the era engendered between conversos' deep involvement in the economic life of the country on one hand, and the profound fear and loathing with which Old Christians regarded New Christians—especially Portuguese conversos and their descendants—on the other. Chapter 3 reconstructs the phenomenon of return within its immediate social and economic contexts. Here I explain the manner in which Jewish religious authorities approached return as a kind of taboo. Through an analysis of selected inquisitorial dossiers, I also present a simple typology of returnees and explain these renegades' behavior and dilemmas vis-à-vis the normative Judaism to which they and other immigrant conversos were exposed in the Sephardi Diaspora. Chapter 4 explicates the premises that guided the interrogation of inquisitorial suspects, and proceeds to construct a collective profile of renegades on the basis of inquisitorial *procesos*. Finally, Chapter 5 charts the religious life of a typical returnee to the point of his reconversion to Christianity. I use that case to explain two aspects. First, I argue that conformity promised renegades an end to social isolation, and hence to an apprehension of solitude and drift; second, I propose that conformity served to ameliorate the vicissitudes that accompanied the struggle for material and psychic security by rendering that struggle into a meaningful narrative. In conclusion, I explain that while many conversos understood their yearning for stability in the pious idiom of their time as a quest for spiritual redemption, and therefore as a purely religious imperative, the yearning was ultimately concerned with life on Earth, with emotional and physical well-being in the here and now, and not with the abstract validity of any theological formula or system of beliefs. Even if the longing for security was self-consciously religious, I continue, its object was the sense of stability afforded by *conformity* indeed by absolute faith in a body of traditional dogmas, rituals, customs, and more importantly, social relations. The goal was not philosophical or mystical truth *as such*.[15] While I acknowledge that at least some converso renegades experienced no conflict in shifting back and forth from one religion to another, I contend that a cause of such shifting, paradoxically enough, was the equivocators' yearning for stability. Renegades found that stability by temporarily embracing and conforming to one community of faith, and then another, as circumstances demanded it. Chapter 6 summarizes these findings and suggests some of their implications for the interpretation of early modern converso and Jewish history.

Historiography, Sources, and Methods

Studies that focus on Judeoconversos, such as this one, do not represent a unitary field of research but a somewhat eclectic subfield of various branches of scholarship. Chief among the latter are Jewish history and literature (especially Sephardi studies and the history of anti-Judaism), Spanish history and literature (especially the history of the Inquisition), Portuguese history, the history of the Netherlands, the economic history of the early modern Levant, the history of European religion(s), and the history of philosophy (especially skepticism and rationalism). The fact that the problem of conversos covers so much academic ground bears witness not only to the geographical mobility of New Christians, but also to their multifaceted cultural and social profile.

During the first half of the twentieth century, historical writing on the subject of Judeoconversos developed along two primary paths. The first path was cleared by peninsular historians who were chiefly preoccupied with identifying and evaluating the role(s) of Judeoconversos within the larger history of Christian Iberia. Historians of *Sepharad* cleared the second path. Unlike their Hispanist counterparts, these scholars paid close attention to converso life (especially crypto-Judaism) in the context of Jewish history as a whole, inside and outside the Iberian Peninsula.[16]

Among peninsular writers, Américo Castro and Claudio Sánchez Albornoz were perhaps the first to dwell on the existence of renegades, chiefly "professional" informers and persecutors of converso origin, and to treat the behavior of these figures as a problem of historical import. Sánchez Albornoz saw the Inquisition as an institutional by-product of a corrupt system of denunciation that, according to him, had characterized the Jewish courts of the pre-expulsion era.[17] Castro concurred with his colleague on the "Jewish" origins of inquisitorial persecution, but insisted that the chief legacy of conversos, was not the corrupting "spirit of the *judería*." Rather, it was a widespread sense of spiritual bifurcation or "psychic fissure." More than other Iberians, the argument went, conversos had experienced "psychic fissure" as a profound insecurity or "disquiet."[18]

On the side of Jewish history, Yitzhak Baer (following Heinrich Graetz) proposed that the mass conversions of 1391–1492 were partially the result of a crisis of leadership throughout Castilian and Aragonese *kehillot*. In Baer's view, prominent Jewish renegades of the thirteenth and fourteenth centuries (Gerónimo de Santa Fe, Pablo de Santa María, and the like) exemplified the culmination of a larger trend whereby educated Jews who lacked the simple, affective piety of the Sephardi masses espoused a spiritually deracinated Averroism, and thus became "ripe" for defection to the Christian enemy.[19] In other words, it was not social, political, or economic forces that had corroded the Jewish elite's sense of national distinctiveness and purpose, but intellectual and moral degeneration in the form of rationalism.

As my brief characterization suggests, Castro and Sánchez Albornoz were principally interested in defining the nature of Spanish nationhood. Both men saw it as crucial to their respective historiographical missions to determine what was fundamentally and authentically Spanish. Today this preoccupation, like the divergent solutions these historians posited, may strike us as a somewhat romantic and heavy-handedly nationalist approach to history, an approach similar to that espoused by patriotic historians elsewhere in nineteenth- and early twentieth-century Europe. The debt of Sánchez and Castro to the German Idealist tradition of Herder (and others) is especially apparent in the two Hispanists' immanentist conception of "the Spanish nation" as an almost primordial, historically continuous entity with a unique character and destiny. For them, what was basic to Spanishness— the *volksgeist* of Spaniards, as it were—gave structure to Spanish history, just as history expressed what was fundamental about the Spaniard.[20]

Similar premises are evident in the work of Jewish scholars—including historians of the "Jerusalem School," such as Baer—whose different perspectives on the "true" character of fifteenth-century conversos may well speak of modern nationalist preoccupations as much as these perspectives shed light on Ibero-Jewish history. According to Baer, most ordinary conversos (as distinct from the traitorous converso elite) were in actuality Jews who were consciously connected to the main body of the Jewish nation.[21] For Benzion Netanyahu, in contrast, almost all conversos became fully absorbed into Christianity during the 1400s, so much so that Judaizing was a negligible occurrence among them. For the first historian, then, conversos served to prove Jewish resiliency in the face of gentile oppression.[22] For the second, they demonstrated the tragedy of national dissolution in exile. As Yirmiyahu Yovel opines, "Both scholars . . . had a tacit ideological (indeed Zionist) agenda, Baer providing the modern national Jewish consciousness with heroes and martyrs, Netanyahu explaining that Jewish life in the Diaspora is fragile and prone to assimilation."[23]

From the late 1960s to the present, historians have begun to shed light on vast areas of converso life that do not fit the sweeping generalizations of earlier histories, for instance Baer's binary model of "corrupt elites" versus "faithful folk" and Castro's notion of collective mentality. Recent studies of inquisitorial dossiers have uncovered more confusion and disunity among the converso rank-and-file than Baer's idealizing view could ever allow. These and other works have also challenged the relatively narrow chronological and geographical parameters of earlier treatments. For example, eminent Hispanists such as Antonio Domínguez Ortiz and Julio Caro Baroja have ventured (however briefly) beyond Iberia to survey the history of exiled conversos.[24] Yosef Yerushalmi, Yosef Kaplan, and Herman Prins Salomon, all students of Jewish history (although Salomon is a linguist and literary critic by training), have produced works that trace the lives of individual conversos before, during, and after they "returned" to Judaism in exile.[25] For their part, students of intellectual and cultural history (Gershom Scholem, Yirmiyahu Yovel, J. A. Van Praag, and Israel S. Révah, to name a few) have explored the manner in which former crypto-Jews and their descendants may have injected distinctively Hispano-Christian concerns into the mainstream of Jewish life.

The blurring of historiographical boundaries that I have sketched reflects at least three important shifts in scholarly approaches to the history of Judeoconversos that have occurred since the 1960s.

First and foremost, the tendency of earlier scholars to measure the moral worth of conversos in light of the latter's supposed adherence to reified notions of Hispanicity and/or Jewishness has somewhat subsided; so too have egregious attempts to claim or disown conversos on behalf of given national camps. These changes should not be overstated, especially as there still exists a marked tendency among some historians to portray conversos as Jewish heroes. Yet the changes do suggest a partial repudiation of grand (national) narratives in favor of more nuanced evaluations that focus narrowly on specific conjunctures of historical factors. With latter-day approaches[26] has come the possibility of confronting Judeoconversos as an analytical challenge in their own right.[27] Today, investigators need not subordinate the study of conversos to explorations of larger and "more important" phenomena—say, the saga of Sephardim or of the Spanish Inquisition. Ironically, by concentrating on the historical particularity of Judeoconversos, scholars may also discern ways in which New Christians resembled their Jewish and Old Christian contemporaries, and thus begin to unearth lines of fundamental continuity in the collective experiences of early modern Jews, conversos, and Old Christians.

Second, a new interest in the complex inner lives of Judeoconversos has emerged. This trend has a precedent in the work of Castro, who underlined the need to take psychological factors into account when formulating historical explanations about conversos. In particular, the challenge of reconstructing the spiritual trajectory of converso refugees as continuous wholes has forced scholars to follow their subjects across Europe, and thus to disregard 1492, the territorial borderline of the Iberian Peninsula, and other such imaginary dividing lines between Hispanic and Jewish history. Fortunately, Castro's successors have demonstrated greater awareness than he of the fact that the behaviors and motivations of conversos spanned a wide spectrum, and that all of these behaviors and motivations were at least partially rooted in larger historical circumstances, not in national essences, as Castro's analysis tends to suggest. Furthermore, some historians now acknowledge as a matter of course that many conversos were, to borrow Van Praag's phrase, "souls in dispute" (or "divided souls") whose self-identity was never a given; indeed, this identity was often in flux.[28] In this regard, Yerushalmi has noted that what is surprising is not that several converso refugees stumbled along the road to Judaism, but that a large number of the exiles adapted to Jewish life without major incident.[29]

Third, a new emphasis on social history has allowed scholars to broaden their analytical scope to include considerations of place, demography, economy, social class, and other causal factors that transcend the traditional foci of older political and intellectual histories. To cite a few examples: Yosef Kaplan, Jonathan Israel, Brian Pullan, James Boyajian, Haim Beinart, and Julio Caro Baroja have made extensive use of communal records, state documents, inquisitorial cases, and private commercial records to compose sociological portraits of, respectively, the Amsterdam Jewish community; Sephardi enclaves and commercial networks throughout Europe and the Americas; the interaction of Venetian Jews and conversos; converso bankers; the New Christian contingent in Ciudad Real; and, finally, Castilian conversos during the reign of Philip IV.[30]

The recent stress on social history promises to correct a traditional overemphasis on the lives and works of highly articulate thinkers and polemicists of converso origin such as Spinoza, Uriel da Costa, and Menasseh ben Israel. The closer investigators have hovered over the rich texture of life among ordinary conversos, the more their studies have revealed variations from the main patterns of converso acculturation. For instance, in his 1983 study on the Venetian Inquisition, Pullan alone unearthed dozens of instances in which otherwise unexceptional conversos failed to develop stable religious identities or were simply incapable of assuming constructive roles within their host communities. One of Pullan's chapters focuses on people who reverted to Christianity after erratic excursions into Judaism.[31] As early as 1943 and 1961, respectively, Cecil Roth and Israel Révah discovered similar examples of "deviance" in Lisbon and Rouen, where New Christian renegades perpetrated wide-scale denunciation against fellow conversos.[32] Much more recently, Jaime Contreras depicted a veritable hornet's nest of informers and counterinformers in his microscopic study of the converso communities of sixteenth-century Murcia and Lorca.[33] For their part, Isaiah Tishby, Yosef Kaplan, and Matt Goldish have unearthed evidence of disaffection and nonconformity among Sephardim of the seventeenth century, particularly among immigrant conversos in London, thus sharpening our view of the difficulties of collective Judaization in that corner of the converso Diaspora.[34] Kaplan is, to my knowledge, the only investigator to have approached the phenomenon of return to the Iberian Peninsula in his pioneering articles, "The travels of Portuguese Jews from Amsterdam to the 'Lands of Idolatry' (1644–1724)" and "The Struggle Against Travelers to Spain and Portugal in the Western Sephardi Diaspora."[35]

The present study both complements and builds upon the efforts of the three last-mentioned authors by broadening and deepening their focus on ostensibly marginal conversos. Without losing sight of the entire western converso Diaspora, I shift attention to France, for which few historical studies on converso dissidents exist. Furthermore, where Tishby, Kaplan, and Goldish merely touch on the economic motivations and activities of marginal conversos, and where the eminent historian of Franco-Judaic life, Zosa Szajkowski, focuses too narrowly on that phenomenon, I devote considerable attention to the mercantile matrix of renegade behavior.[36] By consciously placing the economic activities of returnees at the center of my interpretation I attempt to ground an understanding of the mentality of these dissidents in their mundane circumstances and interests. In this respect my study concurs with and, I believe, confirms Contreras's conviction that the history of sixteenth- and seventeenth-century conversos lies "close to the ground," and is "low and pedestrian" in its horizons, and that therefore this history cannot be properly visualized by recourse to the "grandiloquent conceptions" (collective spiritual malaise, transcendent ethos, and so on) that so dominated the work of historians such as Castro.[37]

Significantly, my study is not concerned with the question of whether conversos were or were not Jews *in essence.* For that matter, the study is not concerned with the question of whether crypto-Judaism was or was not an inquisitorial invention. Most of my subjects lived at one time or another in the Sephardi Diaspora. As a consequence most of them participated in one or another facet of normative Jewish life. Generally speaking, then, my subjects' Judaizing is not at issue.

Of course, my interest in the "low and pedestrian" is a hallmark of social history, an approach to the reconstruction of the past that locates "important" historical events in the realm of ordinary individuals. Because it is ultimately an exploration of the mentalities of ordinary conversos, the present study fits especially well within the branch (or ally) of social history that focuses on the imaginary and symbolic dimensions of experience. Cultural history, as that branch is known, encompasses various studies of identity and its formation. Among these last belong a number of microhistorical inquiries that draw extensively from inquisitorial dossiers.[38] Reuven Faingold's recent article on the inquisitorial prisoner Vicente Furtado comes immediately to mind as an example from the field of converso studies.[39] Because it includes a case study in the self-construction of a typical renegade, the fifth chapter of this book is akin to Faingold's contribution, at least with regard to the theme and documentary source I explore. However, my case study is part of a larger discussion; consequently it goes further than Faingold in relating its main subject, an inquisitorial defendant, to broader historical phenomena. More importantly, the chapter, like the work as a whole, reconstructs the viewpoints of cultural border crossers and attempts to gain insight into the psychology of these dissidents. By contrast, the work of Kaplan, Tishby, and Goldish has reconstructed the impressions of Jewish communal leaders, as well as these authorities' disapproving reactions toward the dissidents. In turn, I examine the testimony of marginal conversos themselves to provide a portrait of the lives and minds of these renegades.[40]

There is yet another subfield of historical scholarship that my work may well advance. I am referring to latter-day studies on southwestern French *kehillot*, notably the voluminous work of Gérard Nahon, that of Anne Zink, and that of Zosa Szajkowski. Along with other students of Franco-Judaica, Nahon has amply documented the existence and legal basis of organized Jewish life in the Portuguese enclaves of early modern France. His articles, however, have focused almost exclusively on the late seventeenth and eighteenth centuries. This focus is consistent with the range of primary sources that the author has chosen to examine—in this case, French governmental material as well as Jewish communal documents. Very few of the latter documents survive that would illuminate the early and middle decades of the 1600s.[41] Here, however, I focus on these very decades through the use of Spanish and Portuguese documents that Nahon has not surveyed. These sources contribute to our knowledge of a formative period in Franco-Sephardi life, chiefly by revealing a conflictive aspect in the evolution of the Judeo-Portuguese Diaspora.

True to his interest in the integrative forces that transformed Portuguese immigrants into French Jews, Nahon has, to my knowledge, never written concerning renegades, much less discussed their economic and personal links to the Iberian Peninsula. For her part, Anne Zink, who has contributed important articles describing the economic profile of converso settlements in the French southwest, has not explicated these communities' pivotal relationship with the Iberian economies.[42] Szajkowski began this project, yet in my view did not bring it to fruition, in his article "Trade Relations of Marranos in France with the Iberian Peninsula in the Sixteenth and Seventeenth Centuries."[43] Neither scholar has discussed cases of social dissidence or focused on the religious lives of conversos who trafficked across the Spanish border. Again, I contribute to existing scholarship by covering this relatively uncharted historical territory. In the process, I expose fissures in the surface of communal Jewish life that are invisible from Zink's and Nahon's more sweeping views.

As for my documentary sources, a few words are in order. Notwithstanding the emergence of novel historiographical approaches, it is clear that every historian who has recently endeavored to reconstruct the behavior of New Christians via inquisitorial dossiers has come face to face with an old methodological puzzle. In short, the question is if and how one can determine whether the testimony contained in inquisitorial *procesos* reflects the true thoughts and experiences of the informants. Another way to present this problem is to ask: To what degree did witnesses and defendants lie to the Inquisition in order to protect themselves and others? Did the declarants' testimonies merely parrot the preconceptions and biases of the inquisitors? Were the declarants' testimonies partially or thoroughly falsified?[44] Alternately, did they reflect a real dialogue (albeit an uneven one) between the accusers and the accused?[45]

The solution I provide in this work is not definitive because it is based on a relatively small sample of inquisitorial cases. Even within that sample, the content, style, and tone of informants' recorded declarations varied. That is why each deposition demanded a fresh assessment of its trustworthiness. Far from excluding any interpretive possibility, much of the testimony I surveyed showed traces of inquisitorial distortion, deliberate omission or prevarication on the part of the informants, as well as plentiful elements of truth.

In evaluating the reliability of informants' depositions, I applied the following commonsensical assumptions: First, that the *sincerity*, and therefore the *basic credibility* of a given testimony are altogether separate from the *plausibility* of its literal content. This distinction, I believe, is critical for the proper interpretation of a decidedly religious, early modern world in which people were routinely conditioned to treat biblical miracles and other blatant impossibilities as literal truths. As an example I offer the defendant Aldonza Cardoso de Velasco. She testified in 1666 that another woman, María Román, had succeeded in "binding" a man—in other words, rendering him sexually impotent—by tying the laces of his undergarments into knots, by reciting an incantation over the knots, and by stomping on the garments in ritualistic fashion. That Román's stratagem had no real power *as magic*, of course, does not mean that Cardoso was lying when she divulged her own belief in that power.[46]

Second, and more importantly, I have posited that an item of testimony is probably (though not *necessarily*) truthful if the declarant did not stand to gain any advantage in offering it to his or her questioners. Along the same lines, a declaration is believable if the declarant was aware (or was probably aware) that rendering it would harm his or her interests. It is a fact that numerous inquisitorial suspects provided basic personal data without which the inquisitors would have found it very difficult to investigate and incriminate them. These data included the suspects' own names and aliases, places of baptism, genealogies, relationships with convicted Judaizers, and the like. Only a stubborn skeptic would argue that much of these data were inauthentic.

Third, I have posited that an item of testimony is generally trustworthy if those who recorded it had no reason to twist or falsify it in any particular way, even if some unconscious distortions occurred in the recording process. There is no consensus among scholars as to why inquisitors and declarants may have wanted to shape what is recorded in the *procesos*. For now, suffice it to say that I address possible motives for distortion as my discussion of the cases (and their contexts) progresses.

Fourth, and most obviously, I have posited that a given deposition is credible if reliable, external evidence supports it. Because direct documentary proof of the credibility of inquisitorial informants is usually unavailable, it is often necessary to rely on circumstantial evidence. Such evidence may not yield total certitude, yet a sense of strong likelihood is attainable and can serve as the basis for sound historical interpretations. It behooves me to warn that the study of inquisitorial *procesos* permits neither perfect reconstructions of historical events nor airtight theories of historical causality. Given this limitation, one must still recognize that a pertinent theory or reconstruction need not be able to repel all possible objections to it in order to be operationally successful; it must simply be able to answer questions that its nearest alternatives cannot.[47]

In what pertains to the problem of identity construction among Judeoconversos, I contend that a sound historical interpretation is one that focuses closely on the complexity of historical events and avoids grand, overambitious ventures; for example, trying to determine how Jewish all Judeoconversos "really" were (or were not). As I will discuss in the final chapter, my findings suggest that no sweeping generalization is desirable concerning the social and religious identities of Judeoconversos. In fact, my research indicates that the questions "How Jewish?" and "How Christian?" are based on a fundamental misconception of what religion meant to most converso renegades during the sixteenth and seventeenth centuries.

My specific findings aside, it is clear that with the exception of works about a few educated skeptics and intellectual luminaries, scholarship has paid relatively little attention to the subject of converso renegades.[48] The theme and scope of this book are consequently new for all intents and purposes. Ironically, my main challenge has not been to unearth archival documents. Many of the records I have worked with are known to specialists, who have tended to underrate, underanalyze, or simply disregard these sources. My chief methodological task has been to configure a distinct body of material from ostensibly disparate files, and to shed a new light on their content.[49] This book constitutes an attempt to interpret the historical experiences and unconventional (though hardly uncommon) choices of ordinary Judeoconversos in a new way.

Terminology

Before embarking upon an examination of the topic at hand, it is crucial to remember that "dissidence," not to mention being a "renegade," is in the eye of the beholder. One can easily surmise that sixteenth- and seventeenth-century Jews, as well as Judaicized[50] New Christians, regarded conversos who reverted to Christianity as odious deserters. Of course, these same "deviants" were nothing less than exemplary penitents in the official estimation of the inquisitors, and probably that of orthodox Catholics in general.

For their part, Christianized conversos, who were as vulnerable to denunciation as actual crypto-Jews, concurred with the normative Jewish view that voluntary informers were ruthless and despicable turncoats. Indeed, New Christian lore produced a stereotypically insidious image of "the informer"—the *malsín*.[51]

In addition to recognizing colloquial usage, I have tried to avoid lexical monotony. Given the relative dearth of purely descriptive terms such as "border crosser," "informer" and "returnee," I have resorted in particular to the less impartial "renegade" (without quotation marks) for purposes of exposition. Whatever stylistic flexibility this and similar non-neutral words afford, it is obvious that they compromise an ideal objectivity: All of them imply an orthodox, thoroughly partisan perspective, be it that of early modern Jews (in the case of "renegade," "nonconformist," and the like) or that of Catholics (in the case of "penitent," "conformist," and similar terms). However, I believe the findings of this study cancel some of the bias inherent in this value-laden nomenclature. They do this by historicizing the actual or probable behaviors (rather than ideal or putative ones) represented by that same terminology.

To cite but one example: In the context of this study, the word "penitent" refers to a Judeoconverso who returned to the fold of Ibero-Christendom by performing certain actions. These actions were calculated to show repentance for past conduct and to demonstrate the actor's renewed, heartfelt adherence to the rules and standards of orthodox Catholicism. Accordingly, one may reasonably argue that the term "penitent" connotes reunion, spiritual restoration, and the actor's essential humility. That is to say, the term itself implies a benign and commendatory view of penitence and, by extension, of the penitent's spiritual state during the process of his or her reentry into the Christian community of faith. This connotational meaning is obviously consistent with the official judgment of the inquisitorial functionaries who welcomed and guided errant sinners back into the bosom of the Catholic Church during the historical period in question.

Looking at the penitents through the lens of historical analysis allows a different view. In the first place, a comparative reading of inquisitorial documents reveals that not all Judeoconverso penitents exemplified humility or were motivated by a previous desire to embrace a Catholic identity. Some "penitents" feigned reconversion; others could not banish their religious doubts despite undergoing formal atonement; a few remained indifferent toward their "recovered" faith, while others—in my view, the majority—embraced it with sincerity if not always with enthusiasm. In the second place, not every converso émigré who came back to the Iberian Peninsula did so with the aim of repudiating Judaism before an inquisitorial tribunal. An important segment of my research suggests that most conversos who returned to Spain and Portugal did so for economic or personal (non-idiosyncratic) reasons: to buy and sell goods, to collect debts, to visit relatives, to seek a livelihood, to help friends in need, to satisfy a deep nostalgia, and so on.

In the end, historical analysis precludes the blanket endorsement implicit in the word "penitent," because all relevant data indicate that penitents were not a homogeneous group. More to the point, "penitent," like "returnee," is a term that glosses over a wide variety of motivations and behaviors. It is this kaleidoscopic yet ultimately coherent array that now deserves our attention.

Chapter 2
Conversos: The Iberian Context

The history of early modern Spain is the story of several paradoxes. First and foremost, it is the story of a group of small Iberian kingdoms that evolved into a vast and fearsome empire, yet whose rulers and literati became so conscious of its economic weaknesses, that some Spanish critics became convinced that the Habsburg colossus could scarcely support itself throughout the very period when it was Europe's only superpower. At a sociocultural level, the history of Habsburg Spain is the story of a society obsessed with notions of honor, nobility, and Christian orthodoxy, which nonetheless produced a large subculture of *dis*honor and impiety known to modern readers through the literary archetype of the *pícaro*. Crucially, early modern Spain was an officially closed and culturally intolerant society that depended considerably on the economic activities of its persecuted minorities. A persistent Spanish preoccupation with the questions of "purity of blood" and "purity of faith" betrayed yet another, more fundamental paradox. This was the fact that early modern Iberian culture, despite its exclusionary bent, had actually incorporated and been deeply influenced by its designated outsiders, first by Jews and Moslems, later by Judeoconversos and moriscos, through centuries of intermarriage, voluntary conversions to Catholicism, forced assimilation, and daily contact.

The seventeenth century, Spain's era of crisis, brought all of these paradoxes into sharp relief as the country's economic and political life accentuated discrepancies between the chauvinistic ideologies that often colored Spanish aspirations on one hand, and the complex realities that shaped the larger panorama of Spanish life on the other. The tumultuous Spanish crisis of the 1600s is important to this study not only because it formed the background against which the drama of Judeoconverso "renegades" played itself out, but because the history of the crisis holds some of the keys to an understanding of the renegades' behavior itself. The purpose of this chapter, then, is twofold: first, to sketch important aspects of a broad historical scenario in order to provide a historical framework for the individual and collective histories of returnees and spontaneous informers, particularly in what concerns these individuals' fateful encounter with the peninsular inquisitions. Second, the chapter aims to place Judeoconversos (including the renegades) in that larger Hispanic context by highlighting key aspects of the economic and sociocultural roles that New Christians played within the Iberian Peninsula.

Spain, Portugal, and Portuguese Conversos

Throughout the latter half of the sixteenth century Spain[1] was the undisputed superpower of Latin Europe. The rich overseas possessions of Philip II (1556–98) dwarfed those of other Christian monarchs, while his European territories, including the Netherlands, Sardinia, Sicily, and the Duchy of Milan, rendered the Spanish crown a formidable force in continental politics. Spanish primacy was nothing new. Much of western and central Europe had experienced it during the regime of the Habsburg emperor Charles V (Charles I of Castile, 1516–58). Toward the end of Philip's reign, however, a series of political and military victories (notably the suppression of the Dutch revolt in 1567–70 and 1579, and the defeat of Ottoman forces at the immense battle of Lepanto in 1571) had made Spanish political preponderance especially palpable.[2]

From the point of view of this study, the most significant Spanish conquest of the late sixteenth century was the annexation of Portugal, which was completed in 1580. This crowning achievement of Spanish empire-building gave concrete political expression to an idea that had shaped the ambitions and institutional self-image of Ibero-Christian kings in the Middle Ages, during the long period of the *reconquista*. I am referring to the concept, more specifically the goal, of *Hispania*: a united peninsular kingdom ruled by Christians and rooted in a "pure" Visigothic heritage.[3]

The unrealistic fantasy of ethnic and cultural "purity" aside, there were several reasons that Spain's annexation of Portugal could not achieve the politicocultural ideal that partially undergirded it, even if Philip II was the first Habsburg to use the official title "King of *España*" after the merging of the two countries. Chief among these reasons was that the political union had been triggered by a dynastic dispute, not by amicable agreement or by a natural, "Hispanic" affinity between the Spanish and Portuguese realms. Furthermore, the union had been forced: Two years after King Sebastian of Portugal was killed in a military expedition to northern Africa, his uncle Philip of Spain invaded Portugal with an army of 37,000 men. A brief war finally realized the Habsburgian claim to the empty throne.[4]

Spain did not assimilate Portugal completely. The culture of the western kingdom, for one, remained virtually independent. Far from trying to Castilianize his new domain, Philip even tried to learn the language of his Portuguese subjects.[5] As for political autonomy, the Spanish state took over some functions of the Portuguese government but left many others in the hands of native elites. Brazil and lesser Portuguese colonies remained under Portuguese control, while Portugal itself experienced relatively little Spanish interference in the internal administration of the country. For example, the wide authority of the Spanish Inquisition never eclipsed that of the Portuguese Holy Office. The Portuguese tribunal enjoyed substantial autonomy throughout the years of Spanish rule, and thus was able to cultivate a notorious ferocity with relatively few constraints.

The annexation of Portugal demands our attention because it greatly accelerated a momentous shift in the geographic distribution of peninsular Judeoconversos. Although the precise dimensions of the shift are not clear, it is indisputable that hundreds and probably thousands of Lusitanian conversos crossed the Portuguese border into Castile, Aragon, and Navarre during the period of Spanish control (1580–1640). In Spain the immigrants became targets of persecution at various levels. Both the newcomers and their descendants fell within the purview of the Spanish Inquisition.

The migrations effectively revived anti-converso persecution in Spain at a time when such persecution was on the wane (trials against alleged crypto-Jews were still legion in Portugal during the middle to late sixteenth century, while in Spain such trials had become comparatively infrequent after the 1490s).[6] Spanish Judeophobia now acquired a distinctly anti-"Portuguese" accent. Not surprisingly, many Lusitanian conversos and their Spanish descendants went into exile, the former for the second time in their lives. A great irony of these developments was that many of the newcomers had left Portugal in order to *escape* intense hostility and, in particular, to avoid inquisitorial scrutiny.

Given the prosecutorial zeal of Lusitanian inquisitors, it is no coincidence that the steady movement of Portuguese New Christians to Spain commenced in the 1540s, just as the newly created Portuguese Holy Office (established in 1536) gathered momentum.[7] John (João) III and his successor, the ill-fated Sebastian (Sebastião), issued several bans against New Christian emigration. Yet a number of conversos were able to sidestep such restrictions and establish firm roots in Castile prior to 1580.[8] After the Spanish annexation the flow of Lusitanian conversos to Spain increased considerably. A new freedom of movement between the previously separate countries afforded members of Portugal's New Christian minority a sterling opportunity to build new lives as residents of Castile, Aragon, Navarre, and other Spanish domains. Philip III gave *cristãos-novos* an added incentive to move eastward when he granted them formal permission to leave their native soil in 1601. In exchange, he exacted a collective payment of 200,000 *cruzados*.[9] Later, he negotiated with the pope to obtain a general pardon for those whom the Portuguese Inquisition had accused of Judaizing.[10] Pope Clement VIII issued the exculpatory brief in 1604, prompting the release of 410 inquisitorial prisoners in Lisbon, Braganza, and Coimbra.[11] The cost to Lusitanian conversos in this case was between 1,700,000 and 1,800,000 *cruzados*, a sum intended to compensate the crown for its loss of inquisitorial confiscations.[12]

Philip's policies did not mean that he was friendly to Judeoconversos as such, but rather that his government looked upon Portuguese New Christians as eminently exploitable resources. To understand the royal approach, it is instructive to remember that Philip's liberality came at a high price. What is more, the king's relative generosity did not apply to Spanish conversos. Neither did it curb the activities of the Spanish Holy Office against Portuguese or any other defendants.

Royal favor made for good policy in a purely strategic sense. At the turn of the sixteenth century, Lusitanian conversos were reputed to possess considerable wealth, while the Spanish crown was experiencing financial difficulties. Although a majority of Portuguese conversos were far from affluent, their total assets, including the fortunes of a few powerful families, may have totaled up to 75 million ducats.[13] In favoring religious amnesty and encouraging immigration, then, Philip sought to draw wealthy conversos toward the Habsburg court so that their economic activities and sheer assets would provide a healthy stimulus to the Spanish economy. Whether the stimulus proved healthy or not, Philip was entirely successful in catalyzing it.

Especially during the middle decades of the seventeenth century the crown tapped the fortunes of Portuguese conversos as a matter of course in order to replenish the coffers of the Spanish state. For some royal officers, bartering governmental concessions for ready cash became a matter of naked self-interest as much as a matter of national economic strategy. Thus, for example, Philip's prime minister, the Duke of Lerma, received an unofficial gift of fifty thousand *cruzados* from moneyed conversos for his role in the negotiations that paved the way for the papal pardon of 1604. For their part, each of the members of the Royal Council for Portugal received sixty thousand *cruzados*.[14]

There is ample evidence that wealthy Judeoconversos took advantage of the royal aperture to Spain, especially after the coronation of Philip IV (1621–65), whose first prime minister, the Count-Duke Olivares, inserted a number of them into the monarchy's financial and administrative machinery.[15] These prominent *hombres de negocios* (businessmen) were very few, however, compared to the multitude of ordinary Portuguese conversos who flocked to Castile and Aragon upon the Spanish annexation. What drew the less affluent *cristãos-novos* to Spain?

As Yosef H. Yerushalmi has observed, Castile-Aragon was wealthier than Portugal, so the lure of economic opportunity must have been substantial to rich and poor *cristãos-novos* alike.[16] From a legal and political standpoint, Spain was most attractive to Portuguese Judeoconversos because the Spanish Inquisition did not punish any crimes committed *in Portugal* against the Catholic faith—even if Spanish inquisitors did make use of evidence collected by their Portuguese colleagues when prosecuting the immigrants for religious crimes allegedly committed *in Spain*. Also, Spanish authorities seldom extradited Inquisitorial prisoners to Portugal.[17] Finally, in Yerushalmi's words, "relative to the fury of Inquisitorial persecution in Portugal, Spain must have appeared . . . almost a refuge."[18] All of these factors meant that Portuguese New Christians enjoyed an enticing measure of legal immunity in Spain at the close of the sixteenth century. Such immunity would have been unthinkable in earlier times, when the Spanish Inquisition was most active against the first generations of Spanish Judeoconversos.

Before delving into the repercussions of the Portuguese migrations and drawing a collective portrait of rank-and-file converso immigrants, we must consider the historical context in which the migrations occurred. The three sections that follow outline the social and economic conditions that awaited Portuguese newcomers in Spain at the beginning of the seventeenth century—and awaited converso returnees throughout that period. A majority of the returnees I have studied were merchants who traveled to and from Madrid, and were living there at the time of their arrest or self-surrender. Consequently I devote the second of the three sections to an overview of conditions in the Spanish capital during the 1600s. The third section pays special attention to the network of commercial roads that converso merchants used, including the highways that linked the metropolis to New Castile, to the rest of Spain, to the neighboring kingdom of Portugal, and to the most accessible of all converso havens in Europe: southwestern France.

Spain at the End of the Golden Age

Historians have referred to the period from 1500 to 1650 as Spain's Golden Age (*edad de oro*) or Golden Century (*siglo de oro*). Among other things, these terms remind us of the fact that during that period Castile extracted vast quantities of gold from America and spent them lavishly in Europe.[19] Arguably Spanish dominance in the European continent, like the empire itself, would have been impossible to maintain without continuous access to the mineral treasures of the New World. At the very least it is evident that the flow of American gold and silver helped the Habsburgs to keep the Spanish economy afloat, to finance an ambitious foreign policy, and to fight several wars.[20]

The sheer bulk of the treasure that Spain absorbed during the Early Modern Period tells its own tale. According to a recent study by Jean-Paul Le Flem, the Spanish economy imported an astonishing 151,561 kilograms of gold and close to 7.5 million kilograms of silver from 1503 through 1600.[21] Especially during the middle decades of the sixteenth century, this unprecedented influx of precious metals triggered a steep increase in prices across Iberia and ultimately throughout western Europe. Despite the resulting inflation, the overall effect of gold and silver imports on the Spanish economy was beneficial at first because Spain's productive capacities and its population had reached a peak in the 1550s. In other words, during the later 1500s there was sufficient demand for food and services that the bullion fueled an economic boom. Higher prices led to increased profits. Inflation also spurred trade and production, and brought more money into circulation. This, among other things, resulted in lower rates of interest and an increase in productive investment.[22]

Throughout the Golden Century various Spanish thinkers interpreted their country's political success and newfound wealth as a sign that Spaniards were God's chosen people. They believed that *España* was the standard bearer of Christianity, since Spaniards had "discovered" and Christianized remote regions of the world while resisting internal and external threats to the (supposed) religious homogeneity of the country. These threats included Moorish power (during the *reconquista*) and Protestant "heresies." In light of Spanish faithfulness, the argument went, was it not right and proper that Spain was the world's strongest Christian state and the avant-garde of the Counter Reformation?[23]

In 1601, for example, the Jesuit political observer Pedro de Rivadeneira explained that God had rewarded Spain with good fortune because in 1492

Ferdinand of Aragon and Isabel of Castile had previously expelled Moors and Jews from Spanish domains. Specifically, Rivadeneira argued that God had showed his pleasure by forever "cleansing" Spain of heretical Christian sects (such as the Protestant groups), and by "giving [Spanish kings] new realms, discovering with His hand a new world with treasures so many and so great that it is one of the greatest miracles that He has bestowed."[24]

From such heroic conceptions of nationhood other commentators inferred that Spaniards would redeem the world in a proximate future. For instance, in 1619 the commentator (and friar) Juan de Salazar concluded that the Spanish nation was heir to God's scriptural promise to the chosen people.[25] "It is very consistent with reason," Salazar wrote, ". . . that at the world's end Spain should be the seat of the Universal Monarchy, which . . . all nations must obey. . . ."[26] To underscore the supposed validity of his prediction, Salazar adduced several items of "proof." The first six of these items are typical of the adulatory triumphalism that gripped many Spaniards of his generation:

First . . . [we know that Spain will redeem the world because of] the situation of the Catholic King [Philip III], which, more than that of any other Christian prince, puts him in position to obtain [the universal monarchy], because he is lord of so many lands and provinces and of so many rich and great realms and states in all four corners of the world. . . .

Second . . . [we can infer the king's divine mission from] the title that the Church has given him, Most Catholic King, which means and signifies universal king.

Third, [we know of Spain's divinely ordained role from] the solid and fundamental causes (godliness, prudence, and fate) that concurred in the creation of the Spanish monarchy. . . .

Fourth . . . [we can infer Spain's divine role from] the catholic and sincere faith that [Philip] professes, without admixture of error or heresy, and [from] the singular obedience he shows to the pope, Vicar of Christ on earth, which...is the foundation and principal basis of the augmentation and conservation of all empires and kingdoms.

Fifth . . . as [the Hebrew prophet] Daniel maintains ...total dominion will be given to the saintly people of the Most High. [As we have seen,] the Spanish nation is God's beneficiary in the Law of Grace [meaning the New Testament], and has assumed the place that the elect [the Jews] had in the time of Scripture [the Old Testament] because it has (like the Israelites themselves) conformed best to the rule of faith enunciated by St. Paul, according to which a Christian's actions must be measured.

Sixth, [we can infer Spain's messianic role from] the prophecies and prognostications [of the prophets Daniel, Obadiah, and others] concerning the diminution of the Ottoman house and the enlargement of that of Spain, which according to common knowledge are the two [houses] that aspire to the universal monarchy. . . . We have already seen fulfilled the first part of [these prophecies] in the marvelous expulsion of the moriscos (last vestiges of the Mohammedans), which the majesty of Philip III accomplished in 1610[;] we may rest assured that the second part [of the prophecies], concerning the ruin of the Turk will also be fulfilled. As Gregory the Great affirms, when many things are announced to us, it is a good sign to see many of them fulfilled, because [this means that] the others too will take their intended effect.[27]

Notwithstanding the hubris and messianic delirium of imperial power, the stark fact remained that Spanish political might rested on a relatively fragile economic base. Numerous events exposed and aggravated this problem during the seventeenth century.

Historians disagree as to what specific incidents triggered the so-called Spanish "decline" of the 1600s.[28] However, there is little dispute about the existence of a multifaceted crisis with economic roots (or, more specifically, a chain of related crises) that brought Spain from its towering position as the military and religious hegemon of the western world to that of an impoverished, second-rate power.

Augured by the state's bankruptcies of 1575, 1596, and 1627, the economic exhaustion of Spain was blatant by the end of the seventeenth century.[29] Gold and silver imports from America diminished considerably throughout the latter 1600s, so much so that in 1654 even the royal court could not find adequate means to pay or feed all of its members.[30]

Perhaps the most obvious symptom of the crisis was the demise of Spain's political supremacy in Europe. Downfall came principally via the revolt and secession of Portugal (1640), the signing of the Peace of Westphalia (1648), and the unfavorable conclusion of war with France (1659). The first of these events revealed that *Hispania* was a romantic illusion. The second event effectively ended the French wars of religion and gave the Dutch provinces their political and religious independence after a draining century of conflict with Spain. The third event confirmed a new balance of power in the continent as Spain ceded parts of Catalonia and the Netherlands to France, the new continental hegemon.[31] The French and Portuguese conflicts were especially significant in that, unlike other imperial wars, they brought death and destruction to the Spanish mainland. Furthermore, both conflicts necessitated the conscription of thousands of Spanish civilians, since most of the country's professional soldiers were fighting the empire's other wars outside the Iberian Peninsula.[32] For its part, the case of the United (Dutch) Provinces provided clear evidence that Spain was incapable of imposing Catholicism on its own imperial turf, much less across the European continent. Finally, all three episodes demonstrated that Spain could no longer shoulder its multiple imperial commitments in Europe.[33]

Aside from these and other geopolitical misfortunes, there were serious domestic crises that imperiled the political stability and cohesion of the Spanish realm at the end of the "Golden Century." Regionalist sentiment and lordly recalcitrance erupted at a time when Philip IV and his chief ministers were attempting to harness the resources of all his Iberian subjects for the expensive task of maintaining the empire. From 1641 to 1652, in the midst of a heated war with France, Catalan peasants and burghers rose against the crown. Royal arms alone could not suppress the rebellion, which subsided only under the double impact of a plague and of French encroachment of Catalan territory. Also in 1641, and again in 1648, powerful lords instigated secessionist plots in Andalusia and Aragon. Both conspiracies failed when their leaders were discovered. Nevertheless, these episodes were like the northern revolt in that they revealed a volatile undercurrent of dissatisfaction with Castilian authority in general, and with the Habsburgs' fiscal demands in particular. Unhappily for the Spanish crown, similar discontent inspired secessionist revolts as far away as Sicily and Naples in 1647 and 1648.[34]

It is not necessary to dwell here on the disasters of the seventeenth-century crisis in order to explain it. After all, the diminution of Spanish power was not the result of particular military or political setbacks. Rather, these setbacks were signs of a structural corrosion; specifically, they showed that the Spanish economy was not strong enough to sustain the country's imperial role.

Spain's economy had at least two fundamental defects that the boom of the 1500s did not eliminate. First, the country suffered from a dearth of cultivable land; second, it suffered from chronically low levels of entrepreneurial investment, especially in industrial ventures.[35] In light of recent historiography on the Habsburg colossus, it is clear that historians have for too long exaggerated these and related deficiencies.[36] Nevertheless, the consequences of the deficiencies cannot be wholly denied. For example, it is clear that by the seventeenth century Spain had developed an abject dependence on imported products. The country's heavy reliance on foreign manufactures sometimes caused local industry to decline, particularly in provincial towns and in cities such as Toledo. In addition, the relative absence of a native class of capitalist investors, coupled with ballooning imperial expenses, made for constant governmental insolvency, a large fiscal debt, and the crown's almost total reliance on the services of foreign financiers and on the sale of local jurisdictions.[37] To make matters worse, the scarcity of arable land heightened the country's relative vulnerability to famine.[38] When severe food shortages occurred, malnutrition left the surviving peasants and townspeople unable to resist epidemic disease. John Lynch has estimated that the total number of plague-induced fatalities for the period 1600–1700 was an astonishing 1,250,000.[39] More than wars and emigration to the Indies, recurrent epidemics caused the decline of the total Spanish population from 8.4 million in the 1590s to barely 7 million a century later.[40] It is not an exaggeration to say that, despite the politically motivated exaggerations of local petitioners to the crown, the seventeenth century saw the dramatic hemorrhaging of Spain.

To the picture of structural weakness and demographic loss we must add two key, exacerbating factors. First, large increases in royal taxation; second, the royally decreed expulsion of moriscos from the Iberian Peninsula in 1609–11.

Let us look at the first factor. Throughout the Early Modern Period, but especially during the seventeenth century, the Habsburg crown imposed increasingly onerous taxes on commoners in order to satisfy the demands of the imperial budget. The state thus deepened socioeconomic cleavages and effectively subsidized wasteful consumption at the royal court.[41] More importantly, heavy taxation drove many peasants to destitution, out of the countryside, and toward urban centers, principally toward Madrid and Seville.[42] The prospect of fiscal exploitation represented a serious, if ultimately surmountable challenge to the economic viability of Castile, where the land was generally arid and infertile relative to that of other regions.[43] In the cities, former peasants and townspeople became part of a burgeoning mass of unemployed or underemployed city dwellers. Unhygenic slums grew at a vertiginous pace, making Spanish cities prime breeding grounds of disease.[44]

As for the second factor: The expulsion of the moriscos was a drastic action that virtually eradicated what Ibero-Catholic chauvinists had for years construed as a principal menace to the religious and physical "purity" of Christian Spain.[45] Crucially, the mass eviction diminished Spain's already limited productive capacities. A high proportion of the nearly three hundred thousand banished moriscos were agricultural laborers. Their sudden dislocation meant the disappearance of a key productive element in the peninsular economy.[46] For the fertile region of Valencia, where moriscos had been a large minority, the expulsion was destabilizing in the short term.[47]

The case of the moriscos is notable (among other reasons) because the victims were of one ethnicity. Yet the Spanish crisis of the seventeenth century took a heavy toll on ordinary Spaniards across all ethnic lines. I have already alluded to the highly lethal and virtually incessant epidemics and wars of the 1600s; to the rapid growth of Madrid; to the fiscal exploitation of the peasantry and townsfolk by royal overlords; and finally, to the economic challenges that faced Castile, where a number of towns became bankrupt. It therefore goes without saying that the human cost of the Spanish crisis was enormous, not only in terms of lives lost, but in material and in psychological terms. A widespread *perception* of systemic crisis undoubtedly conditioned Spaniards' attitudes toward their own society, including, of course, conversos and other disadvantaged groups.

Under what precise circumstances did residents of Castile, Aragon, and Navarre experience the country's tribulations? How did ordinary men and women live in the century of the Spanish crisis? The present overview cannot answer these questions comprehensively. However, I will attempt to provide a limited answer by sketching a socioeconomic profile of two domains, already mentioned, in which converso merchants were especially active: (1) the Spanish metropolis, Madrid, which became the largest single commercial market in the Iberian Peninsula over the course of the late 1500s and the 1600s; (2) the vast network of Iberian trade routes that served the capital and other Spanish and Portuguese cities.

Madrid in the 1600s

Material scarcity and sheer physical discomfort pervaded daily life in the otherwise vibrant Madrid of the seventeenth century. The main reason for this was that the city lay on a dry and semibarren plain and did not have the advantage of a nearby, navigable river by which to receive supplies and dispose of waste matter. Another reason was that the roads that connected the capital to the rest of the country were of poor quality. They slowed the pace of commerce and occasionally aggravated shortages of food and vital commodities.[48] Worse still, the cost of urban living was high for all of Madrid's residents because of the enormous expense of transporting goods into the city on inadequate roads.

Compounding these problems was a demographic explosion that had begun in 1561, when Philip II made Madrid his permanent capital. From that year onward, the city grew at a dizzying pace. In the first half of the sixteenth century, Madrid had been a town of no more than 30,000 people. By 1650, the city had over 150,000 inhabitants.[49] This expansion far surpassed the crown's ability and willingness to create a viable urban infrastructure, much less control the effects of overcrowding.

Despite its considerable growth, the metropolitan economy evolved primarily in response to the needs and wants of the court, not those of the city's ballooning population. As Richard Mackenney has caustically observed, the urban colossus existed only to serve a class of political residents: "A few people made coaches, [and] many more watched them roll by . . . [which highlighted] a curious [parallel] between the unproductive world of the elite and its parody, the unproductive world of the *pícaros*."[50]

In global terms, early modern Madrid exported far less than it imported, and consumed much more than it produced.[51] An artless apologist inadvertently highlighted this fact in 1658 when he wrote, ". . . [O]nly foreigners work on the goods used by the capital, and this very fact proves that all other nations labor for Madrid, the overlord of all other capitals since all of them work for her and she serves none."[52] In other words, the Habsburg capital, like the rest of the country's major cities, was economically and politically formidable, yet grossly dependent on its external suppliers. The latter certainly included converso merchants. Consonant with the inward orientation of the greater urban economy, Madrid's strongest industries did not cultivate foreign demand for their products and services. For example, the crafts of embroidery, gilding, and tailoring thrived only because they transformed imported materials into luxury goods for local courtiers, government officials, and aristocrats.[53]

Madrid's evolution was semichaotic and largely unplanned, hence the city was a grim and uncomfortable place. A majority of its residents were of modest means and lived in squalor, while a significant minority of wealthy denizens lived in private pockets of great luxury. High officers of the church and the royal bureaucracy, influential courtiers, members of the upper nobility, foreign dignitaries, and a handful of affluent merchants comprised the urban elite. Members of this moneyed class were the only ones (besides the royal family) who could afford to own mansions with stone facades, expensive carriages, and protective cocoons consisting of guards and servants.

In terms of its physical appearance, seventeenth-century Madrid offered an array of contrasts between superpatriotic fantasies of Spanish power, wealth, and dignity on one hand, and the reality of economic distress and social disorder on the other. There was considerable irony, for instance, in the fact that the physiognomy of the so-called Capital of Two Worlds (the "Old" and the "New") was the product of a relative negligence.[54] As Madrid's population expanded during the 1600s, the city's avenues, alleys, and footpaths developed haphazardly, forming dark and confusing passages.[55] With the exception of a few main concourses, all streets were unpaved and therefore extremely dusty or muddy depending on the season.[56]

Plain structures of gray brick and earth dominated the city's drab landscape owing to the fact that limestone and other choice building materials were scarce. High municipal taxes all but prohibited the construction of second stories.[57] Most city homes were therefore indecorously low. In addition, a majority of residential dwellings had small, paper-covered holes instead of paned windows because the price of glass was beyond the means of ordinary builders, not to mention the residents themselves.[58] These tiny holes limited the penetration of dust, rain, and extreme temperatures into domestic spaces. Yet the holes also made for dim interiors and could seldom prevent the entry of an endemic stench—the smell of stagnant refuse. As many travelers to the Spanish capital observed, the total absence of a municipal system of waste disposal meant that most *madrileños* dumped their excrement and other trash in the open. Favorite dumping sites included portals, main thoroughfares, and street corners.[59] In addition to fomenting disease, ubiquitous garbage gave the capital an unenviable reputation among foreigners as the filthiest city in Europe.[60]

If Madrid's endemic filth indicated that the city had swelled to unmanageable proportions, periodic disasters provided conclusive proof that the city's sheer size invited total chaos. Epidemic diseases gestated in the unsanitary conditions of the slums, causing many casualties. The fire of 1631 destroyed much of the city's central promenade and marketplace, the Plaza Mayor. It also killed a dozen people and sparked three days of flagrant looting of the surviving property.[61]

The plunder could not have come as a surprise, for despite the city's intense economic activity and sheer economic weight, poverty plagued virtually all areas of the capital. Indigence had become so deeply entrenched over the course of the seventeenth century that there existed an entire underclass of desperate *madrileños*, including beggars, street thieves, prostitutes, and all manner of transients—pilgrims, demobilized soldiers, and the like. A disdainful observer complained, "The streets of Madrid . . . are [always] crowded with vagabonds and loafers who while away the time playing cards, waiting for the soup kitchens of the monasteries to open or to get ready to ransack a house."[62] With similar contempt, a journalist grumbled in 1637 that no one in the capital was safe after sundown because of the large numbers of criminals who prowled the streets.[63] A class of metropolitan *pí-*

caros, then, was not a mere figment of the literary imagination of social satirists; it was an all too real reminder of the harsh reality of the time.

The educated pamphleteers known as *arbitristas* were among the most eloquent observers of Madrid's condition.[64] Several of these polemicists perceived what modern historians have identified as basic faults in the metropolitan economy. For instance, in 1616 the city magistrate Mateo López Bravo argued that the maldistribution of wealth had worsened the economic inefficiency of Madrid by creating too many idlers at the top and bottom of the socioeconomic hierarchy.[65] For their part, the French travelers Barthélemy Joly, Antoine de Brunel, and Francois Bertaut (who were not *arbitristas*) pointed out in 1604, 1655, and 1659, respectively, that Madrid, like Spain as a whole, seemed incapable of producing and accumulating wealth. These tourists' writing paints the insatiable metropolis as a mere channel through which American gold flowed to Spain's European competitors while the latter funneled their manufactures into Spain.[66]

Recent scholarship has confirmed the basic accuracy of assessments such as Brunel's, yet it has also corrected a tendency of the *arbitristas*, of foreign observers, and of several historians to overstate the gravity of the Spanish crisis. New research has shown that while an economic depression was certainly real at the national level, it affected different Iberian regions differently, at different times, and was not always so deep that it embraced all aspects of local economies.[67] Even wars, for instance, did not cause a cessation of Spanish international trade, not even with Spain's wartime enemies.[68]

Though mired in poverty and crime, Madrid had a bustling economy because it was the economic and political nerve center of the Iberian Peninsula. The court alone was an enormous consumer of imports. So too was the large urban population that served it. As the hub of a complex economic system, Madrid had unparalleled access to the wealth of Spain and its far-flung possessions. In return for the service of governing the Habsburg Empire, the city received a host of taxes and revenues. By offering lucrative and prestigious governmental offices, Madrid also attracted nobles from the provinces who brought rents from their estates to the city. The resulting concentration of wealth in the capital was unprecedented in Spanish history. This concentration meant that Madrid had an equally unprecedented power to attract vast resources from beyond the Iberian hinterland. Simply put, Madrid became an enormous consumption-oriented market, and thus a giant magnet for long-distance trade.[69] As we shall see in subsequent sections, Madrid provided commercially inclined New Christians—including Portuguese immigrants, native Spanish conversos, and especially returning exiles of both groups—plentiful opportunities to make a living, even in periods of economic depression.

Beyond Madrid, there were other areas of Spain (encompassing Portugal until 1640) that were economically viable, if not always prosperous, and therefore especially attractive to conversos during the seventeenth century. Seville, the gateway to the riches of the New World, stood apart as the most economically vibrant pivot of the realm. Further inland, a few medium-sized cities functioned as the axes of peninsular commerce. Valladolid remained the economic center of the Leonese province despite the city's loss of preeminence after a brief stint as the seat of the Habsburg court (1601–4).[70] Burgos and Bilbao were main links in the northern trade routes that covered the Basque country and Old Castile. In particular, Bilbao enjoyed a relative reprieve from the hardships that beset major economic centers in the Peninsula because it was a main exporter of iron (crucial for arms manufacturing in an age of constant war) and because it emerged as the wool-exporting capital of Spain during the 1600s, at a time when wool was one of the country's chief products.[71] Zaragoza was economically prominent in the Aragonese interior, while Barcelona and Valencia were the economic capitals of the northeastern and far eastern coasts, respectively. Lisbon, Porto, La Coruña, Cádiz, Málaga, and other ports formed a crucial outer rim of the Iberian Peninsula's commercial and industrial networks (see Map 1). Converso merchants frequented and conducted business in all of these economic centers.

Besides major cities, there were numerous nodes of industrial and agricultural production that continued to function despite the general economic downturn of the 1600s. Most larger cities and principal rural centers were linked by a system of major roads that converged in Madrid, a fact that attested to the geographic and economic centrality of the Spanish capital (see Map 1). These roads were a fundamental component of the economic life of the country, for much Iberian trading was done by land.

Peninsular Trade Routes: Some Salient Aspects

The transportation infrastructure of early modern Spain was an amalgam of different roadways dating from the times of the Romans, the Muslims, and the Catholic monarchs. Toward the end of the sixteenth century most peninsular *carreteras* or *calzadas* (highways) and *caminos* (roadways or trails) were in a state of disrepair. For example, in 1593 the arteries surrounding Valladolid were so deteriorated that according to municipal officials, "people cannot walk on them."[72]

Given copious evidence of the sorry state of Spanish highways, one might conclude that the crown was not interested in maintaining an adequate system of roads, yet that was not entirely the case. Ferdinand of Aragon and Isabel of Castile built some of the main peninsular thoroughfares, while their Habsburg successors invested in ones that linked Madrid to the periphery.[73] The central problem, then, was the upkeep of a vast majority of the country's roads and bridges. That task usually fell upon local authorities such as lords and municipalities.

According to David Vassberg, local agents were not particularly effective in maintaining the country's infrastructure.[74] One reason for this was that the authorities were not always able to secure the necessary manpower to undertake road repairs: Local villagers avoided construction and maintenance work because it was usually unpaid. A second problem was financial. Already impoverished by crushing fiscal obligations, local citizens tended to resist extraordinary taxes earmarked for infrastructural improvements, while travelers were often loath to pay usage tolls since (to paraphrase Vassberg) these levies were meant for the maintenance of somebody else's roads.[75]

Most of Spain's principal thoroughfares were unpaved. Some public highways encompassed stretches that were no more than well-trodden trails.[76] Consequently a number of so-called *carreteras* were barely fit for travel by coach. A French tourist commented in 1659 about the rough paths that led to the capital, "everything arrives [in Madrid] by land, and not by coach as in France, but on asses and mules which is one of the reasons that all merchandise . . . [is] so costly there."[77]

Commerce by overland routes was a predominantly seasonal activity. Because most commercial roads had earthen surfaces, they became very dusty in dry months (August, September, and October) and totally impassable in wet ones (December and January).[78] To make matters worse, the accumulation of snow hindered or totally impeded traffic at high altitudes. Many *calzadas* were thus effectively useless for nearly half of the year. It is not surprising that some highways actually consisted of several alternative routes, each of which was intended to compensate for the frequent closure of the other routes.[79]

Throughout the Early Modern Period, commercial land traffic in Spain consisted mainly of mule caravans and assorted *carretas* (carts). Outside of seasonal peaks, and especially when the weather discouraged traveling, road

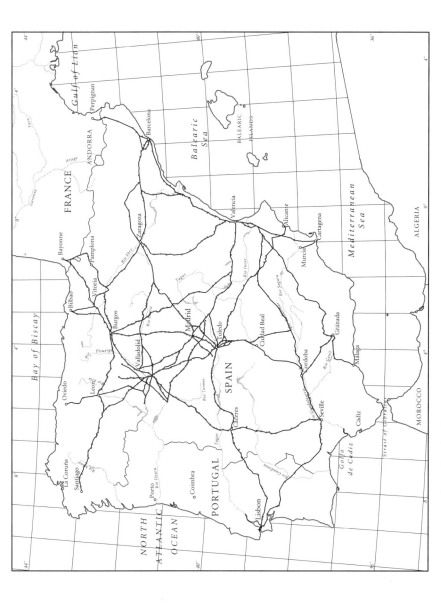

Map 1. Principal Roads of Habsburg Spain, 1608–84. Source: Santos Madrazo, *El sistema de comunicaciones en España, 1750–1850* (Madrid: Ediciones Turner, 1984). The image above is a composite of Madrazo's "Mapa 4" and "Mapa 6." The former is a reconstruction of an itinerary by Ottavio Cotogno (1608); the latter is a reconstruction of a survey by Giuseppe Miselli (1684).

traffic diminished as agricultural laborers retreated to their farms to plow, sow, and harvest.

Itinerant merchants who traversed Spanish highways were known as *arrieros, buhoneros,* and *trajineros.* Of these commercial travelers, rural producers were most likely to use ox-driven carts to transport merchandise. Pack mules and donkeys were easier to handle in mountainous regions, and were commonly preferred by poorer wayfarers and by full-time salesmen whose goods could be borne by one or a few beasts.[80]

Traveling on inadequate roads was an exhausting, time-consuming, and potentially dangerous and expensive affair. *Arrieros* and other voyagers usually had to pay local highway tolls. Merchants who traveled long distances also had to pay royal customs (usually set at 10 percent) at posts located between Castile, the Basque lands, Navarre, Aragon, and the Andalusian province.[81] Of course, traveling *comerciantes* had to meet the additional cost of any merchandise they purchased on the road, not to mention the cost of food and lodging.

Stays at rural and urban inns, usually called *mesones* or *posadas,* were the nightly lot of most merchants who traveled beyond a day's riding or walking distance. Typical hosting establishments were humble places run by peasants or poor city dwellers, and were known for being filthy and generally uncomfortable. *Mesones* offered travelers little more than some straw to sleep on, a modest amount of food for pack-bearing animals, and a stall to keep the animals. Local ordinances in many towns forbade the sale of food by innkeepers. Therefore, in order to have meals, guests often had no choice but to purchase uncooked ingredients at local markets and then ask the innkeepers to prepare the ingredients. Alternately, travelers could go to local taverns, whose keepers were infamous for serving rotten and otherwise revolting food.[82]

The fact that itinerant merchants carried money and commercial goods made these voyagers attractive targets in the eyes of thieves at lodging sites and on the roads. Although Spanish thoroughfares were relatively safe in some areas,[83] road banditry was a manifest danger in regions where the disorder of war and civil uprisings had loosened the grip of law and order. Such was the case in Catalonia, elsewhere along the border with France, and as far south as Valencia, throughout the seventeenth century.[84]

Besides having to beware of bandits, wayfarers had to contend with an understandable sense of isolation as they traveled long distances through alien territory, particularly when they traversed regions as desolate and sparsely populated as early modern Castile. François Bertaut, a traveler from

France, observed in 1659 that Castilian villages were so far apart that one could ride for an entire day without seeing a single person.[85] It is no surprise that many voyagers banded together for purposes of security and companionship. Even this practice, however, could not erase the stigma of being "foreign" in a country where rural and urban folk were typically prejudiced against *forasteros* (outsiders).

As Vassberg has explained, local solidarity in early modern Spanish towns and villages was so intense that it encouraged an exclusionist attitude toward anyone who was not a *vecino*—a taxpaying citizen of the local municipality or federation of municipalities.[86] Prejudice against outsiders took many forms. Some forms were patently discriminatory. For example, local officials often fined *forasteros* more than local residents for violating the same ordinances.[87] Rules governing local marketplaces enshrined the spirit of exclusion in similar fashion. A common municipal policy was to prohibit the sale of outside products until local supplies had been exhausted. A corollary to that approach was to proscribe the sale of inside products to aliens until all internal demand had been satisfied.[88] Through this and a myriad of similar regulations, protectionism became well entrenched in Spanish towns and villages during the Early Modern Era. This form of economic exclusionism worked against non-native, itinerant traders chiefly by limiting their ability to compete. In all likelihood it also encouraged these traders to specialize in the sale of items that were not available locally.

Prejudices against outsiders contributed to the periodic eruption of conflicts between travelers and local citizens. Such disputes were especially difficult to restrain in remote places where the reach of police authorities was limited. For example, in rural Huelva during the mid-1550s, *vecinos* complained that fights between natives and *forasteros* broke out frequently at local inns. According to the worried villagers, such disorders occurred "without justice or punishment," even when the confrontations were lethal.[89]

As if a general distrust of foreigners were not grave enough, the perception that *forasteros* were inimical to local communities acquired a racist coloring where members of marginalized ethnic groups were involved. Popular stereotypes of moriscos, gypsies, and Judeoconversos as inherently dangerous and deceitful were among the oldest ideological lenses through which Old Christians viewed travelers who belonged to these suspect "castes." Portuguese conversos were uniquely vulnerable to ethnic and religious hostility in the roads and cities of Spain because they were doubly conspicuous. Old Christian prejudice marked Luso-conversos not only as *forasteros* (recent Portuguese arrivals often spoke Castilian with a noticeable accent), but also as putative heretics—or more crassly, as "Jews"—by virtue of their Jewish ancestry.

The following episode illustrates some of the perils that Portuguese conversos were liable to encounter while traveling in Spain during the seventeenth century.

The Case of Diego Pereira

On October 15, 1661, two friars appeared uninvited at the house of Francisco Esteban de Cebada, a Toledan inquisitor. The friars, Pedro Mártir[90] and Anselmo de la Huerta, informed Cebada that a Portuguese man who had traveled with them from Andalusia to Castile had "done and said some things" that had made them "suspicious of the [man's] faith."[91]

Later that day, the inquisitor summoned Mártir so that the Dominican could relate his suspicions in detail.[92] Mártir testified that on the previous Sunday he (Mártir), Friar Huerta, and three others were traveling northward through the city of Ecija when a tall man had stopped them to ask how to reach the highway to Cordoba. The man, who was Portuguese, identified himself as Diego de Silva.[93] Mártir told him to follow them, as they too were headed for Cordoba.

The friar continued that when the party stopped to eat at a small country inn, Silva had behaved strangely. According to Mártir, Silva hid behind some wall-matting until the others had finished eating a back of pork. Only then, when the party had totally consumed the pork and the innkeeper brought some cooked rabbits to the table, had Silva emerged from his hiding place to ask if any food remained. When Mártir and the others asked their new road-mate why he had stood behind the matting instead of partaking in the main course of the meal, the latter allegedly did not respond. This made the friar and his companions "suspicious" of Silva.[94] Although Mártir did not explain the group's misgivings, his clear implication was that both he and his traveling partners had smelled the presence of a secret Jew in their midst: Why would a man from Portugal (as opposed to, say, a Spanish morisco) avoid eating pork, unless he were a converso Judaizer?

Mártir recounted that after the group had arrived at an inn in the city of Cordoba, he devised a plan to test Silva. First the friar took out a ham from his road provisions. Then, "with premeditation," he and his comrades maneuvered Silva to a table and pressured him to eat the ham. Friar Huerta later testified about the incident that Mártir told Silva "you will eat [the ham] because there is nothing else to eat," to which the latter "made a very bad face," evidently displeased at the prospect of consuming pork (fol. 7r). Another witness, Diego de Castilla, reconstructed the scene slightly differently. He said that Mártir told Silva that he, Silva, would have to eat the ham "even if he didn't want to" (fol. 8v).

At one point, Mártir continued, a Flemish fellow traveler by the name of Mathias shone a candle under the table and discovered that Silva had not swallowed the ham but had merely tasted it and furtively thrown pieces of it to the floor. According to Mártir, all the members of the traveling cohort were outraged when they saw the half-chewed scraps under the table, and "started calling [Silva] a Jew" (fol. 3r). To this the Lusitanian allegedly responded with the enigmatic statement that their insults did not bother him because he was a prophet (ibid.). According to Mártir, Silva then took some slivers of *tocino* (pig fat) that remained on his plate and put them in his mouth, as though to prove that he was perfectly capable of swallowing pork, but spit them out immediately in apparent disgust (fol. 3r–3v).

By October 14, Mártir could no longer stifle his intense misgivings about the Portuguese traveler. When the group arrived at the Castilian town of Malagón, he confronted Silva by asking him if he knew the tenets of Christian dogma. Silva allegedly said that he did not know religious doctrine, and asked Mártir if he would teach it to him. Naturally, Mártir thought it exceedingly suspicious that a man such as the suspect, who had not denied being a Christian and appeared to be more than forty years of age, should be totally ignorant of Christian beliefs. He therefore tested Silva by asking a simple but highly provocative question: Who is God? Silva allegedly answered that God was "the Eternal Father." Mártir considered this an equivocal rejoinder—he probably interpreted it as a "Judaic" slight of trinitarian doctrine—so he challenged his Portuguese counterpart to say "how many persons were in the Holy Trinity [sic]" (fol. 3v). To this provocation Silva allegedly responded, "Don't people say that they are three?" and duly named the Father, the Son, and the Holy Spirit. The friar then asked Silva which of the three holy persons had died. Silva allegedly stood up to think about the question for a moment, and answered with a tentative query of his own: "Don't they say that it was the Son?" Exasperated and furious at such vacillation, Mártir lashed out at Silva, calling the Portuguese traveler a "Jewish dog," and threatening to denounce him to the Inquisition (ibid.).

This was not all. Mártir also claimed that Silva had uttered the Christian credo on demand, but that he had stopped short of the end after saying the phrase "creator of heaven and earth." The friar stated that when he pressed

Silva to continue reciting the creed, Silva refused. To Mártir this refusal was conclusive proof that Silva was a Judaizer, since the remaining portion of the credo concerned, in Mártir's words, "the sin of the Jews" (namely, their unbelief in Jesus' divinity) and hence contained ideas that a real Jew would be loath to proclaim. Mártir further testified that when he told Silva as much, the latter allegedly repeated his obscure claim that he was a prophet, adding that as such he could live "in whatever law he wanted," meaning that he could follow any religion he pleased (fol. 4r).

In later testimony, the friar stated that he had asked the suspect whether he was traveling northward to escape the Sevillian Inquisition, which had recently taken many people into its custody (presumably under suspicion of heresy). Mártir maintained that Silva did not answer this challenge, but instead asked a young Frenchman who was traveling with them "if there was an Inquisition in France." When the youth told him that there was not, Silva allegedly replied, "Well, then [France] is where I am going" (fol. 4v).

Mártir's deposition continued with a claim that earlier, at a *mesón* in Ciudad Real, Silva had requested a meal and had become agitated when the innkeeper did not give him the food for which he had asked. Cursing angrily, Silva allegedly declared (among other things), "I renounce the Jewish whore who gave birth to me!" Later, on the road to Toledo, Silva's baggage fell from his mule and became soiled, upon which he allegedly began cursing again, saying such things as "I renounce the law of God!" and blaming Mártir for his trouble (fol. 4r).

Following Mártir's deposition, the Toledan Inquisition summoned the friar's comrades to testify about Silva. All of them confirmed the substance of Mártir's testimony, with a few important variations. According to Mathias Pan y Agua, the above-mentioned Fleming, Silva's interaction with his traveling mates had been more volatile and physically dangerous than Pedro Mártir let on. Pan y Agua testified,

When Fray P[edr]o asked [Silva] who was God . . . [Silva] responded that [God was] the Father without saying anything else; seeing this . . . Fray P[edr]o took out the sword of a youth [who was traveling with the group], and putting it naked against the chest of the Portuguese [man], told him that he would kill him unless he declared and confessed by the three persons of the . . . Holy Trinity[;] and then the Portuguese [man], as if under duress, said that God was Father, Son, and Holy Spirit. (fol. 9v)

The record of Pan y Agua's deposition (written, as was customary, in the third person) also contains information about another heated confrontation between the voyagers and their victim:

Having arrived this morning to [the] city [of Toledo] to [a] *mesón*... and presuming this witness and the others from [Silva's] actions [of the preceding days] that the... Portuguese [man] was a Jew, this witness [Pan y Agua] and... Fray P[edr]o took a cross that is attached to the wall of said inn and brought it to the face of [the suspect] so that he would kiss it[;] [the] Portuguese [man] not only refused to kiss it, but he stood up from the stool on which he was sitting, and fled... to the [inn's] hall." (fols. 9v–10r)

Friar Mártir later admitted that the altercation at the Toledan inn had indeed occurred; he also revealed that he had asked Torre to give him a dagger to threaten Silva when Silva had (allegedly) averted his face from the cross (fol. 12v).

Fernando de la Torre, the young French traveler, corroborated the main outlines of Pan y Agua's account. Among other things, he confirmed that Silva had inquired if any Jews lived in France. Torre also claimed that Silva had asked him if Jews were at liberty to pursue their religion in that country. When Torre answered that they were, Silva allegedly said that he wanted to go to France with him. To this Torre responded that if he found out that Silva was Jewish, he would kill him, "as would any other [Frenchman] who found out that that was what he was" (fol. 11r).

Another traveler, Don Diego Manuel de Castilla, a Knight of the Order of Santiago (the most prestigious military order in Spain), concurred with the other witnesses' suspicions that Silva was "Jewish" (*a echo concepto de q el dho portugues es judio*, fol. 5v). Notably, Castilla seconded his comrades' allegations that the suspect had at first given his name as "Diego de Silva," but had later surprised them by identifying himself as "Diego Pereira de Castro y Moscoso" (fol. 5r).

The last witness to testify about the conflict-ridden voyage was Magdalena Martínez. She was the innkeeper in whose *mesón* Silva/Pereira and the informers were staying at the time of the depositions. Martínez was the only one among the witnesses who claimed to have had no contact whatsoever with the suspect; by all appearances at least, she had no reason to be prejudiced against him.[95] In her testimony, Martínez merely acknowledged that three people had altercated in the patio of her inn, among them a friar who was holding a small wooden cross that had been nailed to a wall. However, Martínez said she had not investigated who the persons were and what they were arguing about (fol. 13v).

On the basis of this and the other depositions, Inquisitor Cebada and his colleagues issued an order to arrest Diego de Silva (alias Pereira). Lay assistants of the Holy Office detained the suspect in Toledo and brought him to testify before Inquisitor Joseph Paniagua (no relation to the Flemish witness) in October 17, 1661.

In his first *audiencia* with the Holy Tribunal the defendant identified himself not as "Diego de Silva" but as "Diego Pereira de Castro y Moscoso." He testified that he was an *hidalgo* (nobleman), a soldier by profession, and a war veteran. Specifically, he claimed to have fought in the war of Portuguese independence on the Spanish side (1640), and to have attained the rank of captain in the Royal Spanish Armada in 1654. The defendant noted without shame that he was of Portuguese parentage, and provided a long and detailed personal genealogy. Among his claims were that his paternal grandfather had been an *hidalgo*; that three of his uncles were captains in the Spanish and Portuguese armies, two of whom were knights of the military Order of Christ; and that another uncle was a Jesuit preacher in Lisbon. To the best of his knowledge, all his forbears had been Old Christians, or as he put it, "*limpios*" ("clean ones," namely persons of "clean" blood). He further claimed that none had been the subject of any inquisitorial investigation. Pereira said nothing about his supposed use of the name Silva because, surprisingly, his interrogators did not raise the matter of his alias.

When asked to give an account of his life, Pereira testified that he had spent much of his childhood in Estremoz and Borba, Portugal, but more recently had resided in various Spanish cities, including Madrid, Seville, and Cádiz.[96] From Cádiz, he explained, he had set out alone for Madrid a few days ago because he expected the king to offer him a promotion to the military Order of Christ as a reward for his latest services to the crown (fols. 22r–26r). Pereira indicated that he had started on his journey to the capital when he heard that the Order had concluded its requisite screening procedures and compiled documents known as *pruebas* (literally, "tests" or "proofs"). *Pruebas* were the means by which the military orders of Spain, as well as other exclusive Ibero-Christian societies such as religious confraternities, enforced their statutes of purity of blood. The "tests" were records of internal investigations as to the "cleanliness" of the lineage of prospective members. Such documents often contained additional information concerning the personal character and professional conduct of the applicants.[97] Pereira did not say whether the Order of Christ had determined that his family tree was sufficiently "pure," yet he clearly anticipated that it had or would soon do so—at least that is what the content and tenor of his testimony implies (fol. 26v).

As the interrogation continued, Pereira gave rather halting responses to standard questions regarding his religious education, thereby substantiating Mártir's claim that he (Pereira) had not been properly instructed in the

Catholic faith. The defendant said that he had been baptized and confirmed in Portugal, and that he confessed his sins regularly in church. When his interrogator[98] prompted him to recite the Paternoster and Ave Maria prayers, he did so without any difficulty. Nevertheless, Pereira "stumbled considerably" when reciting the credo (*dijo el credo con algunos tropezones considerables*, fol. 25v). Furthermore, he "did not know the commandments of the Catholic church, or the sacraments, or the articles of the faith, or any articles of Christian doctrine" (fol. 25v).

The rest of Pereira's testimony concerned his fateful voyage from Andalucía to Toledo. Pereira's reconstruction of that journey contrasted sharply with that of his accusers. Regarding the alleged hiding incident, for example, the record of Pereira's deposition reads as follows:

Realizing that he was Portuguese, the people with whom he had been traveling started to say many things to him . . . that he was a so-and-so, and in particular . . . [when] the [inn's] hostess realized that he was Portuguese, she started to say, "Portuguese, Portuguese[!]" and other things, to which this witness replied, "[I am] a nobleman, a very honorable one, as are all my relatives . . ." And they also told him many other [insulting] things, so he became angry and did not wish to eat with them. . . . [Another person in the group], seeing what they were telling him, started saying that [the suspect's] mother was a Jewess, and a whore, and that his relatives were also Jews. In the same manner, while traveling on the road, they told him many things, and in particular they asked him if he was a prophet, to which he responded ironically [*enchança*] that yes, he was a prophet of the king of Spain (fol. 27r–27v).

Like all inquisitorial defendants, Pereira was asked if he knew or presumed why the Holy Office had arrested him. As the above citation suggests, he suspected that his erstwhile companions were the ones who had denounced him. However, Pereira chose to speculate about other possible accusers. In so doing he digressed considerably from the matter of his recent voyage. Toward the end of his deposition, Pereira went so far as to blame some Judeoconversos for his incarceration, referring to them by the popular euphemism "people of the Nation"—*gente de la nación*:[99]

[The defendant] says he presumes that maybe some persons who are called "of the Nation," [had denounced him to the Inquisition]. . . . [H]e had asked [those persons] for alms at the time that he was in Cadiz, in Seville, and in Madrid...when he found himself poor and with nothing to eat. [T]hey did not want to give him [the alms] he asked for, and he treated them badly, saying that they were Jewish *pícaros* and that if he were one of their own they would help him, and that the reason they did not want to give him anything was that he was a nobleman, and that if they were in Portugal they would not dare to stand in front of him with their hats on. [T]hat is why he presumes that some of these persons had denounced him with false testimony, for which he may have been incarcerated [by] the Inquisition. (fol. 27v)

Engaging this spontaneous indictment of Luso-conversos, Pereira's questioner prompted him to identify his presumed accusers by name and to explain why he had called them "Jewish *pícaros*." The inquisitorial notary who assisted Inquisitor Paniagua in the case recorded Pereira's response as follows:

In Cádiz [the defendant] begged Andrés Gómez and Manuel Díaz for alms . . . and [he begged] other people whom he does not remember . . . [yet] he remembers these two because they are *very rich merchants*. Andrés Gómez [is in charge of] the [Royal] Sugar Monopoly, of spice shops, and of many other things, and . . . Manuel Díaz is the administrator of His Majesty's *millones*.[100] . . . [I]n Seville he remembers having asked [one] Dr. Messa for alms—he is a doctor—and [Messa] did not want to give him any, so [the defendant] also called [Messa] a Jew. He also remembers having begged for alms in Madrid from Antonio Henríquez, Portuguese, who is a businessman, who is of the Nation too. . . . [After Henríquez refused, the defendant] told him that he [meaning Henríquez] was *a Jew of the* [Hebrew] *nation*. And the same occurred with Antonio Váez de Guzmán, who [the defendant] understands is a businessman as well. (Emphasis added, fol. 27v)

Pereira's interlocutor was not satisfied by this response. How, he asked, did Pereira know that the merchants, the doctor, and the businessman were "Jewish" if (as the questioner put it) "all the Portuguese appear to be of the same nation"? (fol. 28r). Pereira answered,

In Portugal those who are merchants are held in low esteem; there they live mistreated [*ahajados*] and vituperated by the rest; *and that is why they move to Castile, because* [in Portugal] *they are not considered well-born.* . . . [T]his [attitude] is very common in Portugal. . . . *And since the* [aforementioned individuals] *are Portuguese and they have come to live in Castile, he* [the defendant] *called them Jews,* [although] *he has not seen them do anything against our holy Catholic faith.* (Emphasis added; ibid.)

It was common knowledge in Portugal, Pereira continued, that merchants disliked nobles and disparaged them (fol. 29r). Furthermore, the persons in question had probably testified against him "because they had seen him outside his homeland and impoverished" (ibid.). Here Pereira's implication was that the supposed accusers felt superior to him because of their wealth and their relative comfort in exile. In Spain, Pereira was hinting, such men could not only amass power and property, but they could do so while feeding their bloated commoners' egos and escaping a well-deserved popular backlash.

The final portion of the Pereira dossier records the deposition of the defendant's brother-in-law, Antonio Páez de Santi (or Sandi), a resident of Madrid and knight of the Order of Christ. It is not necessary to rehearse the details of Páez's testimony. Suffice it to say that the information he provided concurred fully with Pereira's declarations. The witness confirmed his prior acquaintance with the prisoner by accurately describing Pereira's physical appearance. Crucially, Páez verified Pereira's statements concerning the latter's identity, his genealogy, and the purpose of his trip to Madrid. Indeed, the witness intimated that he was expecting Pereira's arrival in the capital at the time of the arrest (fols. 36r–37v).

It is disappointing that the Pereira dossier has no formal conclusion; rather, it ends with the narrative record of Páez's testimony. Only one document follows that record, effectively closing out the inquisitorial file. That document is a brief letter written in the defendant's own hand and dated December 15, 1661. In the letter Pereira acknowledges receiving some personal effects, presumably the ones that the Holy Office had confiscated at the moment of his arrest. Thus it appears that, in the end, Inquisitor Paniagua and his assistants set Pereira free. Had the inquisitors realized, on the basis of Páez's deposition, that Pereira had been a victim of libel? Unfortunately, there is no way to answer this question with certainty because the case file does not preserve any document indicating that the process against Pereira had been or would be dismissed, much less suggesting why Pereira had been released. Similarly there is no sign that the inquisitors took any steps to prosecute Mártir *et alia* for offering false testimony.[101]

An Analysis of the Pereira Case

Regardless of how and why the proceedings against Pereira concluded, it is clear that Páez's deposition had brought the inquest to a crossroads. On one hand, the inquisitors had heard a series of mutually supportive and fairly consistent denunciations. Lending weight to these denunciations was the fact, made evident in the course of the inquest, that Pereira barely possessed a rudimentary knowledge of Catholic dogma and did not know several prayers. To make matters worse for the defendant, three of the denouncers were socially respectable individuals whom the inquisitors could not dismiss out of hand as ignorant and conniving rabble: Diego de Castilla was a knight of Santiago, while Pedro Mártir and Anselmo de la Huerta were *religiosos* in good standing. Notably, Friar Huerta was an inquisitorial *calificador*, a theological consultant to the Holy Office who specialized in the identification of heresy. What better qualifications than Huerta's to produce a persuasive deposition in the eyes of his colleagues?

On the other hand stood Páez's testimony, which entirely corroborated key portions of the suspect's deposition. Also bolstering Pereira was his own suggestion that he had successfully undergone *pruebas* as an aspirant to a military honor. By deposing that he had been the subject of a genealogical investigation, Pereira flaunted his confidence that he was without *sangre infecta* (infected blood). More importantly, he intimated that he had the means to prove his "cleanliness" and thus, implicitly, his religious orthodoxy and good character. It is true that genealogical investigations were not foolproof because some individuals (usually wealthy ones) could purchase forged certificates of *limpieza de sangre* in order to obtain favorable evaluations. In any case, "clean" blood did not in itself preclude heresy from the point of view of the Holy Office. Still, *pruebas* were potentially among Pereira's best defensive assets since the Inquisition could easily verify the existence of those documents and thus authenticate a significant part of his testimony.[102] If in fact Pereira had submitted to the scrutiny of the Order of Christ, his *pruebas* could at least raise some doubts as to the credibility of his accusers. At most, the *pruebas* could serve as ancillary evidence of his good faith, even if such records, as fallible instruments, could not prove his *limpieza* or his religious self-identity in a definitive way.

Was Pereira, as his detractors claimed, a dishonest converso and a crypto-Jew? Did Pereira actually dislike *cristãos-novos*, as he virtually boasted to his interrogators, or was he feigning prejudice in order to avoid punishment, in this case by portraying himself as a respectably Judeophobic Old Christian?

To conclude that Pereira was a converso Judaizer who sought to trick his questioners by constructing an elaborate web of lies requires us to suppose that he was a bold and resourceful master of deception. Such an image of Pereira contrasts sharply with the one his accusers drew of him. In their rendering, Pereira was extremely clumsy and volatile: He disclosed his supposed Jewishness in fits of bitterness ("I renounce the Jewish whore who gave birth to me") or through a rather improbable naiveté ("Don't they say [that the second Person of the Holy Trinity] was the Son?").

It is certainly conceivable that Pereira was a rash individual who made some outrageous statements while inebriated or out of a misguided bravado when he felt cornered by a hostile clique. All the same, Pereira's behavior *as his accusers depicted it* grossly overstepped the boundaries of plausibility. For example, it would have required an inordinate and therefore unlikely carelessness or stupidity on Pereira's part to say to a group of strangers that he was entitled to live by whatever religion suited his fancy. Seventeenth-century Spain was a country in which even the mere appearance of religious infidelity was anathema; Pereira must have known this. If he did not, or was so impulsive or demented that he could not control his heretical tongue, he certainly did not have the presence of mind to manufacture a seamless screen of falsehoods, with or without assistance of his brother-in-law.

A historical reconstruction of Pereira must reject the notion that he was at once a calculating, clever rogue and a volatile fumbler who could barely disguise his "Judaism." Pereira could not be both astute and asinine.[103] Thus the most appropriate conclusion one can draw from the available evidence is that even if Pereira was lying about something—his identity, his past, or both—he was not the Judeophobic caricature that his detractors drew of him.[104]

On its face, Pereira's relative ignorance of Catholic dogma and prayer seems to buttress the accusers' contention that he was not a bona fide Christian. As the reader will recall, Mártir's wager was that Pereira could not bring himself to profess Christianity in public because Pereira was secretly so perverse that he denied the Catholic faith altogether.

In reality, however, all that Pereira's ignorance suggests is that he was not a particularly pious Christian. If Pereira had been a skillful liar and a crypto-Jew, he would probably have trained himself in the tenets and verbal formulas of Christianity, for without the ability to repeat these tenets and formulas (however insincerely) he would not have been able to conceal his heresy very well, especially not while living in the midst of an arch-Catholic society such as that of seventeenth-century Spain. (By the same token, if Pereira had wanted to establish his credibility, he probably would not have told the inquisitors that he had previously undergone a genealogical investigation if had he not actually done so: Why would Pereira have risked his future and his reputation by concocting a story that his interrogators could easily disprove?)

Leaving aside questions of plausibility, we must recognize that Pereira's lack of religious knowledge did not necessarily prove anything other than his own ignorance. The records of the Spanish Inquisition offer plentiful examples of defendants—conversos and Old Christians alike—who were far from well versed in official Catholicism. These records also attest to the fact that many self-incriminating Judaizers had not only mastered Christian prayers, but were very familiar with Christian theology.[105] The point is that a defen-

dant's ability or inability to recite creeds and prayers by rote did not necessarily have anything to do with his or her consciously chosen religious identity or, for that matter, with the inquisitors' conclusions regarding that
defendant's real or alleged attitude towards Catholicism.

It may well be that Pereira told his questioners the truth about himself.
Yet, given the absence of definitive proof to that effect, the riddle of his "true"
religious identity and his ethnic origin remains irresolvable. What interests
us here, however, is not the informants' credibility, but the substance of their
testimony as an example of anti-converso sentiment.

Through their depositions, the defendant and his denouncers voiced a
gamut of derisive preconceptions about New Christians that were widespread in the Iberia of the 1600s, as Pereira's own observations about his
homeland suggest. All of the informants, including the accused, appealed
first and foremost to an anti-Portuguese variant of conversophobia, itself a
form of Judeophobia, in order to place blame on conversos (real or imagined) and paint themselves in the colors of innocence and righteousness.

Pedro Mártir and his comrades articulated a rather crude Judeophobia
through a kind of semantic slippage. Instead of defining Pereira as a New
Christian heretic, the accusers referred to him almost obsessively as *el Portugués* occasionally shifting to anti-Jewish epithets such as *perro judío* (Jewish dog). In so doing they not only (mis)used the term "Portuguese" to mean
"converso" and revealed their Judeophobic intent, but they tacitly conveyed
that they were not interested in denouncing heresy in the strictest sense. In
fact, none of the accusers employed such designations as *hereje* (heretic) and
judaizante at all. Instead, the informants insinuated that the person they were
accusing was a full-fledged Portuguese "Jew" who had disguised himself as a
Christian. The focus here was not on the suspect's religious behavior, but on
his presumed nature: In the accusers' eyes it was as if Pereira were ultimately
not a Christian who behaved as a Jew, namely a Judaizer, but a wholly foreign
and unassimilable creature whose essential character was "Jewish." It is noteworthy that Friars Huerta and Mártir were educated men whose theological
training could have allowed them to define Pereira in much more nuanced—
and much more accurate—terms.

Interestingly, Pereira pursued the same anti-"Portuguese" logic as his
accusers. This is highly ironic in light of the fact that Pereira was Portuguese
himself. By his own account, Pereira had previously assailed five supposed
Judeoconversos based on the same prejudiced view of Portuguese immigrants that had, according to him, driven Mártir and the other travelers to
mistrust, curse, and assault him. Specifically, Pereira said that when he had

been a resident of Cádiz, Seville, and Madrid, he had accused two merchants, a doctor, and a businessman of being "Jewish *pícaros*" merely because they, like himself, were Portuguese who happened to be living in Spain. The defendant even admitted that he had insulted the men although he possessed no evidence that they were Judaizers (one suspects Pereira did not even have any proof that his alleged victimizers were New Christians, let alone crypto-Jews). In short, the defendant admitted he had drawn the imaginary equation Portuguese = converso = secret Jew, to which he had fallen prey while traveling from Andalusia to Castile.

In contrast to the travelers' portrait of Pereira, however, Pereira's depiction of the five supposed Luso-conversos reflected a social or class bias as much as it expressed a sense of ethnic and religious opposition between Old and New Christians. The suspect explained that in insulting the alleged *cristãos-novos* he had upheld a popular notion that being *bourgeois* was tantamount to being of Jewish extraction, or at least was as reprehensible as being Jewish. Whether Pereira truly espoused this notion or had merely seized it as a convenient tool with which to level verbal abuse is not immediately relevant. What is more interesting is the mental association that Pereira claimed to have made between members of urban non-noble elites—businessmen, merchants, and professionals—on one hand, and stereotyped images of "Judaic" ignobility on the other.

Pereira's imaginary association entailed four mutually reinforcing premises. The first premise was that a good Christian (by implication, a person of "clean" blood such as Pereira himself) could easily deduce that a given individual was a New Christian, and therefore a Jew, simply by ascertaining that the person was a merchant or businessman of some kind. The second premise was that merchants, and by extension businessmen in general, were easily identifiable by their social behavior, for example by the rudeness with which they treated honorable people. The third premise held, along the same lines, that a Portuguese merchant who acted contemptuously toward his (or presumably her) betters either had Jewish blood or was like someone who did. Conversely—and this was the fourth premise—having Jewish blood predisposed a person to offend the natural and proper order of society by withholding reverence where reverence was due and by embracing beliefs that were contrary to Catholicism. It is significant that Pereira did not pay any attention to the religious beliefs of his alleged libelers, as if to say that the heretical nature of Luso-conversos was well known.

To summarize, Pereira not only presented himself as a Judeophobe, but as an indigent aristocrat who resented low-born individuals (in this case, conversos) precisely because their power over him, like their material wealth, accrued not from the dignity of noble lineage but from the exercise of base commercial or professional skills. Where Mártir and the travelers had collapsed ethnic and religious categories in their testimony ("Portuguese" = "converso" = "Jew"), Pereira conflated two distinct religious classifications ("Jew" and "heretic"), an ethnic classification ("Portuguese of the Nation"), and a socioeconomic one ("businessman" and/or "merchant").[106]

Judeophobia and the Place of Conversos in Peninsular Society

What does the testimony collected in the Pereira dossier tell us about the historical environment from which it sprang? What does the informants' narrative conflation of religious, ethnic, and in Pereira's case, socioeconomic categories reveal about the ways in which Old Christians tended to regard conversos in the seventeenth century?

Above all, the Pereira dossier bears witness to an atmosphere of suspicion that had the potential to mushroom into open animosity against Judeoconversos, particularly against those of Portuguese origin. That such hostility exploded in the face of Diego Pereira, whose outward behavior was probably beyond serious reproach, suggests the fact that at least some bigoted Spaniards (and a few Catholic foreigners like Torre and Pan y Agua) did not require any real evidence of heresy in order to "unmask" and persecute "secret Jews." Pereira confirmed this fact when he indicated that he had not bothered to avail himself of any actual evidence of Judaizing to conclude that certain Portuguese men were contemptible "Jews." All that the accusers' passive bigotry required for it to turn into open abuse was a perception that its object was "Portuguese."

The view that Portuguese immigrants and their descendants were ipso facto New Christians, and that all conversos of Lusitanian origin were secret Jews, arose in Spain in response to the Portuguese migrations of the late sixteenth and early seventeenth centuries. Like most sweeping, derisive generalizations, this double presumption was empirically untenable. Even so, it was not a mere product of bigoted hallucination; rather, it sprang from a small but significant kernel of historical actuality.

As several historians have noted, there is evidence that crypto-Judaism was a lingering reality among Portuguese conversos long after Spanish Judaizing had withered under the cumulative impact of Inquisitorial persecution.[107] Many of the immigrants to Spain were indeed conversos, but, more importantly, it is probable that a number of them were also secret Jews.

Lusitanian crypto-Judaism, whatever its objective resemblance to normative Judaism, owed its survival to the conditions under which Jewish and converso life developed in Portugal. The scope of this study prohibits a thorough review of these conditions, yet the following important aspects are worth mentioning.

The Jews of Portugal pursued a separate social and religious existence in relative peace until 1497. In that year, King Manoel arranged for summary mass baptisms by which an overwhelming majority of them became titular Christians. Once baptized, the former Jews enjoyed legal protection from discrimination and persecution for a period of thirty-six years, in accordance with consecutive royal decrees. The explicit purpose of such protection was to permit the unhindered assimilation of all first-generation "conversos" (the *children* of the converts) and to avert the need to establish an Inquisition in the Spanish mold.[108]

Some scholars have argued that a vast majority of Luso-conversos took advantage of the long legal reprieve to acculturate into Portuguese Christian society.[109] It is certainly the case that some families of *cristãos-novos* penetrated the upper echelons of the Portuguese nobility, the royal bureaucracy, and the financial and commercial elite of the Portuguese kingdom from 1497 until the establishment of the Lusitanian Inquisition in 1536.[110] Still, it is not clear what proportion of Luso-conversos embraced Catholicism sincerely. Some data suggest the possibility that internal converso resistance to Christianization was considerable. For example, the first generations of *cristãos-novos* included several Spanish Jews who had successfully defied conversionist pressure in their native land, and had taken refuge in Portugal in 1492. That those tenacious refugees had not capitulated earlier, under the threat of banishment and expropriation, makes it improbable that they embraced Catholicism wholeheartedly after the sudden and utterly perfunctory mass conversion of 1497.

Perhaps the most prudent assertion one can make about the situation in Portugal prior to 1536, then, is that royal protection allowed those converts who wanted to preserve their Jewish attachments to cultivate and bequeath them in secret, while it also allowed those converts who wished to blend into the fabric of Christendom to pursue the path of assimilation in relative peace.

Sincerely Christian or not, Portuguese conversos became culturally "Ibericized" in the course of the sixteenth century, just as Spanish New Christians had before them. Externally at least, nothing distinguished New Christians from Old Christians in Portugal by the seventeenth century. Portuguese conversos were unique, however, in that their existence, unlike that of the Spanish *cristianos nuevos*, was not the result of a long period of persecution. A key difference between the Spanish and Portuguese Jewries is that the former disintegrated slowly, acrimoniously, and often as a direct consequence of Judeophobic violence, while the latter did not.[111] Portuguese Jewry as a whole ceased to exist in an instant, and only by the most superficial and pragmatic of official acts. Despite episodes of brutality and discrimination, Portuguese Jews suffered nothing comparable to the anti-Jewish riots of 1391 that gave rise to the converso problem in Castile and Aragon.[112] Furthermore, unlike their Spanish counterparts, Portuguese Jews did not have to endure furious waves of conversionist and Judeophobic propaganda. In Portugal there was never any possibility of friction between the converted and the unconverted, as occurred in Spain, since baptism had swept up all the Lusitanian *kehillot*.[113] Crucially, in Portugal most of the converted did not come under inquisitorial scrutiny, though that sorry fate would befall their descendants.

For these reasons, the former Jews of Portugal were able to retain a measure of internal cohesiveness and a sense of continuity with the (Jewish) past. If nothing else, certain group instincts passed by inertia from one generation of Luso-conversos to the next. As late as the seventeenth century, Portuguese conversos still tended to maintain their intracommunal bonds by pursuing endogamous marriage alliances and cultivating tightly knit commercial and professional relationships.[114] In many cases, the familial and commercial networks formed by these bonds resembled or even continued ones that existed among Portuguese Jews prior to 1497. Additionally, *cristãos-novos* inherited many of the professional roles of their Jewish predecessors and thus much of the Jews' social and political position in Portuguese society.[115] When dealing with external authorities, Lusitanian conversos often behaved as a community, and the authorities treated them accordingly. This happened, for example, when conversos pooled together enormous sums of money and solicited João III and the pope through semiofficial representatives in a failed attempt to prevent the establishment of the Portuguese Inquisition.[116] Such communal patterns of activity would be repeated later, for example in the above-mentioned negotiations with Philip II of Spain.

Again, the probability is high that many if not most Luso-conversos retained a consciousness of belonging to an identifiable social group quite distinct from the Ibero-Christian mainstream. Many *cristãos-novos* developed a sense of ethnic difference.[117] This group consciousness probably had roots in an awareness of common descent, and likely derived sustenance from cir-

cumstantial factors. Among these factors were continual social and economic intercourse among *cristãos-novos*, as well as the persistence of Old
Christian prejudice against conversos irrespective of the latter's religious
convictions.

The entry of a sizable "Portuguese" element into the Spanish scene after
1580 was a watershed in the history of all peninsular conversos. By that time,
the virtual disappearance of native crypto-Judaism had caused a shift in
Spanish attitudes toward *cristianos nuevos*. Rather than focusing on religious
behavior per se, these attitudes now focused on the purported ethnic or
racial characteristics of Judeoconversos. So too, words like converso, which
had applied to actual converts during the fourteenth and fifteenth centuries,
had become hereditary labels with predominantly racial or ethnic meanings.
The emergence of collective designations such as *gente del linaje* (people of
the lineage), *esta raza* (this race), *esta casta* (this caste), *esta nación* (this nation), and *gente de la nación* (people of the Nation), underlined the perceptual turn toward racialism that took place in Castile and Aragon during the
sixteenth and seventeenth centuries.[118]

Once in Spain, Portuguese conversos presented a challenge to the conversophobic imagination because they revived the specter of widespread
heresy at a time when racial criteria had become central in Spanish thinking
about human difference and social danger. Not long after the arrival of thousands of Luso-conversos, terms such as *portugueses de la nación*—or simply,
portugueses—came into popular use as a means of differentiating between
Spanish conversos and those of foreign provenance. A practical effect of the
new code words was to define Portuguese New Christians as a dangerous
group in their own right. In time, the appellation "Portuguese" acquired the
same cross-generational meaning that the term *converso* had attained at
the turn of the sixteenth century: by the 1600s, Spaniards typically employed
the word "Portuguese" to identify New Christians who were descended from
Portuguese immigrants. The difference was that the designation "Portuguese" connoted a particularly grave religious menace as much as it connoted a purely racial one.

One result of these developments is the conceptual muddle exemplified
by the narrative testimony of the informants in the Pereira investigation. The
various instances of semantic slippage in that case do not suggest the relatively unambiguous trend toward racial or ethnic definitions of "otherness"
that had taken place during the sixteenth century, but a chaotic ideational
landscape in which several ethnic, racial, religious, and economic conceptions of conversos' "otherness" combined in common parlance to articulate

the paranoid anxieties of a rather bewildered Spanish public. It was a landscape born of the Portuguese influx and the perceptual challenge that the influx posed, namely, how to understand, define, and identify the new converso danger.

Pereira's own avowed dislike of wealthy merchants is an example of a widespread type of anxiety concerning the roles that conversos played—and were *thought* to play—in the economic life of Spain and Portugal. In both countries there were small numbers of conversos who occupied prominent positions in commerce and high finance. This is one reason that a stereotype developed of conversos as powerful and rapacious "businessmen." The Portuguese term *homens de negocios*, its Spanish equivalent, *hombres de negocios* and the bilingual term *mercaderes* gave linguistic expression to this stereotype. By the early 1600s, those terms, like the more generic *hombres de la nación* (men of the Nation) had become popular euphemisms for conversos.

Modern scholars have tended to regard New Christians as a predominantly urban merchant bourgeoisie.[119] On the whole, this generalization is probably accurate given the high proportion of conversos who were city-bound traffickers and retailers. It would skew the record, however, to ignore the fact that conversos also took part in such occupations as soldiering, farming, cattle raising, domestic service, and manual labor, not to mention medicine, bureaucratic administration, tax collection, and diplomacy—four traditionally "Jewish" occupations that did not involve the buying and selling of material commodities.[120] A few conversos even became clerics as late as the seventeenth century, despite repeated inquisitorial purges and the fact that "purity of blood" had become a legal requisite for entering religious orders and for assuming many ecclesiastical posts.[121]

Within the substratum of New Christian *comerciantes*[122] itself there was substantial diversity. From penurious street vendors, to petty shopkeepers, artisans and seamstresses, to relatively comfortable *arrendadores*, it is clear that converso businessmen and merchants did not comprise a homogeneous group. In the world of these conversos, the word *negocios* ("business"—literally, "affairs" or "deals") actually pointed to a variety of mercantile and sometimes non-mercantile activities. As Pilar Huerga Criado has observed, the purview of a single converso businessman could in fact be very broad: "The field in which converso businessmen developed their negocios extended to all economic sectors: Agricultural, artisanal, mercantile, and financial. One who exploited the land, also trafficked in cattle and wine, sold and bought cloths, and administered some rent."[123] Many a New Christian described himself (less often herself) as a *mercader* (or *comerciante*) *de todos géneros*—literally a "merchant of all genres of merchandise."[124] Somewhat reminiscent of the colloquial English term "jack of all trades," this designation underscores the versatility that such individuals developed in order to survive within a variegated economic environment. The point is that New Christians did not form a monolithic class of capitalists or an undifferentiated bourgeoisie. Rather, they were a dynamic and well-integrated part of the Iberian economy whose activities in various fields, many if not most of them commercial, reflected the multifarious nature of that economy.

To be sure, in a country as import-dependent as Spain was during the 1600's, it was only logical that merchants—including those of New Christian stock—were visible mainstays of economic life. In the cities, foreign traders (as well as native traders with foreign connections) were usually the ones who supplied indigenous artisans with raw materials and made foreign manufactures widely available to a commodity-hungry public. Wholesalers met local demand for imports such as tobacco and inexpensive fabrics at local plazas and fairs, while petty tradesmen (many of them smugglers) sold all manner of trinkets, toilet accessories, and trumpery in the streets.[125]

With regard to the economic and ethnic stratification of Spain's predominantly foreign merchant class, Antonio Domínguez Ortiz has noted,

> Between [the] magnates and the miserable *buhoneros* [sellers of bauble] who traversed the dusty roads of Castile there was a whole gamut of intermediate levels in which we can discern a certain specialization by national origin; usually, wholesale commerce was in the hands of [immigrant] Italians and Flemings, while Portuguese and Frenchmen . . . were more numerous in medium and small commerce. But exceptions were so numerous that we think it preferable to abstain from generalizations of that nature.[126]

Converso merchants, including those of Lusitanian origin, tended to dwell within the low and intermediate regions of the commercial sector that Domínguez associates with Portuguese and Frenchmen (in fact, it is conceivable that by "Portuguese" Domínguez actually meant Portuguese Judeoconversos). Again, a handful of Portuguese conversos and their Spanish descendants did belong to the upper economic strata. As royal financiers, administrators, and *asentistas* (royal contractors), wealthy *cristãos-novos* reached the peak of their influence during the reign of Philip IV.[127] To appreciate how important some of these *hombres de negocios* were to the crown, suffice it to note that a mere six years after Philip's accession to the throne—well before Portuguese conversos became his financial backers of choice—ten of them lent the state a total of nearly 1.9 million ducats. That sum represented an imposing 39 percent of the crown's yearly foreign budget.[128] Great financiers and *asentistas*, however, were not typical of Judeoconverso businessmen, who usually took part in relatively minor trades and associated occupations.

Members of the Bernal de Caño family of Ciudad Rodrigo are examples of a middling yet relatively prosperous type of converso merchant. The Caños descended from agricultural laborers who had emigrated from Portugal at the end of the sixteenth century. In Spain, the men of the family became specialists in trades that conformed to the mixed economy of their town. For instance, Juan Bernal purchased wine and cattle from local growers and ranchers in his role as a supplier of taverns and butcher shops in Ciudad Rodrigo. In addition, he served as an *arrendador* of lay and ecclesiastical rents.[129] So too, we find members of the immigrant Piñero family of Ciudad Rodrigo who dealt in textiles, as their immediate ancestors had done in Portugal, yet combined that "traditional" trade with farming, cattle-raising, and rent collection in their adopted country.[130]

Further down the socioeconomic ladder, a host of Portuguese conversos, perhaps a plurality, specialized in what one may vaguely call petty commerce. In reality, these simple *mercaderes* engaged in types of business as diverse but less remunerative than those pursued by the likes of the Bernal Caños and the Piñeros. For example, a converso "stall-keeper" was often also the one who "manufactured" or at least prepared the products he or she sold, such as *aguardiente* (a type of homemade liquor). Like their more prosperous fellows, struggling converso traders congregated in the marketplaces of Madrid, Seville, and other cities to buy and sell food, manufactures, and services.

Many immigrant conversos made a living exclusively by selling items of foreign provenance, either by offering the merchandise from door to door, or by tending a small *estanco* (a small, semipermanent shop or stall) supplied by friends or relatives who brought the merchandise from distant parts. For instance, the small family of Simon Fernández, a Portuguese immigrant, lived almost solely by the petty linen trade in Madrid.[131] Simon and his two eldest sons worked as itinerant linen salesmen. His daughter Isabel was married to another *lenzero* (seller of linens) of Portuguese extraction. Only Simon's brother-in-law, who owned a shop in Madrid's bustling Calle Mayor, sold miscellaneous items, including semiprecious objects made from a type of processed American silver called *solimán*. Despite counting on the stability of this *estanco* the extended Fernández family was not wealthy. Simon's in-laws were totally destitute and "lived from alms" according to Manuel, Simon's second son.[132] Like his father, Manuel had himself had to fend off penury virtually his entire life: He had sold linens in the streets of Madrid well before reaching the age of ten.[133]

New Christians like Simon Fernández, who settled in Madrid during the sixteenth and seventeenth centuries, took advantage of the centrality of the capital and of the sheer volume of goods and services that were exchanged there. Not surprisingly, the records of the Toledan tribunal of the Inquisition, which encompassed Madrid, contain a host of cases against "Portuguese" *lenzeros, estanqueros de tabaco* (tobacco stand-keepers), and *vendedores de paños* (sellers of woven fabrics, usually inexpensive, imported wool).[134] The abundance of such cases gives the strong impression that immigrant conversos were especially numerous in textiles, tobacco, chocolate, and other portable, high-demand commodities. The areas of central Madrid in which Simon Fernández and his sons sold linens, namely the marketplaces and residential streets surrounding the Calle Mayor, seem to have developed something of a "foreign" air with the mass immigration of Judeconversos from Lusitania after 1580, as well as other *extranjeros* (foreigners) throughout the seventeenth century. It is nonetheless unclear whether any areas of the city developed as specifically "Portuguese" sectors.[135]

A possible reason that it is not easy to find such sectors is that relatively few converso merchants stayed in one place along the course of their commercial careers. Economically and geographically, Spain's New Christian minority as a whole was extremely mobile. In that respect, Judeoconversos differed from a majority of Old Christians and resembled a multitude of foreigners, chiefly Flemings, Frenchmen, and Italians, who flocked to Spain throughout the seventeenth century, attracted by the prospect of commerce in American and European imports. Of course, a key distinction between these foreigners and the conversos was that the latter were a very familiar part of the socioeconomic landscape of Iberia. By the seventeenth century, most Peninsular conversos were thoroughly Ibericized, that is to say, they were culturally (if not religiously) "Spanish" or "Portuguese." Their language, public behavior, tastes, and social mores were in line with those of Old Christians of various social classes.[136]

One advantage that *cristianos nuevos* (Portuguese and non-Portuguese alike) had over the immigrant foreigners was that they could avail themselves of preexisting networks of fellow conversos whose presence and support throughout the peninsula made commerce in portable goods an attractive and potentially profitable pursuit. Of course, conversos also differed from the foreigners in that they bore an old social stigma and were often legally disabled by reason of their Jewish ancestry.

Conversos in general, and especially the "Portuguese of the Nation," became the objects of a popular backlash against foreigners as alarm over the political and economic crisis of the Habsburg kingdom grew during the seventeenth century. The backlash manifested itself in various arenas.

Among the educated, eminent social critics struck a xenophobic chord when they bemoaned the fact that immigrant businessmen had become the country's de facto mercantile and entrepreneurial class. Some commentators were particularly distressed that religiously suspect foreigners such as Frenchmen (possible Calvinists) and Portuguese New Christians (presumed Judaizers) prospered, while native Catholics wallowed in debt. Along these lines, the commentator Tomás de Mercado denounced what he called "our senseless subjection to foreigners in giving them control of all the most important things in the country. . . . The best properties are theirs . . . [and] the bulk of the kingdom [is] in their hands."[137] The mercantilist Sancho de Moncada was more specific. For him, the ills of Spain derived from "the new trade of foreigners," the radical cure for which was to prohibit foreign manufactures altogether.[138] Invective against Luso-converso businessmen flowed with particular venom from the pens of various commentators. One polemicist wrote to Philip IV that, "being lords of commerce and of the [customs] of all the ports . . . through the arrendamientos of royal rents, all [conversos] have their wealth outside of [the Habsburg Kingdoms] and the greater part of it in the provinces of your enemies . . . and they bleed these [Hispanic] realms continually, weakening them more every day, and making your enemies more powerful."[139] Such condemnation grossly exaggerated the power of aliens and glossed over the obvious fact that most immigrants were not merchant tycoons. It is true that foreign businessmen had attained prominence in economic life. Frenchmen and Flemings, for example, founded large trading houses in Seville. Genoese bankers, the German Fuggers, and wealthy Portuguese conversos bankrolled the Spanish state at high interest. As mentioned earlier, a few of these conversos also secured the lucrative royal contracts.[140] For all their ire, however, nativist reactionaries could not erase the fact that the commercial activities of the immigrants satisfied Spanish demand that native businessmen and capitalists could not meet, be it demand for credit, administrative services, or foreign goods.

At a popular level, the attitudes of Old Christians toward converso merchants and businessmen during Spain's century of crisis were often tinted by a host of fears about the latter's supposed greed, deceitfulness, and general immorality. Some libelous fictions that circulated freely as late as the 1700s had obvious roots in the mythological *repertoire* of medieval Judeophobia,[141] and had little if anything to do directly with the economic activities of seventeenth-century conversos. For example, in the 1630s a royal bureaucrat by the name of Juan de Quiñones devoted a purportedly scientific treatise to the subject of Jewish male menstruation. Quiñones argued not only that Jewish men and their male descendants menstruated, but that all who descended of Jews emitted a peculiar odor, that they drank Christian blood to alleviate their God-given maladies, and so on.[142] Quiñones's fabulous claims were centuries old,[143] yet they proved remarkably resilient despite the fact that there had been no openly professing Jews in Iberia since the 1490s.

One of the most successful propagators of mythic conversophobia was the Portuguese polemicist Vicente da Costa Mattos. His *Breve discurso contra a herética perfidia do Iudaismo* (1622) was replete with Judeophobic folklore, which is perhaps one of the reasons that the work sold well both in Costa Mattos's homeland and in Spain.[144] The Spaniard Francisco de Torrejoncillo's oft-cited *Centinela contra Judíos,* which dated from the early 1670s, rehearsed the same gamut of anti-Jewish legends for a Spanish public not yet weary of reading about Jews and the evil inclinations and physical monstrosities they supposedly transmitted to their descendants.[145]

Given the currency of conversophobic myths in the Spain of Philip II, Philip III, and Philip IV, it does not seem coincidental that a major outburst of anti-converso hatred occurred in 1632, when a libel known as the *Cristo de la Paciencia* spread throughout Madrid. This cause célèbre centered on a group of Portuguese conversos whom local inquisitors had accused of ritually flogging an effigy of Christ in their "secret synagogue."[146] The inquest into the supposed crimes culminated in a monumental *auto general de fe* in which two of the accused received sentences of death, to the vocal delight of thousands of onlookers.[147]

The image of conversos as bloodthirsty sadists clearly had a wide and lasting appeal. Shortly after the *Paciencia* scandal subsided, another celebrated Judeophobic libel became the subject of a popular literary revival. The libel in question was the late medieval legend of the Holy Child of La Guardia (1492), a gory tale of Eucharist desecration and the ritual murder of a Christlike child by Spanish Jews and conversos. Among latter-day dramatizers of this story were the playwrights Jose de Cañizárez (*La viva imagen de Cristo,* 1641), and the undisputed bestseller of the Golden Age of Spanish literature, Lope de Vega (*El niño inocente,* 1640).[148] For its part, the accusation that conversos relived their ancestors' deicidal bloodlust by whipping statues of Christ resurfaced as late as 1650, in the inquisitorial process against María de Sierra.[149]

By itself, the recurrence of old defamations suggests that Judeophobic images had enormous resonance both as narrative motifs and as accusatory devices to be wielded against conversos. However, during the late 1500s and throughout the 1600s anti-converso sentiment was much more than a perpetuation of medieval hatreds; it was also a product of the specific historical circumstances in which it occurred. Seventeenth-century conversophobia was similar, often identical in form to medieval Judeophobia, yet the meanings that the latter-day bigots attached to their fantasies were not necessarily the same as those the medieval Jew-baiters attached to theirs.

Seventeenth-century Portuguese and especially Spanish conversophobia adhered closely to the essentialist ideology (or ideologies) of *pureza de sangre*. It is not by chance that vociferous defenders of that ideology were at the forefront of anti-converso agitation. In numerous essays, virtually all of them depicted Judeoconversos as greedy, socially ambitious parasites with a hereditary proclivity toward unproductive occupations, such as commodity trading, administration, and (ironically enough) writing. Torrejoncillo, for example, contended that many conversos did not work on the land and were drawn toward commerce and pen-wielding because they descended from the Israelite tribe of Reuben, which God had cursed in such a way that whatever its progeny planted on good soil died within a few days.[150] In 1633, Juan Escobar de Corro provided what could easily pass for a "digest" of common misgivings about conversos when he wrote, "*Hebraei et . . . eorum descendentes abjecti et infames ab omnibus reputantur. Et sunt . . . seditosi, cupidi, avari et perniciosi ad comunitates. . . .*"[151] Unfortunately for conversos, such pejorative evaluations were not the preserve of polemicists. Similar derogations issued from places far removed from debates concerning the purity of blood statutes. In popular literature, for instance, the collective image of conversos did not fare particularly well. Miguel de Cervantes had one of his characters in *El Coloquio de los Perros* exclaim the following:

It is with wonder that one can find among [conversos] one who believes in the sacred Catholic faith in a straightforward manner: their sole intent is to grasp and save money. . . . [A]lways earning and never spending, they...gather up the greatest quantity of money that there is in Spain. . . . They get it all, they hide it all, and they swallow it all. Let it be considered that they are many, and that each day they hide a little or a lot. . . . They steal from us with stealth [*a pie quedo*], and they do so with the fruits of our own inheritance, which they resell to us, becoming rich and leaving us poor. . . . [T]heir science is none other than stealing from us, and they practice it effortlessly.[152]

According to depictions such as the above, conversos despised honest, productive labor. What is more, they were physically weak and incapable of exhibiting valor; thus (among other reasons) they could never equal the honor of *hidalgos*—or, for that matter, that of Old Christian commoners, who enjoyed the comparable dignity of working on the land. Conversos were unworthy, the argument went, regardless of how successful they were in purchasing offices and titles, and in sporting all the external trappings of social success—fine dress, good manners, and the like.[153]

Beyond popular literature, which was, after all, the product of a relatively small number of lettered individuals, there were more pedestrian forms of conversophobic ideation that focused on the supposed materialism of New Christians. Because they circulated freely throughout Iberian society and became part of its folk culture, popular refrains provide impressions of attitudes that were perhaps more widely diffused and deeply held than the comments of assorted literati. In seventeenth-century Iberia, anti-converso refrains not only condensed various ideas about the supposed depravity of these latter-day "Jews," but they "naturalized" those ideas by presenting them as ancient, commonsensical wisdom. I cite here merely a few refrains from those selected by the modern Hispanist José María Perceval.

(1) Regarding the avarice and material appetites of conversos:

El gato y el judío
a cuanto ven dicen mío.

(The cat and the Jew / say "it's mine" of whatever they see.)

(2) On the business acumen and unnatural capacity of "Jews" to amass riches:

El buen judío
de la paja hace oro.

(The good Jew / from hay makes gold.)

(3) On the hereditary cowardice and ignoble lineage of conversos:

Nunca vuestro abuelo mató moro de lanzada
en la vega de Granada.

(Never did your grandfather kill a Moor by lancing him / in the meadow of Granada.)

Just how deeply racialist thinking had permeated public discourse in the 1600s is evident from various other refrains. For instance,

(4) "New Christian" status as an irrevocable, hereditary condition:

¿Sois confeso?
Hasta el hueso.

(Are you a convert? / Unto the bone).

Un asno de diez años es viejo
y un converso de ciento es nuevo.

(An ass of ten years is old / and a converso of one hundred is new.)

To be sure, the existence of folklorically inclined conversophobic works by the likes of Costa Mattos, Torrejoncillo, and Quiñones—all of them literate and otherwise "educated" men who addressed their works to a cultivated as well as a general audience—warns us against drawing too sharp a distinction between "learned" and "popular" conversophobia. Both types of bigotry were closely allied. They left a deep imprint upon the culture of early modern Spain and Portugal.

None of this is to say that Old Christians were unanimous in their utter repugnance toward Judeoconversos. As Henry Kamen has pointed out, the ideology of *limpieza*, perhaps the central legitimator of sixteenth- and seventeenth-century conversophobia, never attained social hegemony "since it had no force in public nor canon law and there was always liberty enough to discuss and question it."[154] In fact, an important segment of educated opinion opposed the purity statutes as immoderate and unjust instruments that stigmatized many innocent people by exaggerating the threat of heresy.[155] Still, it is undeniable that quotidian types of discrimination at least partially offset the relative tolerance of some members of the elite. As Kamen himself has cautioned, "Several institutions operated a system of exclusion without having any formal statutes."[156]

Conclusion

Ordinary conversos with whom this study is concerned, such as the linen salesman Simon Fernández, moved primarily in the lower levels of Spain's social hierarchy. It is here that they encountered informal discrimination of the kind to which Kamen alludes. Seen from a wider historical perspective, the setting in which ordinary conversos navigated was a patchwork kingdom in the midst of an economic, political and social crisis—a crisis that *asentistas* and several historians have called Spain's "decline." The symptoms of the kingdom's material and psychological malaise were plentiful: plague, poverty, a crumbling transportation infrastructure, and a crisis of confidence marked, in some quarters, by nativist reaction and by a stubborn, often nostalgic triumphalism. Reaction rendered conversos of all religious persuasions quite vulnerable. A recrudescent Inquisition, now bent on eradicating "Judaizing" once again, represented what were perhaps the most obvious dangers: persecution, destitution, and public shame. The paradox for the so-called New Christians, of course, is that in the Spain of the last Habsburgs, where they remained pariahs, they also encountered a wide field of economic opportunity and an Iberian social and cultural milieu with which they were intimately familiar. In a word, Judeoconversos were outsiders and insiders at the same time. The chapters that follow seek to explain who these ordinary conversos were, and how several of them reacted to this momentous paradox.

Chapter 3
Exile and Return

One of the claims of Diego Pereira's accusers was that Pereira wished to go to France to escape the Sevillian Inquisition. As I discussed in the previous chapter, much of the pertinent testimony is unreliable. It is therefore reasonable to suppose that Pereira had no intention of fleeing across the border. Yet, the thought that a suspected Judaizer should be eager to leave the Iberian Peninsula was not entirely arbitrary. By the mid-1600s it was common knowledge in Spain and Portugal that many conversos had quit the peninsula and settled in places that were beyond the reach of the Iberian Inquisitions. France, England, the Netherlands, Italy, and the lands under Ottoman control were among the domains where conversos found shelter from the Spanish *Santo Oficio* and its Portuguese analogue.

Many of the conversos who fled from Spain and Portugal adopted normative Judaism in their places of refuge. Iberian conversophobes, who regarded all New Christians as congenital "Jews," saw this as a natural and predictable occurrence. Like these detractors, some modern historians have assumed that a vast majority of the conversos who left the Iberian Peninsula did so because they yearned to practice their ancestral faith in freedom. For example, Haim Beinart has argued that conversos survived as a "distinct Jewish body," because they seldom hesitated to follow a deep-rooted desire to observe the religion of their forbears.[1] As the conversos' Jewish past beckoned, the argument goes, so too their will to escape the Iberian Peninsula was always strong.[2]

According to this and similar interpretations, the yearning for a reunion with Judaism and the Jewish people remained deeply embedded in the hearts of conversos across the generations. And inasmuch as conversos were all "potential Jews" they never left the ken of Jewish history.[3] Seen in this light, the fact that many converso expatriates built new lives within the communal framework of rabbinic Judaism appears as a natural outcome of that history. An important corollary to this reading is the idea that the exiles who *returned* to Iberia and to Catholicism after living as Jews did not do so because they were initially indifferent, ambivalent, or hostile toward the idea of leading a Jewish life. On the contrary, if some conversos slid back into the Catholic fold, it was primarily because they were unable to reconcile an "idealized" concept of Judaism that they had zealously nourished in the Iberian Peninsula with the strict, halakhic way of life that they encountered in the Sephardi Diaspora.[4] In other words, returnees were disillusioned Judaizers. Closely related to this rendering is the notion that there were few religious dissidents among the exiles (hence the label "deviants"), and that therefore most converso "renegades," including repatriates, were historically insignificant.[5]

My research suggests that such an interpretation of the renegade phenomenon is simplistic at best and largely unhistorical at worst. There is considerable evidence that New Christian returnees were not a mere handful of overly "idealistic" malcontents. Rather, they comprised a significant minority of the exiles, particularly among those who settled in southwestern France. My research further suggests that the motives of returnees were not purely ideological or religious in nature but were, depending on the specific case, of a practical economic or social nature.

This chapter addresses the phenomena of exile and return to which Beinart and other scholars have alluded in their work, but which still requires close examination. Using examples drawn from inquisitorial cases, I will draw a very basic typological portrait of converso emigrants who returned to Iberia. My aim will be to highlight two ostensibly strange choices that set their behavior apart from that of their fellow refugees:[6] self-denunciation and, most importantly, return itself. I also intend to show that while religious recidivism and the act of returning to Iberian soil were related phenomena, they were by no means synonymous or necessarily coextensive. In this vein, I will emphasize that the behavior of the renegades seldom fit the stereotypes of religious dissidence and conformity by which the renegades' contemporaries, both Jewish and Christian, defined and approached these supposedly unusual individuals.

The Option of Exile in France

From the sixteenth century until the middle of the eighteenth, hundreds of conversos of Portuguese and Spanish origin emigrated from their homelands to southwestern France in order to avoid inquisitorial persecution. Among the "Portuguese of the Nation" who resided in Spain, even those who had not experienced inquisitorial scrutiny were aware that ethnic and religious prejudice put them in a very dangerous position. One "Portuguese" New Christian from Madrid articulated this awareness when he told the members of his household that "as they already knew, they were all Portuguese—although his wife and sister-in-law were born in [Madrid], but their parents were Portuguese, as were his—and therefore he did not want to live in Spain, subject to [the possibility that] someone would give false testimony about them, denouncing them to the Inquisition, as tends to happen to other Portuguese."[7]

Escaping from Iberia posed numerous logistical challenges. First and foremost there was a legal obstacle to mobility: All conversos required special royal license to travel to foreign lands.[8] As a matter of course, the Spanish and Portuguese governments denied such license to New Christians who were under inquisitorial investigation or were serving a penal sentence. For these reasons, attempts by conversos to flee the Iberian Peninsula were often clandestine.

Escape by sea was an expensive option. In the likely event that exit permits were not forthcoming, prospective escapees had to muster sufficient funds to bribe port authorities and cover the high cost of transportation. Only a wealthy minority of conversos could produce such funds. The least expensive and logistically simplest option was to flee Iberia by land.[9] For obvious reasons of geography, the first destination of conversos who chose or were limited to this mode of escape was southern France.

The French south was no mere transit point for New Christians.[10] In fact, various settlements of converso expatriates developed throughout the areas now known as the Pyrénées-Atlantiques and Les Landes during the Early Modern Era. Western border towns such as St. Jean de Luz, Dax, Bardos, Biarritz, Bidache, and Labastide-Clairence, as well as the Aquitainian towns of Carpentras and Peyrehorade, all received "Portuguese" contingents during the sixteenth and seventeenth centuries.[11] Peyrehorade, Bordeaux, and the Bayonne suburb of Saint Esprit absorbed the largest of these groups. The latter enclave grew considerably during the 1600s, eventually becoming a "small metropolis" of the Sephardi Diaspora.[12]

Demographic data on the converso escapees of the seventeenth century are scarce, but what information does survive shows that patterns of New Christian settlement heavily favored the French southwest. In 1636 a Spanish priest counted twenty to twenty-three families of "Portuguese" in Rouen, six or seven in Nantes, and twelve in Paris. By comparison, his report indicated that there were eighty New Christian families in Labastide, forty in Peyrehorade, forty in Bordeaux, ten to twelve in Dax, and at least sixty in Bayonne. In addition, the informant found that there were a handful of "Portuguese" households in Biarritz.[13] By 1660, according to another source, there were close to four hundred "Portuguese" (around seventy to one hundred households) in greater Bayonne.[14]

The presence of New Christians in southern France was not always stable. For instance, converso immigrants left St. Jean de Luz and Biarritz temporarily, and Tolouse permanently, when their arrival aroused the intense animosity of local residents and religious authorities.[15] Further north in Nantes, the entire expatriate community disintegrated as its members assimilated into French Catholicism or went elsewhere.[16] According to I. S. Révah, the New Christian contingents in Dax and La Rochelle eventually merged into those of larger cities.[17] Nonetheless, the encampments of *nouveaux chrétiens* proved to be permanent and of lasting consequence in other areas. By the eighteenth century, the surviving "Portuguese" communities of the French southwest had become well entrenched. All of them were legal and enjoyed a measure of tranquility under royal protection. Although Judaism had been forbidden in France since the end of the fourteenth century, the country did not have an Inquisition and seldom persecuted "Judaizers" if they maintained a thin veneer of Catholicism—which several of the immigrants did without much difficulty.

Converso communities became rooted in the southwestern corner of France for a number of reasons. First of all, the area was exceptionally accessible. In contrast to the mountainous regions that separate much of northern Spain from southern France, the borderlands in the extreme west form a relatively low corridor that extends from the Spanish Basque country to the southwestern coast of France. In the Early Modern Period, a shifting array of supply routes converged around Vitoria on the Spanish side of the border, turned northward toward the corridor, and extended somewhat smoothly through Irún across the eastern border into Bayonne (see Map 2). A neighboring route led from Logroño, through Pamplona and Burguete, across the Pyrenees, to Bayonne. From Bayonne the way opened to the Aquitanian interior and to the rest of France.[18] Notably, the corridor was directly reachable from Castile, where many of the émigrés resided before their escape (the Basque territory was a province under the direct jurisdiction of Castile, while Navarre and Aragon, which still outline the rest of Spain's northern boundary, were separate royal domains). Aside from the far Catalonian northeast, the narrow southwestern corridor remains the only sector of the French-Spanish frontier in which the Pyrene Mountains fade into valleys or are low enough to allow for relatively easy passage.[19]

In terms of geographic accessibility, Catalonia might have served as a major point of departure for escaping conversos, since eastern Rosselló (Roussillon) formed a continuous plateau with the French lands to its immediate north. However, Rosselló was a major theater of war throughout the Early Modern Period (Spain ceded the province to France in 1648). In addition, Catalonia was beset by civil war for much of the seventeenth century. The Basque country was comparatively peaceful.[20] This is probably one of the main reasons that the road to Bayonne, and not the road to Perpignan, was the conversos' preferred route of escape.

Of course, geography and the turmoil in Catalonia only explain why many escapees arrived in the French southwest, not why they remained there. In order to explain the foundation of permanent settlements of New Christians in southwestern France it is necessary to consider two critical economic factors. First, many if not most of the conversos who settled in that region were poor; some were completely destitute. It is likely that several of them stayed close to the Spanish border simply because they did not have enough money to continue traveling northward.[21] There is no statistical evidence to support this impression, yet various anecdotal data do suggest that wealthier refugees were more likely than their poorer fellows to use the area of the Pyrénées-Atlantiques as a stepping stone toward more prosperous communities of refugees, such as developed in Rouen, Venice, Hamburg, and Amsterdam.[22] To be sure, some indigent conversos did move to wealthier enclaves, especially when word spread that local Sephardim would offer charitable assistance to needy immigrants. Nonetheless hundreds of New Christians stayed near the Spanish border. A large proportion of these settlers came from the lower-middle and poor segments of Iberian society. Other refugees who settled in the area had become poor only recently, either because they had left their property in Iberian lands or because they had forfeited it through bankruptcy or inquisitorial expropriation. In 1636, the "Portuguese" population of Bordeaux, which stood at 260, included 93 persons whom the French government described as indigent.[23] The situation in Bayonne was much worse. In 1660, a resident of that city estimated that no more than 10 of the 400 "Portuguese" living in Saint Esprit were "reasonably prosperous," while the rest survived from charity collected locally or sent from England and Holland.[24]

The second and most important economic factor that accounts for the settlement of conversos throughout the French southwest was the fact that the area was part of an international system of long distance trade whose focal point was the Iberian Peninsula. The contiguity of southwestern France with the road networks of Spain meant that the region was firmly connected

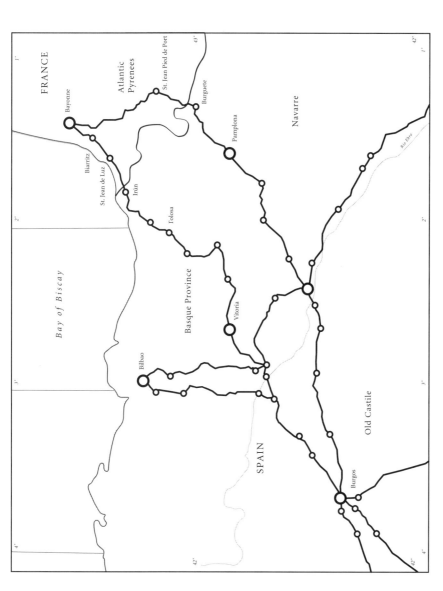

Map 2. Roads in Basque and Navarrese Borderlands. This map is based on a reproduction of a road survey conducted in 1684 by Giuseppe Miselli. The reproduction appears as "Mapa 6" in Santos Madrazo, *El sistema de comunicaciones en España, 1750–1850* (Madrid: Ediciones Turner, 1984).

to the peninsular economy, itself dominated by the Castilian metropolis. Living at or near the terminal points of the Madrid-Bayonne trading axis not only facilitated but encouraged participation in the peninsular market system. As I will detail in the following section, the prospect of launching trading ventures from the safe heaven of Aquitaine into the familiar terrain of Iberia proved very appealing for several of the exiles, particularly if they were desperate enough to disregard the dangers of returning to countries where New Christians were widely distrusted.

During the middle third of the seventeenth century, a unique conjuncture of circumstances injected the refugee communities of southwestern France into the heart of the peninsular system of trade. In 1621, Spain imposed an embargo on Dutch ships, goods, and investments in the Iberian Peninsula. At the time, the viability of the nascent Sephardi community of the Netherlands was largely dependent upon continued economic ties between converso businessmen in Amsterdam and their agents—namely their relatives, friends, and other correspondents—in the peninsula. When the embargo impeded these commercial relationships, Dutch Sephardim came to rely on the communities of converso exiles in France to sustain trade with Spain and Portugal.[25] Owing to their geographic proximity to the Spanish border and to the Bay of Biscay, the "Portuguese" expatriates in France were singularly well positioned to build a complex trafficking network to serve their economic interests and those of the Dutch Sephardim. Jonathan Israel has described this network as follows:

An important contraband system, utilized especially between 1621 and 1635 before France entered the Thirty Years' War against Spain, involved the shipping of goods ultimately intended for the Castilian market to Bayonne . . . a town which attracted a considerable amount of [converso] immigration during these years. The Sephardim of Bayonne, together with others residing in nearby places such as Peyrehorade, Labastide-Clairence and Dax, developed a tortuous overland traffic through which the linens, spices and other valuable goods shipped in from Amsterdam were transported by mule-train over the Pyrenees to the Navarrese capital of Pamplona and from there, through the *puertos secos* (dry ports) of Castile and Aragon to Madrid, Saragossa and Barcelona.[26]

The lifting of the Spanish embargo in 1647 diminished but did not eliminate the flow of merchandise from the Pyrénées-Atlantiques to the Iberian mainland. Ironically, the reopening of licit channels of commerce made it easier for converso exiles to engage in the kinds of trade that had become profitable while the embargo was in effect.[27] An existing relationship of economic interdependence thus solidified between the expatriate communities of the French southwest and the countries from which the refugees had escaped. This interdependence formed the historical matrix within which most acts of return occurred among the exiles.

The Taboo of Return

During the late sixteenth and seventeenth centuries, the return of converso exiles to Iberia scandalized many Old Christians in Spain and Portugal as well as many Jews (including Iberian refugees) in the Sephardi Diaspora. For these critics, return smelled of religious deviance.

As I mentioned earlier, Iberian conversophobes believed that New Christians who escaped from the Peninsula were ipso facto Judaizers. According to this widely held opinion, conversos who returned to Iberia were doubly offensive to Catholicism: they not only mocked Christian vigilance by returning to the scene of their (supposed) crimes, but they threatened to subvert Ibero-Christendom with a Judaic heresy that had been strengthened through the returnees' exposure to diasporic Judaism.

Jewish authorities took a similarly grave view of return. Although there was disagreement as to the halakhic status of conversos, rabbinic arbiters and lay leaders in the Sephardi Diaspora tended to regard New Christians who left the Iberian Peninsula as potential Jews who needed spiritual guidance in order to become suitably observant members of the Jewish people.[28] Accordingly, Sephardi leaders approached the phenomenon of *return* to Iberia much as the peninsular Inquisitions interpreted the phenomenon of *escape* from Iberia, namely as a sign of (or prelude to) religious backsliding. To be sure, a few returnees were beyond suspicion in Jewish circles. I am referring to those who had become rabbis or simply became notorious (deservedly or not) as Jewish missionaries to the "lands of idolatry."[29] Most returnees did not enjoy such a favorable reputation.

A main reason for the Jewish presumption that returnees were either actual or possible recidivists was that their return made it extremely likely that they would transgress Jewish law. It was only logical that returnees would fail to observe the commandments while under the watchful eye of the Spanish and Portuguese Inquisitions. And indeed, several returnees admitted that they had violated the Halakhah while in the peninsula for reasons of safety.

For example, the returnee Felipe Díaz Gutiérrez reported to the Inquisition in 1636 that he had eaten forbidden foods in Castile in order to forestall any suspicion that he was a Judaizer.[30]

From the point of view of Jewish authorities, then, return led to sin. Equally troublesome was the fact that returnees flagrantly contravened pious efforts to incorporate them into the structure of normative Jewish life. By returning to Iberia, these putative renegades seemed to reject their own spiritual and physical liberation from Christian idolatry. And by reversing or at least suspending their public identification with Judaism in "the lands of apostasy," returnees flaunted their freedom to disobey diasporic leaders, not to mention the Halakhah itself. To make matters worse, the returnees opened themselves once again to the influence of Christianity.

At a fundamental level, then, return challenged the notion that remaining within the political, moral, and spatial confines of a *kehillah* was the only appropriate way for exiled conversos to attain spiritual deliverance and social fixity. Return also challenged normative conceptions of the very nature of "Jewish" community. As Yosef Kaplan has observed, the geographic mobility of conversos heightened a simmering contradiction between their supposed religious identity (a "Jewish" identity) on one hand and their social, cultural, and ethnic solidarity on the other.[31] By returning to the Iberian Peninsula to live among fellow conversos, several of whom were faithful Catholics, exiles who had practiced normative Judaism in the Diaspora implicitly gave priority to their familial and ethnic bonds over a supposed loyalty to the *kahal* and to "the God of Israel."[32] In this respect, the behavior of returnees was consonant with that of a vast number of converso refugees who did *not* return to Iberia from the Sephardi Diaspora. Several historians have documented that it was common for such expatriates to correspond with relatives who still resided in the Iberian Peninsula. The "New Jews"[33] in exile even treated conversos who remained practicing Catholics in the peninsula as members of the same Sephardi "Nation" to which they belonged.[34]

Along with rabbinical authorities, the lay governors of the Judeo-Portuguese community of Amsterdam, the most powerful and prestigious Sephardi community of the seventeenth century, typified the official attitude of the diasporic *kehillot* toward the phenomenon of return. The position of these zealous *parnassim* (magistrates or governors) was that any converso's escape from Iberia necessitated his or her unambiguous and permanent embrace of rabbinic Judaism. This prescriptive view was central to the formation of the Amsterdam Jewish colony, owing in part to the fact that most of its founders and subsequent heads were themselves refugees who had undergone a religious metamorphosis in exile. Though they also understood their own individual and collective identities largely in ethnic or "national" terms, the *parnassim* had absolutely no patience for religious equivocation. In this the leaders were different from some ordinary Iberian refugees. Guided by a desire to instill their brand of moral conformism[35] among the Sephardi rank and file, the governors of the Judeo-Portuguese "Nation" took the decisive step in 1644 of barring former members of the *kehillah* who had the temerity to return to Amsterdam after residing as nominal Christians in countries where Judaism was officially forbidden.[36] The Amsterdam *Ma'amad* (governing body) decreed that these double returnees would have to endure penance for a period of four years before they could once again form part of the Jewish community.[37] Between 1655 and 1677, the Jewish communities of Leghorn, Hamburg, and London adopted very similar laws designed to punish those who returned to the "lands of idolatry."[38] (I hasten to add that this form of coercion, however harsh, was mild in comparison to inquisitorial persecution.)

Much like the double returnees targeted by communal regulations in Amsterdam, peninsular refugees who settled in France were in an especially awkward position vis-à-vis the newly Judaicized Sephardim of countries such as the Dutch Republic, where Jews enjoyed freedom of worship and legal rights of residence qua Jews. France did not have an Inquisition, yet Judaism had been illegal there since the end of the fourteenth century. Accordingly, until the 1670s Jewish authorities viewed France as a "land of idolatry," and thus as an undesirable destination for converso escapees. In 1663, Rabbi Moses Raphael D'Aguilar of Amsterdam gave voice to some of these misgivings when he wrote members of the converso enclave in Saint Esprit-lès-Bayonne that no Jew could hope for salvation who remained in France, since that person had to pretend to be a Christian in order to live there. D'Aguilar stressed that it was wrong for the refugees in France to follow Christian ways, to violate Jewish law, or to apply it leniently under the pretext of duress, as nothing prevented them from moving to a country where they could practice Judaism openly and correctly (Catholic France, unlike Spain and Portugal, did not bar the emigration of New Christians). Furthermore, the rabbi declared that economic hardship did not justify dwelling in the "lands of idolatry," for one could easily find one's livelihood elsewhere.[39]

Aguilar's rebuke is one indication that the mere fact of residing in France condemned converso refugees to a semimarginal and at best transitional status in the Jewish world. The rabbi's admonitions also underscored that for all the crypto-Judaic zeal of their self-appointed leaders, the "Portuguese" outposts in France were makeshift colonies composed almost entirely of recent immigrants whose knowledge of and compliance with rabbinic Judaism were understandably inferior to those of Jews in older, more firmly established communities.

The Franco-"Portuguese" colonies did not attain full legitimacy vis-à-vis the rest of diasporic Jewry until they had evolved from a haphazard collection of refugees with a sense of ethnic kinship into coherent social units with formal structures of self-government and clear normative and social boundaries. This evolution was complete only toward the beginning of the eighteenth century.[40] By that time, halakhic Judaism had become so well established that France was no longer perceived as a "land of idolatry" in the Jewish Diaspora, and the façade of Christianity had almost completely vanished.[41] It was not before the legalization of French Judaism in the late eighteenth century, however, that all pretence disappeared entirely.

The prevalence of a halakhically correct (though sometimes semisecret) Judaism among New Christians in the western Diaspora was not preordained. Rather, it was the result of a concerted effort of indoctrination on the part of Jewish leaders in the Diaspora, including some of the most fervent and educated among the New Jews. A host of informal social and economic contacts between Iberian refugees in the Jewish *métropoles* of Venice and Amsterdam and those in the periphery, reinforced Jewish proselytization. These contacts had the cumulative effect of establishing durable and multi-faceted intercommunal relationships whereby the social, political, religious, and economic norms modeled by the major *kehillot* spread to and were adapted by the minor or incipient *kehillot*.[42]

The efforts of Sephardi educators in the *métropoles* to propagandize the refugees in France were intense. From the late sixteenth century, learned emissaries from Venice and later ones from Amsterdam guided the "Portuguese" enclaves of that country toward a solid identification with Jews and rabbinic Judaism. In concrete terms, the task of educating the refugees in normative Judaism consisted of such activities as sermonizing, organizing and supervising communal prayers, supplying Bibles and liturgical works (most of them translated into Spanish), furnishing and caring for ritual objects, circumcising newly arrived male immigrants, and performing a host of rituals that the refugees were not qualified to carry out. Supported by a large cadre of cooperative immigrants and building on a preexisting sense of ethnic solidarity among the "Portuguese," these envoys paved the way for the

adoption of Jewish models of communal organization throughout the settlements of *nouveaux chrétiens* in southwestern France.[43]

The testimony of Jorge Fernández de Castro regarding Jewish practices
in the *faubourg* of Saint Esprit during the mid-1660s provides a glimpse of
the activities of such emissaries, their chief local supporters, and of the environment of righteous piety that both groups promoted. Among other things,
Fernández recounted that members of the Portuguese community gathered
every Sabbath at the home of four "rabbis" (it is not clear, however, whether
these were ordained rabbis; in all likelihood they were simply learned men)
whose main responsibility was to teach them the Law of Moses. There the
congregants recited various prayers for Sabbath including the daily Shema
Yisrael in Spanish, and then

the owner of the house in which they gathered preached to the unmarried people [*la
gente moza*] telling them that they should keep [the Law of Moses] and admonishing
them that he who did not marry someone who kept [that law] would lose the [In-
heritance? Heritage?] of his fathers [or: parents], and he who spoke more [or: badly]
of the [illegible] sinned [?] mortally; and proceeding in that manner [*prosiguiendo
desta suerte*] he exhorted everyone to observe the law of Moses, giving the reasons
there were for doing so. And having finished that preaching, he read from the prayer
book, as this [declarant] and the others listened to him with great attention and in
great silence. . . .

And each Sabbath, praying in the said manner, these meetings took place three
times, once in the morning, once in the afternoon, and the last one by night[;] [In
these meetings] the rabbi whose turn it was to do the preaching and praying dressed
as a Jew [with a long robe with white linen, a head covering, and "some straps around
his wrists"—phylacteries[44]]. . . . [They all observed the Law of Moses three times
daily and on the Sabbath] . . . all of them knowing, one about the others, that they
performed those prayers, because they all let each other know about it [*se daban
cuenta de ello*], and they admonished each other to observe and keep said Law of
Moses with all precision, because it was the good one and the true one, and the one
in which they believed they would be saved.[45]

Fernández's subsequent testimony shed light on the system of ethnic ties that
supported the structures of communal observance and permitted the con-
solidation of the New Christian colony of greater Bayonne as a specifically
Jewish-Portuguese "Nation." This system consisted primarily of informal
contacts mediated by familiar modes of comportment among crypto-Jewish
immigrants from Portugal. As Fernández de Castro described them, these
ways of communicating had the discursive effect of enveloping each immigrant within an implicitly homogeneous and closed cultural milieu complete

with its own code words and interpersonal protocol. To the degree that these modes of communication were efficient, it was because they had existed before the exodus from the Iberian Peninsula and because the immigrants had succeeded in reestablishing them nearly intact in the French Diaspora. As the converso witness Manuel Gómez explained,

The Judaizers had a common style of letting themselves be known amongst those who observed the same law and were of the same nation whenever they entered into a conversation[;] They said, "praised be God," but they never said [as Catholics commonly did], "praised be the Most Holy Sacrament," nor did they say "[praised be] the Virgin," or "[praised be] Jesus Christ"; and then they would ask each other about their places of birth and about their parents and grandparents, and upon knowing that they were *of the Nation* they would say [of each other] "*es dos nossos*" [in Portuguese: "He/she is one of ours"], and later on they would introduce the Law of Moses into the conversation, ending by declaring themselves as followers of it. (Emphasis added.)[46]

A sweeping overview of the development of the "Portuguese Nations" of France and the rest of the Sephardi Diaspora during the seventeenth century might suggest that the trend toward full "Judaicization" was largely unproblematic and inevitable. Yet a closer look at the communities in question reveals the opposite. In Amsterdam, for example, there were a host of refugees who remained on the margins of the organized Jewish community despite maintaining some religious and ethnic ties with those who were not alienated from the *kehillah*. The refugees who returned to Iberia from France were akin to these marginal "Jews without Judaism."[47] In liminal places such as the French southwest a deeper socioreligious ambiguity prevailed among the immigrants until the latter half of the seventeenth century, yet survived until the eighteenth century. In 1630 an inquisitorial informant in France went so far as to note with disgust the "confusion there is between Christians and Jews of this [converso] Nation, in that one cannot distinguish one from the other."[48]

The choice of the renegades to return to the "lands of apostasy" departed from the ideals that in theory constituted the basis of Jewish communities. These ideals, articulated in the language of a venerable "tradition," and supported by ethnic solidarity, were in reality but one ideological component—an official orthodoxy, to be exact—within a much broader and more complex socioreligious reality. The purpose of the following sections is to explain who these returnees were, as well as to describe their experiences and their motivations within that larger reality.

Types of Return to Iberian Lands

It is only prudent to note that I have not set out to quantify the phenomenon of return. In order to accomplish such a task, it would be necessary to cull relevant data from tens of thousands of surviving inquisitorial dossiers, among other sources. The scope of my research has been much narrower. Still, the appearance of scores of returnees in nearly half of the approximately two hundred inquisitorial cases that I have inspected indicates that return was far from an isolated or fortuitous occurrence.[49] More importantly, these records show that returnees were not an undifferentiated body of "Jewish dissidents" or "penitent Christians": In actuality, returnees comprised two overlapping groups of often ambiguous and somewhat indeterminate religious character.

The first group was the largest. It consisted of individuals who traveled to the Iberian Peninsula several times, as a matter of routine, and usually without prior intent to remain there, much less to become reconciled with the Church. I have located inquisitorial records dating from 1609 through 1678 that credibly refer to at least 111 such persons (not including scores of additional, alleged returnees on whom the records contain only minimal information). Most of the 111 individuals in question returned to Castile from the southwest of France (see appendix, Table A, below).

The second group of returnees consisted of former escapees who returned for the purpose of resettling permanently in Spain, Portugal, or Portuguese-controlled Brazil. The dossiers I have studied contain references to at least twenty-seven subjects who fit this description, and an additional handful of subjects who very likely fit it (see appendix, tables A and B, below). Permanent returnees usually came back to Spain from the outskirts of Bayonne or from Bordeaux, although a few traveled from places as distant as Rouen, Antwerp, Amsterdam, Rome, and Venice.

A majority of the chronic or habitual returnees in the dossiers were married men who traveled to and from Iberia on a periodic basis in order to conduct various *negocios*. The ages of these men ranged from the early twenties to the early sixties. Most were medium to petty traders for whom, as one inquisitorial informant put it, "it is very common to come to Madrid with merchandise from France."[50] Some witnesses referred to chronic returnees quite fittingly as traders who "come and go to Spain" (*van y vienen a España*) with commercial goods.[51]

A plurality of the habitual returnees whose cases I have reviewed launched their voyages from the environs of Bayonne. The converso community of that region included various settlers who were not likely to cross the border into Spain, such as women, children, and elderly people of both sexes, owing to the hardships and risks involved. If we consider that the total New Christian population of Saint Esprit was only a few hundred during the seventeenth century, and we note the number of chronic repatriates in my limited documentary survey—more than one hundred for the period 1609 to 1678—we can readily deduce that the proportion of chronic returnees in greater Bayonne was extremely high among young to middle-aged men. Given this high proportion, it is difficult to avoid the impression that the very existence of a New Christian colony in greater Bayonne rested largely on the premise that its young men and "male heads of household" (to borrow a designation from modern census terminology) would be able to cross the border into Spain virtually whenever they wished to do so.

There were a number of conversos who initiated their travels to the Iberian Peninsula from Amsterdam. These individuals seem to have been a minority among habitual returnees.[52] Yosef Kaplan has summarized the phenomenon of chronic return from the Netherlands as follows:

Both in periods of prosperity and in times of crisis, members of the Portuguese Jewish community in Amsterdam played an extremely active part in a network of economic connections between the lands of northern Europe and the Iberian Peninsula. Many of them even participated personally in dangerous journeys to Spanish ports; others exploited their close connections with the communities of secret Jews in Bayonne, Bordeaux, Saint Jean de Luz, etc., and they managed to cross the French border into northern Spain. Some of them tried to find ways of cooperating fully with the Spanish and Portuguese crown; others, despite their loyalty and connections to Judaism, did not hesitate to return to Spain for purely economic purposes, that is, wishing to oversee the management of a network of commercial connections between the center in Amsterdam and the various branches in Spain and Portugal.[53]

Economic Motives

This study focuses primarily on individuals who returned to Iberian lands from France. On the basis of copious anecdotal evidence found in inquisitorial dossiers, it is reasonable, I believe, to surmise that such people comprised the vast majority of returnees, both habitual and permanent, during the seventeenth century.[54]

All indications are that the habitual returnees of southwestern France were generally poorer and handled business of a lesser magnitude than the

Dutch returnees who fascinate Kaplan. In seventeenth-century Bayonne, for example, infrastructural conditions did not allow most of the returnees to engage in commerce on a grand scale. As the historian Anne Zink has remarked,

The conditions of commercial handling [or werehousing] and of transport were such that neither the great producer nor the great buyer was able to make for an economy of scale that would permit large shipments. . . .

In Bayonne mules were loaded up, and small boats were unloaded in order to load the great ships, and vice versa. The role of Bayonne was located, then, at the level of the bundle, the barrel, or even of small packages.[55]

Franco-Sephardi returnees included at least three types of medium-to-petty merchants: smugglers, lawful traders, and other *tratantes* who catered to the legitimate and black markets. Juan de Fonseca is an example of the first type. He allegedly evaded Castilian tariffs by storing contraband at the house of a complicitous friar in Madrid.[56] The following list, which I have taken from the deposition of another habitual returnee (1663), includes examples of the second and third types:

Joseph de San Payo. It is usual for him to come to Madrid by chance [sic], such that he is in Madrid for the greater part of the year with merchandise that he is prone to bring from France, such as *chamelotes*,[57] *rasillas al mizcle*[58] [?] and other things, and with other merchandise he brings from the region of Raya de Portugal, such as tobacco leaves, *cazas*[59] and wax. . . . Recently he brought one thousand books of tobacco leaves from Portugal, and they were confiscated as contraband one league from Madrid[.] . . . He stays there in Baño Street at the Berber's inn . . . [and] goes around in the streets of Madrid dressed in a *bayeta*[60] and on the textiles route he [usually] wears [clothes of] a greenish color.

Manuel, son of [the woman called] La Velota. His most continuous presence, when he comes to Castile, occurs in Valladolid and Rioseco, and sometimes he comes to Madrid. . . . He comes to any of the aforesaid places with merchandise of *chamelotes* and *rasillas* as they become available to him. . . . He does not come at any predetermined time. . . . He [stays] in Madrid at the Puerta del Sol, at the Puerta de Guadalajara, or at the Calle Mayor; and when he brings linens he stays at Postos Street.

Simón Gómez. [He comes back to Madrid with] stockings from England, linens, and other [merchandise] as it is available to him. . . . He never uses a fictitious name.

Don Diego de Amézquita. [He comes to Madrid] with *Cambrais*,[61] *Olandas*,[62] and *Morleses*,[63] and other types of linens, and sometimes he brings fragrances [*olores*]. . . .

Antonio López Pacheco. [He came to Castile in 1660] having brought with him twenty *cazones* of powdered tobacco from overseas[;] each of the *cazones* had sixteen *arrobos*[64] [sic], and he unloaded them in Málaga, and from there he took them to Granada and sold them, and he translated the money he obtained from the sale to Flanders, in writing, and he returned to Bayonne, where [this witness] accompanied him from Pamplona, and on the way [López Pacheco] told him all the aforementioned. . . .

Antonio del Castillo. [He brings] *Cambrais, Olandas, cazas and Bretañas*. . . .[65] [When he comes to Madrid he brings] *Coniquies*[?], *Guineos*[66] [?], and another type of linen from the Portuguese Indies. . . . He goes to Soria and Pastrana. . . . And he comes and goes frequently from France to Castile... always wearing a gabardine.

Diego de Ribas. . . . He [originally] went to Bayonne because he became bankrupt in the tobacco trade, in which he engaged through his store on Amargura Street. [He brings] *puntas, cazas* . . . and stockings from England [and other items from France to] Medina del Campo and Rioseco.[67]

Habitual returnees such as the above-listed *mercaderes* usually moved within a mercantile field whose geographic scope was very broad. They dealt principally in merchandise of northern European provenance, such as inexpensive linens, clothing, and unfinished fabrics. Some of the returnees also dealt in goods from the Spanish and Portuguese Indies, for instance, tobacco, chocolate, cotton, and assorted spices. A number of *mercaderes* returned surreptitiously and traded under fictitious names in order to evade the Inquisition. Other *mercaderes* were not nearly as discreet, which suggests two conclusions. First, the French-Spanish border was so permeable that even members of suspect populations (conversos, moriscos, and foreign spies) could cross it without much trouble.[68] Second, inquisitorial surveillance was not so thorough or cumbersome as to intimidate all prospective returnees.

Commercial opportunities were not the only factors that drew New Christian expatriates to Iberia. Nonetheless, it is clear that economic motives were paramount in all cases of habitual return, as well as in some instances of permanent repatriation. Several returnees articulated these motives clearly, directly, and even with a certain nonchalance.

For example, in 1661 Spanish inquisitors asked the prisoner Joseph Sánchez why he had come back to Spain after living in St. Jean de Luz for several years. He promptly responded that "he had come to Spain to make *aguardiente* to sell it in Málaga."[69] Another defendant, Francisco López Capadocia, allegedly told his friends in Bayonne that he was obliged to return to Spain despite the fact that he was an inquisitorial suspect, "because he had . . . [business] accounts to settle, and [because] he had all his assets there, and if he did not return, he would lose them."[70] (Presumably Capadocia was referring to the possibility that the Inquisition would expropriate his

Castilian holdings.)[71] Echoing this kind of explanation, two inquisitorial witnesses reported that their peer, Román García, had come back to Spain from the Netherlands by way of Bayonne to negotiate the collection of some debts [*dependencias*] that the house of Francisco . . . Solis owed him[.] [These debts] . . . originated in letters [of credit] that he had issued to [Solis]."[72] More specifically, García had returned, "to see his nephew, Don Simon de Solis, to ask for what [Solis] owed him. . . . [García] only came back to collect it [; furthermore,] he came to Spain *because his own wife and child were suffering* [poverty in Amsterdam], and he could not return to Amsterdam without [collecting] what was owed to him" (emphasis added).[73]

I have found that most prisoners who testified that they had returned to Iberia to seek economic relief or to pursue monetary gain were credible in their respective claims of economic motives. The same is true of witnesses who attributed economic motives to alleged returnees.

The basic credibility of economic explanations lies in the fact that they did not exculpate the suspects in any way. In effect, such explanations could even be slightly deleterious to them. As we have seen in the previous chapter, common wisdom in seventeenth-century Iberia depicted New Christian merchants as morally corrupt.[74] From this it follows that escapees who stated—or about whom it was stated—that they had returned to Iberia in order to take advantage of commercial prospects risked putting their rectitude in doubt.

Habitual returnees who had been captured by the Inquisition under suspicion of heresy could easily attempt to forestall such doubt by shifting all blame away from themselves. For instance, they could testify that crypto-Jews had coerced or tricked them into Judaizing, and that they, the victims of machinations, had returned to Iberian territory in order to recover their "true" Christian faith and denounce their victimizers. The potential rewards of deposing in this manner were enormous. Suspected Judaizers who cooperated fully with their interrogators (or who succeeded in giving the impression that they were totally candid and contrite) could avoid being tortured. They could even secure relatively lenient sentences if their judges deemed that their confessions had been especially thorough. For example, Jorge Fernández de Castro testified that his parents had taught him the Law of Moses "since he was so small that he did not have any notice of our Lord Jesus Christ until he had acquired the use of reason." He subsequently provided detailed descriptions of the manner in which the "Jews" of Bayonne observed their religion (see above), including a transcription of portions of their liturgy.[75] For this and for denouncing more than 140 Judaizers, he received a light sentence of one year's imprisonment during which he was obligated to wear a penitential garment.[76]

It is significant, however, that habitual returnees often did not follow Fernández's apologetic strategy. Most of those who did adhere to this approach were *permanent* returnees. The latter typically made no mention of economic motives in explaining their return (see the following section).

Several of the habitual returnees whose dossiers I have reviewed affirmed that they had Judaized willingly and that they had encouraged other conversos to Judaize. What is most interesting is that despite incriminating themselves, these same defendants did not cite their religious status or beliefs in spelling out the logic of their return. These defendants made no pretense of having returned to their homelands for religious reasons, either to renounce Judaism or to promote its practice among local conversos. In other words, the suspects did not explicitly confirm the conversophobic presumption that they (and by extension all returnees) were natural subversives who had reentered Iberian territory with the specific aim of propagating Judaism, even though admitting such motives could actually have *improved* the suspects' chances of avoiding torture—and perhaps even of receiving a forbearing sentence—by making the suspects appear utterly pliant to inquisitorial expectations.

Still, it would be a mistake to take defendants' economic explanations (or those of their denouncers) at face value, if only because it is usually impossible to know the precise extent to which the declarants lied and the way in which the inquisitors may have edited or otherwise distorted the suspects' words. Nevertheless, it would be equally erroneous to discard these explanations out of hand as pure fabrications. First, we should consider that the suspects' religious conduct was the main focus of all inquisitorial interrogations. Economic explanations were strictly unrelated to religious conduct and hence cannot be considered mere echoes of the inquisitors' questions. Second, in and of themselves, references to economic motives were neither particularly damaging nor helpful to the alleged returnees. At worst, any mention of a returnee's economic activities in the Iberian Peninsula *insinuated* that that returnee was morally questionable, but did not explicitly assail the returnee's character as a Christian. The allegations I have quoted regarding Román García, for example, had nothing to do with his religious practices or convictions. Furthermore, they contained verifiable details about his business dealings with the Solis family that were irrelevant to his prosecution as a religious criminal and therefore bear a certain verisimilitude.

Of course, one may object that by explaining acts of return in economic terms, the defendants and their denouncers may have been trying to chart a middle course between incrimination and exoneration. To put it differently, the defendants may have been feigning candor while protecting themselves (or the persons whom they denounced) from the most serious charge of heresy. This objection is not sustainable because, again, habitual returnees usually admitted that they had hereticized. For their part, informers also claimed that the returnees whom they identified had committed religious transgressions (Francisco Capadocia's and Román García's accusers were no exception to this pattern of denunciation). Thus, providing an economic excuse for reentering the Iberian Peninsula did virtually nothing to minimize the gravity of the returnees' testimony or that of their accusers. Admissions and even mere allegations of heresy rendered any economic explanation of return superfluous from the inquisitors' point of view. The informants must have known this, since their interrogators asked them questions that focused primarily on matters of religious belief and practice, not on economic matters *for their own sake* (see my discussion of inquisitorial protocol in the following chapter). It is extremely likely, in my opinion, that economic explanations for return adhered to the truth precisely because they served no discernible ulterior purpose, yet the witnesses provided them nonetheless.

Economically Motivated Returnees: A Few Exemplars

The following are additional examples of individuals who returned to Spain and Portugal in search of a livelihood.

Francisco Núñez Redondo was a mule handler who specialized in transporting fellow conversos surreptitiously from Castile to France through Biscay. Given Núñez's line of work, one may say that he was a habitual returnee par excellence. When he was captured by the Toledan tribunal in 1663 (he was fifty-eight years old at the time), Núñez testified that he had not had a fixed residence outside of Portugal, from which he had immigrated to Spain decades earlier.[77]

Núñez readily admitted that he had Judaized in Iberia and in France. He did not deny that he had encouraged other conversos to Judaize by helping them to escape from the Iberian Peninsula. Even so, at first he did not provide a religious rationale for his dangerous activities or even hint that he had undertaken them for reasons of ethnic solidarity. When inquisitors asked him why he had agreed to transport one Enríquez Pereyra into France,

Núñez simply said, "The reason that he was persuaded to [undertake the trip] was that [Enríquez Pereyra] wrote to him that Manuel Enríquez, [an intermediary], would give him four hundred reales [for his services], *and the fact that* [Manuel Enríquez] *indeed gave the money to him*" (emphasis added).[78] This explanation supports another defendant's impression that the mule-handler was "a poor man who would do anything . . . to earn [a few] reales."[79]

Fernando Gil de Espinosa, a native of Madrid, was another emigrant who returned to Iberia primarily—if not solely—to earn a living. His tortuous trajectory speaks of perpetual transience and constant privation. Such conditions appear to have been the lot of the poorest conversos who escaped Iberia via southern France but later returned in search of greener pastures.

Gil told inquisitors in 1669, when he was twenty-two years of age, that he had left his home in Amsterdam because he could not find work there. Gil did not even hint that he had returned because he yearned to live in Spain or because he wished to embrace Catholicism or because he was disappointed with the Judaism he had practiced dutifully for much of his life.[80] "In order to look for a livelihood in some trade," Gil's deposition reads, "he boarded a ship . . . [in 1667 and sailed] from Amsterdam to look for his father who was [reportedly] in Bordeaux."[81] After fourteen months in Bordeaux, Gil departed for Bayonne, where his mother and sister lived. Shortly thereafter, he boarded a French ship bound for the Spanish port of Cádiz. His geographic backtracking was now complete.

Once Gil was in Andalusia, economic distress forced him to engage in whatever occupation seemed most expedient in light of his lack of occupational training and experience. The record of his testimony reads:

[The declarant] was in Cádiz four days, and because he did not find anyone whom he knew or from whom to receive support . . . he went to the Port of Santa María, where he stopped for two days, and from there he embarked for Seville, where for one month and a half he undertook some jobs with a little money that he had available in order to keep what little possessions he had. . . . [H]e dealt with [a few merchants] in Seville, buying some things from their stores. And after eight and a half months of living in Seville he would go out to earn his living by taking a few petty items [*cosillas*] from Seville to sell [outside the city], and return to that city to buy other such items. He spent five or six months doing this.[82]

In May 1669, Gil left the Andalusian province for Castile, traveling with an adolescent whom he had met at an inn. After the youth left his company, Gil walked alone for twenty days "without becoming acquainted with anybody."[83] Later he sold a few trinkets along the road so as to be able to buy a mule in the town of Plasencia. From there, he rode to Madrid to look for his father, Gaspar de Espinosa, to whom he had written from Seville to see if the older man was still alive.[84] Evidently the two had not had contact with one another for several years. In Madrid, Gil "tried to see if his father could accommodate him in some petty trade [*tratillo*] so that [Gil] would be able to earn a living, but since [Gil] found his father so poor and without means to help him, he was going to return to Andalucía to continue with his own *tratillos*."[85]

Indigent conversos like Gil and his father were certainly not the only ones who returned to their lands of origin. Francisco Díaz Méndez, a defendant of Portuguese extraction, exemplifies a comparatively wealthy type of returnee. Díaz explained his return to Toledan inquisitors as follows:

[From the age of sixteen to the age of thirty, the defendant] was in Bilbao and San Sebastián handling cargoes of merchandise [destined] for Portugal. . . . He [later] came to this court [meaning, Madrid] with his brother with the aim of taking over some of His Majesty's taxes and administering them, but because this aim was not realized, *he left for Rouen . . .* and later, when his brother took over the [administration of the] taxes of 10 percent on wool through an *arrendamiento . . .* [the defendant] *came to assist* [his brother] *at this court in order to help* [his brother] *and to get a share of the taxe*s. (Emphasis added.)[86]

Díaz was somewhat typical of returnees who specialized in medium to high commerce and administration in the sense that he did not always fare well in his professional pursuits. Several other conversos were even less fortunate than Díaz, despite possessing occupational experience and business skills comparable to his. A symptom of Spain's economic instability during the seventeenth century was the frequency with which "Portuguese" businessmen sank into bankruptcy and fled to southern France to try to start anew—only to return to Spain, lured by the prospect of a quick windfall.[87]

Gonzalo Báez de Paiba, a "Portuguese" *arrendador* from Murcia, was one such individual. In the late 1640s Báez sold cattle throughout Andalusia, administered the sale of pepper in Ciudad Real, and managed salt mines in Murcia. He was well off. By 1650, however, all his *negocios* had failed. He had become so insolvent that he chose to confine himself at the Royal Hospital of Buen Suceso (in Madrid) rather than face debt collectors.

Báez remained at the hospital for three years until the police transferred him to a royal prison, presumably because he had still not paid his debts. Lay officers of the Holy Tribunal of Toledo later moved him to an inquisitorial prison to face an unrelated charge.[88] In 1657, Báez was released after serving a relatively brief sentence for Judaizing. Of course, he was still penniless, so he decided to travel to Rome to request the financial assistance of a wealthy relative who lived there. Along the way, Báez heard that a plague had struck the city, so he stopped in Bayonne to wait for conditions in Italy to improve.

The former *arrendador* eventually abandoned the idea of seeking help from his relative and resettled in Saint Esprit, where he admittedly practiced Judaism with other expatriates. He then decided that his wife, Catalina de Paiba, who had remained in Madrid during his travels, should join him in his new home. Báez was hesitant to reenter Castile to escort her to France, however, but not because he was afraid of running afoul of the Inquisition. In fact, Báez later testified that what he feared most was the possibility of being detained by agents of the royal treasury (he still owed the crown some taxes). To solve his dilemma, he sent for Catalina de Paiba through a relative, the returnee Juan Sarmiento.[89]

With his *señora* safe in Saint Esprit, Báez was emboldened and returned to Castile. He was captured by the Inquisition in 1659, in Madrid. Incredibly, Báez testified that he had returned to Spain for the sole purpose of putting himself at the Holy tribunal's mercy and embracing Catholicism. He further claimed that he had not surrendered to the Tribunal immediately after arriving in Madrid because he had stumbled and injured his foot, after which he was forced to spend all his money on medical treatment and convalescence. As if that did not already sound like a feeble pretext, Báez added that he had tarried because he was trying to recover his financial viability by working as a tax farmer (ironically enough), under an assumed name.

Báez's testimony regarding his return smelled of a flimsy excuse, yet he quickly confessed to having Judaized and denounced scores of his supposed accomplices. This approach seems to have helped him considerably. Suffice it to say that Báez received an unusually lenient sentence of "perpetual incarceration and penitential habit." The sentence, which was later commuted, may sound terribly harsh to modern ears. In actuality it was relatively mild: relapsed "Judaizers" such as Báez typically received the death penalty.[90]

What interests us here is the *arrendador's* improbable testimony concerning the reasons for his return. There is little question, in my opinion, that Báez was lying when he claimed that he had entered Spain for the purpose of surrendering to the Inquisition. If Báez had truly wished to confess his sins to the Holy Office, he would not have bothered to travel as far as Madrid. Instead, he could have offered himself to inquisitorial authorities in the Basque city of Irún, which lies immediately across the border from southwestern France.

This is not to say, however, that all of Báez's testimony was false or, for that matter, that it is impossible to reconstruct his actual motives. We need only focus on Báez's verifiable assertion that he was working as a tax officer at the time of his arrest to find the most likely reason for his return: Simply put, Báez returned because he wanted to earn money, presumably by resuming his activities as a fiscal administrator. Judging by the promptness with which Báez obtained a tax commission after his return, it is not surprising to find that one of his denouncers suspected that Báez's ulterior purpose in crossing the border into Spain was "to do business in Castile."[91]

The case of Gonzalo Báez de Paiba, like that of Francisco Díaz Méndez, underlines that New Christians who possessed administrative and commercial expertise could aspire to occupy remunerative posts or engage in lucrative *negocios* if they returned to their countries of origin. As we have seen, even defendants like Núñez (the mule handler) and Gil (the petty merchant), neither of whom was especially well educated or skilled in business, could find the means to stay alive in Iberian lands. Returnees of a third type occupied a middle socioeconomic ground. I am referring to mid-scale, itinerant merchants.

Antonio Rodríguez de Amézquita is an example of this type. He was a moderately successful *tratante* who surrendered to the Spanish Inquisition in 1664. Along with numerous other traders who undertook long-distance trips between southwestern France and the urban centers of Spain and Portugal, Rodríguez de Amézquita was a linchpin of the peninsular system of trade. Indeed, he and his fellow itinerant dealers were a mobile element without which the Dutch-French-Spanish trading network would have collapsed. As the last, pivotal link in a long chain of supply, these merchants transported, sold, and thus stimulated demand for many of the foreign products that the Iberian market absorbed during the Early Modern Period. Needless to say, the merchants also introduced Iberian products to northern Europe. These included Spanish wool and Portuguese sugar.[92]

Rodríguez de Amézquita was born in Valladolid in 1614. He became an itinerant salesman at the age of fifteen, when his father, an immigrant from southern Portugal, became ill and was no longer able to support the Rodríguez family. For over a decade, Antonio sold textiles in Andalusia as well as in his father's native land, chiefly in Lisbon. He moved to Madrid in 1641, where he married Leonor Gómez, a fellow "Portuguese" of New Christian stock. Three years later, he left for Andalusia (without Gómez) to acquire "various genres of merchandise," which he then sold throughout the area, as well as in Madrid. In time, he became an established wholesaler who handled diverse goods, both manufactured and unprocessed. These included saffron, raw cotton, chocolate, and linens of various kinds and origins. Among other things, Rodríguez de Amézquita frequented trade fairs in Galicia (where he bought and sold linens); served as an agent for other "Portuguese" merchants in Castile; sold saffron in Cordova, Ecija, and Málaga; and discharged a temporary commission to collect taxes in Huete (province of Cuenca).

Rodríguez de Amézquita testified in 1664 that he had become a crypto-Jew in the course of his travels, at the urging and with the support of some of his relatives from Málaga. Afraid that his heretical practices would be discovered and that members of his family would be harmed by their association with him, Rodríguez transferred his entire household to France in 1655.

From that year until 1664, the *tratante* returned to Spain at least three times, and twice to Portugal, to conduct various mercantile transactions. His commercial activities consisted mainly of purchasing large quantities of American goods in Spain, shipping the goods from Bayonne to Lisbon, and selling them in Portugal. It is not clear why Rodríguez de Amézquita followed this circuitous trafficking procedure. He did not say, for instance, whether it helped him to avoid paying tariffs. Neither did he explain how he transported the goods from Spain to Bayonne, or why he preferred to ride or walk from Bayonne to Lisbon instead of traveling by sea with the merchandise. The inquisitors who interrogated him were not particularly interested in these details (in this they were not unusual); otherwise they would probably have asked Rodríguez de Amézquita to clarify the minutiae of his business deals. We can speculate, however, that the trader chose to travel by land because it was relatively safer and more profitable than sailing. Road journeys gave him the opportunity to sell merchandise that he had stored in Spain during previous trips or to purchase new merchandise that he could sell upon his return to Bayonne.

In the course of his long deposition, Rodríguez de Amézquita denounced dozens of fellow returnees and local conversos whom he alleged were Judaizers like himself. He also explained that during his forays into Iberian territory he had always refrained from practicing Judaism fully "as he was staying at inns, where he was not at leisure" (*como andaba en posadas no tenía comodidad*).[93] However, he claimed to have kept the Law of Moses as openly and as appropriately as he could whenever he was in France. In this Rodríguez de Amézquita was like the vast majority of the habitual repatriates whose cases I have examined.

Rodríguez de Amézquita may well have preferred to stay in the safety and comfort of Bayonne, yet he never attained sufficient financial success to hire more than one commercial emissary to handle his affairs in Spain and Portugal. Consequently, he had no choice but to serve as his own business agent (so to speak) in the peninsula for much of his career.

The same was not true of more prosperous traders such as Diego Rodríguez Cardoso, Rodríguez de Amézquita's fellow refugee and close acquaintance.[94] In the course of three decades, Rodríguez Cardoso crossed the Spanish border several times to buy and sell merchandise in various parts of the Habsburg mainland. The wealthier Rodríguez Cardoso became, the less he found it necessary to leave his home in Saint Esprit. In the late 1650s he began to employ couriers and commercial agents on a regular basis to conclude the international transactions that he had once handled himself. Many of the agents were habitual returnees. By the time that the Spanish Inquisition had gathered enough information to try him under the charge of heresy, Rodríguez Cardoso was beyond its reach, for he no longer had any need to enter Spain. In fact, he had become so successful that he was one of the wealthiest persons in Saint Esprit, as well as one of the leaders of the Judeo-Portuguese community of greater Bayonne.[95] For his part, Rodríguez de Amézquita continued to earn his livelihood on the roads of Spain and Portugal until his final bankruptcy and eventual detention by the Inquisition in 1665. The two men's divergent paths underscore that the frequency with which merchant refugees returned to Iberia may have been closely related to their economic status. Generally speaking, the needier the merchant, the more likely he was to cross the border into Spain—and to do so often.

I will return to the details of Rodríguez de Amézquita's travels in the Iberian Peninsula in due course. For now, suffice it to reiterate that his frequent border crossing and his commercial activities were typical of economically motivated habitual returnees.

Permanent Returnees

The most obvious difference between the likes of Rodríguez de Amézquita and most permanent repatriates is that the latter made only one journey of return. Like habitual returnees, conversos who came back to Iberia with the intention of settling there articulated a relatively narrow range of motivations. Usually, however, permanent returnees did not cite economic reasons in justifying their return. Another difference is that permanent returnees included a small number of women as well as avid ultra-informers (so-called *malsines*) of both sexes. Two of the four women repatriates whose dossiers I have located in the archives of the Toledo tribunal were married; a third was widowed. The first two testified in almost identical language that their husbands or adult sons had "brought" them back to Spain from southern France. These uniform explanations underscore the fact that, as women in a patriarchal society, the two declarants could not easily travel at will (to do so was dangerous and "unseemly"), and at least in that respect they could not escape their social role as dependents of the adult men in their families. The fourth woman, Gracia Gómez Hurtado, apparently decided to return to Spain on her own. Still, she did not undertake the journey alone, but was accompanied by her twenty-two-year-old brother.[96]

Permanent returnees varied in age and economic background, yet a close look at their depositions reveals certain behavioral similarities. Twenty-five of the permanent returnees I have studied initiated contact with the Inquisition shortly after returning to the Iberian Peninsula. All twenty-five immediately declared their intention to renounce heresy and name other conversos who had betrayed Christendom. A typical self-incriminator declared:

To be good in the eyes of God . . . and with the zeal of the Catholic religion, [the declarant says] he has come from Bayonne of France to this court [of Madrid] without any motive other than to give an account to the Holy Office of what, in the space of eight years, he saw different Portuguese persons do and say against our faith . . . for which reason he presented himself the day before yesterday [at the offices of] the Inquisitor General and put himself at his feet so that he would grant him an audience.[97]

The fact that not all permanent returnees surrendered to the Holy Office suggests that their motivations varied. Those who were arrested by the Inquisition, however, concurred with those who testified voluntarily in one important respect: All of them reported or hinted that fellow expatriates in the Sephardi colonies of the Diaspora had set strict adherence to normative Judaism as an unqualified precondition for social acceptance within those communities. In particular, the declarants complained of the insistence with which former Christians had demanded such adherence from them. Some informants alleged that these demands had led to bitter quarrels between themselves and their exiled peers, neighbors, and next of kin. Predictably, the supposed disputes often centered on the irreconcilable opposition between the informants' own alleged Christian leanings and their counterparts' zeal-ous affiliation with Judaism. For example, Manuel de León testified:

[The Portuguese residents of Saint Esprit] were wont to say of [him], "look what that dog is doing; the devil should take him for doing these things, going to mass and being a Catholic. . . ." And this declarant and [his sister] Doña María de León . . . would respond that no one is saved in any law but the law of our Lord Jesus Christ. . . . [I]n [1658] three [of the Portuguese] tried to pervert them and to set this declarant apart...from the observance of our lord Jesus Christ. . . . And he does not remember what words they said to them beyond than [the fact] that [the Judaizers] called them "dogs" because of the difference in the law they kept.[98]

A similar deposition from 1665 reads:

And when [the declarant] wanted to go to mass [the Jews] did not let him, and they took away his cape so he would not go . . . and from that day onwards, some on one side and some on the other, sought to persuade him to leave the faith of Jesus Christ . . . and the [declarant] resisted for four days, until Sunday arrived, and when he wanted to go to mass they gave him the same reasons, seeking to persuade him to observe the Law of Moses, and then the prisoner surrendered and believed that the Law of Moses was the true one.[99]

Even when they did not specify the reason(s) for their return, several perma-nent returnees hinted that they had left the converso Diaspora to escape the pressure that other refugees had exerted upon them to renounce Christian-ity. In this vein, Francisco Cardoso Ortiz testified in 1641 that "[he] went to Peyrehorade where his mother and brothers live; [but once] there he endured many tribulations with them in connection to their attempts to convert him [to Judaism], and their accusing him of being a renegade with the support of all the Portuguese of Peyrehorade . . . *from which city* [the declarant] *left for Pamplona*" (emphasis added).[100]

   There is no doubt that some informants (though it is difficult to know exactly how many) lied or exaggerated in portraying themselves as innocent Christian victims who had persevered in the face of Jewish pressure. The case of João de Aguila is an example of the egregious use of this rhetorical tactic. Aguila, a young Portuguese returnee, appeared spontaneously before the Holy Tribunal of Lisbon in 1650 to denounce several Judaizers with whom he had allegedly become acquainted in the Netherlands. Among Aguila's claims was that he had clashed with Saul Levi Morteira, one of the leading *hakhamim* of Amsterdam. Aguila testified that as a student in Morteira's class for newly arrived refugees, he had challenged the rabbi's interpretation of

Holy Scripture with a Christological reading of his own. According to the declarant, Morteira did not disprove his lucid and highly detailed exegesis (how could anyone confute the Christian truth?); instead, the rabbi became flustered and banished him from the *kehillah*.[101]

Through a careful analysis of the dossier in question, H. P. Salomon has argued persuasively that Aguila and his inquisitorial interlocutors fabricated the supposed altercation with Morteira.[102] The existence of probable perjurers such as Aguila, however, does not justify a categorical invalidation of all the testimony that permanent returnees rendered to the Inquisition. Even some of the returnees who testified in an apologetic manner depicted some aspects of their experience in the converso Diaspora in terms that circumstantial evidence as well as evidence internal to the dossiers themselves shows to be realistic and quite trustworthy.

The most credible informants told, not of cathartic confrontations with grotesquely malicious "Jews," or of heroic resistance to spiritual coercion, but of their own gradual alienation from the social world of expatriate conversos. Burdened by their own ambivalence, these informants betrayed a sense that living in a predominantly Jewish milieu had led them to question or even redefine their social, ethnic, familial, and religious attachments.

The deposition of Fernando Alvarez is an example of credible testimony that projects this feeling of social alienation and self-doubt. Alvarez, a sixty-four-year-old converso of Castilian origin, was imprisoned by the Santo Oficio in Cuenca after returning from Bayonne in 1663. The defendant testified under cross-examination that he had been a seller of stockings in Seville but had lost his business and had been unemployed prior to his emigration from Spain. He had gone to Saint Esprit, he said, to live with his son, Pedro Alvarez. Given the informant's advanced age and his unemployment, it is probable that he had gone to France to take shelter and find sustenance under his son's roof.[103]

Upon arriving in Saint Esprit Fernando Alvarez found that his son and all but three families of local conversos were fervent Judaizers. Pedro had even attained some prominence as a host of semisecret prayer services. According to Alvarez, Pedro and the Judaizers of Saint Esprit had welcomed him into their community, exclaiming that they were relieved that he had escaped to a land where he could practice the Law of Moses "with more freedom."[104] He also reported that these selfsame neighbors had warned him not to return to Castile lest someone betray him to the Inquisition. Not long thereafter, the neighbors allegedly became intrusive, going so far as to voice "great exhortations" (*grandes persuasiones*) in order to convince Alvarez to submit to circumcision.[105] The *vecinos* had reportedly stressed that if Alvarez died in Spain, where there was nobody who could circumcise him, his soul would at least be saved if he were already circumcised. Taken aback by such pressure, Alvarez refused to consent to the painful and dangerous surgery.

The refugees' admonitions to Alvarez regarding circumcision exemplify what some scholars have identified as a tendency among conversos to view this rite as a kind of sacrament akin to Christian baptism. According to this "sacramental" view, circumcision is a ritual that serves to cleanse believers of sin and thus helps assure their salvation. There is evidence that some refugees also regarded circumcision as a means of restraining potentially rebellious conversos by tying them irrevocably to the Jewish people. One returnee reported that his grandfather had browbeaten him into being circumcised by arguing that he (the grandson) should submit to the procedure "so that he would come out of it a Jew, and so that, *though he may renege, he would not be able to stop being a Jew*" (emphasis added).[106] This view of circumcision, like the "sacramental" understanding of it, was as foreign to Jewish law and tradition in the seventeenth century as it is today. Halakhic definitions of the rite treat it as a covenantal obligation, never as a means of absolution, a prerequisite for redemption, or a soul-transforming ritual of conversion.[107]

More important for our purposes is what the "great exhortations" to which Alvarez alluded indicate about his neighbors' view of the phenomenon of return to Iberia. If we consider that at the time of Alvarez's encounter with the Judaizers of Saint Esprit numerous exiles were crossing the border into Spain on a regular basis, the *vecinos's* alleged warnings to Alvarez that he should consent to a circumcision "in case he died in Spain" do not seem to be mere rhetorical devices calculated to induce his cooperation. Rather, these warnings speak of a perception among the refugees that returning to Iberia, while generally undesirable, was well within the realm of possibility or even necessity, even for those who bound themselves spiritually—and, in the case of the circumcised, physically—to the Jewish community of faith then emerging in the southwest of France.

Taken out of context, Alvarez's testimony regarding the New Jews of Bayonne may seem like a fabrication designed to distance himself from them and thus to allay any inquisitorial suspicions concerning his religious identity. Far from avoiding blame, however, Alvarez claimed that he had been an adherent of the Law of Moses since the age of thirty, when a certain Dr. Reynoso and one Francisco López had introduced him to the world of marranic belief in Castile.

Alvarez testified that López and Reynoso had taught him that fasting on certain days in contravention of Catholic practice was a primary way of keeping the Law of Moses.[108] From this, the defendant said, he inferred that his own wife, Catalina de Alvarez, had been a Judaizer for several years. She too had fasted periodically before Alvarez's religious initiation, a fact he now recognized as a sign of her true religion. Even then, Alvarez added, he never told Catalina de Alvarez directly, and she never told him, what they both knew to be the truth about their fasts. As the defendant put it:

his wife never declared herself as an observer of [the Law of Moses] by word with this witness [Fernando Alvarez]; neither did this witness tell her that he was a keeper of the Law of Moses, [but] with this tacit understanding on two occasions . . . Doña Catalina, his wife, asked him if he wanted them both to fast for God; and although she did not tell him anything else, this witness understood that the fast was of the Law of Moses; and thus both fasted those days; he does not know if he remembers what festivity or what precept the fasts were for. This was when both were alone without anybody else knowing what they were doing. Neither beforehand nor afterwards did they perform any rite or ceremony . . . Nothing happened, and neither one nor the other said a single word about the fact that these were fasts of the Law of Moses, but by the very fact that the fasts were different than those kept by the Christians he knew that his wife knew and understood them to be fasts of the Law of Moses.[109]

Alvarez alleged that he had followed a similar pattern of discretion in Bayonne. Specifically, he claimed that neither he nor his son ever informed one another explicitly that they were observers of normative Judaism, even though the father could plainly see that Pedro Alvarez followed the same practices as the other New Jews of Saint Esprit, and the younger man knew that his father attended Jewish services on a regular basis.

What brings us to the crux of Fernando Alvarez's internal dilemma, then, is what he allegedly *did* tell his son:

[The declarant told Pedro Alvarez that] . . . it weighed on him [Fernando Alvarez] to have gone to that community, *that that was not the place for him, a land totally full of Portuguese observers [of Judaism], and that if he [Alvarez] were not [an observer] they would exert pressure on him;* but that he did not wish to offer any counsel to him [meaning the son, Pedro Alvarez], that [Pedro] could do whatever he wanted." (Emphasis added.)[110]

Interestingly enough, the permanent returnee Fernando Gómez Tejadillos corroborated Alvarez's self-portrayal as a reluctant Judaizer. In a deposition intended for his own trial, Gómez testified that although [Fernando] Alvarez attended services to hear the [Jewish] prayers, it was apparently without much desire or private enjoyment, it was rather to please his son and his niece [another refugee]; [Alvarez] *was warned about this* [by members of the community], yet this witness did not see him keep the Sabbath . . . from which this witness gathered that [Alvarez] acted with unease. . . . [Alvarez] would ask, why should he do things he was not raised to do, since he knew that this was something that was not good for him? (Emphasis added.)[111]

Fernando Alvarez did not directly address the reasons for his return in any of his own testimony. At the same time, the gist of his declarations, as well as Gómez' impression of him, suggest that Alvarez may have left France because he was uncomfortable living among the Judaizers of Saint Esprit. More specifically, Alvarez may have returned to Spain because he resented their attempts to incorporate him into their community on their own terms. Can we know that this was in fact Alvarez's motivation for returning? For that matter, is it possible to ascertain whether any of the information he gave the inquisitors is reliable? More to the point, did Alvarez lie in order to portray himself as a "good" penitent who had only practiced crypto-Judaism under duress?

As I mentioned in the introductory chapter, one way to answer questions such as these is to ask whether the informant would have benefited in any way by providing the *specific* testimony that appears in his or her inquisitorial dossier. In Alvarez's case, the answer to the question is no.

First, Alvarez's statements that he, his wife, and his son communicated tacitly regarding their observance of "the Law of Moses" were irrelevant to his prosecution. All that Alvarez had to say (and did say) to satisfy his interrogators is that he had kept that Law of Moses by fasting with Catalina de Alvarez and by praying in semi-secret "synagogues" with Pedro Alvarez. Yet the defendant went beyond these simple affirmations. He described a very specific modus operandi that was immaterial in the context of his deposition. More importantly, this description did not exculpate him, or his wife and son, or the New Jews of Saint Esprit (except for the three families of "faithful Catholics" Alvarez mentioned at the beginning of his deposition).

It is also worth noting that Alvarez's testimony concerning the secret religion he allegedly observed with his wife prior to his arrival in France depicts a shallow, essentially negative faith that was largely devoid of affirmative theological or ritual substance. This religion was not the rich, colorful stuff of Judeophobic fantasy that the inquisitors had perhaps come to expect from the testimony of various denouncers.[112] More than a fully developed and well-articulated alternative to Christianity, the marranism of the Alvarezes appears to have been a form of anti-Catholicism whose connection to Jewish norms and customs was vague at best. Indeed, the couple's secret practices fit Juan Blázquez Miguel's definition of "residual crypto-Judaism," that is to say a moribund pseudo-religion that survived among Castilian conversos in the late sixteenth and seventeenth centuries after the Spanish Inquisition had nearly extinguished vibrant forms of native crypto-Judaism.[113]

But whether or not Alvarez's religion had a substantive core, it is clear that he did not *need* to portray it as he did, namely as an ultra-cautious exercise in obfuscation. From Alvarez's testimony it appears that both he and his wife were so terrified of being discovered, and were so distant psychologically from one another, that they preferred to leave their tentative adherence to the "Law of Moses" unspoken, and thus plausibly deniable. Why would Alvarez incriminate his spouse and then bother to depict such an elaborate relationship of mutual distrust unless the relationship had actually existed?

Alvarez's assertions that the Judeo-Portuguese majority of Saint Esprit exerted pressure upon him to conform to Halakhah are similarly credible. Had Alvarez claimed to have been a good Christian prior to his encounter with the expatriate community and then justified his return as a response to Jewish coercion, there would be reason to doubt the reliability of his account. Yet Alvarez testified that he had rejected social and ideological pressure despite the fact that he already considered himself a Judaizer before emigrating to France. In other words, Alvarez did not deny or try to minimize his own culpability in any way. His somewhat oblique criticism of the intrusive New Jews of Bayonne was essentially superfluous to the question of his guilt, and therefore was as plausible as the equally redundant details he had provided concerning his secret fasts.

The most crucial information Alvarez furnished in connection to his return to Spain was that which provided glimpses of his attitude toward the New Jews of Saint Esprit. It is impossible to determine with finality whether Alvarez actually developed an aversion to his neighbors (as he hinted) and whether such antipathy had catalyzed his return to Iberian soil. Nonetheless, there are key aspects of his account that lend such an interpretation considerable credence.

First, Alvarez claimed to have suffered something of a culture shock in France, but though he depicted the shock as serious, he did not paint it in overly dramatic colors. For instance, he never indicated that his rejection of the strictures of communal life had led to acrimonious confrontations with his son or with their neighbors. Second, by the same token, Alvarez did not paint his fellow refugees as utterly hateful conversionists. Rather, he portrayed them quite plausibly as a group of overbearing meddlers who were anxious to establish social and religious discipline in their community. We must remember that Saint Esprit was an embryonic colony of Jewish neophytes that still lacked complete internal cohesion, a fully institutionalized authority, and clear normative contours.[114] If anything, Alvarez's testimony suggests that members of the incipient commonwealth overcompensated for these shortcomings by projecting toward recent immigrants their own eagerness to solidify the community's Jewish identity.

Third, Alvarez portrayed himself not as a Christian hero or as a completely innocent victim but as a reluctant subject of communal surveillance. He never claimed to have renounced the Law of Moses while in Bayonne, although, according to Gómez, Alvarez did express some understandable doubts about practicing a religion in which he had not been educated as a child, regardless of the intellectual appeal of that religion. Such hesitation certainly fits well within a range of responses one would expect from someone who had been accustomed to practicing one religion (Roman Catholic Christianity) but had subsequently adopted an exceedingly cryptic and unpopular one (secret "Judaism") at a late age.

What seems to have bothered Alvarez most, then, was not his new neighbors' religion, if we define "religion" narrowly as a set of ideas about the meaning of existence, about the proper order of the universe, accompanied by a gamut of rituals designed to express or realize those ideas in the realm of daily life. Rather, what Alvarez disliked was his neighbors' tight supervision and their continual demands that he conform strictly to their notion of appropriate behavior and belief. As Alvarez put it, he was wary that the New Jews "would exert pressure on him" if he were not observant by *their* standards.[115]

In sum, Alvarez's account was not an implausible fable about good (Christianity) repulsing evil (Judaism). Rather, it was a reasonably verisimilar depiction of his encounter with a community of recent converts to normative Judaism who were anxious to cement their newly acquired collective identity, and who, in their understandable insecurity, placed an especially heavy burden of conformity upon the community's newest members. In essence, Alvarez's testimony sketches his realization that he could not accept the authoritarian system of social relations that this assiduously self-conscious community embodied. As the foregoing suggests, there is no evidence that Alvarez left Bayonne because he was a disillusioned Judaizer in an ideological or philosophical sense. He was certainly not like the arch-dissident Uriel da Costa (ca. 1583–1640), who objected to rabbinic Judaism in principle. Alvarez simply resented being told what to do and what to believe, regardless of whether or not he was a cognizant "Judaizer."

It is important to recall that Alvarez also indicated that he had felt like a Castilian outsider in a predominantly "Portuguese" suburb. Although we cannot certify that this was how he actually experienced life in Saint Esprit, it does not seem farfetched that Alvarez should have felt out of place because of his cultural background. After all, the Sephardi "Nations" of sixteenth- and seventeenth-century France were decidedly Portuguese in a demographic and therefore in a cultural sense.[116] As several scholars have noted, émigré conversos of Lusitanian origin retained Portuguese as their vernacular and their lingua franca.[117] Alvarez, a Castilian, probably did not speak Portuguese as fluently as his new neighbors, most of whom were Lusitanian or of Lusitanian descent. Furthermore, he had no part in the network of intra-"Portuguese" bonds that connected his fellow exiles in the Diaspora and that excluded him for the obvious reason that he was a newcomer to the community and was not of Portuguese stock.[118] While many Castilian conversos, such as Pedro Alvarez, became integral parts of predominantly "Portuguese" collectives, his father's case warns us not to assume that all Castilian conversos were prepared to do the same.

There is yet another factor to consider in connection to Alvarez's ethnic background: exiled conversos such as he felt a deep emotional and intellectual attachment to their countries of origin. It is a matter of scholarly consensus that even when they renounced Christianity, New Jews in Europe and the Mediterranean retained a strong sense of connection with the Iberian lands and cultures that had shaped their collective heritage and personal histories.[119] There is no reason to believe that Alvarez was an exception to this tendency. Thus, if Sephardi expatriates who adjusted well to normative Judaism based their social identity in the Diaspora largely by reference to their old homelands and to a sense of being "Portuguese" or "Spanish," it follows that ambiguous Judaizers or outright malcontents such as Alvarez, who felt they did *not* belong in the Jewish world, had little besides an awareness of their own Hispanicity as a ground on which to anchor their social identity. I suspect this was especially true of misfits who had abandoned Christianity yet failed to replace it with a solid alternative. Arguably, Alvarez's tentative and shallow crypto-Judaism was anything but a viable substitute for full-fledged Catholicism. In this light, his return to Spain appears as a logical step toward reconstituting his sense of social fixity along familiar, Castilian lines.

All indications are that Alvarez was not the only refugee who felt like a stranger among his fellow expatriates and who resented their procrustean approach to new immigrants. The defendant Rafael Méndez, for instance, told inquisitors in 1660 that he had been a crypto-Jew before emigrating to France yet had never told this to his insolent neighbors in Bayonne, precisely because they had accosted him with their conversionist *persuasiones* without even bothering to ascertain, as was supposedly customary, whether he was already *um dos nossos* ("one of ours").[120]

To be sure, other repatriates experienced a more welcoming atmosphere in their respective places of exile than did Méndez and Alvarez. But even these fortunate returnees felt compelled by circumstance rather than by inner conviction to adopt their neighbors' Jewish way of life. The aforementioned Fernando Gómez Tejadillos is an example of this phenomenon. He was among the returnees who did not portray his fellow expatriates as abrasive or hostile. Gómez described his own rather uneasy espousal of halakhic Judaism as the result of a process of social adjustment and gradual indoctrination, not as a surrender to overt intimidation, or, for that matter, as a free and private choice based on an intellectual consideration of the merits of Judaism:

It was around the time [that he was in Livorno, Naples, and Bayonne] that he [Fernando Gómez Tejadillos] became persuaded that [the Law of Moses] was good, *because he saw that so many people of good habits followed it,* and because of what his uncle said to him, but internally [the Law of Moses] stuck to him only a little [*se le pegaba poco*], and thus he was a poor observer of the Law of Moses, because he used to go into the [gentile] hostels and eat sausages and other forbidden things. . . . And when he had a few difficulties [regarding the Law of Moses, his uncle] took him to some principal men (whose names he does not know) so that they would satisfy and solve the difficulty for him . . . and as this confessant was a youth at the time, and had no intelligence for those matters, they convinced him with ease (Emphasis added.)[121]

The dilemma that recent immigrants such as Gómez encountered in their new surroundings is understandable. However hostile to conversos, Iberian society was the soil on which these immigrants had been rooted for much of their lives. Once in exile, the refugees found themselves displaced and in the position of social and religious novices. To make matters worse, they were in the midst of countries that were unfamiliar to them. All of this created an enormous pressure upon the refugees to establish new roots within the socioreligious framework of the colonies of converso expatriates, where at least people spoke familiar Iberian languages. Such pressure was compounded by the communal cadre's attempts to establish and enforce behavioral uniformity among the newcomers. The choice to stay outside the framework implied complete social isolation. Meanwhile, the option to stay within the framework meant gaining some respectability, companionship, and access to the protection of the national-religious collective. In 1618 the informant Bartholomeu Nunes articulated this stark reality. He told inquisitors in the Portuguese colony of Goa that he had been reluctant to admit that he was not an observer of the Law of Moses when he had first settled in Amsterdam for fear that his neighbors "would treat him badly and disfavor him."[122] Some time later he succumbed to loneliness and declared himself a Jew:

Seeing himself disfavored and alone [literally: without anyone] *and seeing that he had no one but the Jews who taught him the law [of Moses], he said that he was a Jew like them in order to please them and so that they would help him and favor him* [;] and he thinks that they believed him . . . and sometimes he went to synagogue with them . . . but when he was behind their backs he did not keep the Sabbath and ate whatever he found. (Emphasis added.)[123]

In the above passage, Nunes, like Gómez, does not portray the New Jews of Amsterdam as particularly aggressive or abusive, merely as inhospitable and uncompromising toward conversos who did not defer to a set of behavioral imperatives. Whether or not Nunes was trying to ingratiate himself to his interrogators by saying that he had secretly violated the Law of Moses is a separate matter. The point to emphasize here is that his observations regarding the Amsterdam *Kehillah* are not the stuff of Judeophobic apologia; rather, they hint of the real vulnerability and defensiveness of what was at the time a small, newly created colony of Catholics-turned-Jews that was straining to establish a creedal identity for itself.[124]

Like much of the testimony I have cited in the present section, Nunes's deposition illustrates that for recent converso escapees social acceptance in the Diaspora hinged largely on their ability to create the *appearance* of conformity with the Jewish collective. While new refugees could choose to practice Judaism halfheartedly, they could scarcely afford to allow their more zealous neighbors to *perceive* them as halfhearted Jews. As far as these *vecinos* were concerned, there was no middle ground: Either an immigrant belonged to the Jewish community of faith and heeded all its commands, both explicit and implicit, or the immigrant was entirely outside of it. Overt dissidence isolated a refugee socially and economically in what was an unfamiliar country. In addition, nonconformity brought shame not only upon the dissident, but upon his or her family, even if the family was fully compliant with the behavioral norms of the Judaizing majority. Expatriate conversos recognized this problem and expended much energy constructing and maintaining a respectably orthodox (or perhaps it is more accurate to say *orthopractical*) image. The returnee Francisco Cardoso Ortiz reported that "in Peyrehorade, [his mother] gave . . . all the other Jews to understand that this declarant was already converted to the Law of Moses, and as she could not [actually] achieve [his conversion], she asked him to at least refrain from going to mass in public in Peyrehorade, so that he would not do a disservice to [her and her other children] and anger the others by singularizing himself."[125]

Of course, defying the Jewish community brought with it the possibility that the renegade would become isolated within his or her own family. Familial ostracism could lead to the rebel's economic marginalization. The returnee Manuel Machuca revealed this double peril in his testimony of 1662. Like Nunes, he noted the intense feeling of isolation that had preceded his capitulation to the demands of the "Judaizing" cohort. Machuca reported that nine years earlier his grandfather, Gabriel Henríquez, and the above-mentioned wholesaler Diego Rodríguez Cardoso had taken him from Bayonne to Peyrehorade so that a Jewish emissary from the Low Countries could circumcise him. During the trip Rodríguez Cardoso allegedly asked Machuca

if [Machuca] knew for what purpose they were taking him [to Peyrehorade]; [Machuca] said he did not, to which his grandfather said: "Look, you are here so that they may circumcise you and you may come out of it a Jew . . . and if you do not [get circumcised], the devil will take you, and I will not take any notice of you, [and] I would sooner bequeath my property to a stranger than to you; [but] if you get circumcised I will leave all of it to you. . . ." [At that point, other Jews joined the grandfather in exhorting the defendant to submit to the circumcision] . . . *and finding himself beleaguered and alone in his feelings [Machuca] consented and allowed himself to be circumcised.* (Emphasis added.)[126]

Gabriel Hernandez's fear that his grandson would become a "renegade" was not out of the ordinary in the converso Diaspora of the seventeenth century. Neither, I suspect, was Hernandez' threat to disinherit Machuca if he did not follow the Law of Moses. Several wills survive in the archives of the Judeo-Portuguese community of Amsterdam in which formerly Christian testators pursue exactly the same approach as Hernández. In their testaments, these New Jews assigned their property to relatives on the express condition that the latter become or remain publicly professing and practicing Jews.[127]

Given the stark choice between social integration and isolation, between respectability and dishonor, and between economic survival and destitution, a number of the refugees who felt that they could not or should not swim

against the current of Jewish communal life returned to the culturally familiar and economically promising world of the Iberian Peninsula. Judging by
their testimony, it would appear that this was especially true of permanent
returnees whom I have studied.

Conclusion: The Relative Banality of "Treason"

In the present chapter I have outlined the phenomenon of return to Iberia by
reference to two major groups of returnees—habitual returnees and permanent returnees. As we have seen, the motivations of the first group tended
heavily toward the economic. These returnees did not fit the Judeophobic
stereotypes that depicted them as anti-Christian provocateurs with a natural
vocation to subvert Iberian society. Neither did chronic returnees fit the
image of moral weakness and degradation that Jews (especially New Jews) ascribed to them. Economically motivated returnees were certainly not all trai-
tors fit for daily curses, or like dogs who return to eat of their vomit
(Christian idolatry), to paraphrase the opinion of the New Jewish intellectual
Immanuel Aboab (ca. 1626).[128]

If anything, the experience of habitual returnees and some economically motivated permanent returnees suggests that for them material subsistence and the quest for prosperity overruled any ideological or philosophical
qualms. Economic security was an immediate and crucial goal that evidently
compelled these individuals to avoid following the letter of Halakhah, and in
so doing adhere to some idealized self-image or compulsory model of community.

Not that these "renegades" behaved especially badly as Jews. In fact, it
seems that most of the habitual returnees observed at least some of the basic
norms of the diasporic *kehillot* that gave shelter to peninsular immigrants.
But for such refugees, normative Judaism was like something activated by an
electric switch: It could be turned on or off according to circumstance. If
decorum, a sense of duty, and religious scruples demanded that the returnees
do such things as attend synagogue, learn proper behavior from Jewish experts, and bury their dead according to halakhic rites while in the Diaspora,
then the renegades did so, whether they felt internally conflicted or not. If, in
contrast, the renegades needed to earn money, they found it perfectly expedient and acceptable—or even absolutely necessary—to violate Jewish law
and behave as Christians while trying to find a job or attempting to sell merchandise during long sojourns in Castile, Aragon, and Portugal.

Habitual returnees were chiefly *economic* refugees who dissented from certain normative social and religious patterns chiefly through their actions and not through their words. These men were not true heretics in the sense that their rebellion against Jewish authority had strictly little if anything to do with questions of religious dogma. Viewed in this light, their frequent remigration to Iberia may appear as something relatively mundane, even banal.

It is reasonable to assume that the poor and middling conversos who comprised the "renegade" cohort in southwestern France would have disagreed with Rabbi Moses D'Aguilar that it was not particularly difficult to leave that area to make a living in countries where "freedom of conscience" was the legal norm. Similarly, economically motivated returnees would probably have disagreed with Immanuel Aboab's position that the spiritual rewards of strict halakhic observance were infinitely greater than the material assets required to move to places such as Amsterdam and Venice, which were comparatively hospitable to Jews.[129] To be fair, Aboab realized that dire poverty was endemic among peninsular refugees. He also acknowledged the high expenses and perils that conversos faced if they chose to relocate from "the lands of idolatry" (including France) to the safer corners of the Jewish Diaspora. In a letter to the refugees of Labastide, Aboab even cited cases in which Jews had taken advantage of converso refugees, so it is clear that his outlook was far from rosy.[130] Yet, as the grandson of one of the last Iberian *hakhamim* and a reasonably prosperous member of the diasporic world, Aboab was clearly incapable of fully empathizing with those conversos less fortunate and less attached to rabbinic Judaism than he. In this he was typical of the New Jewish establishment.

Habitual returnees tended to be as mobile in exile as they had been prior to their escape from Iberian territory. Furthermore, in their role as economic actors, these returnees never ceased to form part of a complex Iberian system of trade. Within that system, they exploited the advantages of belonging to a far-flung, ethnic support network. That the network extended to places like Bayonne and Bordeaux did not alter the fact that the primary cultural, occupational, and economic orientation of these conversos was towards Iberia.

If there were any disillusioned Judaizers among the returnees, they were among the ones who returned to their countries of origin with the aim of settling there permanently. As we have seen, many permanent returnees left the Sephardi Diaspora because, to paraphrase several of them, they "could not find a life" (*no hallaba su vida*) among Jews.[131] The evidence adduced in the present chapter concerning the behavior of such returnees indicates that difficulties in the process of acculturation to Jewish society were the main causes of permanent return. These difficulties applied equally to voluntary delators (*malsines*) and to permanent returnees who did not surrender to the Inquisition of their own volition. Prior to their return to Iberia permanent returnees often walked a fine line between integration and alienation, between wanting to blend into the expatriate communities, and being totally repulsed by the latter's authoritarian posture.

Neither full outsiders nor full insiders of the *kehillot* those who failed to develop stable and comfortable roles in Jewish or proto-Jewish communities opted to solve the problem of their cultural liminality by means of self-repatriation. Whether surreptitiously or as conspicuous penitents, the repatriates sought to establish a lasting truce between themselves and Iberian society. For their part, habitual returnees took a more pragmatic path that allowed them to find economic and social security in constant mobility. The religious malleability of chronic returnees was implicit in their strategy of adaptation, namely in chronic return. These refugees' ability and willingness to shift from one religious community to another and to blend into both, as circumstances required it, was consistent with their participation in an economic system that spanned the socioreligious and geographic divide between normative Judaism and Christianity. The following chapter will examine the accommodationist and the pragmatic solutions to cultural liminality through a closer examination of the religious lives of converso renegades. The chief questions will be the following: How did renegades construct their religious and social identities, and what did identifying with a particular faith or religious law mean to them?

Chapter 4

Interrogation, Confession, and Reversion to Christianity

Not all permanent and habitual repatriates, whose total number is unknown, came into contact with the Inquisition. Those who did were invariably subject to a process of formal re-Christianization. In most cases, this process entailed (1) a public abjuration of heresy; (2) the fulfillment of an inquisitorial sentence involving incarceration, destitution, banishment from certain cities, forced labor, public shaming, flogging, or a combination of these penalties depending on the severity of the crime and the completeness of the declarant's confession; and finally, (3) subjection to a regimen of penitential exercises and religious reeducation under the auspices of the inquisitorial confraternity of St. Peter Martyr.

Obligatory penance was the lot of all returnees who confessed that they had Judaized. This requirement of atonement depended neither on the veracity of the confessants' testimony nor on the sincerity of their repentance. Even so, there is evidence that several returnees' official reconciliation with the church concretized a real shift in their social and religious self-perception. For these earnest penitents, formal acceptance of "the faith of our Lord Jesus Christ" was a true culmination of the process of return. Specifically, the tripartite process of reconciliation cemented in spiritual terms what the penitents had accomplished in the temporal realm by crossing the border into Iberian soil.

To understand the phenomenon of formal re-Christianization it is necessary to examine the system of inquisitorial justice that formed that phenomenon's immediate context. It would be redundant to dwell at length on the procedures that Iberian inquisitors followed in their inquests and trials as modern scholarship has already produced an enormous body of work devoted to that theme.[1] In this chapter I will outline merely a few aspects of inquisitorial *procesos* that shed light on the inner lives of former exiles and thus permit a selective yet substantive reconstruction of their experiences as returnees to Christianity. Specifically, I will concentrate on the interrogations that elicited the bulk of our evidence concerning the lives of Judeoconverso penitents. I will also discuss the premises that underlay the Holy Tribunals' questioning of suspected Judaizers. Finally, I will focus on the testimony that the returnees rendered under examination, concentrating on the declarants' confessions of Judaizing, for these initiated the overt process of re-Christianization and gave voice to some of the penitents' inner reconversion.

A word on my approach to the confessions is in order. In the previous chapter I assessed the likelihood that "renegades" returned to Iberia for economic reasons. I also evaluated the likelihood that some of these putative dissidents returned because they had failed to adapt to the socioreligious world of New Jews. The questions I posed in both cases were aimed primarily at establishing a clear-cut facticity. In essence, I tried to prove that economic motives as well as instances of social maladaptation were not imaginary, but actually occurred. In the present chapter and in the chapter that follows it, however, I will focus on questions of religious identity. These latter questions pertain to the utmost subjectivity, and therefore cannot be properly addressed by reference to a supposedly transparent reality totally extrinsic to and independent of the subject.[2] Neither do such questions necessitate final answers, contrary to what the stark designations "truth" and "falsehood" suggest. Against the simple realism of true/false scenarios, I will approach the religious consciousness of the renegades as ongoing, internal processes of interpretation and reinterpretation that responded to specific historical experiences (the vicissitudes of cultural liminality) and constraints (communal and inquisitorial pressure). A premise of my approach is that the identities of the declarants did not exist *exclusively* prior to and independently of the autobiographical testimonies by which the informants gave momentary shape to those identities. As one historian has put it, "A narrative does not simply 'represent' facts, it participates in their making."[3] In effect, I will argue, renegades created their respective religious self-identities on a contingent basis by emplotting (or reemplotting) their individual lives as meaningful narratives.

As historical outcomes, the identities of renegade informants were largely conditioned by coercion, yet they were not for that reason necessarily insincere. This chapter is ultimately devoted to showing how the cultural matrix in which the penitents experienced their spiritual "return" permitted the coincidence of external coercion and voluntary self-formation.

Interrogation and Its Purposes

Perhaps the most important part of any returnee's inquisitorial dossier from the point of view of the history of popular culture and what modern historians have called the "history of mentality" is the record of the cross-examination(s) that followed the returnee's arrest or voluntary surrender.

Inquisitorial interrogations consisted of a series of standard questions designed to elicit data concerning the suspect's genealogy and his or her religious life. Portuguese and Spanish inquisitors utilized identical sets of mandatory questions to delve into the first of these areas, and totally different ones to explore the second. In addition, both groups of inquisitors supplemented their stock of queries with various others that responded to the peculiarities of each case.

It is my impression that Portuguese dossiers of the seventeenth century are characterized by the dry, repetitive, and exceedingly formulaic testimony that fills their folios. Such testimony reflects the businesslike and target-oriented approach of the interrogators, as well as the relatively narrow scope of the requisite questions themselves. The following is an excerpt from a typical deposition recorded in Lisbon in 1619. I have italicized the portions that appear verbatim in countless other Portuguese cases against suspected Judaizers:

And being both alone making an account of a certain assignment [*the defendant and his associate*] *came to speak about the Law of Moses, and they acknowledged to one another* [*se derao conta hum ao outro*] *that they lived by it and believed in it, saying that it was good, and that they expected to be saved in it, and they did not speak about* [*any*] *ceremonies* [*of the Law of Moses*] or about who might teach one how to perform them; neither did they say to whom they had previously communicated [their adherence to the Law of Moses]; nor did they speak about it before or afterward, *knowing from that instance that they were Jews, distanced from* [*our*] *faith;* [*the defendant also said*] *that they were not relatives and that one had confided in the other because they were friends and of the same nation.*[4]

It is not difficult to infer from the style and content of the excerpt that the material preserved is a legalistic summary of responses the suspect allegedly provided rather than an exact record of his words. The recurrence of verbal formulas in testimony such as the above suggests that Portuguese inquisitors and their notaries may have distorted or even falsified portions of prisoners' depositions. Some scholars have categorically dismissed the confessions of Portuguese "Judaizers" as hoaxes, partly because of the ubiquity of rote language in much of the recorded testimony.[5] The merits and weak-nesses of this sweeping interpretation need not detain us. Still, it would be careless to ignore that formulaic-sounding depositions tell historians more about the interests, biases, and bureaucratic preferences of the Lusitanian in-quisitors than about the actions and personalities of the confessants. At the very least, the formulaic quality of many of the Portuguese records suggests that Lusitanian inquisitors approached their questioning of prisoners as a means of confirming their own preconceptions of what constituted religious criminality, not necessarily as a way of inducing wide-ranging or especially meticulous confessions.

As the quotation exemplifies, the Portuguese officers were chiefly inter-ested in determining the following, in order of importance:

First, *whether a suspect had ever made a declaration (declaração) admit-ting he or she was a follower of the Law of Moses.* The Portuguese inquisitors' stubborn pursuit of "proof" of such declarations gives the strong impression that for them verbalizing an allegiance to "Judaism" constituted a crime in and of itself, regardless of whether the suspect in question had ever practiced any illicit religion, or whether that religion derived from or bore any resem-blance to normative Judaism. If statements of allegiance to the "Law of Moses" fit the inquisitorial definition of a crime, one can easily see why the Portuguese tribunals sought to establish early on that a defendant had ut-tered them: Once the defendant admitted that he or she had made a hereti-cal *declaração*, the trial could proceed expeditiously as there was no need to prove anything else to secure that person's conviction.

Second, *the time that the declaration occurred.* This information helped to draw a chronology of the suspect's religious crime(s) and to determine whether the supposed transgressions were covered by general pardons, which were effective only for limited periods of time. (The Holy See issued pardons for Portuguese "Judaizers" in 1533, 1547, and 1605.)[6]

Third, *the reason(s) the suspect and his or her counterpart(s) had confided in each other that they were observers of secret Judaism.* If the defendant "ad-mitted" that he or she had discussed heresy with his or her accomplice be-cause the latter was a friend, a relative, or simply a fellow New Christian, the admission helped to establish the plausibility of the communication between the suspects. The inquisitors' obvious assumption here was that friends, rel-atives, and members of the Judeoconverso "Nation" were more likely than strangers to exchange sensitive information in confidence. More importantly, the admission served to confirm New Christians' supposed propensity to en-gage in heretical conspiracies. In essence, therefore, the admission bolstered conversophobic prejudices that partially fueled the inquisitorial persecution *of cristãos-novos* irrespective of their actual beliefs and behavior.

Fourth, *what practices the accused performed in fulfillment of the Law of Moses.* Eliciting such information was a basic intelligence-gathering function of the peninsular Inquisitions, whose primary objectives included identifying all forms of heresy in order to suppress them.

Fifth, *who, other than the suspect, held heretical views or had committed heretical acts.* Naturally, the Holy Office considered it vital to determine how far the defendant's heresy had spread, and to prosecute as many heretics as possible lest the heresy spread further—and the coffers of the Inquisition become empty. In Portugal, as in Spain, the Holy Office funded itself principally by confiscating the assets of convicted defendants as well as through various investments and corruption.[7]

Spanish inquisitors of the Early Modern Period were concerned with many of the same questions that preoccupied their Portuguese colleagues. However, the investigative agenda of the Spanish officers included a host of additional questions that delved deeply into the suspects' public and inner lives. Among other things, these questions (which I will identify below) placed a greater emphasis on determining whether the suspects had *practiced* heresy than on ascertaining whether they had merely *professed* it. One may say that the ethnographic curiosity (so to speak) that undergirded these supplementary questions was much deeper than that which guided the Portuguese protocol.

An important characteristic of the Spanish dossiers is their relatively high level of annalistic precision. My impression is that recorded testimony in the Spanish cases consistently reveals a greater fidelity to the flow and style of normal speech than do most analogous Portuguese depositions. Although the Spanish records retain stock language, much of the testimony preserved in them has a natural ring to it, particularly in terms of tone and diction. This unaffected quality suggests a true willingness on the part of the Spanish Santo Oficio to document at least part of what declarants actually said rather than what the tribunal considered the declarants *ought* to say. Notably, the realistic nature of much of the language in the Spanish records makes it difficult to conclude that the Spanish Inquisition of the 1600s was a mere "factory for making Jews," as the historian António José Saraiva famously concluded in his assessment of the Portuguese tribunals.[8]

The following deposition from Madrid (ca. 1625) illustrates the comparative realism of many of the Spanish records (as distinct from the actual veracity of the informants):

And to this [the declarant's mother] *said* [to him] *that, well, what was being a Christian anyway? It only amounted to worshipping a figure made of paper, which, if someone
put it to the fire turned to ashes;* and this [declarant] made an effort to remember
whether his mother burned [such an] image or if she only said those words, and he
does not remember; [but later] he [said he] understands that she must have burnt [a
picture of a crucifix] because he did not see it hanging [on the wall] anymore. . . .
*And he also says that he heard his mother say that our Lady did not give birth remain-
ing a virgin, but that one morning the glorious patriarch [sic] Saint Joseph left home,
leaving the door open, and that a man had entered pretending to be the same Saint
Joseph, and he had had relations with our [Lady], and from that union Jesus Christ was
born;* this he heard his mother say. (Emphasis added.)[9]

Spanish inquisitors typically cross-examined suspected Judaizers in one
comprehensive hearing. The tribunals that conducted the cross-examination
usually consisted of two inquisitors (the principal interrogators), a prosecutor (the *fiscal*), and a legal advisor. Typically these officers were canon lawyers
in holy orders. They were assisted by a constable and other lay staff, including at least one notary.

The primary interrogation session itself, called the first *audiencia*, afforded voluntary declarants the opportunity to explain why they had presented themselves before the Holy Tribunal. It also gave defendants who had
been detained occasion to reveal the crimes they had committed and the reasons they had committed them. From its very outset the *audiencia* was an in-
vitation to confess and to repent, since it did not begin with any accusation
on the interrogators' part, but with their simple request that the declarant
disclose his or her sins.

Absent a spontaneous confession, the interrogation began with questions regarding the suspect's genealogy and his or her family's past encounters
with the Inquisition (if any). Genealogical data and evidence of wrongdoing
by the defendant's forbears and next of kin helped the inquisitors to reconstruct a historical context by which to evaluate the possibility that the suspect
was a religious criminal. Depending on the declarant's responses, such information could highlight a presumptive causal nexus between the declarant's
racial heritage and his or her relatives' reputation on one hand, and the defendant's own heretical proclivities on the other. It is important to caution,
however, that Spanish inquisitors did not treat a person's lineage or close familial relationship to convicted heretics as legal proof of that person's heterodoxy. For example, the defendant Aldonza Cardoso de Velasco, who said she
had lived in Bayonne "until her husband brought her to Madrid," testified
during her first hearing (in 1668) that she was an Old Christian.[10] Her interrogators seem not to have considered this datum very significant. They never

asked her specifically to admit that she was a conversa, even though they strongly suspected that she was a Judaizer and eventually elicited her confession to that effect. In the larger context of her trial, Cardoso's stated ethnic status proved to be relatively unimportant. What mattered most to her judges was bringing about her admission that she was a heretic.

After obtaining information about the lineage and religious background of the defendants, Spanish interrogators asked each declarant if he or she had been baptized and confirmed, and if so, where the baptism and confirmation had taken place. The answers served to clarify the nature of the Holy Tribunal's jurisdiction over the declarant. If, for example, the respondent had never been baptized, then he or she was technically not a Christian and could not be tried as a heretic.[11]

The interrogation continued with a series of questions that appear relatively infrequently in the records of the Portuguese *procesos*. First the inquisitors enjoined the suspect to declare if he or she attended mass and performed confession regularly in accordance with the dictates of the Catholic Church. The inquisitors then prompted the declarant to (1) make and bless the sign of the cross over himself or herself; (2) recite certain basic Christian prayers (usually the Paternoster, the Credo, and the Ave Maria); and (3) recite the Commandments of God (the Decalogue) and the articles of the Christian faith. Lastly, they commanded the declarant to state whether he or she was literate. If the answer was in the affirmative, the questioners inquired how the declarant had learned to read and write. They also asked whether he (not she) had studied a *facultad* (an intellectual discipline such as law, religion, or science), and whether he or she owned or had ever read prohibited books. This section of the interrogation served to produce a cultural portrait of the declarant, and fulfilled the inquisitors' pastoral duty to monitor the religious knowledge of Christians who came under their scrutiny.

The interrogators usually followed their queries about religious education and access to forbidden literature by directing the declarant to state whether he or she had ever traveled outside of Spanish realms. If the declarant had left the Spanish mainland, logically the questions ensued: Where had he or she gone, when, and how many times? Travel to foreign lands, which was usually forbidden without official approval, raised the possibility that the declarant had had contact with Jews, heretics, or with other enemies of Spain, such as foreign recruiters of spies. Traveling to France, Italy, England, or the Netherlands was particularly compromising for suspected crypto-Jews because these countries had become notorious as havens for Iberian "Judaizers" in addition to being strongholds of Protestantism. Any indication that a suspect had made a voyage to such places usually occasioned questions regarding the nature of the trips, the people with whom the declarant had communicated while in foreign territory, and the like.

The next major portion of the interrogation broadened the inquisition's focus on the personal history and religious identity of the suspect. As a first step, the interrogators prompted every defendant to provide a *discurso de su vida*—a narrative account of his or her life. In this "discourse" the declarant could address virtually any aspect of his or her personal experiences, even some that digressed from the matter of his or her religious convictions and activities. While the records often preserve such digressions, the interrogators usually did not demonstrate a sustained interest in pursuing these extraneous matters unless the testimony in question promised to shed light on one or more of the following aspects: First, the religious conduct of the declarant; second, the religious conduct of his or her fellow suspects; third, the existence of property that the Inquisition could confiscate. Thus, for example, one rarely finds any sign in the transcripts of *audiencias* suggesting that the investigators tried to elicit details concerning the declarants' daily economic activities (save perhaps for a few queries regarding the value and location of assets potentially subject to garnishment). Although they prosecuted several returnees who handled contraband, Spanish inquisitors seldom probed into matters related to its transportation, to its sale, or to the widespread problem of tariff evasion. Such affairs, after all, were the province of secular courts.[12]

If a detainee had not confessed to hereticizing by the end of the *discurso*, the inquisitors challenged that person to declare if he or she "knew or presumed" the reason that *familiares* had brought him or her to testify before the Holy Tribunal. The interrogation continued with a formal reprimand if the defendant still failed to disclose any wrongdoing. Specifically, the judges admonished the suspect to "review his [or her] memory" and confess to having hereticized. To this end, they reminded the declarant that "in this Holy Office it is not customary to apprehend any person without first possessing sufficient information that he/she has said, done and committed or has seen other persons do, say, or commit something that is or seems to be contrary to our holy Catholic Faith."[13]

This standard admonition encapsulates the inquisitorial presumption that all detainees who were suspected of heresy were guilty, and that it was incumbent upon them to present evidence to the contrary. As several historians have noted, it was extremely difficult for any defendant to mount an effective defense in the face of such a presumption. According to standard inquisitorial procedures, the names of all denouncers remained secret to everyone except the inquisitors throughout the proceedings. The same rule of secrecy applied to the denunciations themselves, at least until the *fiscal* found it appropriate to issue formal charges against the suspect. Because such charges were always issued *after* the defendant's interrogation, he or she could only guess the substance of the incriminating testimony during the cross-examination itself. In addition, the suspect had no recourse other than guessing the identity of his or her accusers in order to try to discredit them.[14]

If the declarant revealed no crimes after three admonitions (one for each *audiencia*), he or she was liable to suffer judicial torture unless a physician appointed by the tribunal certified that the suspect was too frail to withstand physical coercion.[15] The inquisitors' operational assumption was that any confession obtained through such coercion was genuine and thus legally valid if the prisoner ratified the confession at a later *audiencia*.[16]

How truthful and thorough the inquisitors considered a declarant's confession to be depended on a number of factors. Perhaps the main factor was the degree to which the confession concurred with the testimony by which witnesses in the case had incriminated the declarant during the investigative stages of the *proceso*. It was possible, for example, for a person suspected of crypto-Judaism to confess to several crimes under torture but remain a *negativo*, that is to say "denying" or "uncooperative" in the eyes of the tribunal if he or she did not substantiate every crime that informers had attributed to him or her.

Another supposed sign of true repentance was the number of persons whom the defendant denounced. As mentioned earlier, the greater that number, the greater the likelihood that the declarant's sentence would be light. Fernando Gil de Espinosa alone divulged the names of more than 215 "Judaizers" he claimed to have met in Amsterdam, Bayonne, Bordeaux, and various cities in Spain. For his cooperation, he received an extremely minor penalty of two months in prison and banishment from Madrid and Toledo. Unlike many other persons convicted of Judaizing, he was not required to wear a penitential garment after publicly renouncing heresy. Moreover, he did not have to endure physical punishment of any kind.[17]

The manner in which the suspect expressed remorse constituted a third, though ancillary type of "proof" of his or her veracity. Inquisitors considered certain behaviors to be worthy "signs of contrition."[18] These behaviors included crying, spontaneous prostration, voicing a readiness to receive "Christian" punishment, and begging the Inquisition for merciful justice.[19] On occasion a defendant obtained special clemency by exhibiting these "signs." In and of itself, however, manifest remorse could never override an "incomplete" confession.

If the suspect confessed to having hereticized during any portion of his or her deposition, that disclosure occasioned a host of standard as well as extraordinary questions. The latter questions spoke to the particularities of each declarant's testimony, and thus varied considerably from case to case. The standard questions included the following.[20]

First: Did the defendant know and understand that the Law of Moses was contrary to the Law of Jesus Christ and the teachings of the Catholic Church at the time that he or she had hereticized?

Second: What had moved (*qué le movió*) the declarant to abandon Christianity and adopt the Law of Moses?

Third: What law (that of Christ or that of Moses) did the suspect now consider and hold as "the true one" for the purpose of saving his or her soul, and in what law (*en cual ley*) did the declarant hope to live the rest of his or her life?

If the suspect answered the third question by avowing a renewed commitment to the Law of Jesus Christ, the fourth question followed: What was it that had moved the declarant to abandon the Law of Moses and embrace Christianity once again?

Fifth: Had the defendant ever heard mass, and did he or she believe that the consecrated Host was the actual body of Christ?

Sixth: During the time that the declarant had believed in and observed the Law of Moses, had he or she performed sacramental confession, received the Host at the altar, and if so, "with what intention" had he or she undertaken these actions? If the suspect had confessed sacramentally, had he or she ever admitted to having hereticized?

The immediate aim of these six clusters of questions was to illuminate the confessant's spiritual journey from Catholicism to crypto-Judaism and (depending on the case) back to the threshold of "Our Most Holy Faith." Underlying all of the queries was a keen interest in penetrating the conscience of the suspect so as to compel that person to acknowledge and take responsibility for his or her *specific* religious errors. More importantly for purposes of determining punishment, the questions were designed to ascertain the degree of cognizance with which the confessant had violated the Catholic faith, and to yield responses that would allow the tribunal to measure the authenticity of the declarant's return to that faith.

To be sure, the standard queries were motivated by interests that extended beyond the purely ideological. Recent scholarship has broadened and enriched our understanding of inquisitorial activities by explaining their political and social logic.[21] Still, it is hardly questionable that religious concerns shaped, animated, and were at the heart of the inquisitorial protocol—and of the inquisitorial mission as a whole. After all, the Holy Office was a Catholic tribunal that belonged to a premodern world in which religion still suffused the totality of human experience. Catholicism provided many of the conceptual tools and materials with which the Spanish Inquisition fashioned and described its guiding notions of truth and falsehood, justice and injustice, crime and punishment, recalcitrance and rehabilitation. Regardless of the motivations and levels of piety of individual judges and prosecutors, inquisitorial *procesos* were products of an institutional culture that was overwhelmingly religious. Thus it is not surprising that the trials echoed the practice of auricular confession in their essential design and purpose. In the Santo Oficio, as in the realm of sacramental confession, religious experts administered divine justice by prompting errant Christians to disclose their sins. The experts then prescribed suitable penance, and absolved the penitent. In essence, then, inquisitorial *procesos* were meant to expose a spiritual illness that supposedly lay buried within the souls of religious criminals.[22] As in auricular confession, the interrogation of prisoners served to initiate a process of ideological correction, a type of exorcism of the illness, by which the confessants would be cured of their error. Officially at least, the tribunal's ultimate goal was to realize the heretics' "reconciliation" with the church, that is to say, their ideological conformity, and in so doing to promote "purity of faith" throughout the territories under inquisitorial jurisdiction. From the point of view of the judges and prosecutors, the physical elimination of heretics was never an absolute necessity. Burning heretics at the stake was the tribunal's way of punishing unrepentant recidivists, not all religious criminals, and then only as a last resort. Furthermore, inquisitors did not perform any of the physical punishments, let alone the killing; they merely delivered condemned prisoners to the "secular arm" of the law for execution.

According to the sacramental model that served as a basis of inquisitorial proceedings, the soul of an ideological criminal was malleable and could be refashioned by the tribunal's rigorous yet compassionate hand, for that hand was the terrestrial agent of God's *misericordia.* In order to receive God's love, the sinner's soul had to undergo a deep and genuine transmutation: It had to learn to love God.

In the tribunal's eyes, the spiritual transformation of a Judaizer could be accomplished gently. This occurred whenever the suspect confessed in a prompt, thorough, and remorseful manner. However, if the suspect failed to confess after three admonitions, or if any doubts lingered in the interrogators' minds as to the sincerity or depth of the declarant's confession, the Holy Office had a duty to compel that person's complete "enlightenment" and heartfelt "conversion" to the Catholic faith. As one inquisitor put it, "God's divine love . . . is not satisfied with [mere] reverence toward the dear faith, *but obliges everyone to love the faith by grace or by force*" (emphasis added).[23] Hence the option of judicial torture.

It goes without saying that forced "enlightenment" does not correspond to any modern liberal notion of a criminal's genuine change of heart. The men who staffed the Holy Tribunals, however, admitted no contradiction between their own coercive practices and the free will of confessants. For these officers it was crucial to uphold the idea that yielding to the Christian truth could only be a liberating experience for any sinner, whether or not the sinner had embraced the faith as a result of the inquisitors' application of overt pressure. In order to be consistent with Catholic dogma, the tribunal's functionaries also had to maintain the position that genuine repentance and penitence were the sole antidotes to moral and doctrinal error. Absent these two premises, the inquisitorial endeavor would have lost all credibility and ideological coherence. If the inquisitors had acknowledged that any of their victims had embraced Catholicism insincerely and under duress, the Santo Oficio would not have been able to justify as divine and merciful its authority to determine guilt and dictate punishment. Likewise, had the Holy Office not claimed that it possessed the ability to effect a *genuine* change in wayward souls, how could the same institution possibly convince Christians that God's power was not only just, but wondrously efficacious?

Inquisitorial Ideology and Conversos

Where Judeoconversos were involved, the Spanish Inquisition's understanding of justice contained a distinct element of racial consciousness. As we have seen, the tribunal was not only interested in assessing and correcting the religious behavior and beliefs of suspected Judaizers; it also sought to ascertain the ethnic origin of the suspects. Although an informant's racial stock did not determine his or her guilt, the fact of having New Christian blood could, and in most cases probably did, reinforce an existing presumption of that person's unorthodoxy.

The Inquisition's simultaneous preoccupation with matters of faith and the question of lineage is evidence that the tribunal's predominant approach to suspected Judaizers during the Early Modern Period was actually rooted in two closely intertwined yet logically incompatible interpretations of evil. The first interpretation was largely explicit in the standard *interrogatorio* (protocol) and in much inquisitorial propaganda, for example, in inquisitorial sermons.[24] This view painted evil as ideological deviance, and posited that impurity of faith was curable through confession and repentance under the auspices of inquisitorial judgment, an instrument and earthly guarantor of God's grace. The second interpretation was largely implicit in the *interrogatorio*, specifically in questions related to the "stock and origin" (*casta y generación*) of the suspects. This interpretation held that "Jewish" immorality was a natural attribute carried in the blood. According to this view, impurity of blood was irreversible, and therefore "Judaic" error was incurable.

Lest we see the coincidence of these conflicting interpretations as an intractable conundrum, we should recall that the Spanish preoccupation with purity of blood was not "racist" in the modern sense. The concepts of *casta* (caste or stock), *generación* (origin) and *linaje* (lineage) had absolutely no connection to pseudoscientific notions of race. Such notions did not exist in the Early Modern Period, although the idea that blood transmitted immutable moral traits from generation to generation had made its appearance in Iberia well before that time.[25] Conversophobic prejudice was, at base, an antipathy toward an ethnic group widely reputed to practice a particular religion in secret. The chimera of "infected blood" (*sangre infecta*) allowed prejudiced Old Christians to explain and justify that antipathy to themselves and to their fellows, yet did not cancel a fundamentally religious conception of Judaizing as a *spiritual* malady borne primarily (but not solely) by Judeoconversos. In racialist prejudice, then, the idea of religious deviance was never far below the surface.[26]

The simultaneous application of the ideas of *pureza de fe* and *pureza de sangre* yielded some peculiar results in the context of inquisitorial trials of Judeoconversos. One result was the frequent incidence of the term *judío judaizante*—"Judaizing Jew." This designation appears primarily in the text of the sentences of convicted New Christians, chiefly as means of signifying the convicts' legal and religious status prior to their renunciation of heresy. On occasion declarants of converso origin used the term in the course of their testimony to describe themselves and other alleged crypto-Jews.[27]

On its face, the double designation *judío judaizante* appears to be redundant: How could a Jew not "Judaize"? Actually, the term is incongruous. In the language of early modern Castile, the word *judío* properly denoted a person who professed normative Judaism and formed part of a self-contained and legally recognized Jewish collective. Needless to say, in seventeenth-century Iberia there existed no such licit group. In turn, the word *judaizante* connoted a *Christian* who hereticized by performing Jewish (or Jewish-like) rites and holding "Judaic" beliefs.[28]

The fact that inquisitors saw or admitted no incongruity in the invented term *judío judaizante* suggests their drift toward colloquial usage in their official speech. As I discussed in the second chapter, in common parlance early modern Castilians tended to conflate the terms "Judaizer" and "Jew," (as well as "Portuguese," "businessman," and "merchant") with the synonymous misnomers "converso" and "New Christian."[29] *Judío judaizante* thus preserves in the official records of the Spanish Inquisition something of the intellectual incoherence that marked popular Judeophobic thought in sixteenth- and seventeenth-century Iberia.

This is not to say that popular and official bigotry were always identical. Especially during the acrimonious years that followed the removal of Philip IV's chief minister, Olivares, segments of Spain's intellectual and political elite, including a few high-ranking officers of the Inquisition itself, assailed the random nature of popular conversophobia. They particularly objected to the indiscriminate persecution of New Christians, arguing that there existed considerable evidence to discredit the supposed nexus between familial origin and religious deviance. Commenting on the proliferation of purity of blood statutes, one inquisitorial critic argued in 1624,

The experience of many years shows us today that families who are of this infected [Judeoconverso] race are profoundly faithful Christians, devout and pious, putting their daughters into religion, their sons into the priesthood, living with clear Christian devotion. . . . [I]t is proven that there is no longer any good reason for [the purity of blood] statutes and that with the changing times they have become not simply unjust but totally superfluous.[30]

In response to critiques of racist discrimination, the Holy Office (including the critics in its ranks) struggled to devise and present an ethically and intellectually defensible position vis-à-vis New Christians. This task was complicated by the logical incompatibility of *pureza de fe* and *pureza de sangre,* two of the pillars of inquisitorial thinking about conversos.

Among the supporters of the Inquisition, those who defended racist animus had to explain how it was possible for people to be reconciled to the Roman Church who had unalterably "Jewish" blood coursing through their veins. At the same time, these partisans had to explain the paradoxical fact that divine *misericordia* was not always successful in transforming the souls of sinners—that, in fact, the Holy Office did not secure the conversion of *all* New Christian heretics to "the Dear Faith," and saw no choice but to release recidivists to lay authorities for execution. To confront this dilemma, a lay officer of the Santo Oficio wrote in 1680:

The means that the Holy Tribunal applies to disabuse [the imprisoned heretics] of their errors are sacred, and the proofs that it offers to convince them are so many . . . that none of [the prisoners] can have any pretext other than their voluntary obstinacy for not embracing the Christian religion. *The inclination of blood [el empeño de la sangre] dominates the men of this Nation,* as does [their] arrogance in placing the blindness of their elders in front of the wisdom of the Christian doctors. . . . *Fomented by sensuality and greed,* [this inclination] *makes their eyes blind to reason;* and therefore praises must be given to the infinite clemency of God, who, in view of such ingratitude, gives such powerful succor to some of them that they are subjugated to the loving guild of our mother, the Church. (Emphasis added.)[31]

Here the apologist tried to affirm the supposed ideological integrity of the inquisitorial project by minimizing the discrepancy between "purity of blood" and "purity of faith" while upholding both sets of premises. First, he allowed that "impure" blood had a force all its own. According to him, *sangre infecta* made people "of the Nation" extraordinarily stubborn, rapacious, and indulgent. (Notice that intransigence—a sign of moral blindness—sensuality, and greed were among the faults that Church doctrine as well as popular Christian sentiment traditionally associated with the Jews.) At the same time, the apologist did not entirely abandon the possibility that God's benevolence could cure at least a few hardened "Jewish" souls. The very fact that anyone who belonged to "the Nation" could submit to Christianity by embracing it was to him a miraculous sign of divine strength. The point to emphasize is that in the writer's understanding the path of "conversion" remained open, notwithstanding the pernicious power of blood. This message was consistent with that conveyed by Spanish inquisitors in their interrogation of conversos, namely that if a New Christian suspect wished to save himself or herself from punishment, he or she must overcome nature by quelling innate heretical impulses.

In light of the tribunal's institutionalized bias against people of converso extraction, it is no exaggeration to say that the outcome of investigations against suspected Judaizers was largely preordained if the defendant was "of the Nation." Predictably, most converso returnees confessed to some heretical crime, even if their responses varied in terms of credibility, specificity, and in other respects. Yet, given the inquisitors' insistence that faith could triumph over nature, and their unwavering quest for "full" confessions, it would be simplistic to view the trials of suspected Judeoconversos purely as means of confirming the latter's putative culpability. The main question before the Spanish tribunal was not whether a defendant's guilt could be confirmed. Rather, the question was *how*, that is to say, with what degree of conviction and through what kind of confession, would the defendant vanquish nature by renouncing sin, and thus rejoin the mystical body of Christ. In the end, inquisitorial trials of Judaizers were attempts to induce "natural" sinners to allow God's grace to help them crush an "inborn" Jewishness. Accordingly, the accused faced a stark choice between "conversion" and "damnation," that is to say, between total submission to the imperatives of the Inquisition, and severe punishment.

The following section summarizes some of the ways in which returnees negotiated this stark choice. As we shall see, their behavior under cross-examination reflected the restrictions that inquisitorial exigencies placed upon them. Relatively few respondents in the cases I surveyed were so verbally deft and psychologically resilient as to be able to resist the path of self-incrimination indefinitely, at least not without the aid of allies and favorable circumstances extrinsic to the *procesos*. What is most significant for our purposes, however, is that the testimony of returnees and other renegades revealed much besides their mere realization that they must yield to inquisitorial demands. The confessions of renegades-cum-penitents were not entirely mechanical. Fortunately for the historian, that body of testimony constitutes a window into the subjects' experiences and understanding of religion itself.

An Overview of Common Responses to the Standard Spanish *Interrogatorio*

Habitual and permanent returnees usually provided straightforward answers to the portions of the Spanish *interrogatorio* that dealt with their formal catechization, their secular education, and their basic familiarity with Catholic culture. I consider these answers to be generally reliable. After all, it was impossible for respondents to convincingly feign knowledge of prayers they had not learned, and there was seldom any use for the suspects to lie about such matters as their ability to read and write, or the names of their teachers.[32]

Most of the respondents demonstrated that they had been catechized reasonably well. Nearly all of them knew at least some of the basic tenets and precepts of Tridentine Catholicism. Though several returnees were literate or semiliterate, few of them reported having read (or heard read) any books

aside from "the Bible in Castilian" and Jewish prayer books that Jewish authors had translated into Castilian for the benefit of converso neophytes residing in the Diaspora.[33] The fact that a number of respondents incriminated
themselves by alluding to these works suggests that these same informants
were not lying about their unfamiliarity with other books, or, for that matter, about their ability to read and write (or lack thereof).

While defendants who were suspected of Judaizing usually admitted
that they were of New Christian stock or even "of the Hebrew Nation,"[34] a
few claimed to be of Old Christian descent or denied knowing their *casta y
generación.* Some respondents who had immigrated to Spain from Portugal
or were descended from Portuguese immigrants described themselves simply
as "Portuguese." This response was also common among Lusitanian New
Christians who were not returnees. For instance, the defendant Ana Díaz testified in 1632 that, "she did not know of what stock and origin she and her
parents are, besides the fact that they are Portuguese, and that her parents
and . . . her aunt, had been imprisoned by the Holy Office in Valladolid [for
the crime of heresy]."[35]

The diversity of defendants' responses to questions regarding their
ethno-religious origins may attest to an actual variety in those origins. It is
entirely possible, for instance, that the above-mentioned Aldonza Cardoso
was an Old Christian, as she claimed.[36] However, we cannot discount the al-
ternate possibility that the absence of uniformity in the suspects' responses
reveals differences in the conscious approaches that some of these suspects
adopted toward their interrogators, from near-total mendacity, to absolute
candor, to a combination of deceit and veracity. We must also consider the
possibility that the diversity of responses points to differences in the self-per-
ceptions and emotional states of the declarants during their respective interrogations. Finally, we must consider—as I will detail below—that some
respondents may have been genuinely confused about or ignorant of their
origins.

In response to inquisitorial prodding, most captured returnees testified,
perhaps cautiously, that they did not know why the Holy Tribunal had imprisoned and summoned them to depose. The rest of the defendants in the
case sample answered in a variety of ways. For instance, Aldonza Cardoso answered that she feared she had been brought before the Tribunal because she
had once lived in Bayonne. Obviously she was aware that past residence in
France was ipso facto suspicious from the point of view of the Inquisition.[37]
For his part, the returnee Manuel Méndez Cardoso (no relation to Aldonza),
speculated incisively that the tribunal had summoned him "because [some-

one had] said that he was Jewish, and because he was 'of the Nation,' and because he had dealt with those who were [of the Nation in foreign lands]."[38]

The respondents' accounts of their lives were as diverse as their responses to questions regarding their *casta y generación*. Still, these *discursos*
exhibited key similarities that describe not only a constellation of life trajec-
tories, but certain patterns of acculturation. What gives basic shape to these
patterns is a series of recurring experiences and behaviors. For the sake of
clarity and order, I have grouped these recurrent elements under four inter-
related topics: First, the respondents' familial context; second, their religious
socialization as "Judaizers"; third, their reconversion to Christianity; and finally, their frequent travels in the roads and sea-routes that formed the trading networks of Iberia.

The Familial Relations of Renegades as Reflected in the *Discursos*

By "familial context" I am referring to the subjects' personal circumstances,
including their upbringing and their relationships with family members. Although these circumstances varied according to social class, the personalities
of the people involved, and a host of other highly contingent factors, several
of the testimonies described a peculiar paradox: On the one hand, the respondents relied heavily on networks of kin for purposes of business, marriage, and child rearing. On the other hand, many of these same respondents
knew relatively little about the lives of their ancestors and living relatives, especially when the latter were dispersed throughout the Iberian Peninsula, the
Spanish and Portuguese Empires, and the Jewish Diaspora. Furthermore, in
the renegades' portrayals of their respective families, circumspection,
obliqueness, and mutual distrust often marked the relationships between
men and women, as well as between adolescents and adults.

For instance, the returnee Cristobal Méndez Silveira testified that he was
not certain whether his female cousins in Saint Esprit knew that he prayed
"in the Jewish manner," adding that "if they knew, they dissimulated and did
not let him know of it [*no se lo dieron a entender*]; neither does he know if
they kept the Law of Moses."[39] It is significant that Méndez had no discernible need to exculpate the women, as they were permanent residents of
France who were unlikely to return to Spain, and were therefore safe from direct inquisitorial harassment.

Even when they incriminated each other, some declarants maintained
that they had never acknowledged explicitly their common allegiance to the

Law of Moses. Ana Díaz, the sister of a would-be *malsín*, testified that she had witnessed his observance of the same "Judaic" fasts that she performed. Yet, she continued, the fasting had occurred "without her communicating with him, and he with her" about their secret activities.[40] Díaz also observed that since her brother was a man, it was his custom to leave the house, hence she was unaware of what he did during much of his time. As for her father, the businessman Antonio Montesinos,

> she did not see him [keep any of the heretical fasts], except that one Friday in the evening [as if to celebrate the Sabbath] he wore a clean shirt that she gave to him [upon his request]. . . . She also said that her father was seldom present at home. He left in the morning, and did not return until it was time to eat. In various seasons he was out of Madrid, and thus she surmises that he did not know what she and her siblings, mother, and aunt did; neither did he become involved in matters of the home.[41]

Perhaps Díaz testified as she did in order to appear cooperative while allowing her brother and her father to deny plausibly that they had acted with any intention of observing the Law of Moses. Then again, Díaz's alleged unfamiliarity with the activities of the two men rings true in light of her historical and cultural context. In early modern Iberia "respectable" women such as the declarant spent a considerable portion of their time secluded at home, while men enjoyed far greater freedom of movement—and thus led largely separate lives.[42]

Not surprisingly, the theme of separateness was prominent in the testimony that several of the renegades provided regarding their spouses. A number of respondents claimed to have inhabited psychological spheres vastly different than those of their marriage partners. In particular, these declarants alleged that they had seldom shared key aspects of their religious lives with their wives. The testimony of Fernando Alvarez regarding his wife, Catalina, is a credible example of this type of allegation (see my discussion of the couple in the previous chapter). Another example is the deposition of Manuel Pasaña, whom several witnesses went out of their way to describe as "the only Catholic in Saint Esprit" even while incriminating other returnees.[43]

Reminiscent of many an impoverished returnee, Pasaña reported to the Toledan Inquisition that he had moved from Portugal to France "because of the many needs that he suffered" (*por las muchas . . . necesidades que padecía*).[44] His testimony includes the following allegations: In 1649 Pasaña settled in Bayonne, "where he did not have any money for one year."[45] The following year he returned to the Iberian Peninsula. First he settled in Madrid, then in Pamplona, where "he was occupied in handling tobacco to support himself."⁴⁶ Later he moved to Bayonne yet again. There "he dealt in tobacco and would bring it [across the international border] to Pamplona in order to sell it."⁴⁷ On or about 1655 he married the future Josepha María de Pasaña "in accordance with the Catholic rite" at a Bayonnaise parish. It was not until two years had passed, however, that

> he noticed that . . . his wife was not a Catholic Christian because she did not go to mass frequently and . . . she kept Saturdays as holidays by not working. And having entered carefully [into an investigation of the matter] he tried by good means to do away with his suspicion, and he asked her if she kept the Catholic Law. [She] responded that she did not keep it, and that she was a Jew, and that her mother . . . had taught her the law of the Jews and had persuaded her to keep it at the time that she had entered Bayonne for the first time, and that [because of] those *persuasiones* she had left the Law of our Lord . . . eleven years ago, when her mother had taken her to France. . . . The declarant tried to separate [Josepha María] from the law of the Jews and to subdue her [*reducirle*] to the Catholic Faith. This task took him six months [to accomplish]. . . . Thereafter he subdued her so that she would be a good Catholic Christian . . . and two months hence she has been keeping the Catholic Law, and she asked this [declarant] to take her from among Jews and bring her to Spain to live in a Christian and Catholic manner, as she now does. . . . Seeing his wife's determination, he came back [to Spain even though he was] in poor health.⁴⁸

Here Pasaña did not demonize his spouse, yet incriminated her nonetheless. This virtually assured that the Inquisition would punish her. Of course, the declarant could have easily denounced someone else and painted Josepha as a completely innocent victim of Jewish coercion (as distinct from motherly persuasion). The fact that Pasaña did not opt for total exculpation raises the possibility that he was trying to save his own skin by offering Josepha as a sacrifice to the Inquisition. Then again, the alleged disjunction between Pasaña's religious life and that of his wife was far from improbable. As I mentioned earlier, the separation of men and women in social space was a marked tendency in early modern Iberian culture.⁴⁹ This sexual cleavage became sharper when husbands traveled extensively to earn a living while their wives were left at home to their own devices.

Not surprisingly, the same dossier that preserves Manuel Pasaña's testimony also contains the deposition of an indigent soldier, Gonzalo Correa, who claimed to have discovered after several years of transience that his wife had emigrated to France, where she had become part of the putatively "Judaic" cohort of greater Bayonne. Correa deposed in 1659 that he had been imprisoned in Valladolid for three years because "he had not made a life with his wife," and had cohabited with another woman. He explained that after serving his sentence he did not return to live with his spouse, but like many a nomadic converso, had resided in various parts of the Iberian Peninsula, including Barcelona, Málaga, and Madrid. Eventually the crown mobilized Correa's military unit to Fuenterrabía, immediately opposite St. Jean de Luz on the French-Spanish border. There the soldier allegedly received notice that Barbol Pérez, his wife of seventeen years, had moved from Madrid to Bayonne. In May of 1658 he traveled to Saint Esprit in a futile attempt to locate her. Shortly thereafter, Correa claimed, he had spotted her behind a window at the home of one Marcos Ravelo, next to the bridge that linked Bayonne to the *faubourg* of Saint Esprit across the Adour River. The soldier testified that he had immediately entered the house in question, only to find that Pérez had hidden from him.[50]

It is unfortunate that what remains of Correa's testimony does not reveal whether he and Pérez were conversos, or whether he ever accused her explicitly of having become a Judaizer in France. Yet it seems likely that Correa, who was not an inquisitorial prisoner and told his story to the tribunal voluntarily, was trying to hint at Pérez's guilt by associating her with an infamous group of exiles. Beneath Correa's testimony the question seemed to lurk: Why would a Christian settle in Bayonne, in a community of notorious Judaizers, unless she too were a heretic? The point to underline here is that regardless of Correa's motivations, of his wife's actual or imagined infidelity to Christianity, or of the couple's ethnoreligious origins, the spatial and psychological distance that separated the spouses found expression in his stated suspicions that she was a *religious* deviant.

Marital relations aside, some informants claimed to be completely unaware of the activities and beliefs of various members of their families. Francisco de Aguilar, a returnee and "merchant of all genres," failed even to identify his grandparents, maternal uncles, aunts, and one his paternal uncles when his interrogators prompted him to reconstruct his genealogy. However, Aguilar admitted that he was a converso. He also named another of his paternal uncles who resided "in the Indies" (meaning Spanish or Portuguese overseas colonies), well within the reach of the Iberian Inquisitions. The fact that the suspect exposed his kinsman to inquisitorial scrutiny points to the possibility that Aguilar was not feigning ignorance of the identities of his other relatives. In other words, the merchant may not have been trying to protect these individuals.[51] A further (though less compelling) indication of Aguilar's conceivable sincerity is that during his *discurso* he incriminated a few additional relatives, albeit ones who lived in France. The latter were persons with whom Aguilar claimed to have had more significant contact than with the relatives whose names he had omitted. For example, the suspect alleged that his stepfather, a resident of Tolouse, had threatened to withhold an inheritance if he (Aguilar) did not observe the Law of Moses.[52]

Antonio del Monte was the baptized son of Iberian exiles and a native of France. He settled in Madrid in 1669 and was arrested on suspicion of crypto-Judaism shortly after his arrival. Unlike Aguilar, this defendant identified at least a dozen of his relatives, including his cousins, uncles, and nephews. However, during his first *audiencia* del Monte seemed confused as to the "stock and origin" of his family: "[The defendant] was asked of what *casta y generación* his parents, grandparents, and siblings were. Perhaps it was by mistake that he responded that they were Old Christians. . . . As for his cousins, uncles and aunts, and nephews, he does not know of what *casta* they are, but he presumes they [keep the Law of Moses] since they live in a land where that law is observed."[53] Later, in the course of his *discurso*, del Monte corrected himself, stating that he thought his grandparents had indeed been conversos. As if to apologize he added the observation that "in France it is not easy [to determine a person's status]; neither is it known who is an Old Christian."[54]

Why would del Monte have admitted he was a Judaizer yet hesitated to identify his family as New Christian, when he had already incriminated several of his relatives as fellow Judaizers? One possible answer is that the defendant did not know what ethnic and religious category best described his relatives. Another possibility is that he was either vaguely or not at all aware of his own extraction. A third possible scenario is that while he understood the meaning of the word "Judaizer," he did not perceive clearly what the inquisitors meant by the designation *cristiano nuevo*. Of course, it is also possible that del Monte was actually an Old Christian who testified to that effect, but later changed his testimony in order to comply with what he perceived to be his interrogators' expectations.

Unfortunately, there is no empirical evidence that would point to any of these possibilities as a conclusive solution to the puzzle of del Monte's testimony. All the same, four items of circumstantial evidence suggest that the first three explanations are reasonably applicable to instances in which renegades provided obscure responses to questions concerning their ethnoreligious background.

First, as I have mentioned elsewhere, assimilationist conversos could and often did hide their ancestry by purchasing forged "proofs" of blood-cleanliness (*pruebas de limpieza*). In addition, falsifiers could withhold potentially compromising genealogical information from their own children and grandchildren. Some declarants may have been ignorant or uncertain of their provenance precisely because their ancestors had obscured it if not disguised it altogether.

Second, many "conversos" did not descend from Jews alone. In some cases (for example, the spontaneous delator João de Aguila), "converso" lineages were the product of the repeated intermingling of Old and New Christian bloodlines. In such cases, the subjects' precise ethnic origin may have been so complex as to be utterly opaque and therefore indescribable in the clear-cut terms that Spanish cross-examiners expected (namely, "New Christian," "Old Christian," "Jewish," and "Moorish").[55]

Third, in the sixteenth and seventeenth centuries conversos were among Europe's most mobile and thus geographically dispersed minorities. If confessants claimed to possess only the vaguest knowledge of their provenance and of the lives of their relatives, it is not arbitrary to suppose that in several cases such ignorance was due to the physical distance that separated various branches of the confessants' families. Given that distance, it is likely that some of the informants had never met their *consanguineos* and had only heard scant information about them, if any at all.

Fourth, despite the currency in Iberian society of the notion of *pureza de sangre*, Spaniards of the period of the Portuguese migrations did not always acknowledge or perhaps even understand the denotational difference between terms such as "New Christian" and "Portuguese."[56] In a social and cultural environment where speakers of Castilian habitually tended to use these and a few other signifiers of human difference as synonyms (for example, "merchant," "businessman," and "Jew"), we should not expect that conversos were themselves immune to conflation where linguistic categories of "race," religion and ethnicity were concerned. To take this point a step further, it is unwarranted to suppose that in the seventeenth century, long after the word "converso" had ceased to denote actual converts from Judaism in colloquial speech, all inquisitorial suspects of New Christian stock possessed a clear and unambiguous (let alone accurate) mental image of Jews and Judaism. This supposition holds whether or not the suspects consciously allied themselves with the Law of Moses, whatever that law meant to them. In the end, it is probable, to say the least, that some suspects did not perceive the difference between their ethnicity, their religious heritage, and their place of origin because they had not inherited or developed a clear and conceptually precise consciousness of their social identity. Such respondents would arguably have been more likely than others to describe their *casta y generación* in terms the Holy Tribunal found wanting. The likes of Antonio del Monte come to mind immediately, as do defendants who referred to themselves enigmatically as "Portuguese."

The aim here is not to speculate for the sake of speculating. It is merely to suggest that true ignorance or confusion, rather than a desire to mislead the Inquisition, could well have been behind some of the renegades' incomplete, vague, or equivocal characterizations of their respective backgrounds and families. What I wish to underline is that just as there were a number of conversos who were adept at genealogical obfuscation, there were a number of genuinely assimilated or semi-assimilated conversos to whom identifying and defining their lineage may not have seemed especially problematic until they were interrogated by the Inquisition (or denied entry into a given profession, or barred personally from a given office or title). To such individuals, characterizing their ancestry seems to have been a perplexing task. As one conversa told the Coimbran Inquisition in 1583, "she did not know whether her father and mother were New or Old Christians *and she did not comprehend this* [question], nor would it have ever crossed her mind to ask her mother whether she was a New Christian or an Old Christian, and in this she persisted in spite of being much admonished [by the interrogators]" (emphasis added).[57]

The Religious Socialization of Renegades

As we have seen in the previous chapter, a number of returnees testified that they had rejected entire communities of Judaizers after enduring troubled socioreligious initiations. *Malsines* and would-be *malsines* embodied the most extreme form of disavowal, namely betrayal. In particular, the testimony of young ultra-informers speaks of a deep psychological and social estrangement between adolescent conversos and their elders. In most cases it is difficult (if not impossible) to authenticate the charges of heresy that these accusers leveled against their kin. Quite apart from this it is clear that young *malsines* approached religion as a vehicle of rebellion against familial authority. For these delators, alleging that their parents and relatives had tried to incorporate them into crypto-Judaic life was a way of avenging grievances and claiming a measure of personal independence. It was also a way for the informers to rid themselves of the stigma of "dirty" lineage (at least temporarily) by aligning themselves with a Christian community of faith whose representative, the Holy Office, promised to give value to their voices.

Duarte Montesinos, a fifteen-year-old defendant, was one New Christian who alienated and allegedly threatened to betray his family to the Holy Office. In 1632 the Toledan Inquisition arrested him as part of its investigation of an altercation in which the boy had been severely bloodied. During his first *audiencia*, Montesinos explained that one of his father's employees had beaten him with a stick at the father's command as punishment for following a sacramental procession and helping to solicit donations for the cult of the Eucharist. Several eyewitnesses, including the declarant's sisters, corroborated Montesinos's version of events. However, the witnesses added that Montesinos had vociferously threatened to exact retribution for his assault. Specifically, they said that the boy had vowed to reveal the family's heresy (including his own) to the Inquisition. At first Montesinos denied that he had made any such threats. Later, under further cross-examination, he related that his mother and his aunt had initiated him in the family's crypto-Judaism a few months prior to his detention. Montesinos then acknowledged that he had indeed threatened to denounce his family, but cautioned that he had issued the threats in anger, not because he had actually wished to have anyone prosecuted.[58]

Another young declarant, Enrique de Paz, reacted to his own (alleged) "Judaic" socialization by accusing virtually his entire family. This twenty-year-old converso appeared spontaneously before the Toledan tribunal in 1622. At the time he was a resident of Madrid and worked as a servant to his elder cousin.

After revealing that he had emigrated from Portugal to avoid inquisitorial persecution, Paz testified that three years earlier his parents had introduced him to certain "Jewish" practices. Ever since, the youth alleged, his parents and his cousin, Domingo Gómez Núñez (seconded by Gómez's wife, friends, and converso associates), had repeatedly admonished him to follow the Law of Moses.

Paz did not make clear how closely he had adhered to his family's secret "Judaism" during the three years following his conversion. Yet, like Duarte Montesinos, Paz claimed to have violated at least one major Jewish fast. On the day in question, Paz "went down to a basement, and there filled his stomach with peaches and apples *so as not to do what his father told him to do*" (emphasis added).[59] The youth also claimed that he had criticized a peer for daring to suggest that the Law of Grace (Christianity) was inferior to the Law of Moses.[60]

According to Paz, his final rupture with the family came in the wake of a dispute between himself and Domingo Gómez Núñez:

Today . . . this declarant had a great quarrel with his master and cousin . . . concerning [the declarant's] having made some soap without permission. Another boy-servant retained by . . . Domingo Gómez [Núñez], also Portuguese . . . called Luis de Acosta, told [Paz], how could he have dared to make the soap without his master's permission? And this declarant responded that [the soap] was not for himself, but for a friend, whereupon [Paz] took his cape and left [sic], and Luis de Acosta told him [derisively]: "Why don't you go to your washtub?" *And this declarant responded that he didn't want to be a Jew like his own father.* To this Luis de Acosta responded, "You too are a Jew!" And this declarant told him that his father, yes, *but him—no, because he [Paz] was a Christian, and he believed in the mystery of the Most Holy Trinity. And with this* [the declarant] *went to look for his confessor* [in order to denounce his family]. (Emphasis added.)[61]

A skeptic might reasonably conjecture that Paz invented his family's "Judaism" and inserted it into his account of the quarrels with Gómez and Acosta in order to justify his recourse to the Inquisition (and embellish his account in the process). However, Paz did not have to raise the specter of heresy in connection to these disputes at all, for he had already accused his parents and relatives of being Judaizers throughout his testimony. The tenor and content of the above-quoted portions are altogether strange: Acosta mocks Paz, but Paz replies with disproportionate self-righteousness by damning the supposed religion of his own father. What gives the young delator's odd reaction to Acosta's remarks the ring of authenticity is precisely the fact that the reaction was redundant: Paz's repudiation of Judaizing simply did not follow logically from his supposed anger at his uncle's reprimand or at Acosta's sarcasm. The declarant's non sequitur, I submit, is comprehensible as a spontaneous burst of pent-up resentment against familial power and control.

Of course, given the absence of corroborating evidence, it is impossible to *prove* that Paz did not concoct his family's "Judaism." The same caveat applies to Duarte Montesinos. Conceivably he too accused people who were innocent of heresy. But the point is that the strife that characterized these informers' alleged relationships with their respective families was probably real. As evidence of this we have the fact that Montesinos, without any apparent hesitation, confirmed that he had experienced a violent clash with his father's authority. Furthermore, Montesinos never denied that the clash had occurred outdoors, in full view of various onlookers. Their descriptions of the scuffle varied from Montesinos's own reconstruction only with respect to his alleged threats. Whether the cause of the altercation was the young man's supposed devotion to Catholicism is a separate matter.

As for Paz, it was not strictly necessary for him to mention any of his personal strife to the inquisitors in order to denounce his family. Ironically, Paz's account of his disputes with Domingo Gómez Núñez and Luis de Acosta are verisimilar precisely because they compromised his credibility as a disinterested informer. The delator's bitter descriptions of these quarrels placed his private grievances and emotions at the center of his testimony, thus weakening his denunciation as possibly motivated by prior enmity, not by actual evidence of Judaizing. Here it is worth noting that in accordance with its standard procedures, the Spanish Holy Office was required to disqualify the testimony of personal enemies of the accused.

Despite his occasional protestations that he believed in the mysteries of Christianity, Paz's testimony revealed his desire to rid himself of the adults who controlled his life, not of Judaism per se. Witness his suggestion that he had violated a "Jewish" fast, not because he objected to the Law of Moses as such, but because he wished to disobey his father.

It is instructive to consider that while the Tribunal convicted Duarte Montesinos, who did not denounce anyone spontaneously, it did not prosecute Enrique de Paz, who confessed to crypto-Judaism yet offered his testimony freely. With his former master and other family members imprisoned, Paz was left at relative leisure to do as he wished. The delator sought to leave Spain for the Indies. If he succeeded, this probably would have improved his odds of escaping any retribution his Iberian relatives may have planned.[62] The lesson of the lads' respective fates is that, when faced with Inquisitorial examiners, a New Christian resisted incrimination at his or her peril. Conversely, the path of voluntary denunciation could bring about a young informer's virtual emancipation.

Paz and Montesinos were not entirely typical of renegade conversos inasmuch as the young men were neither returnees, nor merchants, nor businessmen of any kind. Arguably Montesinos does not even deserve the appellation "*malsín*" because he did not denounce anyone spontaneously. In any case, voluntary informers only comprised a small fraction of the subjects in the *procesos* under consideration. In two crucial respects, however, the two declarants were like a majority of the renegades, including almost all the returnees in the group of cases I have surveyed. First, both informants reported that their parents and relatives had introduced them to the Law of Moses in a sudden, superficial, and vaguely coercive manner. Second, both youths testified that their conversions had occurred during their adolescence.

Paz painted his initiation as a brief lecture by his father followed by several admonitions.[63] Montesinos described his as a single and somewhat anticlimactic encounter in a secluded hallway with his aunt and his mother. In this meeting the women allegedly told him, apparently without any explanation, that the Law of Moses was "the true one" and "the one in which he could save his soul."[64] Later, Montesinos inferred by observing their behavior that "Judaizing" consisted of three sets of rather mundane activities: first, preparing a meal and new candles on Friday evenings for Saturday. Second, wearing clean clothes on Friday evenings. Third, fasting occasionally in observance of nondescript "holidays."[65] Lest we dismiss this sketchy "religion" as a mere fiction created from the raw material of inquisitorial suggestions, it is worthwhile to recall Fernando Alvarez's eminently believable testimony regarding his family's own vague "Judaism," a tacit modus vivendi that consisted primarily of fasting whenever Old Christians feasted (see my discussion of the Alvarez family in the previous chapter). What Montesinos described may well have been a variant of this residual crypto-Judaism.

Returnees' tales of crypto-Judaic socialization range from the felicitous to the distressing. Most of the accounts tend toward the latter yet stay clear of outright tragedy. Like Montesinos's deposition, a vast majority of the *discursos* of returnees convey the arbitrariness of the experience from the initiates' point of view. These accounts also speak of the relative theological poverty of the "Judaism" with which the declarants supposedly became acquainted. By contrast, all the narratives emphasize the comparative importance of the familial and other social bonds that the novices implicitly accepted (or solidified) upon entry into the Mosaic orbit.

Interestingly, few of the declarants suggested that they had actually discussed the *meaning* of the Law of Moses with their initiators, as if obedience rather than comprehension were all that their Judaizing counterparts ever required of them. The handful of declarants who testified that they had examined the merits of "Judaism" with their initiators claimed to have adopted the heretical faith as adults, in other words, at an age of relative intellectual sophistication and spiritual autonomy. Unlike those who told of adolescent initiations, adult converts sometimes depicted their first encounters with crypto-Judaism as informal lessons by fellow adults—friends, relatives, or learned men *(hombres doctos)*—who "knew" the Law of Moses. In these lessons, the educators allegedly convinced their disciples of the validity of Mosaic commandments by "bringing to memory many miracles that God had performed for His people [the Jewish nation]."[66] But even these self-described adult initiates painted a rather opaque image of "Judaism." For example, none of them identified the miracles in question.

That ideological sophistication was absent from (or irrelevant to) renegades' "Judaism" is a reasonable conclusion, yet the newly adopted religion was not completely devoid of intellectual or affective substance. In fact, the contrary was true, as I will explain in later sections of this chapter. It is simply that the *procesos* obscure much of the texture and depth of Jewish life as the declarants experienced it. After all, the tribunal's most immediate purpose was not to reconstruct the religious *consciousness* of the suspects, but to identify their accomplices and catalogue heretical practices.[67]

If the theological or mystical basis of Judaizing was largely superfluous to the inquisitors, there is still much the *procesos* illuminate with respect to the religious socialization of the renegades. For example, the testimony of Pedro Henríquez Peteño, a returnee, hints of the confusing suddenness and sense of personal violation that often accompanied young initiates' transition to "Judaism." Henríquez related that his parents had taken him to Bayonne when he was ten years of age and, shortly after their arrival in Saint Esprit, attempted to take away an image of the Virgin of Guadalupe that he had carried with him from Spain. Reluctant to part with the icon, Henríquez resisted, but to no avail. One morning he allegedly discovered that they had removed it while he had been sleeping.[68]

A few declarants told of gentler entries into the world of Mosaic observance. Even so, they usually painted their "conversions" as brief exercises in subordination rather than as processes of deep spiritual, moral, and intellectual transformation. Francisco Núñez Redondo testified that when his parents advised him to follow the Law of Moses, "He gave them credit, and said that he would do as they counseled . . . because it was his parents who had told him to do so, and because it seemed to him that they would counsel whatever was best for him."[69]

Yielding to parental authority was only a first step in many a neophyte's Judaicization. According to several testimonies, a crucial second step consisted of conforming to the behavioral standards of other Judaizers (usually elder family members, friends of the family, and neighbors). The previous chapter examines this aspect at length. I will not address it here except to reiterate that several of the respondents who claimed to have "passed to the Law of Moses" in the Sephardi Diaspora noted the definitive effect that the momentum of communal life had had upon their decision to assume a Jewish identity. As a returnee from Sephardi neighborhoods in Italy and the Netherlands testified, "The scriptural lesson that they caused him to read in the Ghetto of Venice, and the reasons given to him by the rabbis who taught him, *and seeing that so many people followed the Law of Moses*—these were the things that led him to follow that Law, and to believe in it" (emphasis added).[70]

Like the declarant who uttered the above sentence, several renegades related that their proselytizers had enforced adherence to the Law of Moses by modeling proper religious observance (however minimalistic), as well as by monitoring the behavior of novices. Such surveillance was much easier to perform in the relative freedom of the Sephardi Diaspora than in Iberia itself. Occasionally, however, neophytes complained that "Jews" had spied on them even in Spain and Portugal. For example, the returnee Francisco Cardoso Ortiz reported that a stranger had accosted him in the streets of Madrid in an attempt to dissuade him from betraying fellow returnees to the Inquisition. According to Cardoso's description of the encounter, the mysterious converso had not tried to convince him of the error of his Christianizing path by engaging him in an ideological debate. Rather, the man had tried to embarrass Cardoso by alluding to the latter's familial honor. "I am shocked," the man had allegedly told Cardoso, "that [you], the son of such good parents, is involved in what you are involved; that hatred and rancor should bring you to do evil."[71]

Shaming was but one of several options that a Judaicized family or a larger group of Judaizers could exercise in order to prevent the defection of newly initiated individuals to Christianity. As we have seen, members of the collective could also subject rebels to scorn, withhold their inheritance, compel young men to undergo circumcisions, inflict physical punishment, or, as in the case of Francisco Cardoso Ortiz, threaten to marry the potential renegades to more diligent Judaizers:

One of the endeavors that [the declarant's] mother undertook in order to subdue him [*reducirle*] once again into [being] a Jew was to tell him that she would marry him to Felipa or Violante Cardoso, daughters of one of his aunts. [The two unmarried women] live here in Madrid at the home of Diego Cardoso, their brother. Cardoso and his sisters are Judaizing Jews [*judíos judaizantes*]. The declarant knows this from a letter his mother showed him in Peyrehorade forty days ago, written by Felipa and Violante, in which they told their mother and their aunt . . . that they were only waiting to obtain the wherewithal to go to Judaism and leave behind such blindness, by which [the declarant] understood they meant the Catholic religion.[72]

By focusing on familial and communal coercion, explanations such as Cardoso's tend to portray Judaizers as oppressors, thus making the informers look relatively innocent, as in the criminal's proverbial complaint, "I was only following orders" and its corollaries: "I did it for fear of punishment," and "Everyone else was doing it (so I felt obligated to do it too)." Still, the declarants' stated views of their fellow Judaizers should not mislead us into the simplistic conclusion that all the conversion narratives were mere fabrications motivated exclusively by self-interest. While condemnatory in their general content and tenor, the accounts are nonetheless relatively sober—some are even benign—and thus essentially realistic in their portrayal of Judaizers. Most of the devices of "Jewish persuasion" that the declarants described, for instance, the threat of ostracism, disownment, and forced incorporation through marriage, were neither unlikely nor extraordinarily perverse.[73] In fact, these methods of behavioral control were mild compared to the evils Old Christians (as well as Christianized conversos) commonly attributed to "Jews," such as swindling, bribery, ritual abuse, black magic, dissimulation, sophistry, and theological falsification. Relatively few of the Judaizers depicted in the *discursos* display the unnatural stubbornness, covetousness, or sensual appetite of anti-Jewish caricatures. At worst, most habitual returnees assailed their supposed proselytizers as harsh parents, overbearing masters, and intrusive neighbors, in other words, as flawed yet ordinary people to whom the declarants nevertheless owed respect or obedience as a matter of custom or cultural convention.

In sum, most of the conversion narratives are not accounts of grotesque coercion.[74] Neither are they maudlin tales of innocents who internalized deep theological error per se. Rather, these narratives depict reasonably lifelike, almost pedestrian instances of social (re)education and adjustment. The "Judaism" to which the renegades claimed to have succumbed was anchored not on religious ideation but on the (largely implicit) existence of a community of belief, be it a family or a larger collective. "Judaism" represented a set of abstract notions only insofar as that community actualized them by practicing them and enforcing adherence to them. Above all, becoming "Jewish" required that the subjects adapt to the self-definition, the rhythms, and the social relations that made the community distinct. In the practical terms of everyday life the community alone, rather than a holy book or imaginary "church," embodied "the Law of Moses." As the returnee Rafael Méndez testified about Jewish Bayonne, "He does not know for certain what cause [the Judaizers of Saint Esprit] may have had for catechizing him and persuading him to keep the Law of Moses . . . *but he suspects it may have been the fact that over there the said Law is observed publicly among the Portuguese, and [the fact] that they all know each other and are Portuguese*" (emphasis added).[75] This is a momentous statement. It suggests Méndez's opinion that the New Jews of Saint Esprit did not treat the Law of Moses as compulsory because they were convinced of its morality, transcendence, or truth. Rather, they, a group exiles, had adopted that law to express in ideological terms the group's prior existence and recent development as a functioning community. This makeshift collectivity was not founded on religion, but rather on familial ties, ethnic bonds, and circumstance. Indeed, as Méndez put it, the exiles "all know each other and are Portuguese." Furthermore, as New Christians they were all victims of social prejudice. Only then did they *become* collectively "Jewish."

It is appropriate that declarants often employed the term *reducción* (in Portuguese, *redução*) to describe their passage to the Jewish world. Literally translatable as "reduction" or "diminishing," the term denotes two contrary meanings. Ironically, both meanings are applicable to the phenomenon of Judaicization as the renegades described it. First, *reducción* signifies *subjection* or molding to a particular pattern. This meaning emphasizes the binding of an individual conscience by external forces or agents. Second, *reducción* denotes *persuasion* through reasoned argument.[76] This meaning acknowledges the freedom of an individual to inquire and choose between particular propositions or stances. *Reducción* thus encapsulates a fundamental paradox conveyed in the *discursos*, namely, that obedience and routinization—in a word, social conditioning—were paramount in the self-definition of the renegades as *autonomous* keepers of the Law of Moses. For the renegades the adoption of a religious identity was, so to speak, a form of *self*-subjugation.

Confession and Reconversion

Permanent and habitual returnees typically confessed to Judaizing well before their interrogators found it necessary to threaten them with torture. The respondents articulated their desire to confess in a variety of ways.

Some confessants explained themselves in a formulaic manner. For instance, Cristobal Méndez Silveira, who indicated he had once returned to Spain to escort his mother and sister to Bayonne, first requested a hearing "to confess his guilt and ask God for pardon and the Holy Office for penitence with mercy."[77] This and similar phrases (for example, "he wishes to depose in order to unburden his soul") abound in the recorded confessions of suspected Judaizers. It is therefore likely that the exact wording of such statements had been predetermined, perhaps under the direction of counselors appointed by the Tribunals, so as to conform to inquisitorial notions of correctness.

There were, however, entire confessions and large parts of confessions that did not observe stylistic formulas—at least not as closely as Méndez's statements. The following citations exemplify relatively spontaneous sounding (if not entirely accurate) declarations by which conversos expressed their readiness to divulge their sins. The quoted portions are from depositions recorded in 1625 and 1662, respectively:

It has been two years since [the defendant, Diego de Lima], without having consulted with anyone but with divine inspirations, came to consider the mysteries of our Holy Faith and to read the life of Christ our redeemer and those of the saints; and he gathered with exemplary Old Christians, and in particular, at one time he was faced with the book *El símbolo de la fé* by Fray Luis de Granada, where he found great thoughts and warnings about his [own] errors, and thus he determined to follow and die in our Holy Catholic Faith, and later he confessed fully at the [Jesuit monastery in Madrid], although he withheld for the present confession the fact that he was of the Law of Moses, and [the fact] that he had followed some of its errors. . . . And this confessant frequently confessed and received the Holy Sacrament when he was with one Francisco Prieto, who was very much a servant of God, and he never dared to confess or declare himself [a Judaizer] to . . . Prieto so as not to scandalize them [*sic*], and because [the declarant] had the intention to [leave France and] come to Spain to convert his parents to our Holy Faith.[78]

While in Bayonne around the end of the year [1662], [the defendant, Jorge Fernández de Castro] had begun to doubt whether the Law of Moses, which he followed, was good, and [to ask himself] whether the law of our lord Jesus Christ was good. Given the fact that those who followed the Law of Moses were always so wretched [*andaban siempre arrastrados*] . . . and that those who possessed understanding had left it of their own accord [*de su motivo*] . . . and also considering that the speeches the *hakham* of Saint Esprit delivered neither bound nor unbound, nor convinced his understanding, as did the sermons [the declarant] later heard in Madrid, he began to realize that he had erred in following the Law of Moses, and [he returned to Spain] with the intention of converting to the law of our Redeemer . . . and to ask for penitence, confessing his guilt. Yet shame and fear prevented him from doing so *until recently, when, having been imprisoned by the Holy Office, he asked for a hearing.* (Emphasis added.)[79]

Here Diego de Lima and Jorge Fernández de Castro portrayed themselves as voluntary candidates for Christian penance who had long harbored doubts regarding the worth of Judaism. Both men claimed they had independently come to the conclusion that they wished to be good Christians. This line of self-justification was common among permanent returnees, though a few habitual returnees articulated it as well.

Notably, Fernández's disclosures approximate several confessions in which declarants linked their own "enlightenment" to the very experience of captivity and interrogation. Respondents who drew this linkage typically conveyed that they had perceived the eternal and absolute truth of Christianity at the very moment they had become wards of the Inquisition (or shortly thereafter). For example, Cristobal Méndez Silveira testified that

he has kept the Law of Moses *until he entered as a prisoner into these inquisitorial prisons; that seeing himself a prisoner, our Lord illuminated him so that he would know the Truth*; and considering that Catholics are so many and that among them there are persons so wise and understanding, it was not possible that so many were mistaken, and that the Jews, being so few, could be the ones who were correct; and thus he resolved to separate himself from [the] Law of Moses and return to the one of our Lord Jesus Christ, which Christians hold, and which he had once held, and in which he had been raised; and with that [intent] he had determined to ask for a hearing and to confess his guilt. (Emphasis added.)[80]

Méndez's testimony as to the relative worth of Christianity and Judaism is interesting in and of itself—and does not seem as formulaic as his earlier-cited statements. What I wish to highlight here, however, is the declarant's somewhat oblique message that his experience and abject status as a prisoner had catalyzed his reconversion. Testifying in 1664, the defendant Fernando Gómez Días described his experience in terms similar to Méndez's. Yet unlike his fellow prisoner, Gómez made explicit his realization that imprisonment was a just consequence of his supposed religious transgressions: "*after having been imprisoned* he has distanced himself from said Law [of Moses], and has subjugated himself [*se ha reducido*] to the belief in our holy Catholic faith, in which he protests he will live and die, *it seeming to him that his sins have brought him to the [undesirable] state he is in, and that he is suffering in this prison because of the errors that he has committed against our Holy Catholic Faith*" (emphasis added).[81] In like fashion, the returnee Fernando Gil de Espinosa testified that

since he has been imprisoned he has considered that [his incarceration] is due to God's permission . . . and that by His infinite mercy He has thus permitted it so that he might know his sin and separate himself from his errors and return to embrace the Law of our Lord . . . which he kept until the age of seven . . . when he lived in [Madrid], where he was born and was baptized at the parish of Santa Inés, and [where] he was raised and instructed in prayer and in sufficient Christian doctrine. Because of his young age, as a frail child he was perverted by the advice and persuasion of . . . his mother and of other persons, and it weighs on him that he has committed the sins he has committed . . . and *from the time that he has been in this prison he has firmly proposed to keep the law of our Lord Jesus Christ.* (Emphasis added.)[82]

Like Méndez, Gil and Gómez conveyed that they had deduced that following the Law of Moses was wrong from the fact that Judaizing had been the grounds of their arrest. Neither defendant portrayed his embrace of the Catholic faith as based on fear of further punishment or as forced in any other way. Surprisingly, none of the defendants seemed to consider the alleged timing of their embrace of Christianity at all problematic. All three stated that they had realized their error at or near the very moment of their imprisonment, as though this fact could not put in question the sincerity or the depth of their religious reversion. Notably, the inquisitors did not call attention to the matter of timing either. Although the officers' stance could at times be harshly skeptical,[83] they seem to have accepted the notion that the defendants were sincere, even though the latter had made their avowal of Christianity at the very last minute and under the implicit threat of torture and severe sentencing. In this the inquisitors merely accepted confessions that were consistent with the tribunal's official understanding that coercion could produce true "enlightenment."

As for Gil, Gómez, Méndez, and similarly minded detainees, it is certainly tempting to argue that they testified as they did in order to meet what they perceived to be their interrogators' desires, and not because the defendants had truly reconsidered their "errors." This theory assumes that the respondents knew (or thought they knew) what the inquisitors expected of them. It also assumes that the respondents' actual (as opposed to stated) interpretation of their imprisonment was necessarily different than the inquisitors' own reading. To test these premises, I will turn to the interesting case of Antonio Rodríguez de Amézquita in the following chapter.

Before undertaking that crucial task, however, I would like to complete my overview of the *discursos* by highlighting the most consistent element in the collective profile of the renegades. I am referring to the subjects' remarkable geographic mobility.

Renegades as Perpetual Transients

Traveling was an important aspect of the collective experience of Judeoconversos in the seventeenth century. As we have seen, a high proportion of New Christians were itinerant businessmen, while hundreds if not thousands of conversos experienced the trials of emigration and resettlement, especially following the Spanish annexation of Portugal. Thus it is not by coincidence that the renegades' *discursos* include numerous anecdotes of important events whose immediate backdrop were the roads and maritime routes of Spain and Portugal.

Some renegades reported that they had fallen into bankruptcy while on the road, partly as a result of the harsh conditions that prevailed there. Other renegades claimed to have experienced religious doubts for the first time, or rediscovered old doubts in the loneliness of the *caminos*. A few suspects reported experiencing profound spiritual revelations during their travels. Yet others described pivotal roadside meetings with fellow conversos who possessed knowledge of "Judaism" or were convinced Catholics. Finally, a number of declarants were captured by inquisitorial *familiares* while traveling.

As New Christians, renegades existed in the margins of Ibero-Christian society. That many of them frequently found themselves traversing peninsular roads (or the sea-routes that were Iberia's economic lifelines) is quite logical: In a cultural sense, these *caminos* were themselves marginal places. Specifically, they were places where social outcasts and those who lacked a fixed social and religious identity (such as ambivalent conversos) could maintain a low profile and thus find a measure of safety, and where those who had a relatively fixed identity (such as fully Christianized conversos and Old Christians) could lose their moorings. The travails of Don Quixote and Sancho Panza along the dusty roads of the Spanish hinterland are perhaps the most famous literary reflections on the social marginality of perpetual travelers in early modern Spain, and by extension on the marginality of the roads themselves.

Of course, Iberian highways were marginal in the literal sense that they lay mostly outside of population centers. For our exceedingly mobile subjects, most of whom were merchants, this meant that having a "home" in a given city afforded relatively little real stability. For itinerant *comerciantes* in particular, spending most days riding a mule or walking on badly kept, often desolate thoroughfares and sleeping at woefully uncomfortable *posadas* was the norm rather than the exception.

The dizzying geographical trajectory of Francisco Cardoso Ortiz illustrates the almost constant mobility that shaped the lives of most renegades who testified before the Holy Office. Cardoso was born in 1615 to a family of Judeoconverso émigrés in Saint Esprit, Bayonne. Seven years later his parents returned with him and his siblings to Iberia, where they settled in Medina del Campo, a commercial center of Old Castile. The following year Cardoso moved again, this time with an uncle to Madrid. Approximately two years later, in 1625, Cardoso made a brief return to France with an adult companion. Subsequently the boy, presumably accompanied by another adult, traveled to Livorno to visit Jewish relatives. He remained in Italy for one year. In 1626 he returned to France, and stayed there for two months. He spent the following four months in Amsterdam participating in the commercial enterprises of his local relatives. Though barely a teenager, toward the end of the year Cardoso helped to transport tobacco and other merchandise to northwestern Africa on a boat his uncle had chartered. After staying in the coastal cities of Saleh and Tetouan, Cardoso entered the Moroccan hinterland "to see the country and the *juderías* of Portuguese and Old Jews [*judíos antiguos*] that are in Barbary."[84] In 1627 he returned to Amsterdam. A year later he moved to northeastern Brazil to serve as a spy and translator for the Dutch government of Pernambuco. The colony would prove to be his first true home. A decade after his arrival Cardoso was baptized in the port of Paraíba under the tutelage of a Franciscan monk. In 1640 he embarked for Holland, where he stayed until the following year. Reportedly disgusted with the pro-Jewish, conversionist posture of Amsterdam's Portuguese community, Cardoso then embarked for La Rochelle. Upon arrival he traveled by land to Bayonne and Peyrehorade, where various members of his family allegedly assailed his conversion to Catholicism. Completely alienated, Cardoso then crossed the Iberian border into Pamplona. He eventually continued to Madrid, where he told his story to the Toledan tribunal in 1641.

In all, Cardoso Ortiz had been traveling for more than half of his life until the moment of his deposition. The young man's tortuous course was relatively typical for a traveling renegade except in that it included a term of residence in the Indies. The travels of Jorge Fernández de Castro, a "Portuguese" merchant from Peyrehorade, were much more typical of renegades' itineraries. This *tratante* seldom went far beyond the Iberian Peninsula, and evidently never stayed outside of it for more than one or two years.[85] Jerónimo Gómez, another itinerant businessman, is similarly illustrative of habitual returnees. He reportedly traveled to and from southern France thirty times in the years prior to his incarceration.[86]

Stories such as Cardoso's, Fernández's, and Gómez's are too many (and too similar) to review here. What remains is the task of ascertaining the significance, if any, of the renegades' remarkable mobility. Did frequent traveling, with all its attendant difficulties, inform the renegades' self-perception? If so, did mobility condition the renegades' social and religious behavior in any way? In the following chapter, I will propose answers to these questions based on an examination of the *proceso* of Antonio Rodríguez de Amézquita, a chronic traveler whom I introduced in the third chapter.

Rodríguez de Amézquita's case is interesting for several reasons. First and foremost, despite its particularities, the defendant's account of his life is highly typical of the *discursos* of other habitual returnees, and of the renegades' biographies generally. Second, the case affords a rich view of the circumstances that surrounded the defendant's reconversion to Catholicism, and thus offers an opportunity to reconstruct the historical logic of confession and *reducción* to Christianity. Third, although he was to a considerable extent representative of habitual returnees, Rodríguez de Amézquita grappled with his circumstances in ways that were very much his own. An examination of his choices in their highly specific context allows us to focus on the human dimension of the phenomena of return and reconversion more closely than the above overview of the *procesos* permits.

Chapter 5

The Conversion and Reconversion of Antonio Rodríguez de Amézquita

Earlier I suggested that a key to the formation of a "Jewish" identity among the renegades was the acceptance on faith of a set of socially sanctioned behaviors. The story of Antonio Rodríguez de Amézquita presents three such instances of *reducción*. First Rodríguez adopted crypto-Judaism in Andalusia. Later he accepted the incipient, normative Judaism of the "Portuguese" community of Saint Esprit. His subsequent return to orthodox Catholicism began in the month preceding his surrender to the Inquisition, and came to fruition during his trial in Madrid. The present section will trace Rodríguez de Amézquita's arduous spiritual and social trajectory from his childhood to that third conversion.

A few facts concerning the defendant's life and familial background are worth reviewing at the outset. Near the time of his first deposition (1664), Antonio Rodríguez de Amézquita was a middle-aged man about fifty years of age. Witnesses described him as a person of "good stature," with large or hunched shoulders (*cargado de espaldas*), a thick body, a white complexion, and graying black hair.[1] A fellow returnee commented that he had always thought Rodríguez was Portuguese "because he mixed many Portuguese words into the Castilian he spoke" (fol. 10r).

Actually, Rodríguez de Amézquita was a Spaniard. Born in 1614 in Valladolid, he had spent his formative years in Castile and Andalusia as a merchant's apprentice to his father. The suspect's parents, Balthasar Rodríguez and Ana López, were transplants to Spain from northern Portugal. Both died in their adopted country decades before their son faced the rigors of inquisitorial examination.

Rodríguez named the following as his siblings: The first was Manuel Rodríguez, who had died at the age of three. The second was Isabel Rodríguez, a native of Valladolid. She had died in 1638. Her husband, Francisco López, had been a fellow "Portuguese" and a "merchant without a store" who, like the defendant, frequently transported merchandise to Galicia from his home in Madrid. The third sibling was Beatriz Rodríguez, who had married the Portuguese artisan Martin Rodríguez. I shall say more about this couple in the pages that follow.

The declarant said he had never met his grandparents, and had never cared to know anything about them. He attributed this lack of curiosity to the fact that he had been born and reared in Castile while they had lived in Portugal and died there, presumably before his birth. Rodríguez said he had not tried to obtain any of their biographical information during his many trips to Portugal, "for he did not know what their names were, and because [after their deaths] there did not seem to be any use in asking about them" (fol. 85r).

Concerning his aunts, uncles, and their descendants, the defendant was not as ignorant as he claimed to be about his grandparents. In fact, he furnished copious information regarding several of his relatives. In the process he conveyed the unmistakable impression that the Rodríguez de Amézquita and López families were spread widely across the Iberian Peninsula, and that members of both groups seldom maintained contact with each other.

Regarding his paternal aunt, for instance, Rodríguez said she had lived in Mogadouro (in northeastern Portugal), where she had married a local native surnamed Mota. The couple's son, Juan Rodríguez Mota, had once visited the declarant in Madrid for a few days in 1652 or 1653. Rodríguez Mota had later settled in Toledo, where he married a woman who owned "some kind of small store."[2] Apparently the two cousins did not meet again after 1653, much less develop a close relationship.

In all, Rodríguez de Amézquita said he had (or had had) relatives in cities, towns, and villages as far-flung and diverse as Madrid, Valladolid, Toledo, Seville, Antequera, Porto, Vilaflor, and Viseu. Some of the data he furnished would have allowed the Holy Office to investigate the relatives in question had anyone accused them of heresy. For example, the suspect disclosed the names and places of residence of a living aunt, a cousin, and a nephew from Valladolid, of several nephews from Viseu, and of a niece from Madrid.

Then again, not all of the information Rodríguez supplied was conclusive or particularly helpful to the inquisitors. For example, he said he did not know the name of his eldest paternal uncle, "but he heard it said that his uncle went to the Indies of Castile, and he does not know if he is alive or dead" (ibid.). The suspect testified in almost identical terms about one of his paternal aunts: He had heard that she lived in Porto, but he was not certain whether or not she was alive (fol. 86r).

Rodríguez's Portuguese wife, Leonor Gómez, was residing in Bayonne at the time of his deposition. Given his alleged ignorance of key details of her life, it does not appear that the spouses had developed a close relationship. For instance, the declarant testified that he was not certain whether she was a native of Sao João de Pesqueria or Vilaflor (nonetheless, he identified her brother, Vasco Fernández, as a native of Vilaflor). Confusing matters further, elsewhere he intimated that she had been born in Madrid (fol. 87r, cf. 49r).

Rodríguez and Gómez were the parents of one child, six-year-old Balthasar, who had been born and baptized in Bayonne. The suspect's extra-marital liaison with a French (presumably Christian) woman had resulted in the birth of a second child, five-year-old María. She too lived with her mother in Saint Esprit.

Rodríguez testified that he did not know his *casta y generación*, but declared that to the best of his knowledge all his deceased and living kin were (or had been) good Christians. Furthermore, he stated that none of them had ever faced Inquisitorial prosecution. Later he contradicted all but the last of these claims.

During his initial *audiencia* the defendant indicated that he had been baptized in Valladolid and had last confessed in Zaragoza, immediately preceding his incarceration and transfer to Madrid. He made the sign of the cross on command, and recited the Ave Maria, the Credo, and the Commandments of God correctly. He also enumerated the Articles of Faith and Works of Mercy, though with some difficulty. Finally, the suspect admitted he was literate and had been schooled in Castile (fol. 88v). He gave no indication that his parents had reared him as anything other than an orthodox Catholic.

In his *discurso* Rodríguez testified that he had spent the first eleven years of his life in Valladolid, where his mother died in 1620. The family had moved to Madrid in 1625, upon the marriage of the defendant's sister Isabel to Francisco López. Five years later the family moved again, to Zafra in southwestern Spain, when the declarant's father, an itinerant salesman of linens, experienced financial difficulties. (The defendant explained that Pedro de Amézquita, a relative from Extremadura, had rescued Balthasar Rodríguez by donating merchandise to him, thereby enabling Balthasar to resume his trade in that region.)

Three years after establishing his family in Zafra, the elder Rodríguez became incapacitated owing to an illness. By that time the declarant had gained some experience as his father's assistant, and was thus able to assume the role of principal breadwinner in his family. In 1633 Balthasar Rodríguez's health so deteriorated that the family (including his second wife, the Portuguese Violante da Silva) set out for the baths of the Alfama in southern Portugal. There, the father hoped, he would be able to soothe his physical pain. On the way to Portugal, however, his condition worsened and he could not complete the trip. The voyagers had no choice but to settle where they had stopped, namely in Antequera, near the coast of Málaga (fol. 89r–89v). In the ensuing eight years Antonio Rodríguez de Amézquita sold linens in the vicinity of Antequera. Thus he expanded his already considerable participation in a trading network manned primarily by fellow Portuguese merchants.

After marrying fellow "Portuguese" Leonor Gómez in 1641 and settling in Madrid, the declarant embarked on a series of extended business trips across the Iberian Peninsula. Through these excursions he established a solid reputation as an effective wholesaler and administrator. Meanwhile, Gómez remained in Madrid with her mother and the mother's sister-in-law. In his travels Rodríguez primarily covered Galicia and Andalusia. During a trip to the latter region his religious life underwent the first of three momentous changes.

Around 1647 Rodríguez traveled to Málaga to sell some merchandise he had purchased in Seville. In the former city he lodged at the home of his sister, Beatriz Rodríguez, and her husband, Martín Rodríguez.[3] On one occasion, after a meal, the host allegedly read from a book containing Jewish prayers in Castilian, including ones the declarant later learned were the "Semá" (Shema) and "Amidad" (Amidah) orations of the daily Jewish liturgy. Francisco Rodríguez, a friend of the hosts and no relation to the family, was present at the meal. He allegedly initiated a discussion of the subject of crypto-Judaism by telling the defendant that it was a mistake to follow the Catholic faith, and that if the declarant wished to save his soul he should follow the Law of Moses. According to the suspect, "Francisco Rodríguez persuaded him with so many reasons that this declarant started to wonder whether the Law of Moses was the true one" (fol. 44r). Contributing to the suspect's uncertainty was the fact that his sister and her husband supported their friend's position (ibid.).

In the months that followed this pivotal discussion, Rodríguez de Amézquita, Francisco Rodríguez, and their hosts set out together on several business-related trips. According to the defendant, the three Judaizers usually discussed crypto-Judaism and continually exhorted him to abandon Christianity as they walked or rode their mules along the roads of Andalusia. Unfortunately, the declarant did not describe the specific content of these collective discussions.

Whenever he and Francisco Rodríguez rode alone, they too spent much time speaking of the Law of Moses. Here is the defendant's only detailed recollection of his companion's conversionist efforts:

Francisco Rodríguez explained the chapters of Genesis especially, [saying] that in the beginning God created heaven and the earth. [Francisco Rodríguez] continued pondering through all the days of creation, [saying] that everything had been made by God, and that He was one and only [*uno solo*], and that in order to govern everything no substitute was necessary, neither [was it necessary] to bestow His divinity on another because He was all powerful, and that, it being so, how was it possible that three or four thousand years later Jesus Christ had come to the world, and that, born of a woman, [Jesus] should be God? [Francisco Rodríguez also said] that [Jesus] had . . . blings and that the Messiah promised in the Law had not arrived, and that when he comes he will not be God, rather a man sent by God to be the leader of the Hebrew people, as Moses was. . . . Francisco Rodríguez read passages to [the declarant] from a book he possessed written in Castilian, thus proving [each of] his points. And he gave [the declarant] other very pressing [or narrow] reasons [*razones muy apretadas*], which [the declarant] does not remember in particular; [and] as [the declarant] is a layperson [*seglar*] and . . . Francisco Rodríguez was very learned and wise in many subjects, he convinced him and subjugated him [*le redujo*] to the observance of said Law [of Moses]. (fol. 74v)

It was from this and other such disquisitions that Rodríguez de Amézquita allegedly gathered that Francisco Rodríguez had been instrumental in persuading his sister and brother-in-law to Judaize (fol. 44r).

Eventually the four travelers settled in Seville. They remained there for one year, living in an austere and somewhat discreet fashion, or as the suspect phrased it, "without any servants" (fol. 47r). Still plagued by religious doubts, Rodríguez de Amézquita reportedly began to worry that abandoning the Law of Grace "was not licit, seeing as he was a Catholic Christian, and baptized, and he had always followed the Law of Jesus Christ, so it seemed to him that perhaps Francisco Rodríguez was deceiving him" (fol. 44v).

The declarant subsequently related his apprehensions to his sister and her husband, adding that he was considering revealing his misgivings to a priest. Beatriz and Martín Rodríguez grew alarmed at this. They tried to dissuade their kinsman with tearful pleas "not to reveal anything, for the love of God, for he would expose them and they would be burned" (ibid.). Allegedly moved by their supplications, the defendant withheld his confession. Thereafter his companions "persuaded him with many reasons and *persuasiones*" to leave the law of Jesus Christ once again (ibid.). As a result he became fully convinced that Francisco Rodríguez was a "very wise and versed man" compared to an "unlearned" man such as himself ([*un*] *hombre que no sabe de letras*) (ibid.).

So deep was the effect of his companions' entreaties, the defendant claimed, that he had followed the Law of Moses consistently for eleven months. Specifically, Rodríguez de Amézquita said that he had prayed the "Semá" three times daily, chanted psalms to conclude his prayers, observed the Sabbath by refraining from work, celebrated certain Jewish "feasts," and eaten *carne desencebada* (meat hewed so as to remove its excess fat) (fols. 45r–46v).

If the defendant had acquired a certain knowledge of halakhic rituals and dietary restrictions, it is nonetheless obvious that his alleged observance was extremely fragmentary and somewhat confused. For example, the meat he ate was not slaughtered or bled as required by Jewish law. Among the "feasts" Rodríguez allegedly celebrated was a "festival" he called the Día Grande. Suspected Judaizers who referred to it usually did not describe this "Great Day" as a feast, rather as a day of fasting and atonement. Simply put, Día Grande was a crypto-Judaic version of Yom Kippur. By his own account Rodríguez fell even outside of this marranic understanding.

As if following a clandestine religion were not difficult enough, Francisco Rodríguez had allegedly told the defendant and Martin Rodríguez that their secret devotion would not be accepted by God unless they were circumcised (fol. 47r). However, there is no indication that Rodríguez de Amézquita engaged his teacher on the subject of circumcision, much less entertained the possibility of submitting to the procedure.

In any event, the declarant left his companions behind when he departed for his home in Madrid in 1648 or 1649. Much later he heard that his sister and brother-in-law had succumbed to the plague. He never saw or heard of Francisco Rodríguez again.

While in Madrid, the defendant allegedly kept the Law of Moses "in his heart," but did not observe any of its ceremonies lest his wife and the other members of his household discover that he had become a crypto-Jew. Under the circumstances, the most Rodríguez felt he could do to uphold his adherence to the Law of Moses was to recite some (unidentified) psalms he had memorized during his stay in Seville. He allegedly rehearsed these psalms in silence and alone, mostly while roaming the streets of the Habsburg capital and the land that surrounded it. Whenever he engaged in these silent recitations at home—which was seldom—he allegedly retired to a separate room as if to do something else. In order not to call attention to himself, he ate "any dishes he was given," including foods prepared with *tocino* (pig fat). In addition, he pursued his usual *negocios* on the Jewish Sabbath (fol. 48r).

One day, while walking in the streets of the Spanish capital, Rodríguez chanced upon Diego Gómez. The latter was a Portuguese New Christian and friend of Rodríguez, who, as the declarant later discovered, had been penitenced by the Holy Tribunal. On the day in question, Gómez allegedly engaged Rodríguez in innocent conversation, but suddenly asked a pointed query: Did Rodríguez know when the fast of the Día Grande should be observed? Rodríguez testified that he was not sure how Gómez could have guessed that he, Rodríguez de Amézquita, was a follower of the Law of Moses, unless "on some occasion a word might have slipped," by which Gómez had inferred it was safe to ask him such a question. In any case, the declarant and his friend agreed to meet at a plaza and spend the "Great Day" walking and avoiding all food until sundown. They later carried out their plan in the Prado de San Gerónimo, a long promenade in what was then the relatively undeveloped eastern perimeter of Madrid.[4] The Día Grande had finally become a solemn fast in Rodríguez's secret religious itinerary.

Gathering courage from his meetings with Gómez, Rodríguez allegedly decided to revitalize his newly adopted faith and become circumcised. To accomplish these goals he proposed to leave the Iberian Peninsula altogether. Although they were not aware of his ulterior purposes, Rodríguez's wife and mother-in-law quickly accepted the decision to move, as they did not have anyone other than him to support them financially (*como no tenían otro amparo*) (fol. 50r).

In 1655 the family rented a few mules in Madrid and set off for Pamplona. Twenty-year-old Juan Compra, Rodríguez's trusted assistant, accompanied the traveling group. When the voyagers reached Navarre, Rodríguez obtained permits from vice-royal officers and an inquisitorial commissioner to cross the international border into Bayonne (fol. 50v). In Bayonne the travelers arrived at a small plaza where Portuguese immigrants frequently gathered. A few merchants who had become acquainted with Rodríguez in Madrid (including one of his wife's uncles) recognized him there.

Simon López, one of the merchants, invited the traveling party to stay at his home. That evening he showed his guests an unfamiliar prayer book and told them, "in this tome are the prayers that are customarily read around here, which serve to save souls" (fol. 51r). Somewhat confused, Rodríguez's wife, mother-in-law, and Juan Compra responded that they were ready to pray, as they had brought their rosaries with them. However, when they heard the prayers that López, his wife, and the declarant intoned, the three travelers were "extremely surprised and frightened," for they realized that they were among Judaizers, and worst of all, that Rodríguez de Amézquita was a heretic himself. Shocked at this discovery, Leonor Gómez allegedly began to cry "with great extremity," exclaiming to her husband, "Where have you brought me?" Rodríguez tried to console her by telling her that "she did not know what this [kind of praying] was all about, and that she should not be so extremely frightened, and that once she recognized those prayers, and saw that what was said in them was good and holy . . . she would realize how to follow the true path" (fol. 51r–51v).

In the next few days, several residents of Saint Esprit visited Rodríguez and his family at the home of Simon López. While welcoming their new neighbors, the visitors also took pains to gauge the latter's socioreligious orientation. Several of the men who greeted Rodríguez asked him whether he liked his new surroundings, and more probingly, what he thought of the (Jewish) prayer books used "in those parts" (fol. 52r). Other visitors were even more forward. The women who visited Leonor Gómez, her mother, and Juan Compra blatantly cajoled them to follow the Law of Moses. All three newcomers acceded to the visitors' *persuasiones* "in a matter of four or five days. And *as they were in the house of Simon López they said that all they had been told seemed good*, and that all the prayers [their neighbors recited] in the daily service appeared to them to be very holy and very good, *and that since [the visitors] observed that [religion], they would observe it as well from then onward*" (emphasis added; fol. 52v). The pressure to conform had taken its intended toll. As Rodríguez described the episode, all the members of his household had finally capitulated, not out of conviction, but out of courtesy to Simon López and deference to their new neighbors.

Once Rodríguez and his cohort had moved to a separate domicile in Saint Esprit, their acclimatization to the Judeo-Portuguese world of southwestern France began in earnest. Leonor Gómez, who had not been fully literate before her emigration from Spain, started to improve her reading skills, presumably by following the text of the translated Jewish prayer book along with other worshippers. For his part, the defendant expanded and corrected his previously sketchy knowledge of the Jewish liturgical calendar (he wrote a lengthy description of several Jewish holidays and customs, perhaps at the request of his interrogators). He also learned normative Jewish worship, yet, as the following passage suggests, his religious acculturation was laborious and somewhat infantilizing despite his enthusiasm:

I too wished to learn [to read the daily prayers in Hebrew] and I began to read but I never knew how to construct sentences, and as I had a poor memory it was very hard work for me [*me costaba mucho trabajo*], and I desisted even though I had a Bible in Hebrew. Sometimes at home I would read from it, though very badly and very slowly. . . . [In contrast, young novices] learned very quickly, and after they learned they would pray from Hebraic books, as well as other ones in Castilian [*romance*]. Yet, because I read so slowly and tentatively, I only recited one prayer in Hebrew—the one they call the Canticle of Moses [*El Cántico de Moisés*]. I used to say this prayer on the Sabbath because they chant it very slowly. (fols. 32v–33r)

Finally, Rodríguez underwent a circumcision a month after his arrival in France, thus marking his second religious transformation. The suspect's *mohel* (ritual surgeon) was Abraham ben Israel, an emissary from Amsterdam or Livorno. Echoing Francisco Rodríguez, this learned envoy allegedly told the defendant and two other patients after performing their circumcisions that God would now hear their prayers, for, as newly circumcised men, they were cleansed of sin "as in the hour they had been born" (fol. 55v). Ben Israel's typically marranic implication seems to have been that before circumcision a Jewish man did not enjoy full access to God. In this interpretation, of course, there is a strong hint of the "sacramental" view of *brit milah* I discussed in the third chapter.

Among other things, Rodríguez de Amézquita noted that the expatriate community of Saint Esprit was replete with fellow religious novices (in the course of his depositions he named a total of forty-eight supposed Judaizers he had known in Spain, Portugal, and France). Their congregational activities included praying, almsgiving, and listening to the homilies of preachers such as Ben Israel and a certain Dr. Avila. The latter envoy drew a salary from the community for his services as the first *hakham* of Saint Esprit.[5]

According to one witness, one of the preachers had stressed to his listeners that eating *tocino* and violating the Sabbath were the worst sins a Jew could commit against the Law of Moses.[6] If this and similar (alleged) recollections are at all accurate, it would seem that the envoys—and by extension the communal leadership that had welcomed them to suburban Bayonne—sought to instill the most basic halakhic rules. Saint Esprit, after all, was a community of neophytes. As the defendant remarked, "Since Don Avila has resided in Bayonne, knowledge of the ceremonies of the Law [of Moses], *which [the residents] did not know previously*, has increased greatly, and he has taught many people the Hebraic language" (emphasis added; fol. 70r).

The precise extent to which the immigrant rank and file followed rabbinic law is unclear, yet it is logical to suppose that religious ignorance and laxity were unexceptional in Saint Esprit. Rodríguez revealed an aspect of this laxity when he remarked that several New Jews bowed to economic reality rather than follow the letter of Halakhah:

Whenever in the neighborhood of Saint Esprit there was someone who knew how to slaughter meat [sic] in the Judaic manner [the residents] bought it. . . . But [Rodríguez] has noticed that there are some . . . Judaizers who, although there be meat available that has been slaughtered in the Jewish manner, do not want to buy it because it is more expensive than that which is not slaughtered in that fashion . . . and they eat the [nonkosher meat], saying that by cutting off the fat and bleeding [the meat] . . . they are complying with the Law. (fol. 53r)

The declarant did not identify with religious backsliders, rather with those who endeavored to conform to the predominant ways, rules, and customs of the nascent kehilla. As he put it, he and his family observed all Jewish holidays "in the same form and manner as the other Judaizers perform and celebrate them" (ibid.). Furthermore, Rodríguez developed friendly relations with Diego Rodríguez Cardoso, an economic and political pillar of the New Jewish enclave whose home often served as a makeshift synagogue. In time, Rodríguez de Amézquita's dwelling became the site of communal religious services as well.

Notwithstanding his evolution into a respectable Judaizer, it is clear that the declarant was no model of neo-Judaic orthodoxy. Though at first he returned to Iberia sporadically and sent Juan Compra to Spain as his commercial agent, Rodríguez de Amézquita eventually became a chronic returnee. In fact, the wholesaler pursued his commercial activities virtually as though he had never left Iberia. What is most significant for our purposes is that during his trips to and from the Iberian Peninsula he admittedly reverted to the minimalistic crypto-Judaism to which he had become accustomed in Madrid. At times he even suspended his observance of his newly adopted religion altogether. Crucially, violating Halakhah does not appear to have caused Rodríguez any guilt. Neither did he ever care to ask Compra whether he (Compra) kept the Law of Moses during his forays into Soria, Pastrana, and Madrid (fol. 59r).

Returning to Iberia on a regular basis entailed considerable risks for Rodríguez, and consequently for his family. Furthermore, by frequently sending Juan Compra to Iberia Rodríguez endangered the safety of a person for whom he felt such fondness that he called the young man "nephew." Compra had been part of the merchant's household for years. Although there was no genealogical relationship between the employer and his employee, the younger man fully reciprocated Rodríguez's affection by addressing him as "uncle." This mutual affection entailed a considerable sense of trust. Around 1657, for example, the defendant sent Compra to retrieve a load of cocoa worth approximately fifteen hundred ducats—a small fortune for a lone merchant by the standards of the day. Unfortunately for both men, someone misdirected the load and it was lost seven leagues from Bayonne.

When Juan Compra died unexpectedly during a subsequent business trip to Pastrana, Rodríguez was left with the difficult task of recovering the merchandise he had entrusted to his ill-fated protégé (in this case, Compra had been transporting a load of cinnamon). Standing in Rodríguez's way was the ducal government of the city, which had appropriated Compra's posses-sions on the grounds that the young agent was a foreigner to that jurisdiction and had no heirs to claim the merchandise. As if Compra's death on the road had not highlighted the vulnerability of traveling *mercaderes* sufficiently, Ro-dríguez was now forced to compensate—in essence, to bribe—the duke of Pastrana in order to secure the release of Compra's goods. This humiliating transaction cost the wholesaler at least five hundred ducats (fol. 61v). We can only speculate about how much the loss of his beloved "nephew" cost the de-clarant in emotional terms, yet it is reasonable to suppose that Rodríguez suf-fered considerable grief.

Without Compra to help him the merchant now had to work harder to keep himself and his family economically viable. Instead of hiring a new agent, Rodríguez undertook lengthy trips to the Iberian Peninsula to pro-cure, ship, and sell various kinds of merchandise in bulk. He was no stranger to such journeys. For instance, before Compra's demise Rodríguez had shipped five hundred pounds of saffron from Bayonne to Lisbon. While the ship sailed its course, the declarant had traveled by land to Portugal to wait for the arrival of the merchandise. Before reaching Portugal he stopped in Orense (in Galicia) to claim thirty-three *tafetanes* (pieces of a thin silk) that he had sent from Madrid to a local consigner. Upon his arrival in Portugal Rodríguez received notice that the ship that carried the saffron had been waylaid by Algerian pirates. Left only with the *tafetanes*, he sold them and used the proceeds to purchase and ship additional merchandise to Bayonne, as well as to fund the initial stage of his journey back to France. The return trip was extremely slow and circuitous. In an attempt to rescue some mate-rial profit from his unfortunate excursion, the defendant stayed in Spain for a staggering seven months before reaching his home in Saint Esprit. During that period he allegedly avoided all Judaic practice.

Following the death of his trusted agent, Rodríguez de Amézquita undertook additional voyages. Toward the end of the 1650s he purchased a large load of raw cotton from his friend, the magnate Diego Rodríguez Cardoso, and shipped it to Lisbon. Once again the defendant traveled there by land from southwestern France. After receiving the cotton, disposing of it, and shipping other merchandise to Bayonne, Rodríguez set out for Saint Esprit, retracing the route he had followed to the Portuguese capital. By the summer of 1663 he had reached Zaragoza, where he lodged at the home of a widow. It was there, in the heart of the kingdom of Aragon, that Rodríguez allegedly experienced the beginning of his third religious transformation.

To support himself in Zaragoza, Rodríguez recalled, he had purchased two hundred pounds of chocolate pieces, yet he was only able to sell the merchandise slowly and at a low price because at the time "he was handling few matters skillfully" (*porque amañaba en poco*) (fol. 60r). Slowly Rodríguez's material resources dwindled to the point that he did not even possess the means to pay his daily rent to the widow. A crisis of confidence thus beset the weary and destitute traveler—or so he claimed. Later he testified that religious doubts had come to haunt him at the moment of his utmost misery:

On different occasions during his stay in Zaragoza he has considered that in all the time that he followed Our Holy Catholic Faith Our Lord granted him many mercies [*le hizo muchas mercedes*], endowing him with luck in every business deal his hand touched, for in all these business deals he had benefited considerably, so much so that at the time he immigrated to Bayonne, France, he found himself in possession of seven or eight thousand ducats. . . . But later he saw that after entering Bayonne and becoming circumcised . . . he has not put his hand on anything he has not [eventually] lost. (fols. 61r–61v)

To illustrate the last point, Rodríguez recounted several of his commercial misfortunes. He recalled the five hundred pounds of saffron he had shipped to Lisbon but had been seized by Muslim pirates; the similarly expensive load of cocoa that Juan Compra had failed to retrieve from Spain; and the five hundred ducats Rodríguez had been forced to pay the duke of Pastrana to recover Compra's baggage and personal effects after the latter's untimely death. In addition, the declarant alluded to "several other losses he has suffered, that he does not recall right now" (fol. 61v). Finally, he stated that

he [has suffered business failures] to the point that he has lost all his assets and today finds himself . . . so poor that he still owes . . . twenty days' rent to the widow Juana de Amor, such that he has entered into serious considerations, and it seems to him that all of these losses were punishments that Our Lord had sent him for having done wrong, and for having offended Him so much by leaving our Holy Catholic Faith and following the Law of Moses. (fol. 62r)

Without any apparent pressure on the part of the inquisitors, Rodríguez continued by intimating that his spirit had been enlightened thanks to the religious environment of Zaragoza, a town that bore the deep imprint of its inhabitants' fervent Catholicism. Rodríguez hinted that he had been particularly impressed with the emotive power of local shrines devoted to Our Lady of the Pillar, the Master of Epila, and the Martyrs of Santa Engracia, respectively.

As if to relive the inklings of an epiphany, the defendant also told his interrogators of an occasion in which he had been conversing with a local shoemaker named Antonio near the shrine of the Cross of Coso. In their dialogue, the two men had allegedly spoken of the great number of relics contained in the shrine and in the votive sites that led from the Cross to the Church of Santa Engracia. Delving into the subject of the conversation, the cobbler had related the following story: A Zaragozan priest traveled to Rome to conclude official church business and procure some relics. When the pope heard that the visitor was from Zaragoza, he reprimanded him: "Being from Zaragoza, why do you ask me for relics, since you have so many there already?" To demonstrate the redundancy of his subject's request, the pontiff then commanded the priest to bring him "a little soil" (*un poco de tierra*) from the street that led from the Cross of Coso to the Church of Santa Engracia (namely the very street on which Rodríguez allegedly heard the cobbler's story). When the priest returned to Rome with the sample of earth, the pontiff "took it in his hand and squeezed it, and blood ran from it so fresh that it was as if the martyrs [of Santa Engracia] had just spilled it" (fol. 62v). The pope then told the priest, "Look, why do you need relics, when you have a street soaked with the blood of martyrs?" With this, the priest returned to Zaragoza full of joy and certain of the miraculous piety that pervaded his native city.[7]

This was not all. Rodríguez also recalled that he had witnessed and heard of moving religious processions and rogations in Zaragoza. He noted, for example, that local Capuchin monks had twice marched barefoot to the Shrine of the Holy Christ of Calatrava, an exercise that had taken them more than thirty kilometers from their city. Along the way, Rodríguez continued, the friars had left vivid bloodstains as traces of injuries to the soles of their feet. Rodríguez said he had realized that in order to demonstrate such self-sacrificing devotion the Capuchins must have been "just, virtuous, and

saintly men who followed the path of truth" (fol. 63r). The defendant concluded his anecdote with the momentous declaration that, "given all these
things [he had witnessed in the city], it seemed to him that God had brought
him to Zaragoza so that he would know the bad state in which he was, and
abandon the Law of Moses" (ibid.).

Rodríguez went on to claim that he had become an obedient Catholic
six months prior to his deposition, albeit after a period of vacillation during
which he had attended mass and confessed to a local priest, yet without revealing the worst of his sins for fear of being punished by the Inquisition
(fols. 63v–65v).

The interrogators would have none of this. How, they demanded, did
Rodríguez expect them to believe that he had reconverted to Catholicism and
observed it sincerely during the previous six months, when earlier in his testimony he had shamelessly admitted that he had failed to divulge his heresy
to his Zaragozan confessor? Furthermore, the inquisitors noted that it was
impossible to believe that someone who had admittedly apostatized on the
basis of Jewish propaganda could now return to Catholicism wholeheartedly
without first rejecting the false doctrines that Judaizers had taught him, and
explaining how he had come to the conclusion that those doctrines were
false.

The defendant replied somewhat meekly that he was an *hombre romancista*—in other words, a mere speaker of the Castilian vernacular and
therefore an unlearned man—who did not understand subtle biblical interpretation. He further protested that he had returned to Catholicism and
stayed in Spain of his own accord. To prove this he stressed that if he
had truly wished to return to a life of heresy in France he could have easily
asked one of his fellow Portuguese merchants to lend him some merchandise, which he (Rodríguez) could then have sold to cover the expense of a relatively short journey from Zaragoza to Bayonne. The defendant continued
that he could also have tried to pay for such a journey "with the charity that
observers of the Law of Moses give to poor and uneducated men" (fol. 77v).
Both claims carried considerable plausibility. As we have seen, the French-
Spanish border was extremely permeable. Converso smuggling networks
rendered escaping from and returning to the Iberian Peninsula a virtually ordinary occurrence. We also know that in later years the immigrant community of Saint Esprit counted with a special budget to help indigent conversos
settle in southwestern France.[8] Whether such a budget existed in 1664 or not,
the will to provide help may well have existed. Rodríguez could easily have

sent word to Bayonne that he was in trouble and needed immediate economic assistance.

After alleging pure intentions, Rodríguez requested a writing instrument and two sheets of paper. In a steady and careful hand, he later wrote what his interrogators had implicitly requested of him, namely a thorough avowal of the validity of Catholic doctrine and a rejection of Judaic "error." In this largely apologetic exposition Rodríguez demonstrated a general knowledge and understanding of the Gospels and of Christian doctrine. He also demonstrated an acquaintance with Jewish polemical exegesis and with arguments Christians might deploy against the latter. For instance, Rodríguez wrote,

At the beginning of creation of the world God says, "let us make man," [*hagamos hombre*] and by this it is understood that He is speaking with the Holy Trinity, although the Hebrews say that He was speaking to the four elements, to which I say that in this . . . [the Jews] are in very great error, because to speak to the elements was not necessary, and to go and say "let us make man" is to speak in the plural. Thus I declare and confess that He was speaking to the most holy Trinity—Father, Son, and Holy Spirit—and they are one and the only true God. . . . Now as for [the Book of] Isaiah, I see that there are a few verses . . . where it is said that God does not forgive the sin of those who sold the just [into captivity], and it is easy to see quite clearly that [the passage] is referring to my Savior, Jesus Christ, since, as we know, he was sold by Judas for a mere thirty coins. Yet the Hebrews say that [the verses] referred to [the Patriarch] Joseph. I say that . . . [the Jews] commit a great error. Although it is true that they were in the captivity of Egypt, it was a very short-lived captivity, and anyway [God] forgave them [and freed them] . . . because of Joseph . . . however, we see that the verse [in Isaiah] says "I will not forgive the sin." (fols. 79r–79v)

Obviously, the defendant was conversant in the Christian discourse that his captors had demanded he embrace. Whether in the course of his life in Spain, during months of alleged misery and religious doubt in Zaragoza, under inquisitorial tutelage, or in all three instances, Rodríguez had learned the official ideology of his judges and prosecutors. As a result he was perfectly capable of justifying himself in the language of their worldview.

Evidently satisfied with the defendant's written statement and probably pacified by his denunciation of scores of individuals, the inquisitors imposed a relatively mild sentence on him. It entailed one year's imprisonment, to be followed by one year's reeducation as well as banishment from Madrid, Toledo, Seville, Málaga, and Zaragoza. In their decision, the judges remarked that the defendant's confession had been wholehearted (*de todo corazón*) and had been accompanied by tearful expressions of remorse. Thus Rodríguez's trial concluded relatively well for him. One of the documents appended to his dossier certifies his subsequent completion without incident of a program of penitence and catechization. That is the last we read of his fate.

The Challenge of Interpretation

As we have seen, Rodríguez de Amézquita constructed an elaborate and detailed portrait of himself. At times extremely plausible, at others suspiciously vague and contradictory, this self-depiction is so complex that it defies facile notions of his credibility or lack thereof. To illustrate this point I submit the crucial example of his alleged Judaicization and subsequent return to Catholicism.

If, for the sake of argument, we adopt a skeptical view that Rodríguez lied with regard to his conversion and reconversion, we implicitly posit at least two possible explanations of his mendacity: First, that he lied because in his heart he was a convinced Jew. Second, that he lied because he was an opportunist who swore a superficial allegiance to whatever religion suited his interests at given moments. In either case, this skeptical view supposes that the defendant's return to Christianity was a desperate ruse calculated to save his skin. By the same token, this view posits that many if not all of the highly plausible anecdotes he related were consonant with his attempt to deceive his interrogators (an example of such anecdotes is his comment that a number of New Jews preferred to buy forbidden meat because it cost less than the kosher variety).

An immediate problem with this scenario is that in order to construct such an artful and specious facade Rodríguez would have had to be exceedingly shrewd and cold-blooded. The declarant was no fool, but in light of his highly nuanced deposition I believe it is unrealistic to cast him in the role of masterful fabricator. It simply does not stand to reason that Rodríguez should have concocted so many remarkably lifelike yet legally meaningless scenes, such as the one in which the members of his household, prompted to worship in an unfamiliar fashion, say in their confusion that they are ready to pray with their rosaries; or the anecdote concerning his own inability to follow the recitation of Hebrew prayers.

A stubborn skeptic might object that through these and similarly innocuous-seeming "recollections" the defendant was trying to make his confession sound thorough and realistic while hinting that he and his family had apostatized halfheartedly or even reluctantly. Yet, as we have seen, Rodríguez did not eschew harsher forms of incrimination, including self-incrimination. Furthermore, at the time of the deposition Juan Compra was dead and thus in no danger of being prosecuted. For their part, Leonor Gómez and her mother were safe in Bayonne, so there was no need for Rodríguez to protect them. In all likelihood neither woman had any garnishable property left in Iberia (again, Rodríguez alleged that he was their sole supporter). However, if the women did have such property, then the defendant would have to have been implausibly naive to suppose that his inculpating testimony—however "softened" by clever hints—could shield the property from confiscation. Had the inquisitors suspected Rodríguez of withholding information about his family's assets, they would have asked him about these assets. More importantly, if Rodríguez was so naive, then the original premise that he was a subtle and successful liar is untenable.

Once again for the sake of argument, let us suppose that Rodríguez's testimony regarding his conversion and reconversion was entirely consistent with fact. This scenario unravels more easily than the first. Witness the declarant's early assertion that none of his relatives were or had been heretics, which he later contradicted by relating that his sister and her husband had introduced him to crypto-Judaism. For obvious reasons this contradiction alone renders absurd an unqualified belief in the defendant's reliability. Perhaps worse, the contradiction provides no clue as to which of his assertions, the earlier or the later one, corresponded to his relatives' actual religious identities.

An alternative position that Rodríguez's narrative contains elements of "truth" and deliberate "untruth" is not satisfactory either, because it fails to illuminate key ambiguities in his testimony. For example, in the process of explaining his reconversion to Catholicism Rodríguez initially chose to speak about his commercial misfortunes and about how inspiring he had found the piety of Zaragozans. Only later did he renounce Jewish theology under pressure from his interrogators. By omitting such an abjuration at first, had Rodríguez hidden his "real" motives—that is to say, had he "lied"—or had he told the truth? If, as the hypothesis dictates, he had somehow done both, what aspect of his omission had been "candid" and what aspect of it had been "disingenuous"?

By now it should be clear that neither of the three scenarios—namely, "Rodríguez lied," "he half-lied," and "he told the truth"—elucidates the complex religious mentality that his wide-ranging testimony brings into view. Apart from the reasons already mentioned, the three hypotheses are ultimately insufficient because they are attempts to measure the authenticity of his self-portrait against a hypostatized image of his "real" self, one ostensibly separate from and independent of the self he described in his testimony. It is simplistic, for example, to ask whether Rodríguez "truly" reverted to Catholicism since his religious consciousness was not a perspicuous entity comprehensible *only* in terms of its fidelity (or infidelity) to given extrinsic and incontrovertible facts.

None of this is to say that Rodríguez and other renegades were incapable of consciously misrepresenting certain verifiable data about themselves, or that it is impossible to explain the behavior of the renegades by reference to their objective circumstances. I am not trying to suggest that personal identity has no objective referent, is somehow ephemeral, or is entirely discontinuous. I am simply proposing that the notion of a perfectly hermetic, "real" identity totally distinct from self-perception and self-revelation is illusory, inasmuch as selfhood is not a fixed fact *entirely distinct from the subject's point of view*, namely that person's unique and evolving perspective of life given his or her changing circumstances. If we understand the confession of a "renegade" as a contextually determined *fashioning* of his or her religious selfhood (as opposed to a deliberate concoction of a public self), we may avoid recourse to positivistic extremes such as "the defendant lied" and "the defendant told the truth." The question then becomes, not what that "renegade" *was* in some essentialistic sense—either a "Jew" or a "Catholic"—but *how* that person conceived of "the Law of Moses" and "the Law of Grace," and more crucially, *what* he thought of himself or herself in relation to "Judaism" and "Christianity" as he or she understood them.

I consider Rodríguez de Amézquita's testimony to be a profound *interpretation* of his spiritual history as a significant and coherent narrative. Because Rodríguez fashioned that narrative under the extreme stress of inquisitorial questioning, we should not exaggerate the degree to which he developed his story in logical and rational ways.[9] As the foregoing suggests, my position is that Rodríguez is not reducible to the stereotype of a calculating cynic. But then neither was he an ideal penitent, always spewing forth an ideal and obvious "truth" about himself. Rather, he was a complex man laboring under the burden of his circumstances who made sense of his life by selecting, organizing, and molding his memories and wishes into a self-portrait. Again, the sheer depth and complexity of that portrait prohibits that we dismiss it as simple "perjury."

An Interpretation of Rodríguez as a Religious Actor

In the course of his account Rodríguez described himself repeatedly as an unlearned man who had bowed to the great wisdom and virtue of his religious superiors, whether they happened to be "erudite" laypersons (Francisco Rodríguez), legal experts (Abraham ben Israel and Dr. Avila), or vague groups of supposedly pious individuals (including the barefoot Capuchins of Zaragoza, the lay ritualists of that city, and the Judeo-Portuguese "Nation" of greater Bayonne).

As we have seen, the fact that Rodríguez called himself a mere *hombre romancista* did not mean that he was incapable of reconstructing Francisco Rodríguez's biblical lesson on the validity of Judaism. In fact, the defendant was even able to analyze Holy Scriptures to build a reasonably coherent argument in favor of Catholicism. Therefore, what Rodríguez actually revealed when he intimated that he was an ignoramus was clearly not a lack of knowledge or sophistication per se. Rather, he revealed the fact that he was inclined to subordinate his intellect, indeed his entire outlook, to the ideological prescriptions of individuals to whom he imputed religious authority.

Rodríguez's attitude should not surprise us. Like other Europeans of the Early Modern Period, he inhabited a social world defined by strict hierarchies of power and prestige.[10] At each level of these hierarchies people looked for someone to do, think, and interpret what they alone could not.[11] According to Rodríguez, experts in sacred law and other exemplary pietists had fulfilled that role in his religious life—as they did in the lives of other ordinary believers.

The defendant revealed relatively little concerning the theological lessons he had learned through his exposure to religious experts. Still, he claimed to have embraced in good faith whatever sacred doctrines these men had presented to him. One may wonder why lessons regarding, say, the "true" structure of divinity (a Holy Trinity or not?) did not strike Rodríguez as utterly superfluous. After all, such questions were far removed from his mundane existence. More specifically, they had no direct bearing on his constant struggle for economic security. Why, then, did the merchant care to learn from his proselytizers?

The answer, I believe, is that scriptural exegesis and theology *as such* were not what made Rodríguez susceptible to conversionist discourse. That pious specialists represented "the truth" to him probably had less to do with the intrinsic intellectual appeal of their claims than with the sheer spiritual power that, in his eyes, these teachers radiated. It is significant that although he was capable of reconstructing a few of his educators' "reasons and persuasions," the defendant preferred to emphasize the men's intellectual *stature*. For example, Rodríguez noted that Abraham ben Israel and the *hakham* Avila were familiar with sacred books and spoke Hebrew, an arcane biblical language. The defendant was especially keen to convey that Francisco Rodríguez was unusually intelligent and wise "in many subjects."[12] It is as though Rodríguez wished to communicate that he had been impressed and intimidated, not by certain ideas in and of themselves, but by his educators' mastery of a type of knowledge that was beyond his own capacities.

The merchant did not characterize his interrogators as impressive or self-possessed (at least not explicitly) yet there is reason to suspect that he "read" them too as legitimate and respectable authorities on religion. It is significant that these functionaries exceeded the requirements of wisdom and persuasiveness that Rodríguez had posited in his description of Jewish proselytizers. In addition to being legal experts, speakers of Latin, and officers of the church and state, the inquisitors counted with the mystique of secrecy that shrouded the Holy Office and was among its most potent weapons of social control.[13] Needless to say, the jurists also possessed the legal capacity to decree serious punishment. Rodríguez probably feared them for that very reason. Quite apart from this, however, it is clear that he was conscious of the inferiority of his intellectual status and prestige relative to theirs, both within the context of Ibero-Christian society as a whole, and within more immediate context of his trial: "Should there be some errors in what I have written [Rodríguez wrote], I beg that this Holy Tribunal pardon them. My God knows that I have taken up the pen with all the affections of my soul in an attempt to get everything right, *despite the fact that I am not a latinist and possess a rough understanding*" (emphasis added).[14]

One of the most telling aspects of Rodríguez's depositions is that he did not satisfy the inquisitors until they pressed him to produce a theologically "correct" confession. This suggests, among other things, that the defendant had not known a priori what testimony would appease them. Was his final, written confession, then, anything more than an attempt at appeasement? More specifically, did Rodríguez write his statement on the validity of Catholic dogma entirely without conviction? Was that statement merely a reflexive reaction to fear and an exercise in bootlicking?

To answer these questions, it is only prudent to remember that religious cynicism and false reverence were nothing new in Rodríguez's Iberian milieu. Various satirists of his time portrayed these attitudes through the fictional medium of the *pícaro* (meanwhile, readers enjoyed these same attitudes vicariously). It strikes me as arbitrary, however, to impute the almost modern, skeptical sensibility of that literary archetype to the likes of Rodríguez. As middling merchants in a nonfictional world, the defendant and most of his fellow renegades were not members of a resentfully hopeless underclass. Neither were they part of the disaffected intelligentsia that created and enjoyed the provocative figure of the *pícaro*. Except for the very poor among them, merchant-renegades swam in the economic mainstream of Iberia, whether legally, semilegally, or illegally. For that reason we must not overstate their social alienation and misunderstand their practical cast of mind as utter cynicism. In this vein, it is noteworthy that in their work even some bitterly critical converso intelligenti, including the polemicist Fernão Alvares Melo and the poet Antonio Enríquez Gómez (a permanent returnee), tended to portray conversos as dutiful subjects of Catholicism who had fallen victim to the Holy Office's abuse of its religious authority. In these authors' view, it was the inquisitors who were religiously hypocritical, not the suspected Judaizers themselves.[15]

To return to Rodríguez, it is true that his written confession is mostly apologetic. But unless we adopt the naive position that he was a mere liar of convenience, his verbal contrition only bolsters the impression that he regarded his interrogators as religiously *authoritative* (not necessarily just or perfectly virtuous) in comparison to himself. To regard them in that way, after all, was to accept the conventional wisdom of his time that religious savants were responsible for explaining God and the cosmos, while the main duty of mere laypersons was to believe in God and to obey His law.[16]

A sense of awe towards exponents of sacred knowledge need not have been the *only* cause of Rodríguez's religious pliancy. We must also take into account his perfectly natural receptiveness to the religious tastes and customs that were predominant in his social milieux.

Like some of his contemporaries, Rodríguez was capable of breaking with religious conventions. He admittedly did so by leading a perilous double life in Seville and in Madrid. In his middle adulthood, however, Rodríguez opted for social and religious conventionality.[17] Within the Jewish environment of greater Bayonne he achieved respectability as a well-known observer of the Law of Moses. By the end of the 1650s he had become such an integral part of the New Jewish mainstream that his home was one of a handful of dwellings in which the converso expatriates of Saint Esprit gathered to pray as a full-fledged congregation. Because it defined him as a "reliable" convert, Rodríguez's public role within the nascent *kehillah* was probably a reason that the stigma of return did not damage his social standing. In any event, crossing the border into Spain was an ordinary occurrence among his fellow refugees. Even the local worthy of Saint Esprit, Diego Rodríguez Cardoso, was a habitual border crosser until the late stages of his mercantile career.

In Zaragoza distress drove Rodríguez toward the safety of conformism once again. There he became part of yet another community of faith by partaking of its highly evocative religious culture. Much of what Rodríguez said he had witnessed, learned, and performed within that culture pertained to the sphere of popular devotion and folklore, including the rites of mass and auricular confession. The defendant conveyed that he had experienced Zaragozan Christianity much as he had lived Judaism in Saint Esprit, namely at a practical, communal, and largely pretheoretical level.[18]

To the extent that "high" theology ever influenced Rodríguez at all, it did so because the Law of Grace and the Law of Moses (as he depicted them) each purported to locate his life—indeed, all human life—within a meaningful and transcendent universal order. That order was concretized in the terrestrial realm by given communities of faith.[19] In the case of crypto-Judaism, the defendant allegedly learned from his initiator, Francisco Rodríguez, that God would only accept the devotion of men who entered into a physically irreversible compact with Him. Once the defendant had been circumcised, Abraham ben Israel reportedly confirmed that notion by assuring the merchant that the path to God was finally clear: After circumcision, Rodríguez could participate as a full member in a community ruled by God himself via a host of commandments.[20] (In the present context it is irrelevant that Ben Israel's understanding of the power of circumcision was inconsistent with rabbinic tradition.)

Later on, while pondering his misfortunes in Zaragoza, Rodríguez became exposed to a culture of public piety whose central motif was the transformation of human suffering into an unworldly power. By participating in that culture, however peripherally, Rodríguez absorbed the implicit message that a worshipper who surrendered to that power basked in its glory and gained its protection. As the cobbler's story hinted, and the barefoot Capuchins had supposedly demonstrated, mental and bodily penance nurtured faith and brought a devotee close to the divine.

The point is that for Rodríguez "the Law of Grace" and "the Law of Moses" did not merely represent clusters of vague, ethereal propositions. Rather, these laws described paths to communion with specific blocs of the faithful, and by extension with the transcendent. To embrace "the law" meant establishing a "right" relationship with a sacred order or, to paraphrase Rodríguez, to embrace and follow the "True Path."[21] What did following such a "path" mean to Rodríguez in light of his personal history? What purpose did establishing an "appropriate" relationship with God serve for him?

To answer these questions fully, it is only sensible to note that Rodríguez had little choice but to become at least nominally incorporated into a Catholic or Jewish community of "correct" belief depending on whether he found himself among Catholics or Jews. Open neutrality and negation were highly dangerous options. Both were subject to severe reproach in Jewish society, more so in the Catholic world of seventeenth-century Iberia. Because he stood trial as a heretic, Rodríguez's final option in favor of Catholic penitence was probably inevitable. Nevertheless, the depth and character of the connection Rodríguez forged with each of the "True Paths" he encountered was always partially within his control. Like any other "renegade," the defendant had the ability to develop and express a particular understanding of his experiences in relation to whatever orthodoxy his circumstances compelled him to adopt.

Apart from his impressions of Francisco Rodríguez and Dr. Avila, we can glean relatively little of the defendant's rationale for adopting the Law of Moses in Seville and in greater Bayonne. Fortunately we know more about his reversion to Catholicism. According to Rodríguez, his final illumination had occurred in Zaragoza, under the shadow of bankruptcy. One may question whether his economic woes had been as dire as he depicted them. Yet, the general validity of the claim that he was experiencing poverty at the time of his incarceration is indisputable, since most of his pertinent allegations were verifiable. For example, the inquisitors could have easily ascertained whether Rodríguez owed rent to his landlady. So too they could have investigated the outcome of at least a few of his commercial transactions. At issue, therefore, is not Rodríguez's basic sincerity or insincerity, but the shape and meaning that he lent to his reconversion as an *internal* spiritual process.

In recounting his final illumination, Rodríguez could have easily provided an ideologically "correct" confession from the beginning. True to form, his examiners deemed his testimony complete only after he had outlined the *doctrinal* basis of his reconversion in writing. I am interested, however, in Rodríguez's earlier, oral confession precisely because it amounted to a spontaneous (or semi-spontaneous) "reading" of his spiritual trajectory quite distinct from abstract theology. Here Rodríguez did not dwell directly on matters of religious doctrine. Instead, he concentrated on a defining feature of his adult life: his commercial career.

In his oral confession, the declarant approached his commercial fortunes as a gauge of his spiritual status and of the appropriateness of his relationship to God. Specifically, Rodríguez explained that he had read the outcomes of his professional activities as empirical evidence of God's judgment of his soul. In so doing the merchant described a profoundly practical understanding of his place in the cosmos. In this understanding, God acted upon the world in direct response to human actions. With the proper illumination, a person could intuit this, and hence perceive the "True Path."

The defendant's interpretation speaks of what anthropologists have described as a "traditional" or "mythological" conception of life. Peter Berger has characterized such a worldview as one in which sacred forces permeate human affairs.[22] For its part, that conception of the world was characteristic of the pre-modern society to which Rodríguez belonged (notwithstanding the cynicism of various literati and other of his disenchanted contemporaries). We have already seen the manifestation of that worldview in the Inquisition's approach to justice as a process whereby the miracle of divine kindness transformed corrupt souls. Rodríguez's oral confession is another expression of magical thinking, in this case applied to the challenge of personal identity formation. Here, Rodríguez depicted God as a direct participant in his personal history who had revealed that certain behavioral choices led to salvation while others led to perdition. More concretely, belief in divine intervention allowed Rodríguez to achieve a sense of the "wrongness" of his social behavior as a self-identified observer of the Law of Moses. That sense lent his commercial failures, his incarceration, and all the distress these occurrences caused him the appearance of ultimate meaning by attributing random events in his life to a supreme logic: Suffering was divinely ordained; it was God's way of pointing the sufferer in the "right" direction. In this way Rodríguez recast his history as a private theodicy.

The defendant did not specify what aspect of God's all-knowing power had revealed to him the meaning of his suffering. Yet, his testimony leaves little doubt that he was speaking of a supernatural force akin to the inquisitors' *misericordia*, inasmuch as he understood his fortunes to be agents of divine *judgment*. That Rodríguez framed his personal crisis in terms of his extreme susceptibility to God's justice is understandable. At the time of his deposition he stood accused of religious crimes as the prisoner of a religious tribunal. It does not require an imaginative leap to see that that tribunal's awesome power vis-à-vis individual defendants like himself lent the Holy Office what must have seemed like a godlike stature, at least from the vantage point of the accused. What more immediate and appropriate metaphor than God's judgment for Rodríguez to articulate his hopes and apprehensions as to the significance of his fate?

There is an even deeper level to consider. Captivity and economic ruin confronted Rodríguez with the fragility of whatever social and economic security he had attained prior to his detention. Perhaps most painfully, Rodríguez's predicament laid bare the fact that his hard-earned membership in a halakhic community had failed to assure his well-being. The eternal compact he had supposedly forged with the God of Israel in Bayonne had come to naught. So too had his pragmatic modus operandi as a trans-border merchant. Rodríguez was now forced to reassess his actions. Looking back, he now acknowledged—albeit implicitly—that geographic, economic, and especially social transience had been constant facts of his life, arguably the central facts. Disaster, then, called into question Rodríguez's notion of his place in the world and made finding a new place an urgent necessity.

It goes without saying that in Rodríguez's confession we do not have a penitent's *unforced* reassessment of his life. But then, as I have already proposed, neither was that testimony merely a bundle of cleverly packaged lies. On the contrary, I believe the confession describes a complex process of self-fashioning accomplished under the severe psychological stress of imprisonment. That process had reached a pivotal stage at the very moment of Rodríguez's detention, namely when his life of traveling came to a brutal halt. To ignore the psychological severity of that moment, I believe, would be to miss a fundamental aspect of the prisoner's experience, and thus to overestimate the degree to which his testimony expressed a deliberate strategy of defense. Of course, Rodríguez may well have been trying to say what he thought might appease his captors. Perhaps he said things he would have regretted under different circumstances. Yet, as I have tried to demonstrate, his interrogators did not dictate the entirety of his confession. Whether or not Rodríguez was trying to achieve a particular result by testifying as he did, it was *he* who determined exactly how to relate that his life had ultimately *made sense*. Furthermore, it was he who determined *how* he would explain his relationship to God.

A clear indication that Rodríguez was not a polished liar is the manner in which he professed a renewed faith in the Law of Grace. Little of what he chose to say in that regard recommended him to the Inquisition. On the one hand, the defendant depicted himself as a kind of *iluminado*, namely as a freethinker who placed his private religious intuition before adherence to the dictates of the Catholic Church. According to him, it had been God, through the medium of events, and not an eloquent priest or an inquisitor through the medium of dogma, who had opened his eyes to the error of his heretical ways.[23] On the other hand, the religious importance Rodríguez ascribed to his economic wellbeing placed him in yet another category of "heretical"— though rather common—thinking about human fate. I am speaking of a fundamentally *materialist* cast of mind.

Given the precarious state of the Habsburgian economy in the decades during which Rodríguez pursued his mercantile career, it is understandable that he should have associated economic security with spiritual merit. In a context of acute scarcity, survival and prosperity must have seemed like divine gifts (who controlled human fortunes if not God?). Well before the period of Spain's economic crisis under Philip IV, however, it was not rare for the Holy Tribunal to hear testimony from ordinary believers to the effect that wealth was a sign of divine favor. In 1568, for example, the defendant Benito de Solera reported that he had once been working in a vineyard when his companions related to him the scriptural admonition that "it is no more possible for the rich to enter heaven than a camel through the eye of a needle." Outraged by this maxim, "[Benito] thought that they meant his father and father-in-law, who are rich, so he replied, 'They can so enter [heaven], and what's more, they're better equipped for it because they've got property. The Gospel wouldn't say such a thing!'"[24] Years earlier, a converso allegedly declared in a more acidic vein, "Acquiring is everything, there is no paradise but property."[25]

The case of Rodríguez presents a similarly pragmatic understanding of the nature of salvation. For our defendant poverty was a mark of divine *disfavor*. In other words, spiritual failures were apprehensible precisely because they manifested themselves in bad fortune *here and now*, irrespective of what would happen in the hereafter. Conversely, being sure of one's future salvation meant feeling certain of the rightness of one's way in the present. Knowing where one stood in relation to the "True Path" offered consolation for a life of struggle precisely because it clarified one's place in the world *today*. This was not a skeptical or a "careerist" viewpoint; it was a deeply religious, if unorthodox one.

Rodríguez and the Phenomenon of Reconversion

Various cultural anthropologists have posited that religion is a basic means by which human beings attempt to explain and hence psychologically withstand the vicissitudes of life. Whether Rodríguez's case supports that thesis is for the reader to decide. In this section my question is a narrower, historical one: Does the case of Antonio Rodríguez de Amézquita shed light on the phenomenon of religious conversion and reconversion among his fellow renegades? One way to answer this question is to examine one crucial way in which the defendant's spiritual biography was typical of the *discursos* of other "Portuguese" merchants.

Perhaps the most significant resemblance between Rodríguez's *discurso* and that of other *mercaderes* concerns the manner of his conversion to and limited observance of crypto-Judaism. The defendant's tale of Judaic indoctrination along the roads of Castile is reminiscent, for example, of the testimony of Diego Rodríguez de Leon, another son of Portuguese immigrants to Spain.

In 1661, Rodríguez de Leon told his interrogators that six years earlier he had been traveling from Madrid to Portugal to sell linens. While crossing the Leonese region of Medina de Rioseco, he met Cristobal de Paz, another "Portuguese" salesman. "As they were alone" on their way to a local village, Paz allegedly convinced his fellow "with much efficacy and so truthfully" (*con mucha eficacia y tan de veras*) to keep the Law "that God had given to Moses and to the Hebrew people."[26] Among Paz's alleged *persuasiones* was that the Virgin Mary and the saints were unworthy of belief as there was only one almighty God (fol. 67r).

Two years later the defendant allegedly had a similar roadside encounter with a second "Portuguese" Judaizer, possibly a returnee. The latter too displayed a considerable knowledge of the Law of Moses. For instance, the traveler knew the Hebrew names of Jewish holidays such as "Rosaná" (Rosh ha-Shanah). Seeing that Rodríguez de Leon was himself "Portuguese," the traveler allegedly asked him whether he believed in the Law of Grace. Not wishing to expose himself, Rodríguez answered (or so he claimed) that he was a faithful Catholic. To this his companion responded that "he should not believe in the Virgin Mary, because she was [merely] an image that any sculptor or painter could make" (fol. 69v).

Much like Rodríguez de Amézquita, Rodríguez de Leon said he had observed the Law of Moses primarily by fasting. In that sense at least, the testimony of both men hinted that their crypto-Judaism was an interiorist religion of negation rather than one of affirmation. Furthermore, both men noted the isolation they had endured because of their adopted faith. Though he incriminated other supposed heretics, Rodríguez de Leon said that in six years he had fasted entirely alone, "due to the fact he had been traveling from place to place earning his living, without having a fixed residence, and because of the secrecy to which [his initiator] had sworn him" (fol. 68r). The declarant also noted that he had refrained from walking on the Sabbath even when he had been on the road. Nonetheless, he continued, his dire material circumstances had prevented him from observing other Mosaic proscriptions. For instance, "when he had nothing else to eat besides *tocino*, rabbit, and hare, he ate them."[27] As we have seen, Rodríguez de Amézquita's experience was very similar: Prior to his wife's conversion to the Law of Moses, he ate any forbidden food she prepared for him.

As for Rodríguez de Amézquita's eventual admission of guilt and embrace of the Catholic faith: it too resembles the confessions of his fellow returnees. In the previous chapter I have cited a few of these confessions (see page 138, above). Each of the defendants in question echoes three of Rodríguez's most important claims: First, the defendants convey that they had examined their respective fates and those of fellow Jews; second, that in light of those fates they had concluded that their allegiance to Judaism had been an error; third, that their incarceration was a main consequence of that error. Clearly Rodríguez was not alone in articulating an essentially pragmatic view of his spiritual trajectory.[28] True, he was merely one returnee among several. There is no way to demonstrate conclusively that his motivations and self-understanding matched those of other imprisoned returnees. Yet, if Rodríguez was not archetypical, his testimony does serve as cautionary evidence against a facile historiographical approach that would treat renegades as either perfectly transparent or extremely cunning. More importantly, I believe, the defendant's words speak of the fact that it was possible for renegades to interpret and recount their lives in terms that made sense to *them*, given their dire circumstances, rather than to the inquisitors alone, or, for that matter, to scholars interested in measuring how "Jewish" or "Christian" conversos really were. Rodríguez's case further suggests that a defendant's capability to define himself in profoundly religious terms obtained despite his predisposition to bow to normative religious authority, to yield to social pressure, and to view religion itself just as his proselytizers and adjudicators did (or purported to do), namely through a mythological lens. The phenomenon of "renegades," thus, is at once one of subjugation to power and of self-definition under that power's long shadow.

Chapter 6

Conclusion: On the Historical Significance of Renegades' Self-Subjugation

The present study has been an attempt to describe and interpret the behavior of ordinary conversos who confronted a host of onerous circumstances during the late sixteenth and seventeenth centuries. To reiterate, these conditions included the conversos' own cultural liminality, their geographical transience, and their dispersion. In addition to these realities, the conversos in question had to contend with the recrudescence of inquisitorial persecution in Spain after the annexation and subsequent secession of Portugal. When they entered the growing Sephardi Diaspora, conversos faced yet another set of pressures. There they encountered a climate of dogmatic conformism (however uneven in reality) that eventually transformed makeshift colonies of peninsular refugees into disciplined, permanent *kehillot*. Finally and most significantly, these conversos had to negotiate a dangerous and unsteady economic environment. Ironically, the Iberian system of trade offered them abundant opportunities despite (or perhaps because of) Spain's chronic economic instability. Together, these conditions contributed to the formation of a set of behavioral patterns I have called "renegade behavior."

From afar, exile, return, and especially reconversion to Catholicism—the hallmarks of renegade behavior—may appear to be little more than instances of opportunism and dissimulation. Deceit, of course, is a strategy that several writers of historical surveys of "marranism" have attributed to conversos, often without distinguishing sufficiently between the first generations of New Christians and their more Christianized descendants.[1] By contrast, I have argued that the movement of individual conversos from one purportedly impermeable community of faith to another and back was not a stratagem, but an earnest choice born of a specific historical context and guided by a pragmatic religious mentality firmly rooted in that context.

In light of relatively credible instances of reluctant Christianization and crypto-Judaism among New Christians, the position is hardly debatable that a number of first- and second-generation conversos were "potential Jews."

This, in fact, is how one of the most illustrious students of crypto-Judaism has characterized them.[2] The phenomena of recidivism that I have surveyed here, however, are evidence that by the late sixteenth century several conversos were as much potential Christians, so to speak, as they were potential Jews. In effect, one of the primary purposes of the compulsory religious socialization to which renegades were frequently subjected was to suppress the ambiguity implicit in that dual potentiality.

Because neither orthodox Catholicism nor rabbinic Judaism condoned cultural "in-between-ness," the social stigma that renegades bore by virtue of being border crossers was severe. Yet even in an age of religious intolerance that saw the "confessionalization" of vast regions of western and central Europe, "renegades" were often able to accommodate to two mutually exclusive religious communities despite inspiring suspicion as putative dissidents. Notwithstanding the efforts of clerical and political elites to create disciplined communities of "pure" belief, "renegades" actually confounded the notion characteristic of medieval and early modern societies of an integral social identity.[3]

To be sure, renegades remained socially liminal only as long as they avoided close scrutiny. Constant traveling allowed a number of them to maintain a safe distance (and hence independence) from their more orthodox contemporaries. At the moment of scrutiny, however, intense pressures forced renegades to make a wrenching choice between a Jewish and a Catholic identification. That choice implied a second one between total social isolation and incapacitation on one hand, and the possibility of survival and prosperity within a community of faith on the other. In the case of inquisitorial trials the results were easily predictable: The defendants would conform to Tridentine Catholicism and thus become incorporated into the flock of (presumably) right-thinking Christians. If this outcome did not always obtain in southwestern France vis-à-vis rabbinic Judaism, it was because before the end of the seventeenth century the "Portuguese" enclaves of the Pyrénées-Atlantiques were too vitally connected to the peninsular economy and to the peninsular cultures to achieve a total insulation from Ibero-Christendom. In any case, all incipient *kehillot* lacked an institutional apparatus of control as sophisticated as the Inquisition.

Of course, by converting to Judaism and reconverting to Catholicism the "renegades" ultimately succumbed to institutional and/or corporate forces that were stronger than themselves. Yet the process of acculturation to given communities of faith did not entail a mechanical or merely superficial adoption of absolutist models of belief and comportment on the part of the renegades. In the gap between ideal conformity and stereotypical heresy survived the cultural border crossers' native ability to interpret their experiences as logical, purposeful, and morally comprehensible stories.

Arguably, the more profound a renegade's acculturation, the more it required that he or she construct a rationale to support it. In the fourth chapter, I proposed that unless one were able to prove that most of the declarants in question were callous fabricators, it is reasonable to maintain that the task of self-transformation had to make *some* sense to each of them in light of their respective experiences. Otherwise these dissidents' predicaments and their suffering would have seemed utterly meaningless to them. Evidently the anomie of not belonging to a religiously delineated community was too awful for some renegades to contemplate. Rather than merely simulating conformity, then, renegades appear to have at least tried to rationalize their acculturation. They accomplished this chiefly by drawing a momentous inference from their realization that nonconformity made them extremely susceptible to dishonor as well as complete social isolation. Simply put, the renegades inferred that nonconformity was immoral. As one declarant put it, "seeing that the Holy Office punishes those who observe the Law of Moses, [I] recognized that [I] had been wrong, and left it."[4]

At first glance, this manner of self-justification, which I have called "self-subjugation," appears too convenient to be creditable. However, the very fact that renegades articulated such a seemingly flimsy rationale at all prohibits our careless dismissal of that rationale as a useful "lie" or an absurdity. True, it is impossible to ascertain the ultimate motivations of *every* renegade who testified before inquisitorial authorities. It is also true that conformity was a very convenient means to achieve social inclusion. From these facts it does not necessarily follow, however, that renegades were "lying" when they spoke of their decisions to conform.

I have suggested that even if we deem it more "forced" than "voluntary," the mental contortion whereby "renegades" subjugated themselves to a way of life was genuine inasmuch as that contortion was part and parcel of their struggle to understand their lives by creating emotionally satisfying and useful narratives out of various memories and apprehensions. Such narratives expressed the renegades' realistic acceptance of their possibilities and limitations given their circumstances. In this regard it is crucial to remember that neither of the dominant ideologies with which renegades came in contact—normative Judaism and counter-reformist Catholicism—tolerated religious ambiguity, let alone the duality implicit in being bicultural. By subjugating themselves to both ideologies as conditions required, renegades not only yielded to intolerance, but they explained away the utter relativity of religious "Truth." If a given abstract belief (or set of beliefs) will save me from punishment and social isolation *now*, the declarants seemed to be saying, that belief *must* be the Truth. Moreover (the rationale continued) if so many respectable people in my milieu uphold that Truth, who am I to say that that Truth is not valid? As one defendant observed, "[I] became persuaded that [the Law of Moses] was good, *because* [I] saw that so many people of good habits followed it" (emphasis added).[5] Another dissident opined, along the same lines, "considering that Catholics are so many . . . [I concluded that] it was not possible that so many were mistaken, and that Jews, being so few, could be the ones who were correct."[6]

Understood as exercises in pragmatic acculturation, the testimonies of imprisoned renegades do not appear to be the product of ironic skepticism, but rather of realistic adaptation. An ironic outlook may well describe the "disenchanted" condition of modernity. In light of the present study, it is far from clear that such an outlook characterized the traditional religious mentality of ordinary Iberian merchants of the seventeenth century. By the same token, the study suggests that the question "how Jewish or Catholic were the conversos?"—a question so often posed by students of crypto-Judaism—imposes an erroneous interpretive framework upon the phenomenon of renegade behavior. By positing absolute categories of identity, the query merely summons inflexible and unrealistic models of belief and behavior similar to those with which various keepers of the faith, from Bayonnaise *vecinos* to Spanish inquisitors, assailed the renegades. Moreover, the question treats such models rather than actual human behavior as the chief measure of historical reality. It is worth repeating that the dissidents I have discussed here were not "Jewish" and were not "Christian" in any ideal sense; nor did they match stereotypes of religious treachery. "Renegades" were quite ordinary people who found ways to survive and mold their self-concept(s) to those of dominant elites as much as possible, while simultaneously experiencing the complexities and ambiguities of "real life" (to use a very apt colloquialism). In this, I suspect, renegades were like the rest of their Christian and Jewish contemporaries.

At base, self-subjugation afforded "renegades" a modicum of safety— the safety of belonging to a cohesive, normatively structured community within which spiritual indeterminacy was officially impossible. Such safety implied the possibility of survival and prosperity—psychic, social, and material. In religious terms, being safe meant being certain of "salvation." Conversely, renegades' search for salvation was fundamentally a quest for social and material security in the present. Hence my contention that dissidents such as Antonio Rodríguez de Amézquita exhibited a religious cast of mind that was deeply pragmatic without being cynical, and at once this-worldly *and* lofty in its aspirations.

When framing their religious conversions as matters of salvation, renegades invested these changes with transcendental meaning. Coming to terms with communal Judaism and hegemonic Christianity thus acquired for the dissidents an other-worldly significance beyond the essentially mundane scope of their own ideological and social acclimatization. The will to spiritualize what was an essentially social experience accorded fully with a mythological worldview that guided much (if not all) religious ideation in early modern Europe.

To the extent that the renegades harnessed (and distorted) official religion to interpret their individual situations, they were not mere subjects, but actors in a larger drama of social disciplining and confessional indoctrination.[7] Does that mean that converso renegades were wholly autonomous creators of their religious lives? Clearly not. Much of the evidence I have presented in this study supports the conclusion of the cultural anthropologist Benjamin Beit-Hallahmi (and others) that religious identity is the product of social learning, not conscious choice.[8]

As members of a culturally liminal group, renegades were nearer to and hence probably more conscious of the possibility of religious transformation than most of their Old Christian and Jewish contemporaries, who had been born into their respective faiths. At the same time, the renegades' encounters with secret Judaizers in the Iberian Peninsula, with Jews and New Jews in the Sephardi Diaspora, and with inquisitors upon return to Iberia inaugurated distinct processes of social education and adaptation, not of intellectual persuasion as if in a mental vacuum. To be sure, many of the learners in question (especially habitual returnees) were able to navigate the gray areas that existed between faith communities that cast themselves in drastic opposition to each other. In so doing, these putative dissidents merely fulfilled whatever social and economic roles their difficult circumstances allowed or even encouraged them to fulfill—for example, the roles of smuggler, legitimate importer-exporter, commercial agent, informer, and so on. Crucially, the incidence of self-subjugation among renegades reveals that even these habitual risk takers ultimately had little choice but to internalize the authoritarian notion, rather common in their time, that a free conscience is immoral and dangerous. The frequent recourse to self-subjugation may even indicate that freedom of conscience was scarcely tenable or even imaginable for the rene-

gades given the religious climate of their day (as distinct from the socioeconomic realities of their day).

My primary conclusion with regard to the historical environment that
gave rise to renegade behavior is that renegades' unsanctioned crossing of
territorial and cultural boundaries reflected the actual permeability and flu-
idity of those boundaries as they existed during Spain's era of crisis. In the
context of seventeenth-century Iberia and Sephardi France, border crossing
was highly "transgressive," not because it defied cultural or spatial demarca-
tions that were actually rigid, but because such behavior violated imaginary
models of social and religious conformity. The strict rabbis, zealous New
Jews, rabid Iberian xenophobes, and dutiful inquisitors who upheld these
models all complained of rampant greed and religious betrayal among the
border crossers. The fact remained that as economic actors and as products
of Iberian and Judaic cultures, these so-called "renegades" were an integral
part of peninsular society *as well as* the Sephardi Diaspora. The paradox, as I
have noted repeatedly, is that returnees participated in both spheres but were
full members of neither.

If putative "deviants" such as "renegade" conversos could adopt the ideologies of their catechizers and persecutors, either momentarily or permanently, it stands to reason that the socioreligious identities of these dissidents
were highly contingent. This study shows that the behavior of renegades was
a response to a historical context, more specifically to conditions of extreme
stress. Such behavior was unique in that it contained an element of feasibil-
ity. Renegades were functionally bicultural, hence they could conceive of and
achieve numerous escapes (and returns) to "the other side." Ordinary
Catholics and Sephardi Jews of the Early Modern Period seldom did the
same, perhaps because their identities were less ambiguous and therefore less
flexible than those of conversos. For "mainstream" Jews and Catholics social
identity was not at issue, at least not to the degree that it always was for conversos. For those in the mainstream, identification with Judaism or Catholic
Christianity was the natural consequence of birth and participation in an integrated and relatively insular world of religious laws and customs. Is this to
say that renegades were wholly exceptional? Does the study of such individuals illuminate merely their own marginality? Were the patterns of renegades' identity-orientation and reorientation isolated phenomena lacking
any structural or historical connection to more common behaviors? If so,
what is the use of studying such outlandish behavior as return and reconversion?

I cannot answer these questions in depth here, but I can underline two principal factors that warn against treating renegades and renegade behavior as "exotic." First, as I have shown, the phenomenon of repeated cultural and territorial border crossing among conversos was in all likelihood much more common than scholars have acknowledged; thus the notion that renegades were utterly marginal is highly questionable. Furthermore, we have seen that a relationship of economic symbiosis developed between the communities of the western Sephardi Diaspora and Ibero-Catholic society; this despite the mutual repulsion that characterized their respective official stances. Both sets of communities maintained that relationship largely through the agency of converso returnees. Thus, for all the ire that the orthodox directed toward them, renegades played central, mediating roles within both the Sephardi and the Ibero-Catholic realms.

Second, renegades did not exist in a behavioral vacuum. They were part of broader communities in which religious recidivism stood out as an egregious but certainly not the only possible form of transgression. In Spain and Portugal during the sixteenth and seventeenth centuries conversos who had been accused of crypto-Judaism formed a small fraction of all inquisitorial defendants. Most of the latter were minor moral criminals such as bigamists and blasphemers, not heretics.[9] Anecdotal evidence from the Sephardi Diaspora indicates, along the same lines, that returnees and informers were only the most extreme of dissidents. As I observed in the third chapter, ordinary non-conformists in the Jewish metropolis of Amsterdam included individuals who did not participate in Jewish religious life even though they retained an identification with the Judeo-Portuguese "Nation."[10]

My point is that renegades represented only an extreme set of reactions to a given historical environment. These reactions, I suspect, fit as a kind of pole within a larger range of fundamentally similar responses to the challenges of social and religious acculturation. To pursue this point at length would be to go beyond the intended scope of this study. Suffice it to say that one way to approach renegade behavior is to view it as an exaggerated version of a more quotidian phenomenon of religious and social education— neither heroic nor treacherous. We must remember that renegades were only "renegades" to one religious community insofar as they became (or were thought to become) reconciled to another community. In other words, there always existed a curious dialogue between "conformity" and "dissidence," and hence between the opposing polities that defined these terms.

If we approach "conformity" and "dissidence" historically as human constructions, it becomes clear that neither of the two religious paths converso renegades encountered offered them ultimate philosophical or spiritual

"Truth." Rather, these paths offered "truths" that gave ideological expression to two distinct communities and to those communities' respective ways of life. The renegades' accommodation to the communities amounted to little besides rationalizations of subjective truths as absolute Truth. Only after willing their own belief or assenting to it could the renegades fully appropriate the names "Christian" and "Jew."

Appendix

The two tables below are arranged chronologically. They are by no means comprehensive. For example, in several instances the records surveyed do not offer much information beyond the names of alleged returnees. In several other cases it is not entirely clear whether the subjects in question returned to Spain and/or Portugal repeatedly or permanently. In still other cases the subjects were at first chronic returnees, yet the records indicate (or at least hint) that these subjects later became permanently repatriated. Despite these lingering uncertainties, I believe the information below offers a reliable impression of the general scope of the phenomenon of return, as well as bases for a preliminary reconstruction of the collective sociological profile of the returnees.

TABLE A

Chronic Returnees Named in Inquisitorial Dossiers	Documentary Source(s) Name of the chief defendant tribunal, dossier (file), year	Occupation (if provided)	Precise or Relative age (if provided)
1. Pedro Fernández*	Francisco Díaz Méndez Toledo, 142 (3), 1609–10	—	—
2. Fernán Franco*	Francisco Díaz Méndez Toledo, 142 (3), 1609–10	wool merchant	—
3. Manuel Méndez*	Francisco Díaz Méndez Toledo, 142 (3), 1609–10	—	—
4. Diogo Núñez*	Luis Vas Pimentel Lisbon, 2305, 1612	none (penniless)	26
5. Nuno da Oliveira	Luis Vas Pimentel Lisbon, 2305, 1612	none (aspiring soldier)	"youth"
6. Luis Vas Pimentel	Luis Vas Pimentel Lisbon, 2305, 1612	none	22
7. Luis Lopes	Manuel Méndez Cardoso Toledo, 166 (6), 1622–25	lapidary	a "youth"

8. Manuel Méndez Cardoso	Manuel Méndez Cardoso Toledo, 166 (6), 1622–25	royal envoy, contractor	50
9. Bartholomeu Nunez	Manuel Méndez Cardoso Toledo, 166 (6), 1622–25	lapidary	23
10. Diego y Pedro Hurtado de la Vega†	Elissa Eliano et al. Toledo, 144 (1), 1629	voluntary informer	31
11. Antonio de Acosta de Paz	Pedro Enríquez Fastio Toledo, 145 (9), 1634 Juan Rodríguez Faro Toledo, 180 (6), 1635–50	merchant, voluntary informer	40
12. Manuel de Arrocha*	Pedro Enríquez Fastio Toledo, 145 (9), 1634	—	an "unmarried youth"
13. Pierre de Arrocha*	Pedro Enríquez Fastio Toledo, 145 (9), 1634	—	an "unmarried youth"
14. Andres Díaz Lima*	Pedro Enríquez Fastio Toledo, 145 (9), 1634	merchant	—
15. Pedro Enríquez Fastio	Pedro Enríquez Fastio Toledo, 145 (9), 1634	merchant	—
16. Jaime Luis*	Pedro Enríquez Fastio Toledo, 145 (9), 1634	merchant	—
17. Francisco Serrano	Pedro Enríquez Fastio Toledo, 145 (9), 1634 Juan Rodríguez Faro Toledo, 180 (6), 1635–50	fabrics merchant, *familiar*	an "unmarried youth"
18. Francisco Baez Isidro*	Juan Rodríguez Faro Toledo, 180 (6), 1635–50	fabrics merchant	—
19. Diego Baz Faro*	Juan Rodríguez Faro Toledo, 180 (6), 1635–50	—	—
20. Juan Rodríguez Faro	Juan Rodríguez Faro Toledo, 180 (6), 1635–50	wholesaler	—
21. Nuño Pereira*	Juan Rodríguez Faro Toledo, 180 (6), 1635–50	—	40
22. Felipe Díaz Gutiérrez	Felipe Díaz Gutiérrez Toledo, 142 (2), 1636	businessman	40
23. Juan de Oporto*	Felipe Díaz Gutiérrez Toledo, 142 (2), 1636	—	—
24. Diego T[h]omás	Felipe Díaz Gutiérrez Toledo, 142 (2), 1636	—	—
25. Antonio Fernández de Acosta	Alvaro Gómez Medina Toledo, 151 (1), 1636–45	merchant	26
26. Alvaro Gómez Medina	Alvaro Gómez Medina Toledo, 151 (1), 1636–45	merchant	55
27. Luis Alvarez de Silva*	Isabel de Silva Toledo, 184 (13), 1636–39	broker	(deceased)

28. Pantaleón de Silva*	Isabel de Silva Toledo, 184 (13), 1636–39	—	40
29. Antonio Rodrigues	Antonio Rodrigues et al. Lisboa, 16302, 1637	—	35
30. Don Antonio Martínez	Diego Rodríguez Cardoso Toledo, 177 (11), 1641–78	various mercantile trades	23
31. Pedro Enríquez Peteño	Diego Rodríguez Cardoso Toledo, 177 (11), 1641–78	tax commissioner	23
32. Simon Enrique Rodríguez	Diego Rodríguez Cardoso Toledo, 177 (11), 1641–78	itinerant salesman	20
33. Antonio Enríquez	Diego Rodríguez Cardoso Toledo, 177 (11), 1641–78	merchant	39
34 Manuel Fernández Rodríguez† (a.k.a. Rodríguez Sampayo)	Diego Rodríguez Cardoso Toledo, 177 (11), 1641–78	buyer-seller	50
35. Jorxe de Figueroa	Diego Rodríguez Cardoso Toledo, 177 (11), 1641–78	salesman	30
36. Domingo Gutiérrez/ Rodríguez*	Diego Rodríguez Cardoso Toledo, 177 (11), 1641–78	merchant (?)	—
37. Fernando Gómez Días	Diego Rodríguez Cardoso Toledo, 177 (11), 1641–78	administrator of royal rents	44
38. Juan López Arias	Diego Rodríguez Cardoso Toledo, 177 (11), 1641–78	merchant	50
39. Manuel Machuca	Mateo Méndez de Leon et al. Toledo, 166 (8), 1664	merchant (?)	—
40 Rafael Méndez	Diego Rodríguez Cardoso Toledo, 177 (11), 1641–78	bauble seller	32
41. Simon Núñez Nieto	Diego Rodríguez Cardoso Toledo, 177 (11), 1641–78	merchant	53–55
42. Diego Núñez Silva	Diego Rodríguez Cardoso Toledo, 177 (11), 1641–78	—	—
43. Manuel Rodrigues Franco	Diego Rodríguez Cardoso Toledo, 177 (11), 1641–78	administrator of tobacco stores	32
44. Jorge Rodríguez Peteño*	Diego Rodríguez Cardoso Toledo, 177 (11), 1641–78	merchant (?)	—
45. Diego Rodríguez Pinnero	Diego Rodríguez Cardoso Toledo, 177 (11), 1641–78	merchant	37
46. Joseph Sánchez	Diego Rodríguez Cardoso Toledo, 177 (11), 1641–78	distiller of liquor	—
47. Rafael de Silva	Diego Rodríguez Cardoso Toledo, 177 (11), 1641–78	merchant	—
48. Manuel Suárez	Diego Rodríguez Cardoso Toledo, 177 (11), 1641–78	*arrendador*	32

49. Luis Trevino	Diego Rodríguez Cardoso Toledo, 177 (11), 1641–78	seller of jewelry, owner of market stall	23
50. Francisco Rodríguez Ydaña	Diego Rodríguez Cardoso Toledo, 177 (11), 1641–78	merchant	27
51. Luis de Acosta*	Balthasar Rodríguez Cardoso Toledo, 177 (2), 1650–53	—	—
52. Manuel de Acosta*	Balthasar Rodríguez Cardoson Toledo, 177 (2), 1650–53	—	—
53. Luis Alvarez*	Balthasar Rodríguez Cardoso Toledo, 177 (2), 1650–53	—	—
54. Baltasar Arias*	Balthasar Rodríguez Cardoso Toledo, 177 (2), 1650–53	—	—
55. Juan Báez*	Balthasar Rodríguez Cardoso Toledo, 177 (2), 1650–53	—	—
56. Francisco Cardoso Ortiz, ‡a.k.a. Abraham Cardoso	Balthasar Rodríguez Cardoso Toledo, 177 (2), 1650–53	merchant, sailor translator, spy	26
57. Andrés Dias de Lima*	Balthasar Rodríguez Cardoso Toledo, 177 (2), 1650–53	—	—
58. "El Frade"***	Balthasar Rodríguez Cardoso Toledo, 177 (2), 1650–53	merchant (?)	—
59. Gaspar Enríquez*	Balthasar Rodríguez Cardoso Toledo, 177 (2), 1650–53	merchant	—
60. Henrique Fernández*	Balthasar Rodríguez Cardoso Toledo, 177 (2), 1650–53	rent collector at a port	34
61. Simon López Manuel*	Balthasar Rodríguez Cardoso Toledo, 177 (2), 1650–53	—	—
62. Jorge Méndez*	Balthasar Rodríguez Cardoso Toledo, 177 (2), 1650–53	merchant	—
63. Manuel de Morais*	Balthasar Rodríguez Cardoso Toledo, 177 (2), 1650–53	merchant (?)	—

64. Rodrigo de Morales*	Balthasar Rodríguez Cardoso Toledo, 177 (2), 1650–53	merchant (?)	—
65. Antonio Pacheco*	Balthasar Rodríguez Cardoso Toledo, 177 (2), 1650–53	smuggler of precious metals	—
66. Alonso de Paredes	Balthasar Rodríguez Cardoso Toledo, 177 (2), 1650–53	—	—
67. Alvaro de Payba*§	Balthasar Rodríguez Cardoso Toledo, 177 (2), 1650–53	merchant (?)	—
68. Diego Peixote*	Balthasar Rodríguez Cardoso Toledo, 177 (2), 1650–53	merchant (?)	—
69. Cristobal Rodríguez de Acosta*	Balthasar Rodríguez Cardoso Toledo, 177 (2), 1650–53	merchant, mule handler (?)	—
70. Francisco Vaes de Acosta	Balthasar Rodríguez Cardoso Toledo, 177 (2), 1650–53	—	—
71 Francisco de Aguilar‡	Francisco de Aguilar Toledo, 131 (10), 1652, 1654	merchant/ smuggler	22
72. Simon Baez de Olivero*	Francisco de Aguilar Toledo, 131 (10), 1652, 1654	merchant	—
73. Rafael Díaz de Fras(?)*	Francisco de Aguilar Toledo, 131 (10), 1652, 1654	merchant	—
74. Juan de Fonseca*	Francisco de Aguilar Toledo, 131 (10), 1652, 1654	smuggler	—
75. Francisco Gómez de Acosta*	Francisco de Aguilar Toledo, 131 (10), 1652, 1654	merchant	—
76. Luis López†	Francisco de Aguilar Toledo, 131 (10), 1652, 1654	merchant	50
77. Pedro López de Olivera†	Francisco de Aguilar Toledo, 131 (10), 1652, 1654	merchant/ courier	40
78. Alvaro Méndez†	Francisco de Aguilar Toledo, 131 (10), 1652, 1654	merchant	25
79. Madalena Méndez*	Francisco de Aguilar Toledo, 131 (10), 1652, 1654	—	—
80. Miguel Méndez*	Francisco de Aguilar Toledo, 131 (10), 1652, 1654	merchant	—
81. Diego Méndez Chávez*	Francisco de Aguilar Toledo, 131 (10), 1652, 1654	merchant	—
82. Enrique de Paz*	Francisco de Aguilar Toledo, 131 (10), 1652, 1654	merchant	—

83. Gaspar Petiño*	Francisco de Aguilar Toledo, 131 (10), 1652, 1654	merchant	—
84. Felipe Rodrigues Cardoso*	Francisco de Aguilar Toledo, 131 (10), 1652, 1654	merchant	—
85. Jorge Rodrigues Pardo*	Francisco de Aguilar Toledo, 131 (10), 1652, 1654	merchant	—
86. Diego Rodrigues Piñero*	Francisco de Aguilar Toledo, 131 (10), 1652, 1654	merchant	—
87. Joseph Rodríguez*	Francisco de Aguilar Toledo, 131 (10), 1652, 1654	merchant	—
88. Francisco Fernández*	Francisco Lopes Capadocia Toledo, 161 (5), 1653–55	merchant(?)	—
89. Francisco López Capadocia‡	Francisco Lopes Capadocia Toledo, 161 (5), 1653–55	merchant	22
90. Juan Suarez de Azebedo	Francisco Méndez-Brito Toledo, 142 (6), 1653–57	—	31
91. Diego de la Peña	Gonzalo Vaez de Paiba Toledo, 136 (5, 6, 7), 1654–57, 1659–60, 1661	merchant(?)	50
92. Francisco Pimentel	Francisco López Pimentel et al. Toledo, 161 (7), 1660	—	—
93. Joseph Garcia de Leon §	Cristobal Méndez Silveira Toledo, 165 (12), 1661–71 Jorge Fernández de Castro Toledo, 147 (1), 1663–65	administrator	44
94. Cristobal de Ayala (a.k.a. David Méndez, "Pastelada")	Cristobal Méndez Silveira Toledo, 165 (12), 1661–71	—	34–36
95 Román Garcia	Cristobal Méndez Silveira Toledo, 165 (12), 1661–71	—	—
96. Cristobal Méndez Silveira	Cristobal Méndez Silveira Toledo, 165 (12), 1661–71	merchant	38
97. Francisco Roldan†	Cristobal Méndez Silveira Toledo, 165 (12), 1661–71	merchant	46
98. Diego Rodríguez de Leon†	Diego Rodríguez de Leon Toledo, 177 (12), 1661–62	baker, smuggler	23
99. Diego Fernández de Castro*	Jorge Fernández de Castro Toledo, 147 (1), 1663–65	merchant	—
100. Fernando de Castro	Jorge Fernández de Castro Toledo, 147 (1), 1663–65	soldier	24
101. Jorge Fernández de Castro‡	Jorge Fernández de Castro Toledo, 147 (1), 1663–65	merchant	32

102. Manuel Gómez	Jorge Fernández de Castro Toledo, 147 (1), 1663–65	(unemployed)	22
103. Manuel de Leon§	Jorge Fernández de Castro Toledo, 147 (1), 1663–65 Mateo Méndez de Leon Toledo, 166 (8), 1664	itinerant businessman	30
104. Diego Nunez Silva§	Jorge Fernández de Castro Toledo, 147 (1), 1663–65	*arrendador*	41
105. Duarte de Olivera*	Jorge Fernández de Castro Toledo, 147 (1), 1663–65	—	—
106. Don Diego de Amézquita*	Francisco Núñez Redondo Toledo, 169 (10), 1663–68	merchant	approx. 40
107. Salvador Cardosso*	Francisco Núñez Redondo Toledo, 169 (10), 1663–68	—	—
108. Antonio del Castillo*	Francisco Núñez Redondo Toledo, 169 (10), 1663–68	merchant	30
109. Don Jorge de Figueroa*	Francisco Núñez Redondo Toledo, 169 (10), 1663–68	merchant	35
110. "Gaspar," brother-in-law of Antonio Hidalgo (see 113, below)*	Francisco Núñez Redondo Toledo, 169 (10), 1663–68	merchant	24
111. Gabriel Gómez*	Francisco Núñez Redondo Toledo, 169 (10), 1663–68	merchant	24
112. Simon Gómez*	Francisco Núñez Redondo Toledo, 169 (10), 1663–68	merchant	30
113. Antonio Hidalgo*	Francisco Núñez Redondo Toledo, 169 (10), 1663–68	merchant	—
114. Domingo Luis*	Francisco Núñez Redondo Toledo, 169 (10), 1663–68	merchant	(deceased)
115. Manuel, "hijo de 'la Velota'"*	Francisco Núñez Redondo Toledo, 169 (10), 1663–68	merchant	24
116. Diego Núñez*	Francisco Núñez Redondo Toledo, 169 (10), 1663–68	merchant	28
117. Francisco Núñez Redondo	Francisco Núñez Redondo Toledo, 169 (10), 1663–68	lessor of mules, road guide, smuggler	58
118. Simon Núñez "El Ganso"*	Francisco Núñez Redondo Toledo, 169 (10), 1663–68	merchant	19
119. Thomas Núñez*	Francisco Núñez Redondo Toledo, 169 (10), 1663–68	merchant	25
120. Antonio López Pacheco*	Francisco Núñez Redondo Toledo, 169 (10), 1663–68	merchant	35
121. Diego de Ribas*	Francisco Núñez Redondo Toledo, 169 (10), 1663–68	merchant	—

122. Antonio Rodríguez "El Alto"*	Francisco Núñez Redondo Toledo, 169 (10), 1663–68	merchant	over 50
123. Juan de Salas†‡	Francisco Núñez Redondo Toledo, 169 (10), 1663–68	smuggler, mule handler	35
124. Joseph de Sampayo*	Francisco Núñez Redondo Toledo, 169 (10), 1663–68	merchant, smuggler	40
125. Manuel Albarez de Castro	Mateo Méndez de Leon et al. Toledo, 166 (8), 1664	merchant	—
126. Diego de Andrada	Mateo Méndez de Leon et al. Toledo, 166 (8), 1664	merchant	—
127. Antonio Carballo	Mateo Méndez de Leon et al. Toledo, 166 (8), 1664 Antonio Carballo, Blanca Pereira Toledo, 138 (10), 1671–74	merchant	(deceased)
128. Antonio Cardoso	Mateo Méndez de Leon et al. Toledo, 166 (8), 1664	merchant	—
129. Jorge de Castro	Mateo Méndez de Leon et al. Toledo, 166 (8), 1664	merchant	—
130. Henrique Gómez	Mateo Méndez de Leon et al. Toledo, 166 (8), 1664	merchant	—
131. Matheo Méndez* (not to be confused with the chief defendant, Mateo Méndez de Leon)	Mateo Méndez de Leon et al. Toledo, 166 (8), 1664	merchant	—
132. Mateo Méndez de Leon	Mateo Méndez de Leon et al. Toledo, 166 (8), 1664	businessman	30
133. Gaspar Rodríguez (?) de Payba	Mateo Méndez de Leon et al. Toledo, 166 (8), 1664	merchant	—
134. Gaspar de Torres Payba	Mateo Méndez de Leon et al. Toledo, 166 (8), 1664	—	—
135. Juan Compra*†	Antonio Rodríguez de Amézquita Toledo 177 (1), 1664–70	merchant	a "youth"

136. Antonio Díaz de Acosta*	Antonio Rodríguez de Amézquita Toledo 177 (1), 1664–70	merchant	—
137. Rafael Gómez de Herrera	Antonio Rodríguez de Amézquita Toledo 177 (1), 1664–70	merchant	42
138. Fernando Henríquez de Vega†	Antonio Rodríguez de Amézquita Toledo 177 (1), 1664–70	merchant	25
139. Diego Luis*	Antonio Rodríguez de Amézquita Toledo 177 (1), 1664–70	merchant	—
140. Antonio Rodríguez de Amézquita	Antonio Rodríguez de Amézquita Toledo 177 (1), 1664–70	merchant	50
141. Diego Rodríguez Piñedo* †	Antonio Rodríguez de Amézquita Toledo 177 (1), 1664–70	—	—
142. Antonio del Monte‡§	Antonio del Monte Toledo 167 (9), 1669–70	—	21
143. Fernando Gil de Espinosa	Fernando Gil de Espinosa Toledo 150 (17), 1669–70	itinerant merchant	22
144. Jorxe de Medina Cardoso	Flora de Salazar Toledo 183 (2), 1674–78	wholesale merchant	48

* The subject was neither a witness nor a defendant in the case.

† The subject's genealogical status ("Old Christian" or "New Christian") is uncertain or unknown. In the former case, circumstantial evidence (such as the subject's close association with New Christian individuals and communities) suggests that he or she was of New Christian origin, or at least partially identified with people of that stock.

‡ The subject was the baptized son of native Iberian conversos who had taken refuge in France (or elsewhere). He spoke Spanish and/or Portuguese as his first language, as did the refugee conversos among whom he lived in the Diaspora. Therefore I consider the subject a returnee for purposes of this study, despite the fact that he was reportedly or admittedly born in France.

§ The record in question suggests that the subject eventually became a permanent returnee.

Table B

Permanent Returnees Named in Inquisitorial Dossiers	Documentary Source(s) Name of the chief defendant tribunal, dossier (file), year	Occupation (if provided)	Precise or Relative Age (if provided)
1. Alvaro Gomes†	Heitor Mendes Bravo Lisbon, 12493, 1618	—	—
2. Heitor Mendes Bravo	Heitor Mendes Bravo Lisbon, 12493, 1618	peddler, bauble seller	26
3. Esteban Ares de Fonseca	Estevão Arẽs Lisbon, 3070, 1621 Francisco Méndez-Brito Toledo, 142 (6), 1653–57	soldier	26
4. Gonzalo Vaez (Baes) de Paiba (Payba)	Gonzalo Váez de Paiba Toledo, 136 (5,6,7), 654–57, 1659–60, 1661	merchant and tax farmer	40
5. Isabel de Silva	Isabel de Silva Toledo, 184 (13), 1636–39	—	70
6. Manuel Gómez Machuca	Diego Rodríguez Cardoso Toledo, 177 (11), 1641–78	—	23
7. João de Aguila	João de Aguila Lisboa, 7938, 1650	—	20
8. Fray Antonio de Villegas†	Balthasar Rodríguez Cardoso Toledo, 177 (2), 1650–53	friar	—
9. Carlos Méndez‡	Don Carlos Méndez Toledo, 165 (11), 1622–23	none	34
10. Gonzalo Correa†	Jorge Fernández de Castro Toledo, 147 (1), 1663–65	soldier	38
11. Doña María de Leon	Jorge Fernández de Castro Toledo, 147 (1), 1663–65	—	26
12. Josepha María (de Pasaña)	Jorge Fernández de Castro Toledo, 147 (1), 1663–65	—	—
13. Manuel Pasaña†	Jorge Fernández de Castro Toledo, 147 (1), 1663–65	former soldier, merchant	36
14. Fernando Albarez/ Alvarez	Gracia Gómez Hurtado Toledo, 152 (6), 1663–65	merchant	64
15. Gracia Gómez Hurtado	Gracia Gómez Hurtado Toledo, 152 (6), 1663–65	—	22

16. Fernando Gómez Tejadillos	Gracia Gómez Hurtado Toledo, 152 (6), 1663–65	—	26
17. Aldonza Cardosa de Velasco†	Aldonza Cardosa de Velasco Toledo, 138 (12), 1668–70	—	21
18. Don Luis Márquez Cardoso	Aldonza Cardosa de Velasco Toledo, 138 (12), 1668–70	administrator of tobacco storehouses	36
19. Francisco Díaz Méndez	Francisco Díaz Méndez Toledo, 142 (3), 1609–10	businessman, aspiring *arrendador*	approx. 42
20. Manuel (Manoel) Rodríguez‡	Pedro Enríquez Fastio Toledo, 145 (9), 1634 Balthasar Rodrígucz Cardoso Toledo, 177 (2), 1650–53	baker	22
21. Manuel de Leon	Mateo Méndez de Leon, et al. Toledo, 166 (8), 1664	itinerant dealer	30
22. The wife of Manuel Rodríguez	Mateo Méndez de Leon et al. Toledo, 166 (8), 1664	—	—
23. Francisco Domingo de Guzmán	Cristobal Méndez Silveira Toledo, 165 (12), 1661	—	—
24. Juan Fernández de Acuña	Antonio Rodríguez de Amézquita Toledo, 177 (1), 1664–70	merchant, owner of tobacco stand	—
25. Dyonisio/Jacob de Aguiar‡	Antonio Rodríguez et al. Lisboa, 16302, 1637	—	28
26. Abraham do Porto/ Fernando Albarez	Antonio Rodríguez et al. Lisboa, 16302, 1637	—	70–80
27. Isabel/Rachel Rodrigues	Antonio Rodríguez et al. Lisboa, 16302, 1637	—	23
28. Isabel/Sarah Rodrigues	Antonio Rodríguez et al. Lisboa, 16302, 1637	—	50
29. João Rodrigues/ Isaac do Porto	Antonio Rodríguez et al. Lisboa, 16302, 1637	—	24
30. Juliana/Esther Rodrigues	Antonio Rodríguez et al. Lisboa, 16302, 1637	—	20

* The subject figured neither as a witness nor as a defendant in the case.

† The subject's genealogical status ("Old Christian" or "New Christian") is uncertain or unknown. In the former case, circumstantial evidence (such as the subject's close association with New Christian individuals and communities) suggests that he or she was of New Christian origin, or at least partially identified with people of that origin.

‡ The subject was the son of native Iberian conversos who took refuge in France or elsewhere. He spoke Spanish and/or Portuguese as his first language, as did the refugee conversos among whom he lived in the Diaspora. Therefore I consider the subject a returnee for purposes of this study, despite the fact that he was reportedly or admittedly born in France (or in Istanbul, in the case of Don Carlos Méndez).

Notes

Chapter 1

1. AHN, Inquisición de Toledo, leg. 165, exp. 12 (1661–71), fols. 2r, 43r–56r, 63v.

2. Historians do not agree as to when the Early Modern Period begins. For my purposes, the period comprises the years 1497–1789. By outlawing Judaism in his kingdom in 1497, the Portuguese monarch completed a process whereby conversos throughout Iberian domains were largely or completely cut off from normative Jewish life. The date of the French Revolution, 1789, can be considered to inaugurate the Modern Period.

3. I will use the term to denote the ethnic identity of formerly Jewish Christians *and their descendants*, including those who became professing Jews (but excluding most of their Jewish descendants, whose place within the Jewish mainstream was clear). This use is consistent with the meaning ascribed to the term in Spain and Portugal to this day. I am aware that, strictly speaking, the word "conversos" may apply to converts from Islam (also called *moriscos*) and their progeny. However, I will use "conversos" and "Judeoconversos" interchangeably. This, again, is in agreement with correct scholarly and historical uses.

4. The rabbinic principle is set forth in Tractate *Sanhedrin* 44:a of the Babylonian Talmud. Simha Assaf has surveyed rabbinical responsa on the subject of conversos in *Be'Oholey Ya'akov* (Jerusalem: Mosad ha-Rav Kuk, 1943), 145–80. A more recent treatment that confirms the absence of unanimity among medieval and early modern rabbinical authorities concerning the status of conversos is Simón Schwartzfuchs, "Le retour des Marranes au judaisme dans la littérature rabbinique," *Xudeus e conversos na historia, actas do Congreso Internacional Ribadavia, 14-17 de outubro de 1991,* ed. Carlos Barros (Santiago de Compostela: La Editorial de la Historia, 1994), 339–47.

5. Even If the Spanish and Portuguese Inquisitions were designed to locate and extinguish *religious* irregularities among conversos, it is also true that the mere hint of Jewish *descent* was enough to raise suspicions of heresy. A number of the conversos tried and condemned by the Iberian Inquisitions do not appear to have had any real knowledge of or conscious personal connection with Judaism. There is even significant evidence that inquisitorial persecution did more to awaken conversos' interest in Judaism than any sense of cultural ancestry. For a terse and stimulating exposition of this view, see H. P. Salomon, Introduction, *Portrait of a New Christian: Fernão Alvares Melo (1569–1632)* (Paris: Fundação Calouste Gulbenkian, Centro Cultural Portugues, 1982) (hereafter cited as *Portrait*). My point is that in the moralistic worldview of the Holy Office, as in Ibero-Christian society at large, all New Christians fell under a blanket presumption of crypto-Judaism. The fact that Old Chris-

tians stained all descendants of converted Jews with the inaccurate appellation *conversos* (converts) or *cristianos nuevos* (New Christians)—not to mention more pejorative names—speaks of the deep sense of alienness that anything purportedly Jewish occasioned among many Spaniards and Portuguese of Christian stock.

6. See Yosef Hayim Yerushalmi, "The Re-education of Marranos in the Seventeenth Century," *The Third Annual Rabbi Louis Feinberg Memorial Lecture in Judaic Studies, March 26, 1980* (Cincinnati: University of Cincinnati, 1980) (hereafter cited as "The Re-education of Marranos"). Yosef Kaplan discusses various aspects of the reeducation enterprise in *Judíos nuevos en Amsterdam: Estudios sobre la historia social e intelectual del judaísmo sefardí en el siglo XVII* (Barcelona: Gedisa, 1996) (hereafter cited as *Judíos nuevos*). On the pro-Jewish polemical output of émigré conversos see the following major works: Id., *From Christianity to Judaism: The Story of Isaac Orobio de Castro*, trans. Raphael Loewe (Oxford: Oxford University Press, 1989) (hereafter cited as *Orobio*); Cecil Roth, "Immanuel Aboab's Proselytization of the Marranos," *Jewish Quarterly Review*, n.s., 23 (1932–33): 121–62 (hereafter cited as "Immanuel Aboab"); and Yosef Hayim Yerushalmi, *From Spanish Court to Italian Ghetto: Isaac Cardoso: A Study in Seventeenth-Century Marranism and Jewish Apologetics* (New York: Columbia University Press, 1971) (hereafter cited as *Cardoso*).

7. Although a causal nexus between converso origin and ideological dissent is not certain, the presence of Judeoconversos among religious dissidents in the Iberian Peninsula and elsewhere is well documented. See for example Marcel Bataillon, *Erasmo y España: Estudios sobre la historia espiritual del siglo XVI*, trans. Antonio Alatorre (Mexico City: Fondo de Cultura Económica, 1950) (hereafter cited as *Erasmo y España*); Elke Selke, "El iluminismo de los conversos y la Inquisición. Cristianismo interior de los Alumbrados: resentimiento y sublimación," *La Inquisición española: Nueva visión, nuevos horizontes*, ed. Joaquín Pérez Villanueva (Mexico City: Siglo XXI, 1980), 617–36.

8. The phenomenon of religious heterodoxy among Judeoconversos appears to have been relatively frequent throughout the early modern Mediterranean basin. Needless to say, contrary to inquisitorial presumptions, not all Judeoconversos who deviated from normative Christianity were crypto-Jews.

9. António José Saraiva, Antonio Domínguez Ortiz, and Julio Caro Baroja have even referred to Judeoconversos—particularly Portuguese conversos—as a distinct socio-economic "class." See Saraiva, *Inquisição e cristãos-novos*, 5th ed. (Lisbon: Editorial Estampa, 1994) (hereafter cited as *Inquisição*); Domínguez Ortiz, *Los judeoconversos en España y América* (Madrid: Ediciones Istmo, 1971) (hereafter cited as *Los judeoconversos*); and Caro Baroja, *Los judíos en la España moderna y contemporánea*, 3rd ed., 3 vols. (Madrid: Ediciones Istmo, 1986) (hereafter cited as *Los judíos*).

10. See Jonathan Israel, *Empires and Enrepots: The Dutch, the Spanish Monarchy, and the Jews, 1585–1713* (London: Hambledon Press, 1990) (hereafter cited as *Empires and Entrepots*); id., *European Jewry in the Age of Mercantilism, 1550–1750* (Oxford: Clarendon Press, 1989), 87–184. See also Daniel Swetschinski, "Kinship and Commerce: The Foundation of Portuguese Jewish Life in Seventeenth-Century Holland," *Studia Rosenthaliana* 12 (1978): 55-87.

11. See for example Domínguez Ortiz, *Los Judeoconversos*, 219–53, or his discussion of Portuguese (Judeoconverso) businessmen in *Los extranjeros en la vida Es-*

pañola durante el siglo XVII y otros artículos (Sevilla: Diputación de Sevilla, 1996), 23–36, 89–102 (hereafter cited as *Los extranjeros*).

12. Early examples of these articles include David Kaufman, "Jewish Informers in the Middle Ages," *Jewish Quarterly Review* 7 (1895–96): 217–38; Francisco de Bofarull, "Los judíos malsines," *Boletín de la Real Academia de buenas letras de Barcelona* 11.41 (1911): 207–16. More recent work includes Elena Lourie, "Mafiosi and Malsines: Violence, Fear, and Faction in the Jewish Aljamas of Valencia in the Fourteenth Century," *Crusade and Colonisation: Muslims, Christians and Jews in Medieval Aragon* (Hampshire: Variorum, 1990), 69–102; Asunción Blasco Martínez, "Los malsines del reino de Aragón: Una aproximación," *Proceedings of the Eleventh World Congress of Jewish Studies, Jerusalem, June 22–29, 1993* (Jerusalem: World Union of Jewish Studies, 1994), 83–90.

13. However, Caro Baroja, *Los judíos,* includes brief chapters on *malsines* (converso informers) and other socially "maladapted" conversos. Yosef Kaplan has contributed what are, to my knowledge, the only articles that concentrate on the phenomenon of conversos' return to the Iberian Peninsula. Id.,"The Travels of Portuguese Jews from Amsterdam to the 'Lands of Idolatry' (1644–1724)," *Jews and Conversos: Studies in Society and the Inquisition,* ed. Yosef Kaplan (Jerusalem: Magnes Press, 1981), 197–224 (hereafter cited as "The Travels"), and id., "The Struggle Against Travelers to Spain and Portugal in the Western Sephardi Diaspora" (in Hebrew), *Zion* 64,1 (1999): 65–100 (hereafter cited as "The Struggle").

14. See my discussion of existing historiography on these questions, below.

15. The highly atypical cases of converso intellectuals such as Isaac Cardoso, Menasseh ben Israel, Uriel da Costa, and Benedict (Baruch) Spinoza (a Jewish son of conversos) are the exceptions that demonstrate this rule.

16 To be sure, it is only natural (and prudent) that investigators who specialize in Iberian history should examine Judeoconversos from the point of view of European or Iberian history as a whole, just as historians of the Jews tend to approach conversos from the perspective of Jewish history.

17. Claudio Sánchez Albornoz, *España, un enigma histórico,* 2 vols. (Buenos Aires: Editorial Sudamericana, 1962), 2:255.

18. See Américo Castro, *La realidad histórica de España* (Mexico City: Editorial Porrúa, 1954); id., *The Structure of Spanish History,* trans. Edmund L. King (Princeton, N.J.: Princeton University Press, 1954); id., *España en su historia: Cristianos, moros y judíos* (Buenos Aires: Editorial Losada, 1948). For a brief recapitulation of the author's concept of *inquietud,* see id., prologue to *El Ingenioso Hidalgo Don Quixote de la Mancha* by Miguel de Cervantes (Mexico City: Editorial Porrúa, 1979), xli–xlii.

19. See for example Yitzhak Baer, *A History of the Jews in Christian Spain,* trans. Louis Schoffman, 2 vols. (1959–61; reprint, with an introduction by Benjamin R. Gampel, Philadelphia: Jewish Publication Society, 1992), 2:210–24, 253–77. In response to Baer's position, Norman Roth has observed that while many rabbis converted, no medieval Sephardi philosopher is known to have defected to Christianity. Id., *Conversos, Inquisition, and the Expulsion of the Jews from Spain* (Madison: University of Wisconsin Press, 2002), 11.

20. On Claudio Sánchez Albornoz's approach to the role of Jews in Spanish history, for instance, see Benzion Netanyahu, "Sánchez-Albornoz' View of Jewish His-

tory in Spain," *Toward the Inquisition: Essays on Jewish and Converso History in Late Medieval Spain* (Ithaca, N.Y.: Cornell University Press, 1997), 126–55. On Américo Castro's historiographical vision see Aniano Peña, *Américo Castro y su visión de España y de Cervantes* (Madrid: Gredos, 1975). See also Ronald E. Surtz, Jaime Ferrán, and Daniel P. Testa, eds. *Américo Castro: The Impact of His Thought: Essays to Mark the Centenary of His Birth* (Madison: Hispanic Seminary of Medieval Studies, 1988), especially the essays on Castro and historiography, and on his view of the Muslim and Jewish contributions to Hispanicity in 117–41 and 163–91.

21. See Baer, 2:270–77.

22. See especially Benzion Netanyahu, *The Marranos of Spain: From the Late 14th Century to the Early 16th Century, According to Contemporary Hebrew Sources*, 3rd ed., rev. and exp. (Ithaca, N.Y.: Cornell University Press, 1999).

23. Yirmiyahu Yovel, "The New Otherness: Marrano Dualities in the First Generation," *The 1999 Swig Lecture, September 13, 1999* (San Francisco: The Swig Judaic Studies Program at the University of San Francisco, 1999), 1. For a broader discussion of Baer's evolution as a scholar see Israel Jacob Yuval, "Yitzhak Baer and the Search for Authentic Judaism," *The Jewish Past Revisited: Reflections on Modern Jewish Historians*, ed. David N. Myers and David B. Ruderman (New Haven, Conn.: Yale University Press, 1998), 77–87. On Baer and the "Jerusalem School" see David N. Myers, *Re-Inventing the Jewish Past: European Jewish Intellectuals and the Zionist Return to History* (New York: Oxford University Press, 1995).

24. Domínguez Ortiz, *Los judeoconversos*; Caro Baroja, *Los judíos*.

25. See Yerushalmi, *Cardoso*; Kaplan, *Orobio*; Salomon, *Portrait*.

26. Preceded, to be sure, by surveys such as Cecil Roth, *A History of the Marranos* (Philadelphia: Jewish Publication Society, 1932).

27. A noteworthy attempt to explicate the historical problem of Judeoconversos *in toto* is I. S. Révah, "Les Marranes," *Revue des etudes juives* 118 (1959–60): 29–77 (hereafter cited as "Les Marranes"). Révah's position that crypto-Judaism was widespread among New Christians opposes the interpretation offered by António José Saraiva, *Inquisição*. The famous (and quite heated) debate between the two historians, carried on in various issues of the *Diário de Lisboa* appears as an appendix in Saraiva, 5th ed., 213–91.

28. J. A. Van Praag, "Almas en litigio," *Clavileño* 1 (1950): 14–26.

29. Yerushalmi, "Conversos Returning to Judaism in the Seventeenth Century: Their Jewish Knowledge and Psychological Readiness" (in Hebrew), *Proceedings of the Fifth World Congress of Jewish Studies* (Jerusalem: World Union of Jewish Studies, 1972), 2:201–2.

30. Kaplan, *Judíos nuevos*; Israel, *Empires and Entrepots*; Brian Pullan, *The Jews of Europe and the Inquisition of Venice, 1550–1670* (Oxford: Blackwell, 1983); James C. Boyajian, *Portuguese Bankers at the Court of Spain, 1626–1650* (New Brunswick, N.J. Rutgers University Press, 1983); Haim Beinart, *Conversos on Trial: The Inquisition in Ciudad Real*, trans. Yael Guiladi (Jerusalem: Magnes Press, 1981) (hereafter cited as *Conversos on Trial*); Julio Caro Baroja, *La sociedad criptojudía en la corte de Felipe IV* (Madrid: Real Academia de la Historia, 1963). Two important works focusing on conversos and their cultural milieu appeared while the present work was being prepared. Both are noteworthy for their thoroughness and skillful mining of Spanish archives:

Bernardo López Belinchón, *Honra, Libertad, y Hacienda: Hombres de negocios y judíos sefardíes* (Alcalá de Henares: Instituto Internacional de Estudios Sefardíes y Andalusíes, Universidad de Alcalá, 2001), and Juan Ignacio Pulido Serrano, *Injurias a Cristo: Religión, politica, y antijudaísmo en el siglo XVII* (Alcalá de Henares: Instituto Internacional de Estudios Sefardíes y Andalusíes, Universidad de Alcalá, 2002).

31. See Pullan, *The Jews of Europe*, 243–312. His earlier article, "A Ship with Two Rudders: Righetto Marrano and the Inquisition in Venice," *The Historical Journal* 20.1 (1977): 25–58, is a case study of the phenomena the author addresses in his above-mentioned chapter. See also id., "The Inquisition and the Jews of Venice: The Case of Gaspare Ribeiro, 1580–1581," *Bulletin of the John Rylands University Library* 62 (1979–80): 207–31.

32. Cecil Roth, "The Strange Case of Hector Mendes Bravo," *Hebrew Union College Annual* 18 (1943–44): 221–45; id., "Les Marranes à Rouen: Un chapitre ignoré de l'histoire des juifs de France," *Revue des etudes juives* 88 (1929): 114 –55; I. S. Révah, "Autobiographie d'un Marrane: édition partielle d'un manuscrit de Joâo (Moseh) Pinto Delgado," *Revue des etudes juives* 119 (1961): 41–130.

33. Jaime Contreras Contreras, *Sotos contra Riquelmes* (Madrid: Anaya and M. Muchnik, 1992).

34. Isaiah Tishby, "New Information about the Community of Conversos in London According to the Letters of Sasportas of 1665" (in Hebrew), *Galut Ahar Golah: Studies in Jewish History Presented to Professor Haim Beinart in Honor of his Seventieth Year*, ed. Aaron Mirsky, Avraham Grossman, and Yosef Kaplan (Jerusalem: Mehkon Ben-Tsevi le-heker kehilot Yisra'el ba-Mizrah, 1988), 470–96; Yosef Kaplan, "The Jewish Profile of the Spanish-Portuguese Community of London During the Seventeenth Century," *Judaism* 41.3 (1992): 229–40; Matt Goldish, "Jews, Christians, and Conversos: Rabbi Solomon Aailion's Struggles in the Portuguese Community of London," *Journal of Jewish Studies* 45.2 (1994): 227–57. On marginally attached Jews in Amsterdam see also Yosef Kaplan, "Wayward New Christians and Stubborn New Jews: The Shaping of a Jewish Identity," *Jewish History* 8.1–2 (1994): 27–41 (hereafter cited as "Wayward New Christians").

35. See note 13 above.

36. Jonathan Israel has in many ways brought Szajkowski's project to fruition in "Crypto-Judaism in 17th-Century France: An Economic and Religious Bridge Between the Hispanic World and the Sephardic Diaspora," *Diasporas within a Diaspora: Jews, Crypto-Jews, and the World Maritime Empires (1540–1740)* (Leiden: Brill, 2002). Israel's treatment broadens Szajkowski's own by shedding considerable light on the relationship between the economic history of the converso communities of the French southwest and their complex religious profile. Largely on the basis of secondary sources, Israel notes the religious divisions and uncertainties that beset these communities throughout much of the 1600s. In what concerns economic history, Israel's article foreshadows and surpasses my own analysis (see especially chap. 3). However, Israel does not attempt a meticulous reconstruction of the refugees' *mentalité*. Neither is his treatment of the social and psychological realities of cultural liminality based on a direct and systematic analysis of Spanish documents.

37. Jaime Contreras Contreras, "Criptojudaísmo en la España moderna: clientelismo y linaje," *Inquisição: Ensaios sobre mentalidade, heresias, e arte*, comp. Anita

Novinsky and Maria Luiza Tucci Carneiro (Sao Paulo: EdUSP, 1992), 272 (hereafter cited as "Criptojudaísmo").

38. See for example the seminal work of Carlo Ginzburg, *The Cheese and the Worms: The Cosmos of a Sixteenth-Century Miller*, trans. John Tedeschi and Anne Tedeschi (New York: Penguin Books, 1982). See also Richard L. Kagan, *Lucrecia's Dreams: Politics and Prophecy in Sixteenth-Century Spain* (Berkeley: University of California Press, 1990).

39. Reuven Faingold, "Searching for Identity: The Trial of Portuguese Converso Vicente Furtado, 1600–1615" (in Hebrew), *Pe'amim* 46–47 (1991): 235–59.

40. With the exception on work regarding the converso author and returnee to Spain Antonio Enríquez Gómez, I am not aware of any work that discusses the motivations of returnees in sustained fashion. On Enríquez Gómez see for example I. S. Révah, "Un pamphlet contre l'Inquisition d'Antonio Enríquez Gómez: La seconde partie de la 'Politica Angélica' (Rouen, 1647)," Revue des etudes juives, n.s., 4.1 (1962): 83–168 (hereafter cited as "Un pamphlet"); Constance H. Rose, "The Marranos of the Seventeenth Century and the Case of the Merchant Writer Antonio Enríquez Gómez," *The Spanish Inquisition and the Inquisitorial Mind*, ed. ángel Alcalá, (1984; New York: Columbia University Press, 1987), 53–71; Charles Amiel, introduction, El siglo pitagórico y vida de don Gregorio Guadaña by Antonio Enríquez Gómez (Paris: Ediciones Hispanoamericanas, 1977); Michael McGaha, "Biographical Data on Antonio Enríquez Gómez in the Archives of the Inquisition," *Bulletin of Hispanic Studies* 69.2 (1992): 127–39. More generally, see Glen F. Dille, *Antonio Enríquez Gómez* (Boston: Twayne, 1988); Nechama Kramer-Hellinx, *Antonio Enríquez Gómez: Literatura y sociedad en* El siglo pitagórico y vida de don Gregorio Guadaña (New York: Peter Lang, 1992) (hereafter cited as *Gómez*); Carsten Lorenz Wilke, *Jüdisch-christliches Doppelleben im Barock: Zur Biographie des Kaufmanns und Dichters Antonio Enríquez Gómez* (New York: Peter Lang, 1994) (hereafter cited as *Jüdisch-christliches*). A fruitful attempt to reconstruct the psychology and motivations of early modern religious dissidents, in this case Ashkenazic converts to Christianity, is Elisheva Carlebach, *Divided Souls: Converts from Judaism in Germany, 1570–1750* (New Haven, Conn.: Yale University Press, 2001).

41. See for example Gérard Nahon, ed., *Les 'nations' juives portugaises du sud-ouest de la France (1684–1791): Documents* (Paris: Fundaçâo Calouste Gulbenkian, 1981). The earliest Jewish document in this collection is from 1684. Meanwhile, Nahon's analytical articles on the colonies of conversos in France focus on a slightly later period. See for example, id., "La nation juive portugaise en France, XVIeme–XVIIIème siècle: Espaces et pouvoirs." *Revue des etudes juives* 153 (1994): 353–82. Despite its title, the article deals primarily with developments in the 1700s. The same is true of id., "La 'nation juive' de Saint-Esprit-Les-Bayonne du XVIe au XVIIIe siècle: Escale ou havre de Grace?" *L'exode des juifs d'Espagne vers Bayonne: Des rives de l'Ebre et du Tage à celles de l'Adour*, comp. Maïte Lafourcade (Bayonne: Faculté pluridisciplinaire de Bayonne-Anglet-Biarritz, 1993) (hereafter cited as "La 'nation juive'"). For a more panoramic view see the articles gathered in id., "*Métropoles et périphéries Sepharades d'occident: Kairouan, Amsterdam, Bayonne, Bordeaux, Jérusalem* (Paris: Les Editions du Cerf, 1993); id., "From New Christians to the Portuguese Jewish Nation in France," *Moreshet Sepharad: The Sephardi Legacy*, ed. Haim

Beinart, 2 vols. (Jerusalem: Magnes Press, 1992), 2:336–64 (hereafter cited as "New Christians"); id., "The Sephardim of France," *The Sephardi Heritage*, ed. R. D. Barnett and W. M. Schwab, 2 vols. (Grendon: Gibraltar Books, 1989), 2:46–74 (hereafter cited as "The Sephardim"). For information regarding Franco-Sephardi communities and their relations with other diasporic centers in the eighteenth century see Evelyne Oliel Grausz, "Relations et reseaux intercommunautaires dans la diaspora sefarade d'occi-dent au XVIIIe siecle," Ph.D. diss., University of Paris, 1999.

42. See for example Anne Zink, "L'activité des juifs de Bayonne dans la seconde moitié du XVIIe siecle," *L'exode des juifs d'espagne vers Bayonne: Des rives de l'Ebre et du Tage à celles de l'Adour*, comp. Maïté Lafourcade (Bayonne: Faculté pluridisci-plinaire de Bayonne-Anglet-Biarritz, 1993), 85–107 (hereafter cited as "L'activité"); id., "Une niche juridique: L'installation des juifs à Saint-Esprit-lès-Bayonne au XVIIe siè-cle," *Annales, Histoire, Science Sociales* 49.3 (1994): 639–69 (hereafter cited as "Une niche"); id., "La comunidad judía de Bayona y su contexto," *El Olivo* 49 (1999): 55–64.

43. Zosa Szajkowski, "Trade Relations of Marranos in France with the Iberian Peninsula in the Sixteenth and Seventeenth Centuries," *Jewish Quarterly Review* 50.1 (1959): 69–78. Regarding Jonathan Israel's latest and very germane contribution, see note 36, above.

44. Saraiva, Inquisição is a classic exposition of the view that the Inquisition concocted most evidence of crypto-Judaism in accordance with the Holy Office's own ideological, political, and more importantly its economic interests.

45. A main proponent of this view is Carlo Ginzburg. See id., "The Inquisitor as Anthropologist," *Clues, Myths, and the Historical Method*, trans. John Tedeschi and Anne C. Tedeschi (Baltimore: Johns Hopkins University Press, 1986), 156–64.

46. AHN, Inquisición de Toledo, leg. 138, exp. 12 (1668–70), fol. 85r.

47. In this I follow the formulation of the New Testament scholar John Dominic Crossan, *Who Killed Jesus? Exposing the Roots of Anti-Semitism in the Gospel Story of the Death of Jesus* (San Francisco: HarperSanFrancsico, 1996), 28–29. In a similar vein, another scholar has observed that, "Historical 'proof' in the scientific sense is rarely available in historical reconstruction, because the objects themselves are 'subjective'; human . . . behavior [is] not 'lawlike' except in trivial ways, and thus [it] is not pre-dictable, as for instance the behavior of particles might be in physics; there are too many unknown variables in trying to determine historical 'causation.'" Thus, the his-torian must often content himself or herself with "the balance of probability." It may not offer definitive proof of what events occurred and why they occurred, "but to overturn that would require a more likely scenario, replete with new and superior in-dependent witnesses." William G. Dever, *What Did the Biblical Writers Know and When Did They Know It? What Archeology Can Tell Us about the Reality of Ancient Israel* (Grand Rapids, Mich.: William B. Eerdmans Publishing Company, 2001), 107–8.

48. Recent work on religiously uncommitted or minimally committed conver-sos outside Iberia who were not members of social elites includes the articles by Ka-plan, Goldish, and Tishby that I mentioned earlier. See note 34, above. For earlier work of Roth and Révah on conversos who returned to the Iberian Peninsula to be-come arch-informers see note 32, above. Neither author examined the lives and mo-tivations of their respective subjects.

49. To be more specific concerning my sources, I surveyed approximately two

hundred inquisitorial dossiers that are archived in Madrid and Lisbon. A vast majority of these dossiers include extensive excerpts from dossiers compiled at various regional tribunals (not merely those of Toledo and Lisbon). Of all the dossiers surveyed, I found approximately one hundred in which witnesses identified renegades (chiefly returnees), or in which renegades deposed as witnesses and/or defendants themselves. I located most of these one hundred relevant cases by drawing simple connections between them. Thus, for example, if case "A" included a returnee's deposition taken from case "B," I proceeded to locate case "B"; I examined "B" in order to find information concerning the defendant, as well as the names of other possible renegades (for instance, relatives, business partners, and friends of the defendant). Then I proceeded to locate the dossiers pertaining to individuals whose names I had just obtained from "B," and so on.

50. I will use the terms "Judaicize" and "Judaicization" throughout this work to refer to the process by which converso refugees and their children adopted normative Judaism and became part of normative Jewish communities in the Diaspora.

51. The following refrain hints of the dread and hatred that figure inspired:

No vivas con *malsín*, y si le vieres
calla delante del, mientras le oyeres.

(Do not dwell with a *malsín*, and if you should see him / be silent in front of him, and listen meanwhile.) *Biblioteca de autores españoles*, 62:364, quoted in Caro Baroja, *Los judíos*, 1:299.

The Judeoconverso author Antonio Enríquez Gómez, himself a target of Inquisitorial persecution who returned to Spain after taking refuge in France, was even more caustic:

[El *malsín*] era hippocrita vil con tanto exceso
Que rezava en las cuentas de un proceso,
Persegia Inocentes,
Aunque fuesen sus deudos o parientes
Y en [tribunales] acusava por su modo
A diestro y a siniestro, el Mundo entero
sin perdonar (en uno y otro sexo)
La infancia alegre, el venerable viejo,
La doncella mas casta y mas honrada,
Ni la virtud de la Muger casada.

([The *malsín*] was a hypocrite of such excess / That he prayed during a trial / He persecuted innocents, / Although they be his relatives or ancestors / And in [tribunals] he accused in his way/ This one and that one, the whole world / without forgiving (in one or another sex) / Happy children, the venerable elder, / Neither most well-bred and honest maiden/ Nor the virtue of a married woman.) Antonio Enríquez Gómez, *El siglo pitagórico y vida de Don Gregorio Guadaña* (1644), quoted in Caro Baroja, *Los judíos* 2:281.

As the citations suggest, delators of converso origin were unofficially known as *malsines* (singular: *malsín*), a Spanish distortion of the Hebrew term *malshin*. In rabbinic usage, *malshin* denoted a Jewish person who appealed to gentile authorities against fellow Jews, thus betraying the *kehillah* and its governing elites. For instance, a Jewish man who bypassed rabbinical judges by asking secular (Christian) courts to resolve a dispute between himself and other Jews was regarded as a *malshin*. In contrast, a Jewish apostate who helped Christians to persecute his former correligionists was considered a *meshummad*, namely an opponent to Jewish law who deserved extinction, not an informer in the juridical sense. The earliest rabbinic definitions of *malshinut* (slander, informing) include Midrash *Tehillim* to Psalm 120, and the *Targum* for psalm 52, 4. Marcus Jastrow, comp., *A Dictionary of the Targumim, the Talmud Babli and Yerushalmi, and the Midrashic Literature* (New York: Judaica Press, 1992), 794.

Needless to say, the denouncer-conversos, like most of their victims, were Christians from the point of view of canon law. It follows from all this that the terms *malshin*, and hence *malsín*, are technically inaccurate as descriptions of Judeoconversos who willingly collaborated with the Holy Office. I employ both terms in this study, but merely in order to acknowledge their colloquial use by conversos, inquisitors, and Ibero-Christians at large.

Chapter 2

1. Henceforth, I will use "Castile and Aragon" and "Spain" interchangeably to denote the conglomerate entity commonly known by the second term. In the Early Modern Period that entity included Castile (more specifically, Old Castile and New Castile) and Aragon, the principal kingdoms, as well as lesser provinces and kingdoms: Andalusia, Asturias, Catalonia, Extremadura, Galicia, León, Murcia, Navarre, Valencia, and the Basque territory.

2. Fortunate events for Spain during the late sixteenth century included, first, the civil wars that erupted in France during the 1560s, which effectively neutralized that country as an immediate threat to Spanish hegemony in western Europe until the seventeenth century. Second, between 1567 and 1570 Spanish forces under the Duke of Alba suppressed a major revolt in the Dutch provinces. Later, in 1579, another Dutch uprising subsided after Spain gained the support of Catholic districts under the Union of Arras. Third, in the New World, the viceroy of Peru put an end to large-scale Inca resistance. Further south, Spaniards reestablished the colony of Buenos Aires, an economically important node of imperial strength, in 1581. Meanwhile, successful expeditions into North American territory promised to broaden the already wide scope of Spanish power in the Western Hemisphere. Fourth, Spanish arms completed the subjugation of the Philippine Islands in 1571. Fifth, in the same year the Holy League, led by the Spanish navy, imposed a crushing defeat upon the Ottoman Empire in the Battle of Lepanto. In this apocalyptic encounter the Muslim armies— the cutting edge of the world's only other superpower—sustained an overwhelming majority of the losses, while Spanish forces left the battle relatively unscathed. It is worth noting that although England would destroy the "invincible" armada in 1588, the defeat did not exhaust the vast reservoir of imperial resolve. As early as 1596 and

1597, and despite the chronic infirmity of the Spanish economy, Philip II sent two additional fleets against Ireland and England. Happily for these northern kingdoms, neither of the new armadas reached its destination owing to poor weather. Henry Kamen, *Spain, 1469–1714: A Society of Conflict* (London: Longman, 1991), 131–34 (hereafter cited as *Spain: 1469–1714*).

3. Isidore of Seville (659–67) was perhaps the first to glorify *Hispania* in a work of "national" history, his *Historia de regibus Gothorum, Wandalorum, et Suevorum.* (Despite its title, the chronicle devotes more attention to the Goths than to any other people.) In the tenth century, Leonese kings projected their desire for peninsular hegemony through their appropriation of the title *Imperator.* Simultaneously they strove to revive Visigothic law and rituals. The neo-Gothic ideal acquired an even more blatantly "Hispanic" coloring in the eleventh century, when Alfonso VI styled himself *Imperator Hispaniae.* With the division of peninsular territory into culturally distinct kingdoms in the High Middle Ages, the Leonese archetype of *Hispania* became totally unfeasible. Still, the pivotal concept of *España (Hispania)* survived. According to Joseph F. O'Callaghan, it became entrenched as a symbol of future unity. See id., *A History of Medieval Spain* (Ithaca, N.Y.: Cornell University Press, 1975), 86, 120–21, 255, 428.

4. Kamen, *Spain: 1469–1714*, 126–27.

5. Ibid.

6. The first period of intense anti-converso activity by the Spanish Inquisition began in the 1480s and did not wane until the first quarter of the sixteenth century. See Henry Kamen, *Inquisition and Society in Spain in the Sixteenth and Seventeenth Centuries* (London: Weidenfeld and Nicolson, 1985), 184. The table in question does not appear in the revised version of this work, id., *The Spanish Inquisition: An Historical Revision* (London: Weidenfeld and Nicolson, 1997) (hereafter cited as *The Spanish Inquisition*). Jean-Pierre Dedieu has shown that the activity of the Toledo Tribunal against Judeoconversos was most intense from 1483 to 1530. During that period, the Santo Oficio conducted more than twenty-five hundred trials against alleged Judaizers. According to Dedieu's data, the only remotely comparable upsurge of anti-converso activity by the same tribunal occurred between 1621 and 1700. Close to nine hundred alleged Judaizers were prosecuted between those years. Id., *L'Administration de la foi: L'Inquisition de Tolède, XVIe–XVIIIe siècle* (Madrid: Casa de Velázquez, 1989), 239–41. As for Portugal, a high percentage of all defendants processed there during the sixteenth century were alleged Judaizers. For example, according to the *livro das denuncias* (an inquisitorial index) 90 percent of those accused within the jurisdiction of the tribunal at Porto before 1547 fell under that category. María José Pimenta Ferro Tavares, *Los judíos en Portugal* (Madrid: Editorial MAPFRE, 1992), 199 (hereafter cited as *Judíos*).

7. Several historians have observed that the prosecutorial harshness of Portugal's Inquisition matched and often exceeded that of its Spanish counterpart. See for example Yerushalmi, *Cardoso*, 9. See also Pulido Serrano, 76–86. Regarding the influx of conversos to Spain prior to 1580, see Pilar Huerga Criado, *En la raya de Portugal: Solidaridad y tensiones en la comunidad judeoconversa* (Salamanca: Ediciones Universidad de Salamanca, 1993), 33, 35.

8. Huerga Criado, 31–35. As the author relates, João III barred conversos from

emigrating in 1532 and 1547; Sebastião I did the same in 1567, 1569, and 1573. Paradoxically, Sebastião also issued the first permission to emigrate in 1577.

9. Salomon, *Portrait*, 41. See also Pulido Serrano, 52, and Domínguez Ortiz, *Los judeoconversos*, 63.

10. Domínguez Ortiz, *Los judeoconversos*, 63–64.

11. Salomon, *Portrait*, 43.

12. Ibid., 44. See also Domínguez Ortiz, *Los judeoconversos*, 63 and Pulido Serrano, 53–54.

13. Domínguez Ortiz, *Los judeoconversos*, 63. See also his essay "Los extranjeros en la vida española durante el siglo XVII" in *Los extranjeros*, 17–181.

14. Salomon, *Portrait*, 44. See also Domínguez Ortiz, *Los judeoconversos*, 63–64.

15. Domínguez Ortiz, *Los judeoconversos*, 67. For an in-depth treatment of this phenomenon vis à vis the wealthiest New Christian businessmen from Portugal see Boyajian, *Portuguese Bankers*. On converso bankers and major *asentistas* see also Pulido Serrano, 37–50, 65–70. A more comprehensive treatment is López Belinchón, 67–168.

16. Yerushalmi, *Cardoso*, 9.

17. Ibid. Here Yerushalmi notes that as late as 1630 there was no provision for extradition.

18. Ibid. Commenting on the power and prestige of Portuguese inquisitors, Father António Vieira (though by no means a disinterested observer) commented in 1673 that "here it is said publicly that in Portugal it is better to be an inquisitor than to be king." Vieira, quoted in Carl A. Hanson, *Economy and Society in Baroque Portugal, 1668–1703* (Minneapolis: University of Minnesota Press, 1981), 70. Luso-converso notables sent a series of specific complaints against the comparative harshness of the Portuguese tribunal to Philip IV. On these complaints, and Philip's equivocal responses to them, see Pulido Serrano, especially 79–108.

19. "Golden Age" also refers to a cultural effervescence that is most evident in the literary and pictorial output of the time. Much of this artistic harvest, however, coincided with the *decline* of Spain as a military and political hegemon, so it is not entirely clear whether the harvest was a symptom or a departure from the earlier development and projection of Spanish power. Jean-Marc Pelorson, "¿Cómo se representaba a sí misma la 'sociedad española' del 'siglo de oro'?" *La frustración de un imperio, 1476– 1714*, by Jean-Paul Le Flem et al. (Barcelona: Editorial Labor, 1982), 295–97.

20. Dominguez Ortiz has observed that sixteenth-century Castile, which would remain the nucleus of the Habsburg Empire for centuries, owed its dynamism chiefly to the invigorating effect of acquiring overseas possessions. Id., *The Golden Age of Spain, 1516–1659*, trans. James Casey (New York: Basic Books, 1971), 173 (hereafter cited as *Golden Age*). See also Kamen, *Spain: 1469–1714*, 89.

21. Le Flem et al., 70–77. See especially the table on p. 70. Le Flem's analysis summarizes those of Ramón Carande, Pierre Chaunu, Earl J. Hamilton, and Pierre Vilar.

22. Kamen, Spain: 1469–1714, 98–99, 168.

23. Yosef Kaplan, "Jews and Judaism in the Political and Social Thought of Spain in the Sixteenth and Seventeenth Centuries," *Antisemitism Through the Ages*, ed.

Shmuel Almog (New York: Pergamon Press, 1988), 155 (hereafter cited as "Jews and Judaism").

24. Pedro de Rivadeneria, *Tratado de la religion y virtudes que debe tener un principe cristiano* (Madrid, 1601), *Antología de escritores politicos del siglo de oro*, ed. Pedro de Vega (Madrid: Taurus, 1966), 149.

25. Juan de Salazar, *Politica española* (Madrid, 1619), quoted in Yosef Kaplan, "Jews and Judaism," 155.

26. Juan de Salazar, *Politica española* (Madrid, 1619), quoted in Pedro de Vega, ed., *Antología*, 203.

27. Ibid., 196–97.

28. For a traditional explanation of the crisis based on an analysis of finance and monetary policy see Earl J. Hamilton, "The Decline of Spain," *Economic History Review* 8.2 (1938): 168–79. A more thorough examination of structural deficiencies in the Habsburg economy, as well as their social origins and repercussions, is Antonio Domínguez Ortiz, *Crisis y decadencia de la España de los Austrias* (Barcelona: Ariel, 1984). James Casey, "Spain: A Failed Transition," *The European Crisis of the 1590s*, ed. Peter Clark (Boston: Allen and Unwin, 1985), 209–28, suggests that an unsuccessful shift to an urbanized economy from the fifteenth to the sixteenth centuries planted the seeds of collapse. Henry Kamen has argued that in actuality there was no "decline," as there was never any real ascent; the Spanish economy was so structurally weak that it could only attain a superficial prosperity. Id., "The Decline of Spain: A Historical Myth?" in *Crisis and Change in Early Modern Spain* (Brookfield: Variorum, 1993), 24–50 (hereafter cited as *Crisis and Change*). Cf. Helen Nader, *Liberty in Absolutist Spain: The Habsburg Sale of Towns, 1516–1700* (Baltimore: Johns Hopkins University Press, 1990). By demonstrating the flexibility and ultimate buoyancy of the economy of Habsburg Spain, Nader's work is perhaps the most devastating counterpoint to theories of "decline."

29. By "exhaustion" I do not mean a total and irreversible collapse. As Lynch notes, a number of light industries and entire cities such as Bilbao (the wool exporting capital of the country) survived the worst economic depressions in reasonably good shape. Id., *Spain Under the Habsburgs*, 2 vols. (New York: Oxford University Press, 1969), 2:153–54. As James Casey has summarized the phenomenon, "What seems to have happened over the Early Modern Period was a significant weakening of the front-line industries—those which had once a national and international market—and a reversion to instead to smaller centers." Id., *Early Modern Spain: A Social History* (London: Routledge, 1999), 63 (henceforth cited as *Early Modern Spain*).

30. Diego de Velázquez, comptroller of the Habsburg palace under Philip IV, complained in 1654 that the crown owed him his entire salary for that year, as well as half a year's salary for the previous year. Reflecting on the lamentable effects of fiscal disorder he added, "The sweepers have stopped work and, what is worse, there is not a *Real* to pay for logs for His Majesty's apartment." Id., quoted in Marcelin Defourneaux, *Daily Life in Spain in the Golden Age*, trans. Newton Branch (Stanford, Calif.: Stanford University Press, 1970), 56.

31. Kamen, Spain: 1469–1714, 209–10.

32. See Lynch, 104, 129.

33. See Kamen, *Spain: 1469–1714*, 162–65. Here the author outlines the balloon-

ing costs of empire maintenance that brought the Spanish treasury to its knees during the reigns of Philip II and Philip III. See also Casey, *Early Modern Spain*, 61–86.

34. On the regional revolts see Kamen, *Spain*, 236–40.

35. See Kamen, *Spain: 1469–1714*, 169–71, 225. See also Lynch, 138, 178. The second deficiency was perhaps not a structural fault, but was nonetheless a serious economic weakness rooted in various factors that need not detain us. The question of why Spain had such a small (or, at any rate, ineffectual) native bourgeoisie is still open to scholarly debate. For a brief appraisal of traditional and recent discussions of that weakness (among other aspects) see Miguel Avilés Fernández, Siro Villas Tinoco, and Carmen García Cremades, *La crisis del siglo XVII bajo los últimos austrias (1598–1700)*, vol. 9 of *Historia de España* (Madrid: Gredos, 1988), 11–24. More recent approaches to the question of the supposed Spanish "decline" and its root causes are included in I. A. A. Thompson and Bartolomé Yun Casalilla, eds., *The Castilian Crisis of the Seventeenth Century: New Perspectives on the Economic and Social History of Seventeenth-Century Spain* (Cambridge: Cambridge University Press, 1994).

36. See evidence against key elements of the "decline" thesis in Nader.

37. Regarding the role of foreign financiers, see Boyajian; Domínguez Ortiz, *Los extranjeros*, 23–36. On the question of economic dependence see Kamen, *Spain: 1469–1714*, 169–71. See also id., *Crisis and Change*, 24–50. On the sale of jurisdictions see Nader.

38. Domínguez Ortiz, *Golden Age*, 175; Lynch, 127.

39. Ibid.

40. Ibid. See also the well-tabulated analysis of "the demographic drama" in Avilés Fernández, Villas Tinoco, and García Cremades, 92–99.

41. Kamen, *Spain: 1469–1714*, 167, 202. The author reports that from 1559 to 1598 the burden on the ordinary Castilian taxpayer rose 430 percent while income rose only 80 percent. Defourneaux, 54, cites anecdotal information that the court spent lavishly beyond its means even during its worst financial crises. For instance, the crown expended three hundred thousand ducats to celebrate the accession of Ferdinand III to the Austrian throne in 1637. In reaction to criticism of such waste, the crown issued an official explanation that the lavish display of wealth was not for its own sake, but to show Cardinal Richelieu that Spain was wealthy enough to be a formidable geopolitical and military rival to France.

42. Antonio Domínguez Ortiz, *La sociedad española en el siglo XVII*. 2 vols. (Madrid: Instituto Balmes de Sociología, 1963), 129–40 (hereafter cited as *La sociedad española*).

43. Lynch, 127.

44. Ibid.

45. An example of anti-morisco chauvinism is the earlier-cited statement of Juan de Salazar in his work of 1619, *Politica española* (see notes 26 and 27 above). On the image of moriscos as a dangerous "race" with unique physical attributes and behavioral proclivities see also José María Perceval, *Todos son uno: Arquetipos, xenophobia, y racismo: La imagen del morisco en la monarquía Española durante los siglos XVI y XVII* (Almería: Instituto de Estudios Almerienses, 1997), 128–38, 167–73, 202, 234, 242–60, 272. For a global treatment and overview of much existing work on the

moriscos see Antonio Domínguez Ortiz and Bernard Vincent, *Historia de los moriscos* (Madrid: Revista de Occidente, 1979).

46. Kamen, *Spain: 1469–1714*, 174, 222.

47. Ibid., 222–23.

48. In 1659 the French traveler François Bertaut wrote regarding Madrid, "It is a marvel how this city can subsist. It is as large as the *faubourg* of St. Germain in Paris, or as Bordeaux, yet because it lacks any river that can carry boats and barges, everything reaches [Madrid] by land, not by carriage as in France, but upon asses and mules, which is one of the reasons that all genres and merchandise are so costly there." Quoted in José Deleito y Piñuela, *Solo Madrid es corte: La capital de dos mundos bajo Felipe IV* (Madrid: Espasa-Calpe, 1942), 149.

49. Domínguez Ortiz, *La sociedad española*, 1:155 (Graph 3). See also Casey, *Early Modern Spain*, 154.

50. Richard Mackenney, *Sixteenth-Century Europe: Expansion and Conflict* (New York: St. Martin's Press, 1993), 94–95.

51. Defourneaux, 66.

52. Ibid.

53. Ibid.

54. Cf. Claudia W. Sieber, "The Invention of a Capital: Philip II and the First Reform of Madrid," Ph.D. diss., Johns Hopkins University, 1985. The author demonstrates that the Habsburgs invested in Madrid's infrastructure and luxuries. However, it seems to be a matter of scholarly consensus that by the reign of Philip IV, the city had burgeoned so dramatically that it had overtaxed that infrastructure.

55. Deleito y Piñuela, 29. Many of these serpentine passageways survive in the oldest section of the city.

56. David Vassberg, *The Village and the Outside World in Golden Age Castile: Mobility and Migration in Everyday Rural Life* (Cambridge: Cambridge University Press, 1996), 37. See also Defourneaux, 96.

57. Deleito y Piñuela, 25.

58. This according to the French traveler Antoine de Brunel, *Voyage d'Espagne* (1655), quoted in Deleito y Piñuela, 25.

59. Ibid., 28, 128–33. Defourneaux, 62–63. Casey reports that a network of sewers was not built in Madrid until the late eighteenth century. Id., *Early Modern Spain*, 33.

60. Deleito y Piñuela, 129.

61. Ibid., 41.

62. Pedro Fernández Navarrete, quoted in Defourneaux, 68. The textual source of the quotation is obscure. I suspect it is Navarrete's *Conservación de monarquías y discursos políticos* (1626).

63. José Pellicer, *Avisos* (1637), quoted in Defourneaux, 68.

64. These critics were perhaps the most contentious analysts of the condition of Madrid, and of the Spanish realm as a whole. The very concept of an era of Spanish decline derives from the writing of these men, whose efforts were primarily devoted to explaining Spain's dwindling political fortunes and prescribing ways to preserve Spanish power. See Kamen, *Spain: 1469–1714*, 233.

65. Ibid., 235. (Kamen's reference is to Bravo's *De Rege et regendi ratione* [1616]).

Along the same lines, the pundit Martín González de Cellorigo opined, "We [Spaniards] lack people in the middle who are neither rich nor poor but follow their natural occupation. And the cause of this defect is our inequitable system of taxation." González de Cellorigo, quoted in Lynch, 138.

66. Defourneaux, 26. For a discussion of "dependence" as a model by which to understand the Spanish economy during the sixteenth and seventeenth centuries see Kamen, *Crisis and Change*; id., *Spain in the Later Seventeenth Century, 1665-1700* (London: Longman, 1980), 67–68, 127–31. See also id., Spain: 1469–1714, 228–30.

67. Kamen, *Spain: 1469–1714*, 225, 255–57. See also Lynch, 152; Casey, *Early Modern Spain*, 63; Nader, 99–157, 207–9.

68. Defourneaux, 20; Lynch, 154.

69. David Ringrose, *Madrid and the Spanish Economy, 1560–1850* (Berkeley: University of California Press, 1983), 314. On Castile see also Nader.

70. Philip III moved his court to Valladolid in 1601 yet moved it back to Madrid in 1604-1606. Kamen, *Spain: 1469–1714*, 200.

71. Lynch, 154.

72. Bartolomé Benassar, *Valladolid en el siglo de oro: Una ciudad de Castilla y su entorno agrario en el siglo XVI*, 2d ed. (Valladolid: Ambito, 1989), 82–86. Le Flem, 75, has observed that in the days of the last Habsburgs it took forty days to transport 460 kilograms of wool on an ox-drawn *carreta* from Guadalajara or Segovia (New Castile) to the Basque ports San Sebastián or Bilbao (a distance of 500 kilometers).

73. Domínguez Ortiz, *Golden Age*, 177. See also Vassberg, 42–43 and David Ringrose, *Transportation and Economic Stagnation in Spain, 1750–1850* (Durham, N.C.: Duke University Press, 1970), 17–18.

74. Vassberg, 42–43.

75. Ibid., 43, 45.

76. Ibid., 45.

77. François Bertaut, *Journal d'un voyage d'Espagne* (1659), quoted in Deleito y Piñuela, 149.

78. Vassberg, 37.

79. Ibid., 45.

80. See ibid., 34, 37, 39. Vassberg's discussion suggests that mule-drawn and ox-drawn carts were preferred by farmers who sold merchandise seasonally rather than on a year-long basis.

81. Lynch, 148.

82. See Vassberg, 131–33, 134.

83. For instance, this was so in the outskirts of Valladolid during the late 1500s, according to Benassar, *Valladolid*, 86–87.

84. See Kamen, *Spain: 1469–1714*, 140–41, 242. See also Henry Kamen, "Public Authority and Popular Crime: Banditry in Valencia, 1660–1714," *Journal of Modern History* 49 (1977): 210–30.

85. Bertaut, quoted in Defourneaux, 17. Barthélemy Joly, writing fifty-five years earlier, noted that Aragon was, in parts, even more arid than Castile. *Voyage of Barthélemy Joly in Spain 1603–1604*, paraphrased in Defourneaux, 17.

86. Vassberg, 14–15.

87. Ibid., 18.

88. Ibid., 23.

89. Ibid., 133. The author quotes residents of the village of Cumbres de Enmedio, from a report in the Archivo General de Simancas, EH, 269. Nevertheless, as Nader points out, however accurate in essence many such reports may have been, they were calculated to motivate the crown to remove towns from clerical or seigneurial control and place them under royal jurisdiction. Once "rescued" by the Habsburg state, the townsfolk could (and often did) purchase legal autonomy for their towns from the cash-strapped crown.

90. Interestingly, the friar was a namesake of the patron saint of the Holy Office.

91. AHN, Inquisición de Toledo, leg. 174, exp. 17 (1661), folio 2r.

92. I summarize the friar's testimony with the caveat that his deposition amounted to a series of unproven and probably unprovable allegations as to what he, his companions, and the Portuguese suspect said and did. For reasons of style I do not always qualify Mártir's statements as allegations (or as versions of alleged events) within my summary. For example, I do not always write such phrases as "Mártir alleged that the Portuguese man said. . . ." I trust that the readers will remember that whenever I refer to something that happened, or something that the Portguese man "did" or "said," I am actually referring to what Mártir claimed had occurred.

93. Mártir only remembered the apellation de Silva. This is evident from the fact that he called the defendant "fulano de Silva." Other witnesses remembered the suspect's alleged given name, Diego.

94. AHN, Inquisición de Toledo, leg. 174, exp. 17 (1661), fol. 3r.

95. Ibid., fol. 13r. Unlike Mártir's peers, Martínez told her interrogators that she did not know why she had been summoned to testify, and that she had not witnessed anyone commit any acts against the Catholic faith.

96. Ibid., fol. 26r. The defendant indicated that he had been born in the Indies but had been brought to live in Estremoz at the age of two.

97. On the procedures and other details of genealogical investigations of *pureza* see for example the detailed discussion regarding the cathedral chapter of Murcia in Juan Hernández Franco, *Cultura y limpieza de sangre en la España moderna: Puritate sanguinis* (Murcia: Servicio de Publicaciones, Universidad de Murcia, 1996), 90–135.

98. This was either an inquisitorial prosecutor or Inquisitor Paniagua himself.

99. Similar anti-converso euphemisms included "Portuguese of the nation" (*portugueses de la nación*). "Men of the nation" (*homens da nacão*) and "businessmen" (*homens de negócio*) were among euphemisms current in Portugal at the time. Whether "nation" referred specifically to "the Jewish nation" or more narrowly to a nation of New Christian Judaizers is not clear. The meaning was pejorative in either case.

100. *Millones* were taxes on basic foodstuffs such as vinegar, oil, wine and meat. Introduced in the sixteenth century, these levies aroused popular resentment as they increased the cost of subsistence for a majority of Spaniards. Lynch, 141; Kamen, *Spain: 1469–1714*, 166.

101. So the questions remain: Did the inquisitors abandon their investigation in midcourse, as the dossier's abrupt termination suggests, or has an original, concluding portion of the dossier been lost?

102. Even if Pereira were a skillful liar, why would he have risked his future by concocting a story that his interrogators could easily disprove?

103. Unless he suffered from a peculiar form of dementia. We could posit manic depression for the sake of argument, but to do so would be, in my view, exceedingly speculative.

104. I doubt Pereira was a shrewd fabricator. Even though it is impossible to reconstruct his motives definitively, I suspect the inquisitors recognized, on the basis of Páez's declarations, that Pereira had been a victim of libel, and they set Pereira free. Páez's deposition and Pereira's letter allow us maintain this position with a robust measure of certainty. The first of these documents offered reasonably credible evidence that the denouncers' allegations about Pereira were bogus while Pereira's own counter-claims were at least fundamentally sincere, if not exonerating in every detail. The second document, while not very informative in itself, permits a reconstruction of the circumstances surrounding the conclusion of Pereira's case. These circumstances are perhaps the strongest indication that Pereira's deposition was essentially truthful.

Any conclusion the inquisitors may have reached about Pereira's veracity hinged largely on whatever credence they gave to Páez's testimony. Although the latter made no pretense of impartiality (he said he was related to the suspect and seemed to know him personally) I believe that there is sufficient reason to believe that the information Páez gave the Holy Office concerning Pereira was not only genuine but fundamentally accurate. A skeptic might object that Pereira could have contacted Páez from prison, advised Páez of his predicament, and prepared Páez to testify in a manner fully consistent with his own. Such a scenario assumes two things. First, that Pereira knew that Páez (or another ally or relative) would be called to testify in his case. Second, that Pereira was able to communicate with Páez from jail. Both premises are farfetched. Pereira could not know who, if anyone, would appear to depose in his favor. Although according to basic inquisitorial procedure, he was free to summon witnesses as part of his defense, he could only do so after the prosecution had issued formal charges against him. Pereira did not convoke any witnesses because the Holy Office never charged him with any crime. It was Inquisitor Paniagua who summoned Páez to Toledo. As for the second premise: In all probability Pereira was not in a position to conspire to produce false testimony. Like all other prisoners of the Holy Tribunal, he was not allowed to correspond with anyone outside his cell (aside from functionaries of the Inquisition). Moreover, Pereira was under the constant surveillance of the tribunal's *familiares*, whose standard practices included watching detainees through peeping-holes and advising inquisitors about any suspicious behavior. *Familiares* certainly possessed the capability to detect prisoners' attempts to smuggle information out of prison. Scores of intercepted messages survive among the pages of inquisitorial dossiers, bearing witness to the efficacy of inquisitorial spying. See for example the transcriptions of numerous such intercepted messages in David Willemse, *Un "portugués" entre los castellanos: El primer proceso inquisitorial contra Gonzalo Báez de Paiba, 1654–1657* (Paris: Fundação Calouste Gulbenkian, 1974). The point is that in order to make contact with any of his friends, relatives, or other potential allies from his prison cell, Pereira would have had to evade close and persistent inquisitorial scrutiny. Specifically, he would have had to find an accomplice among his guards or among outgoing prisoners; arrange for the accomplice(s) to carry or relay his message(s) from Toledo to Madrid, in total secrecy, to the appropriate party (Páez); and finally, transmit the message(s) in a relatively short period of time—enough time for the intended recipient to memorize a highly specific but fictitious biography and be able to repeat it flawlessly before a panel of professional interrogators. Surely it is reasonable to consider it improbable that Pereira, or anyone else for that matter, could realize such a logistically formidable scheme of evasion from one month to the next while being held *incommunicado*.

Before we abandon the question of Pereira's credibility, let me posit for the sake of argument that Pereira was, after all, a converso and a crypto-Jew who had always lived a double life, and whose family had skillfully burrowed itself in Old Christian society through marriage alliances and fraud even prior to Pereira's birth. Let me further assume that because Pereira had always supplied false information about himself he did not need to contact Páez from prison in order for Páez to furnish that information to the inquisitors, since Páez was already familiar with Pereira's bogus information (whether Páez knew the information to be false is irrelevant). To test the scenario, let me focus on one aspect of Pereira's story. If Pereira wanted to falsify his genealogy in order to gain admission to the Order of Christ, then he would have had to obtain a counterfeit certificate of *limpieza*. Yet the cost of such certificates was high. Wealthy conversos were usually the only ones who obtained them. Pereira had relatively little money. We know that he was not wealthy from the fact that in the days before his arrest he had been traveling by mule and not by horse or by coach, as a gentleman of means probably would. The relatively modest possessions that Pereira had been carrying during his voyage further attest to his low economic status. From the list of confiscated items preserved in the dossier, it appears that the defendant was neither destitute nor well off. In that respect at least Pereira was in the same position as many a demobilized soldier of the time. We must also recall that Pereira claimed he had been completely penniless in Cádiz, Madrid, and Seville. For some impressions on the widespread phenomenon of demobilized soldiers in Golden Age Spain see Defourneaux, 67.

It is conceivable, one may object, that Pereira's self-portrayal as an indigent noble and occasional beggar was part of a painstaking plan to hide his true identity. But why would he *specifically* paint himself as a pauper, when he could have easily described himself in different terms, all without compromising his ostensible innocence? If Pereira wished to obscure the fact that he was capable of paying his way into the Order of Christ, he certainly did not need to go to the extreme of inventing a story about his own mendicancy. Such a story would have been redundant in any case, since Pereira had already informed the inquisitors of the occupations of each of his living relatives, and hence it was readily verifiable that all of them were persons of modest means. Pereira must have been aware that much of the information he provided the inquisitors could be investigated. Was Pereira so sure that all of his friends or relatives, if they were summoned to testify, would hold up the complex veneer of lies that he had so fastidiously erected? Again, given the sheer implausibility of that caricature, and given Páez's reasonably credible testimony, I believe it is unlikely that Pereira lied about his identity. Even if the man's ancestors included Jews and conversos in some long-forgotten or purposely effaced past, it is doubtful that Pereira was himself a crypto-Jew and that he was conscious of having converso ancestors.

In sum, the reason we must discard the "Pereira-as-fabricator" theory is not that it is totally implausible—it certainly is not—but that it lacks verisimilitude. A lifelong sham of that magnitude would require such daring, such cunning, such vigilance and good luck, that it strains the imagination to picture how anyone could sustain it for long, especially under an inquisitorial microscope.

105. An example of this familiarity is Manuel Méndez Cardoso, the defendant in AHN, Inquisición de Toledo, leg. 166, exp. 6. (1622–25), not foliated.

106. The key rhetorical slippage, then, was in essence a conscious or unconscious failure to distinguish between the formal meanings of the terms "Jew," "converso", and "Judaizer." The first term properly denoted an unbaptized member of a Jewish community who professed the Jewish religion. Virtually no such people remained in Iberia after the expulsions of the 1490s. For its part, the term "converso" literally meant "convert" and in that sense denoted nothing about private (as opposed to public) religious affinities. "Judaizer," in contrast, denoted a baptized Christian who behaved as a Jew regardless of his or her ancestry.

107. See for example Révah's influential article, "Les Marranes," 29–77. A very effective summary and defense of Révah's position is Yerushalmi, *Cardoso*, 3–50; see especially 21–40.

108. See Ferro Tavares, *Los judíos en Portugal*, 173–86 and Salomon, *Portrait*, 17.

109. Salomon, *Portrait*, 17-20. Here the author consciously follows the position of Alexandre Herculano, *Da origem e establecimiento da Inquisição em Portugal* (Lisbon, 1854–59).

110. Ferro Tavares, *Los judíos en Portugal*, 174–78.

111. The story of the riots and forced conversions that gave birth to the converso phenomenon has has been told several times, but perhaps most famously by Baer, A *History of the Jews in Christian Spain*, 2:95–424.

112. The only Portuguese event arguably comparable in terms of its disastrous results to the anti-Jewish violence that Jews and conversos experienced in Spain was the anti-converso riot of Lisbon of 1506. See Yosef Hayim Yerushalmi, *The Lisbon Massacre of 1506 and the Royal Image in the Shebet Yehudah*, Hebrew Union College Annual Supplements 1 (Cincinnati: Hebrew Union College, 1976). Pulido Serrano, 100–101, relates that anti-converso violence resurfaced in several Portuguese cities in January of 1630, after Old Christians accused conversos of stealing religious effigies from the church of Santa Engracia in Lisbon.

113. Yerushalmi, *Cardoso*, 6-7.

114. For a discussion of converso endogamy see Huerga Criado, 67–77, and López Belinchón, 260–63. López notes that *paisanaje*—namely, provenance from given cities or villages—was a basis of Luso-converso solidarity. An example of endogamy is the family of Gonzalo Báez de Paiba. See Willemse, XLVII. For a discussion of converso familial alliances see also Jaime Contreras y Contreras, "Estructuras familiares y linajes en el mundo judeoconverso," *Solidarités et sociabilités en Espagne*, ed. Raphael Carrasco (Paris: Les Belles Lettres, 1991), 187–241.

115. See for example Ferro Tavares, *Los judíos en Portugal*, 174–77, 261–62, 265–68.

116. Yerushalmi, *Cardoso*, 8.

117. Studying the case of Braganza, Claude Stuczynski has argued that the collective identity of Braganzan conversos, like their crypto-Judaism, was based primarily on their sense of ethnic difference and interconnectedness. Id., "Libros y técnicas de lectura entre los cristianos nuevos portugueses: El caso de Bragança, Siglo XVI," working paper, A Literatura Judaico-Portuguesa, Cursos da Arrábida, Arrábida, Portugal, 22 July, 1997. For a discussion of conversos as an ethnic group see Thomas F. Glick, "On Converso and Marrano Ethnicity," *Crisis and Creativity in the Sephardic World, 1391–1648*, ed. Benjamin Gampel (New York: Columbia Univ. Press, 1997), 59–76. Glick has applied sociological models of ethnic relations to the case of conversos. Much recent work has explored the affinity of conversos toward Iberian culture and their sense of Hispanic ethnicity even outside the Iberian Peninsula as crucial elements in their collective and individual self-perception. See for example Kaplan, "Exclusión y autoidentidad," in *Judíos nuevos*, 56-77. See also Miriam Bodian, *Hebrews of the Portuguese Nation: Conversos and Community in Early Modern Amsterdam* (Bloomington: Indiana University Press, 1997) (hereafter cited as Hebrews).

118. Miriam Bodian, "'Men of the Nation': The Shaping of *Converso* Identity in Early Modern Europe," *Past and Present* 143 (1994): 49–76 (hereafter cited as "'Men of the Nation'"). The coincidence of words denoting race and ethnicity to describe conversos is not surprising if we agree that medieval conceptions of race and nation were tightly linked. On that linkage see Robert Bartlett, "Medieval and Modern Concepts of Race and Ethnicity," *Journal of Medieval and Early Modern Studies* 31.1 (2001): 39–56.

119. This is how António José Saraiva and Julio Caro Baroja, for example, have characterized them. See Saraiva, *Inquisição e cristãos-novos*, 44, 127–40. Caro Baroja, *Los Judíos*, 2:13–49. For a useful discussion of the role of conversos as a predominantly mercantile class in Portugal see Hanson, 44–48, 71– 105. A useful, multilayered discussion of the economic and social relations between conversos is López Belinchón.

120. See Huerga Criado, 98–99, and her more general discussion of the occupational profile of conversos, 95–128. See also Ferro Tavares, *Los judíos en Portugal*, 261–88; Bruce A. Lorence, "Professions Held by New Christians in Northern and Southern Portugal during the First Half of the Seventeenth Century," *History and Creativity in the Sephardi and Oriental Jewish Communities*, ed. Tamar Alexander, et al. (Jerusalem: Misgav Yerushalayim, 1994), 315–26.

121. Domínguez Ortiz, *Los extranjeros*, 35–36, mentions Manuel Cortizos de Villasante, a converso of Portuguese descent who became an inquisitor in 1642. For additional examples of conversos among the clergy and in the religious orders see Caro Baroja, *Los judíos*, 227–33, 241–43.

122. Literally, people engaged in commerce.

123. Huerga Criado, 97–98.

124. For example, the defendant Cristobal Méndez Silveira used this term to describe himself. AHN, Inquisición de Toledo, leg. 165, exp. 12 (1661–71), fol. 43r.

125. Defourneaux, 66.

126. Domínguez Ortiz, *Los extranjeros*, 37.

127. See Boyajian. See also López Belinchón, focusing on the career and socioeconomic milieu of the contractor Fernando Montesinos and his family.

128. Genoese bankers and the Fuggers supplied the remaining 61 percent. Domínguez Ortiz, *Los extranjeros*, 26–27.

129. Huerga Criado, 100.

130. Ibid., 98–100.

131. AHN, Inquisición de Toledo, leg. 147, exp. 5 (1651–52), fols. 31r–32v.

132. Ibid., 32r.

133. Ibid., 33r.

134. Markus Schreiber has written in German and Spanish regarding the familial networks and economic activities of conversos in seventeenth-century Madrid. See for example his "Cristianos nuevos de Madrid," *Historia de la Inquisicion en España y América* (Madrid: Biblioteca de Autores Cristianos, Centro de Estudios Inquisitoriales, 2000), 3:531–56.

135. Nonetheless, López Belinchón observes that the northern neighborhoods (barrios altos) of Madrid "concentrated a good part of the Lusitanian microsociety in [the city]," including recent arrivals and veteran madrileños. The area of highest Portuguese density extended north of the axis formed by the Calle Mayor, the Puerta del Sol, and the Calle de Alcalá, between San Bernardo Street and San Barquillo Street. This area lay at the margins of major arteries such as the avenues of Hortaleza and Fuencarral, and covered parts of the parishes of San Luís and San Martín. Many Lusitanians settled in secondary and rather humble residential streets within the area, such as the Calle de la Madera, Calle de la Ballesta, and Calle de San Antón del Barco. Id., 273.

136. Numerous works discuss the cultural Iberian-ness of sixteenth and seventeenth-century conversos as a foundational element of their individual and collective self-perception in exile. See Henry Méchoulan, *Hispanidad y judaismo en tiempos de Espinoza: Edición de* La certeza del camino *de Abraham Pereyra* (Salamanca: Ediciones Universidad de Salamanca) (hereafter cited as *Hispanidad y judaismo*). See also Van Praag, 14–26. Recent works include Kaplan, *Judíos nuevos* and Bodian, "'Men of the Nation.'"

137. Tomás de Mercado, quoted in Kamen, *Spain: 1469–1714*, 171.

138. Sancho de Moncada, quoted in Kamen, *Spain: 1469–1714*, 234.

139. The original source of this quotation is a memorial addressed to Philip IV. It appeared under the tendentiously inaccurate title "Los Judíos españoles y portugueses en el siglo XVII," in *Boletín de la Real Academia de Historia* 49 (1906): 87–103. Here I have quoted and translated an excerpt from that article that appears in López Belinchón, 306. The latter scholar's apparatus does not identify the author or date of the *memorial*. For similar and better documented examples of anti-converso polemics that focus on the economic roles of the "Portuguese," see id., 306–10.

140. On the role of powerful New Christian *asentistas* see Caro Baroja, *Los judíos*, 2:45–142; Domínguez Ortiz, *Los extranjeros*, 23–36; and López Belinchón.

141. Numerous editions of Francsico de Torrejoncillo's searingly Judeophobic *Centinela contra judíos* were published in Spain between 1674 and 1691. The work was probably based on Vicente da Costa Mattos's *Discursos contra a herética perfidia do Iudaismo* (Lisbon, 1622), a diatribe that also met with much popularity and was reissued several times. The former work restates numerous items of medieval, anti-Jewish folklore, including the accusation that Jews have tails; that they are incapable of spitting

(because they supposedly descend from those who spit upon Christ, and have been punished accordingly); that they murder Christian children ritualistically; that Jewish bodies inhibit the growth of grass over their tombs, and so on. Albert A. Sicroff, *Los estatutos de limpieza de sangre: Controversias entre los siglos XV y XVII*, trans. Mauro Armiño (Madrid: Taurus, 1985), 204–5. Proving the resiliency of such myths, Antonio Contreras's *Mayor fiscal contra judíos* (Madrid, 1736), flagrantly plagiarized Torrejoncillo's work while exceeding its venom. Domínguez Ortiz, *Los judeoconversos*, 105 n.1.

142. Yerushalmi, Cardoso, 127–28.

143. The association of Jews with evil in the medieval Christian imagination has been explored by Joshua Trachtenberg, *The Devil and the Jews: The Medieval Conception of the Jew and Its Relation to Modern Antisemitism*, 2nd ed. (New York: Meridian, 1943). On the origins of Christian Judeophobic attitudes and myths in late antiquity see Marcel Simon, "Christian Anti-Semitism," in *Essential Papers on Judaism and Christianity in Conflict: From Late Antiquity to the Reformation*, ed. Jeremy Cohen (New York: New York University Press, 1991), 131–73.

144. See Sicroff.

145. Ibid., 202–5.

146. Perhaps the most exhaustive treatment of this affair and its aftermath is that of Pulido Serrano.

147. The most complete account of the auto in question is Josef Vicente del Olmo, *Relación histórica del auto general de fe que se celebró en Madrid este año de 1680* (Madrid, 1680).

148. Both works appear in Manuel Romero de Castilla, ed., *Singular suceso en el reinado de los Reyes Católicos* (Madrid: Ediciones Rubí, 1946). Pulido Serrano, 82–83, notes that Sebastián de Nieva Calvo, a member of the Holy Office, published his own literary version of the libel, *El niño inocente* (1628), thus anticipating Lope's version by several years.

149. AHN, Inquisición de Toledo, leg. 184, exp. 12 (1651–53). López Belinchon, 342, mentions yet another case—AHN, Inquisición de Toledo, leg. 1931—in which the defendant Violante Rodríguez was accused and convicted in 1654 of flogging and burning an effigy of Christ.

150. Sicroff, 204.

151. Juan Escobar de Corro, quoted in Caro Baroja, *Los judíos*, 2:325.

152. Cervantes, quoted in Perceval, 274. The translation of Cervantes, however, is mine. A dated but reliable study on anti-Jewish references in Spanish literature of the Golden Age is Edward Glaser, "Referencias Antisemitas en la literatura peninsular de la edad de oro," *Nueva revista de filología hispánica* 8 (1954): 39–62.

153. For a discussion of accusations by sixteenth- and seventeenth-century writers that Jews were cowardly and unworthy of their supposed refinement and status, and that peasants and hidalgos were worthy of both attributes, see Sicroff, 161, 167, 198, 204, 249, 336–43.

154. Henry Kamen, "A Crisis of Conscience in Golden Age Spain," *Crisis and Change in Early Modern Spain* (Brookfield: Variorum, 1993), 7.

155. Ibid., 9. Here Kamen argues that a majority of the Spanish elite opposed *pureza de sangre* statutes in the 1580s.

156. Ibid., 4.

Chapter 3

1. See for example Haim Beinart, "The Converso Community in 16th and 17th Century Spain," *The Sephardi Heritage*, ed. R. D. Barnett, 2. vols. (London: Valentine, Mitchell, 1971), 1:476 (hereafter cited as "The Converso Community").

2. Ibid., 462–63; Révah, "Les Marranes," 29–77. Révah tends to assume conversos' desire to escape to lands where they could practice Judaism freely. See especially pp. 59–70. Along the same lines, Yosef Hayim Yerushalmi has argued that "the flight [of conversos to the Sephardi Diaspora] was itself already an act of intense Jewish commitment. . . . And this was true not only of those who fled voluntarily, but even those who . . . fled to escape arrest [by the Inquisition]." Id., "The Reeducation of Marranos," 2.

3. Révah, "Les Marranes," 55. Here the author follows a position articulated by Carl Gebhardt that a New Christian was by definition "a Catholic without belief and a Jew without knowledge, but by will, a Jew." Gebhardt, quoted in Miriam Bodian, *Hebrews*, xi.

4. Beinart, "The Converso Community," 462–63.

5. Except for a small number of sophisticated heretics such as Uriel da Costa, whose rationalistic critique of traditional religion foreshadowed modern outlooks, relatively few converso renegades have commanded scholary attention. The relative lack of interest in converso dissidents is surprising given the fact that several scholars have acknowledged the existence of returnees. It is as if the phenomenon of return had been judged so rare a priori, that it is not considered worthy of sustained discussion.

6. Cecil Roth's use of the word "strange" to describe the behavior of the returnee and super-informer Heitor Mendes Bravo is an example of the implicit notion that "renegade" behavior was bizarre. Id., "Hector Mendes Bravo." In fact, there were several returnees who presented themselves before inquisitorial authorities to denounce as Judaizers virtually everyone they had known in the Jewish Diaspora. I have found close to two dozen such men (and one woman) in a small and semi-random survey of dossiers. While these delators were a minority, their behavior was by no means "strange" in the connotational sense of "unusual" and "inexplicable."

7. AHN, Inquisición de Toledo, leg. 177, exp. 1 (1664–70), fol. 50r.

8. Uriel da Costa, for instance, reminded his readers in his autobiography that it was illegal in his day to leave the Iberian kingdoms without a royal permit. Uriel Acosta, *A Specimen of Human Life*, n. trans. (1687; New York: Bergman Publishers, 1967), 13.

9. Cf. Pulido Serrano, 58. Here the author maintains on the basis of a *memorial* sent to Philip III by Luso-converso notables that "whosoever wished to abandon Hispanic realms could and continued to do it with greater ease from Portugal than from Castile, from which the frontiers were more distant." I reiterate that flight by sea was not an easy option for conversos who were not wealthy.

10. Révah, "Les Marranes," 66, states that southwestern France was an "escale sur les chemins qui conduisaient aux juiveries de Turquie, d'Italie et du nord de l'Europe." Yet this was certainly not true for all immigrant conversos. See also Nahon, "New Christians," 337. Here Nahon observes, "A way station, France welcomed the

Spanish and Portuguese Conversos before redirecting them to other countries." This generalization is surprising in light of the fact that several of Nahon's own superb (and more nuanced) studies on the southwestern French *kehillot* contradict such a characterization. Even if many converso immigrants to France moved on, it is clear that many others remained to found communities that were not mere tributaries to the Jewish métropoles of Amsterdam and Venice (or to other important Sephardi centers such as Kairouan, Hamburg, and Jerusalem). The impression that the New Christian communities of the French southwest were essentially transitory or instrumental, I suspect, rests on a prejudgment of the intent of the escapees from Iberia. If one posits that the motivation of these exiles was a desire to "return" to mainstream Judaism, the assumption follows that they preferred (or would have preferred) to settle in the main centers of normative Jewish life. "Peripheral" places such as Peyrehorade and Bayonne are thus imaginable—however fleetingly and in contradiction of the evidence—as mere conduits for recently liberated Jewish souls.

11. In addition, there existed important settlements of New Christians in Nantes, Rouen, and Paris. Gérard Nahon, "Les rapports des communautés judéo-portugaises de France avec celle d'Amsterdam aux XVIIe et XVIIIe siécles," in *Métropoles et periphéries Sefarades d'occident: Kairouan, Amsterdam, Bayonne, Bordeaux, Jérusalem* (Paris: Les éditions du Cerf, 1993), 99–103 (hereafter cited as *Métropoles*).

12. The term "petit métropole" is Nahon's. Id., "Bayonne dans la diaspora Sefarade d'occident (XVIIe-XVIIIe siecle)," *Métropoles*, 259.

13. Révah, "Les Marranes," 66-67.

14. Nahon, *Métropoles*, 121. The source in question is a seventeenth-century memorandum cited (or wholly contained) in E. Dulaurens, *Inventaire sommaire des Archives communales antérieures à 1790, ville de Bayonne* (Paris, 1894–97), Archives de Bayonne, GG, 229. The author of the memorandum writes, "il n'y en a pas dix [juives á Saint Esprit] qui ayent du bien raisonnablement, tout le reste ne vivant que des charitës qui se font parmy eux et que leurs frères d'Hollande et D'Angleterre leur envoyent." From this Nahon concludes that the memorandum does not date from 1600, as the *Inventaire* indicates, but from a later date since, "les communautés d'Amsterdam et sourtout de Londres ne disposaient pas de l'organisation que postule ce document." For her part, Anne Zink comments that the handwriting of the *inventaire* may well be that of a local clerk whom the city of Bayonne employed in the 1670s. Id., "Une niche," 665 n.142. However, the research I present in this chapter suggests that during the seventeenth century much of the income of the refugee community of Saint Esprit derived from the mercantile activities of habitual returnees, and hence originated in Iberia. The refugees may not have been eager to admit this to a hostile Christian such as the author of the memoire given, first, the illegality of much transborder trade, and second, the social stigma that attended to the act of return within the refugee community. It is therefore entirely possible that the chronicler did write his impressions during the first quarter of the seventeenth century, albeit on the basis of unfounded assumptions or misinformation that all the refugees lived mainly by the charity of other *kehillot*, when in fact a considerable portion of their sustenance was of Iberian provenance. The surviving *inventaire* may well be a copy of the earlier original.

15. Nahon, *Métropoles*, 99–103. An example of the volatility of popular sentiment

toward the immigrants is the following episode that Manuel Rodríguez, a "Portuguese" from Biarritz, recalled in his testimony before the Inquisition of Toledo in 1632: Christian sailors in Biarritz had seen Triana Zelaya, a Frenchwoman, cast into the sea a mixture of unleavened bread, raisins, and fresh fruit, as if to put a spell on the water. At that instant, the sea became so turbulent that three beached vessels containing much merchandise were lost or damaged. When the sailors confronted the woman about the incident, she replied that her employers, three Portuguese men, had instructed her to throw the mixture of food into the sea. The sailors then approached the men, who were nearby, and threatened to denounce them as sorcerers. The three men—Cristobal Rodríguez, Franco Vaes de Acosta and Cristobal de Acosta—succeeded in bribing their assailants into silence. Fearful that local authorities would nevertheless hear of the incident, the alleged evildoers promptly escaped across the Navarrese border. Officials in Biarritz eventually tried and convicted the three men in absentia. Unappeased, "the residents of the town were indignant because of this affair and wanted to burn the homes of the Portuguese, and would have burned the Portuguese themselves had the authorities not intervened." AHN, Inquisición de Toledo, leg. 177, exp. 2 (1650–53), fol. 39r–39v. A discussion of another incident of popular hostility is Zosa Szajkowski, "An Autodafé against the Jews of Tolouse in 1685," *Jewish Quarterly Review*, n.s. 49 (1958–59): 278–81.

16. Regarding the disappearance of the "Jewish" cohort of Nantes see Jules Mathorez, "Notes sur le la colonie portugaise de Nantes," *Bulletin hispanique* 15 (1913): 316–30. With regard to the assimilation of Iberian refugees elsewhere in France see also Zosa Szajkowski, "Population Problems of Marranos and Sephardim in France, from the 16th to the 20th Centuries," *Proceedings of the American Academy for Jewish Research* 27 (1958): 83–105. Szajkowski's position is that a majority of the New Christians who immigrated to France from the sixteenth century to the beginning of the seventeenth became integral parts of French Catholic communities. In "Les Marranes," 65–67, Révah disputes this view, arguing that a majority of the refugees eventually emigrated from France or died there as Judaizers.

17. Révah, "Les Marranes," 65-66.

18. "Les routes menant à Bordeaux, celles par Labouheyre et les Grandes landes et celle par Roquefort et les Petites Landes, confluaient á vingt-cinq kilomètres au nord de l'Adour. Sur le pont de Saint Esprit . . . passait ainsi la route qui joignait Madrid à Paris et aux Flandres." Zink, "Une Niche," 643. For reproductions of various geographical surveys of early modern Spanish roads see Santos Madrazo, *El sistema de comunicaciones en España*, 1750–1850, 2 vols. (Madrid: Ediciones Turner, 1984).

19. From the eastern to the central sectors of the Pyrennean region, the mountain chain rises nearly 9,800 feet. Passes lower than 6,500 feet exist only in the far west, where the chain begins to blend into the Cantabrian range. These western passes alone permit travelers (non-alpinists, at any rate) to cross the Pyrennean range itself. *Britannica.com, Encyclopaedia Britannica*, January 8, 2000 <http://britannica.com/>, s.v. "Pyrennees."

20. While the Treaty of the Pyrenees (1659) affirmed the territorial integrity of France and Spain in principle, it did not define the territorial boundary between the two states. In effect, earlier, local arrangements such as grazing treaties between villages and individual villagers had for long set the actual political borders of the two

kingdoms throughout the western Basque region. More importantly, these local treaties shaped and gave expression to the fundamentally peaceful political environment of the western Pyrenees. To foment trade among (mostly Basque) mountain dwellers and valley dwellers, these traditional agreements protected the free circulation of persons and goods across the region. From the fifteenth century until the nineteenth, regional treaties pledged the residents of the Pyrennean valleys to eternal peace irrespective of any conflicts between the Spanish and French sovereigns. Such was the preexisting sense of cohesion among Basque and Navarrese villagers on both sides of the international border that for three centuries they frequently refused to fight for their respective sovereigns and countries, and thus kept their mountainous area relatively peaceful. Daniel Alexander Gómez-Ibáñez, *The Western Pyrennes: Differential Evolution of the French and Spanish Borderlands* (Oxford: Clarendon Press, 1975), 13, 44–49.

21. Nahon furnishes various data that support this position in *Métropoles*, 107, 121. The former page (n. 98) includes a citation from the *Livro dos termos da ymposta da nação*, a document dating from the 1620s, in which the Amsterdam *kahal* made it clear that it would not help conversos immigrate to the Netherlands from France.

22. For example, several witnesses accused Juan Rodríguez Faro, a dynamic and successful wholesaler, of emigrating to St. Jean de Luz in 1632, then moving (in chronological order) to Bayonne, Bordeaux, and Amsterdam. From the latter city the suspect allegedly returned "sometimes" (*algunas veces*) to Madrid and Seville to conduct various transactions. AHN, Inquisición de Toledo, leg. 180, exp. 6 (1635–50), fols. 12r–21r. Manuel Méndez Cardoso, a Portuguese envoy of the king of Spain and probably a mid-level *asentista* as well (hence a relatively affluent man) immigrated directly to Flanders. From there he transferred his family to Amsterdam, where he allegedly became a Jew. AHN, Inquisición de Toledo, leg. 166, exp. 6 (1622–25), not foliated. In a letter to converso residents of southwestern France (ca. 1626–27), Rabbi Immanuel Aboab recorded for posterity some of the economic reasons that compelled poorer refugees (at least in their view) to remain in that region: "Others say," the rabbi complained, "that . . . if they do not do what they should and profess . . . what the Lord commands . . . [it is because] things are so difficult and business is so futile in [southern France] that if they were to depart [from there] . . . they would spend a good portion of their assets, and they would later have to endure a penurious existence." Aboab, British Museum MS OR. 8698, fols. 275–97, quoted in C. Roth, "Immanuel Aboab," 145. The translation of Aboab's words from Castilian is mine.

23. Bodian, *Hebrews*, 141.

24. See note 13 above.

25. Jonathan I. Israel, "The Sephardi Contribution to Economic Life and Colonization in Europe and the New World (Sixteenth–Eighteenth Centuries)," *Moreshet Sepharad: The Sephardi Legacy*, ed. Haim Beinart, 2 vols. (Jerusalem: Magnes Press, 1992), 379–80.

26. Ibid., 380. A more thorough treatment of the relationship between the embargo and the development of Franco-Sephardi communities in the French southwest is Israel's article, "Crypto-Judaism in 17th-Century France: An Economic and Religious Bridge Between the Hispanic World and the Sephardic Diaspora." It appears as chapter 7 in id., *Diasporas within a Diaspora: Jews, Crypto-Jews, and the World*

Maritime Empires (1540–1740) (Leiden: Brill, 2002) (hereafter cited as *Diasporas within a Diaspora*).

27. Travelers did not have to cross the Pyrenees at high altitudes unless they wished to avoid customs posts altogether. It was possible, for instance, to enter France by way of the border city of Irún. Testifying in 1609, the returnee Francisco Díaz Méndez recalled, "It has been three years since [the defendant] left . . . Madrid to go to Rouen of France, where he intended to settle his household and have [commercial] correspondence with Portugal, with Castile and with Flanders. . . . [A]long the way he passed through Vizcaya to St. Jean de Luz and Bordeaux, which [are along] the Royal Highway. . . . [A]bout two months ago he came back here to Madrid by the same route." AHN, Inquisición de Toledo, leg. 142, exp. 3 (1609–10), not foliated. The defendant was clearly familiar with the key parts of the highway system that linked the Low Countries with Madrid via Paris, Irún, Burgos, Valladolid, and Medina del Campo. Other important routes included that which connected Lisbon and the Pyrenees via Valladolid and Burgos. María Matilla Montáñez, *El correo en la España de los Austrias* (Madrid: Consejo Superior de Investigaciónes Científicas, Escuela de Historia Moderna, 1953), 53. The merchant and inquisitorial spy Antonio de Acosta de Paz deposed in 1633 that his fellow returnees habitually employed Irún, Maia (?), and Burguete as their principal points of entry into Spain. AHN, Inquisición de Toledo, leg. 145, exp. 9 (1634), not foliated.

On the mercantile network linking conversos in the Netherlands to those in Spain (especially Madrid) via conversos in France in the years following the Spanish embargo, see Jonathan Israel, "Some Further Data on the Amsterdam Sephardim and Their Trade with Spain During the 1650s," *Studia Rosenthaliana* 14.1 (1980): 7–19.

28. I reiterate that in the 1600s there did not exist a perfect rabbinical consensus as to the religious status of conversos and hence as to the manner in which they should be integrated into diasporic Judaism. Some rabbis advocated the outright *conversion* of immigrants to normative Judaism; others proposed integration through repentance and atonement alone, thus implying that the immigrants were already Jewish. Still others combined both approaches. According to Simón Schwartzfuchs, however, the first approach became dominant in the Sephardi Diaspora during the seventeenth century. By then several generations separated immigrant conversos from normative Judaism. This probably rendered these conversos less palatable as errant "Jews." Id., "Le Retour des Marranes," 339–48. Disagreeing with Schwartzfuchs, Yosef Kaplan states in an unpublished review of the manuscript of this book, dated November 27, 2002, that rabbis regarded the conversos who adopted Judaism as "forced converts who returned to the bosom of Israel."

29. One of the most famous cases of "martyrdom" is that of Isaac de Castro Tartas. He was captured by the Brazilian Inquisition while allegedly in possession of Jewish religious artifacts. His subsequent execution in Lisbon in 1647 stirred the passions of former Christians throughout the Sephardi Diaspora. On Castro see for example Elias Lipiner, *Izaque de Castro: O mancebo que veio preso do Brasil* (Recife: Fundação Joaquim Nabuco, 1992). Negligence or a foolish craving for martyrdom seems to have motivated another transient, the religious equivocator Abraham Reuven, to travel to Iberian lands from Amsterdam. Like Castro, this self-described Jewish educator was carrying objects that his inquisitorial captors interpreted (in this case quite plausibly)

as evidence of his intent to spread Judaism among peninsular conversos. One of the objects in question was a printed Hebrew alphabet such as one would expect a teacher of children (and religious novices) to use as a training tool. The defendant's dossier preserves this document as part of an unfoliated appendix. It is conceivable that Reuven had learned to recognize Hebrew characters from such an alphabet, if not from the very one his captors confiscated. AHN, Inquisición de Toledo, leg. 134, exp. 18 (1624–25). On Reuven, see Haim Beinart, "The Travel of Jews from Morocco to Spain in the Early Seventeenth Century" (in Hebrew), *The Jubilee Volume in Honor of Salo W. Baron on the Occasion of his Eightieth Birthday* (Jerusalem: American Academy for Jewish Research, 1974).

30. "Y si alguna vez comía [alimentos prohibidos por la Ley de Moises] era por estar delante algunas personas." AHN, Inquisición de Toledo, leg. 142, exp. 2 (1636), not foliated.

31. Yosef Kaplan, "Wayward New Christians," 30.

32. Ibid.

33. This is how Yosef Kaplan, among other scholars, has described them. See for example id., "Wayward New Christians." There is curious evidence, however, that seventeenth-century Iberians used the term themselves to refer to converts to Judaism. For instance, the defendant Jacinto Vásquez Araujo testified in 1687 that he had wanted to become a *judío nuevo* despite the fact that all his ancestors had been Old Christians. AHN, Inquisición de Toledo, leg. 187, exp. 4. (1687–88), fol. 228v.

34. Kaplan, "La comunidad sefardí de Amsterdam en el siglo XVII: Entre la tradición y el cambio," *Judíos nuevos*, 28–33.

35. Ibid., 38. The phrase "morality of conformism" is Kaplan's.

36. Kaplan, "The Travels," 205–6.

37. Ibid.

38. Yosef Kaplan, "The Struggle."

39. Kaplan, "Wayward New Christians," 33. See also id., "The Role of Rabbi Moshe D'Aguilar in His Contacts with Refugees from Spain and Portugal in the Seventeenth Century" (in Hebrew), *Proceedings of the Sixth World Congress of Jewish Studies, Hebrew University of Jerusalem, August* 13–19, 1973 (Jerusalem: World Union of Jewish Studies, 1975), 2:95–106 (hereafter cited as "Moshe D'Aguilar").

40. There is no doubt that communal Jewish life in the French southwest existed in some fashion prior to the eighteenth century. It is nonetheless suggestive of the underdeveloped state of the *kehillot* in question that aside from tombstones bearing traces of Jewish names, the Iberian refugees did not bequeath documents attesting to their formal organization as specifically Jewish colonies until the eighteenth century. See Nahon, *Métropoles*, 97–98. As for the eighteenth century, the only internal, Jewish source available is a log-book of the "Portuguese nation" of Bordeaux. Its interesting but limited contents have been published by Simón Schwartzfuchs, *Le Registre des délibérations de la nation juive portugaise de Bordeaux (1711–1787)* (Paris: Fondation Calouste Gulbenkian, 1981). A communal document from greater Bayonne is also extant. Gérard Nahon, "Une délibération de la 'Nation portugaise de Saint-Esprit' relative aux synagogues (1776)," *Revue des etudes juives* 124 (1965): 422–27 (hereafter cited as "Une délibération"). Despite the fact that, as I indicated earlier, the refugee outposts of the southwest were not mere "way stations" on the road to more openly Ju-

daicized centers of the converso Diaspora, Israel is ultimately right to state that in the cultural sense "the crypto-Jewish network which developed in the late sixteenth century and early seventeenth in south-west France remained over many decades insecure, furtive, and transitional." Id., *Diasporas within a Diaspora*, 247.

41. According to Gérard Nahon, the earliest extant document proving that French authorities formally recognized the "Portuguese" community of greater Bayonne as Jewish dates from 1684. Nahon, "The Sephardim," 2:52. For information regarding the shifting attitudes of Jewish communal authorities toward France and other predominantly Catholic places in the Iberian Diaspora that were cultural thresholds for conversos, such as Antwerp, see Yosef Kaplan, "The Struggle."

42. Nahon, *Métropoles*, 111. "[I]l semble," Nahon writes, "que la venue á Bayonne du Rabbin italien Raphael Meldola ait determiné l'adoption du rituel de priéres de Livourne dans les communautés françaises." Ibid., 143. On later relations between various Sephardi communities, including those in France, see Oliel Grausz.

43. Nahon, *Métropoles*, 143. I hasten to add that however much rabbinical and other social pressure was brought to bear on conversos in southwestern France to join the Jewish community, there is no evidence that Jewish authorities ever used the kind of blatant coercion that was the Inquisition's chief currency. Orthodox rabbinical Judaism was far from a Jewish mirror image, as it were, of counterreformist Catholicism.

44. The declarant's possible formulation, *[pecar]ía mortalmente*, would appear to be an example of residual Catholicism, so to speak. There was and is no such thing as a "mortal sin" in rabbinic Judaism. Also, the declarant seems to have been somewhat confused or ignorant regarding the use of tefillin (phylacteries), which by rabbinic law are only worn on weekdays, not on the Sabbath. Was Fernández's error a reaction to inquisitorial probing regarding these artifacts? Did memory serve Fernández badly, or was he so uninterested in (or ignorant of) matters of ritual that he would have been incapable of correcting his own error in any case?

45. AHN, Inquisición de Toledo, leg. 147, exp. 1 (1663–65), not foliated.

46. Ibid., 38r. See also nonfoliated portions. The testimony is that of Manuel Gómez, an unemployed native of Oporto, an erstwhile resident of Bayonne, and, at the time of his deposition, a resident of Madrid. He testified "of his own accord" (*de su voluntad*).

47. Kaplan, "Wayward New Christians," 29.

48. Diego de Cisneros, quoted. in Israel, *Diasporas within a Diaspora*, 260.

49. Cf. Kaplan, "The Travels," 204.

50. See for example the testimony of Francisco Núñez Redondo in reference to the trader Joseph de Sanpayo. AHN, Inquisición de Toledo, leg. 169, exp. 10 (1663–68), fol. 76r.

51. See the testimony of Francisco Roldán in AHN, Inquisición de Toledo, leg. 165, exp. 12 (1661–71), fol. 36r. Roldán testified that he had dealt with several merchants in Amsterdam who "come and go to Spain with merchandise" (*van y vienen a España con las mercadurías*). Another returnee, Francisco Díaz Méndez, reported: "he has . . . seen other people in St. Jean de Luz who are prone to come and go from there to here and from here to there. . . ." (*también ha visto [a] otras personas en St. Jean de*

Luz que suelen ir y venir de aqui allá y de allá aqui). AHN, Inquisición de Toledo, leg. 142, exp. 3 (1609–10), not foliated.

52. I reiterate that I have not attempted to quantify the phenomena of return. Given the fact that not all returnees were captured by the peninsular Inquisitions, and considering the sheer number of inquisitorial cases one would have to review to arrive at statistically significant conclusions (not to mention the embryonic state of scholarly research on the subject), I believe that a definitive quantification of return is not currently attainable. In this work I nonetheless provide an educated impression of the phenomenon (and of its relative dimensions) based on the inquisitorial cases under consideration.

53. Kaplan, "The Travels," 203.

54. After all, frequent travel between northern Europe and the Iberian Peninsula was more expensive, more time consuming, and entailed longer distances than returning from southwestern France.

55. Zink, "L'activité," 92. The translation from Zink's French prose is mine.

56. AHN, Inquisición de Toledo, leg. 131, exp. 10 (1652–54), fol. 39r. The delator's reference is to the returnee Francisco de Aguilar. Inquisitorial records tell us little else about Aguilar, yet various additional testimonies allow us to infer the wide scope of the commercial and social activites of his fellow customs-dodgers. For instance, Pedro López de Olivera, a merchant-returnee, said of another smuggler:

When [López] was [in Madrid] . . . he saw a Portuguese man . . . from the [suburb] of Santispiritus in Bayonne, now living in Bordeaux of France, where [the man] worked as a courier. . . . The [witness] knows the man is married in this court [of Madrid] to a Portuguese . . . midwife who lives in San Anton [Street]. . . . [The man] is usually occupied with bringing smuggled merchandise from France to Castile. . . . [López asked the smuggler] how he had fared in his recent trip to Aix-en-Provence from said suburb of Santispiritus, from which the witness had seen him depart on that journey in the company of [another merchant], who used to be a resident of this court and lived next to the [Plaza] of San Anton Martín . . . [where] he sells tobacco, chocolate, and other things with his wife and family.

AHN, Inquisición de Toledo, leg. 177, exp. 2 (1650–53), fols. 49v–50r, 51r.

57. *C[h]amelote*: a strong and impermeable woolen fabric. *Diccionario de la lengua española*, Real Academia Española, 21st ed., s.v. "camelote" (hereafter cited as *Diccionario*). According to the lexicographer Sebastián de Covarrubias Orozco (1539–1613), a *camelote* is made of camel hair. Id., *Tesoro de la lengua castellana o española*, ed. Felipe C. R. Maldonado (1611; reprint, rev. by Manuel Camarero, Madrid: Editorial Castalia, 1995), s.v. "camelote."

58. *Rasilla*: A thin, woolen cloth similar to *lamparilla* (a fabric used in the manufacture of summer dresses and capes). *Diccionario* s.v. "rasilla."

59. *Caza*: a very thin type of linen similar to gauze. Ibid., s.v. "caza."

60. *Bayeta*: A loosely woven woolen cloth. Ibid., s.v. "bayeta."

61. *Cambray*: From Cambray, a city in France. A type of slight, white linen. Ibid., s.v. "cambray."

62. *Olanda*: From *Holanda* [Holland], the fabric's place of origin. A very fine linen used to make shirts, bedsheets, and other items. Ibid., s.v. "holanda."

63. *Morlés*: From Morles, a city in Brittany. A linen fabric, not very fine, made in Morles. Ibid., s.v. "morlés."

64. *Arroba*: Weight equivalent to 11 kilograms and 502 grams. In Aragon, 12.5 kilograms. Ibid., s.v. "arroba."

65. *Bretaña*: A fine linen manufactured in Brittany. Ibid., s.v. "bretaña."

66. *Guinga*: From the Portuguese, *guingão* (of Malasyan origin). A type of cotton fabric. Imitations of this fabric include varieties of flax and silk. Ibid., s.v. "guinga."

67. AHN, Inquisición de Toledo, leg. 165, exp. 12 (1661–71), fols. 76r–78v.

68. For a discussion of the peaceful social and commercial environment of the Basque Pyrenees and their valleys see Gómez-Ibáñez, 44–49.

69. AHN, Inquisición de Toledo, leg. 177, exp. 11 (1641–78), fol. 13r. *Aguardiente* refers to a kind of liquor distilled from wine (among other substances). *Diccionario* s.v. "aguardiente."

70. AHN, Inquisición de Toledo, leg. 161, exp. 5 (1653–55), fol. 55r. The defendant was probably the same Francisco Lopes Capadosse whom Jewish authorities of Amsterdam threatened to place under a ban in 1622 if he did not become affiliated with the Jewish congregation and have himself and his sons circumcised. The reasoning of the communal authorities was that Lopes should be incorporated into the *kehillah* because he was a member of the Hebrew nation who professed the unity of God. Lopes reportedly reacted with disdain to the ultimatum, saying that the community could do whatever it wished. Kaplan, "Wayward New Christians," 28–29. See also Bodian, *Hebrews*, 112–13.

71. A similar account appears in AHN, Inquisición de Toledo, leg. 147, exp. 1 (1663–65), fol. 28v. Here Gonzalo Correa testifies that in France the defendant, Jorge Fernández de Castro, had publicly complained that "a relative he had over here [namely, in Madrid] . . . had all his assets and that he had not been able to take anything [to France] besides the shirt he was wearing, and that this would force him to come to Spain to take the assets away from [his relative], although it was so risky to return."

72. AHN, Inquisición de Toledo, leg. 165, exp. 12 (1661–71), fol. 66v.

73. Ibid., 30r.

74. Several Old Christians employed the term "merchant" pejoratively to mean "converso," while others considered all merchants, especially ones who dealt in foreign goods, as leeches who selfishly attached themselves to a healthy body (Ibero-Christian society) and sapped its strength. Already in the sixteenth century, the figure of "the merchant" had assumed a dishonorable hue in several comedic, tragic, and political portrayals. The commentator Tomás de Mercado echoed several critiques when when he stated in 1568, "The merchant is not a man desirous of the good of his own homeland . . . but a lover of his own money and someone who covets that of others." Id., *Suma de tratos y contratos (Madrid, 1568)*, quoted in Michel Cavillac, *Pícaros y mercaderes en el Guzmán de Alfarache: Reformismo burgués y mentalidad aristocrática en la España del siglo de oro,* trans. Juan M. Azpitarte Almagro (Granada: Universidad de Granada, 1994), 204–5. See also ibid., 193–95. Cavillac argues that the negative portrayal of merchants in Spanish culture of the Golden Age masked a latent mercantilism in Spanish society.

75. AHN, Inquisición de Toledo, leg. 147, exp. 1 (1663–65). For example, an un-foliated section of this dossier includes a record of the defendant's verbal reproduction, from memory, of what he called "the morning prayer" of the Jews. In fact the prayer he intoned is almost entirely consonant with the beginning of the daily afternoon service, the *minḥa*: "Mi Dio me dio el alma, que diste en mi limpia, tú la criaste [sic], tu la formaste, tu la soplaste [?] . . . Adonay Dio mio, Dio de mis padres, señor de todas obras, señor de todas almas, bendito tú Adonay, y nuestro Dio, rey del mundo, haces tornar almas a cuerpos muertos . . . hazme apartar de inclinación mala." Ibid., not foliated.

76. Ibid., not foliated.

77. AHN, Inquisición de Toledo, leg. 169, exp. 10 (1663–69), fols. 48r, 51v.

78. Ibid., fol. 60r.

79. Ibid., fols. 37v–38r.

80. AHN, Inquisición de Toledo, leg. 150, exp. 17 (1669–70), fol. 27v.

81. Ibid.

82. Ibid., fol. 29r–v.

83. Ibid., 30r–v.

84. Ibid., 30r.

85. Ibid.

86. AHN, Inquisición de Toledo, leg. 142, exp. 3 (1609–10), not foliated.

87. See Willemse, XLIV. Cf. Caro Baroja, *Los judíos*, 2:60–61. Caro attributes return to an "obsessive" greed among New Christian merchants. The Judeophobic overtones of Caro's position and language in this respect bear an eerie resemblance to early modern conversophobic canards, and are vaguely reminiscent of the well-known antisemitism of Caro's own relative, the novelist Pío Baroja.

88. AHN, Inquisición de Toledo, leg. 136, exp. 5 (1659–61), fols. 44v–47r, 70r–77v.

89. Ibid., fol. 30v.

90. In addition, by the seventeenth century the Holy Office commuted the sentences of "perpetual" imprisonment after a few months. Such sentences rarely exceeded three years if the prisoner showed signs of repentance. Kamen, *The Spanish Inquisition*, 201.

91. This is according to the witness Joseph García de León. AHN, Inquisición de Toledo, leg. 136, exp. 5 (1659–61), fol. 7r–7v.

92. See Zink, "L'activité," 233; Edgar R. Samuel, "The Trade of the New Christians of Portugal in the Seventeenth Century," *The Sephardi Heritage*, ed. R. D. Barnett and W. M. Schwab (Grendon: Gibraltar Books, 1989), 2:100–113 (hereafter cited as "The Trade"). Another merchant who typified habitual return is Juan Rodríguez Faro. AHN, Inquisición de Toledo, leg. 180, exp. 6 (1635–60). See especially fols. 1r–16v.

93. In addition, the defendant claimed that he had prayed in silence (and in abbreviated form) while he had been alone. AHN, Inquisición de Toledo, leg. 177, exp. 1 (1664–70), fol. 58v.

94. Despite their common last name, Rodríguez, all appearances suggest that the men were not related.

95. AHN, Inquisición de Toledo, leg. 177, exp. 11 (1641–78). See also Caro Baroja, *Los judíos*, 2:145–64.

96. Gómez's dossier is AHN, Inquisición de Toledo, leg. 152, exp. 6 (1663–65). Al-

donza Cardosa de Velasco's case is AHN, Inquisición de Toledo leg. 138, exp. 12 (1668–70); that of Isabel de Silva is AHN, Inquisición de Toledo, leg. 184, exp. 13 (1636–39). For information regarding María de León, a major witness in the dossier on the defendant Jorge Fernández de Castro, see AHN, Inquisición de Toledo, leg. 147, exp. 1 (1663–65). The names of a few additional women who were permanent returnees occur elsewhere, though the information regarding these subjects is minimal. See appendix, table B, below.

97. AHN, Inquisición de Toledo, leg. 147, exp. 1 (1663–65), fol. 18r (labeled 14r). The delator in question was Manuel Pasaña (1662).

98. AHN, Inquisición de Toledo, leg. 166, exp. 8 (1664), fols. 4r–5v. The cited testimony is that of Manuel de Leon, a witness.

99. AHN, Inquisición de Toledo, leg. 177, exp. 11 (1641–78), fol. 204r. The cited testimony is that of Simón Núñez Nieto, an inquisitorial prisoner at Logroño (1665).

100. AHN, Inquisición de Toledo, leg. 177, exp. 2 (1650–53), fol. 48v. The cited testimony is that of Francisco Cardoso Ortiz (1641).

101. ANTT, Inquisição de Lisboa, proc. no. 7938 (1650), fol. 8r.

102. H. P. Salomon, *Le procès de l'inquisition portugaise comme documents littéraires, ou du bon usage du fonds inquisitorial de la Torre do Tombo* (Lisbon: Torre do Tombo and Estudos Portugueses-Homenagem a António José Saraiva, 1990).

103. The defendant's age was "advanced" by the standards of his time, place, and culture.

104. AHN, Inquisición de Toledo, leg. 152, exp. 6 (1663–65), fol. 2r.

105. Ibid., 2v.

106. AHN, Inquisición de Toledo, leg. 177, exp. 11 (1641–78), fol. 215r. The testimony cited is from the deposition of Manuel Machuca (1662).

107. Evidence of conversos' peculiar views on circumcision includes the exchange of letters between Rabbi Moses D'Aguilar and David Manuel Isidro, a member of the "Portuguese nation" of Bayonne (ca. 1663). Somewhat confused by the notion that circumcision posessed salvific power, Isidro asked what would happen to the souls of conversos who died circumcized but were buried in Christian cemeteries in accordance with Christian rites. D'Aguilar responded adamantly that circumcision did not save, purify, or spiritually transform men who wished to become Jewish. Kaplan, "Wayward New Christians," 32–33; id., "Moshe D'Aguilar," 99–101.

108. For impressions of alleged initiations and marranic fasting see David M. Gitlitz, *Secrecy and Deceit: The Religion of the Crypto-Jews* (Philadelphia: Jewish Publication Society, 1996), 191, 224–28, 321, 391–402, 507–8, 628.

109. AHN, Inquisición de Toledo, leg. 152, exp. 6 (1663–65), fol. 6r–6v.

110. Ibid., 5v.

111. Ibid., 12v.

112. Cf. AHN, Inquisición de Toledo, leg. 147, exp. 5 (1651–52), fol. 5r–7v. Here a Portuguese prisoner accuses his New Christian friends and employers of holding a bizarre ceremony in which they ritualistically spit on him. For an example of imaginative Judeophobic accusations see also AHN, Inquisición de Toledo, leg. 174, exp. 17 (1661), and my discussion in the previous chapter.

113. Juan Blázquez Miguel, *Inquisición y criptojudaismo* (Madrid: Kaydeda, 1988), 149. See also Kamen, *The Spanish Inquisition,* 285. Cf. Contreras Contreras, "Cripto-

judaísmo," 288. Contreras's analysis suggests that by the sixteenth century residual crypto-Judaism was limited primarily to large Spanish cities, less so to small towns and rural villages, where familial alliances were stronger and active crypto-Judaism was consequently more difficult to eradicate than in the cities.

114. It would be a mistake to assume from later evidence that throughout the seventeenth century the "Portuguese" refugees of Saint Esprit comprised an *entirely* cohesive (as opposed to a largely institutionalized) *kehillah*. No Jewish archival documents exist to support such an assumption. All but one of the extant records concerning the "nation" of Saint Esprit are French municipal and royal documents. The exception is a record that dates from 1776. See Nahon, "Une délibération." Even though it is very likely that during the 1600s the community had instituted at least the rudiments of a full-fledged *kahal*, a burial society, and other such organizations, it would be erroneous, given the data I offer in the present work, to assume that the refugees themselves exhibited a high level of religious discipline and political unity in the 1600s. Incidentally, Nahon maintains that "le registre [communautaire] de Bayonne a disparu." This assertion implies the author's certainty that such a record existed. Id., *Métropoles*, 98. An important (if unanswerable) question, however, is, *when* did the community begin to keep its own records? I would be surprised to find that it did so prior to the mid-seventeenth century.

115. AHN, Inquisición de Toledo, leg. 152, exp. 6 (1663–65), fol. 6r–v.

116. It is not accidental, for instance, that Louis XIII officially referred to the Iberian refugees in the provinces of the *Pays-Bas* as "les Marchands Portugaises." Nahon, Métropoles, 154.

117. This was true even when refugees accorded the Castilian language a semisacred status. According to Henry Méchoulan (among others), in most parts of the Sephardi Diaspora Castilian was a language of Jewish prayer and educated discourse second in prestige only to Hebrew. See id., *Hispanidad y judaísmo*, 40–42.

118. Perhaps the most famous of Castilian conversos who decided to abandon predominantly "Portuguese" milieux was the poet Antonio Enríquez Gómez (1600–1663). The writer's successful installation in the "Portuguese" communities of Bordeaux and Rouen, like his political support of the secessionist house of Braganza, suggest his ability to thrive in a Lusophone mainstream. Nonetheless, Enríquez returned to Spain, apparently with the intention of remaining there indefinitely. In 1661 the Santo Oficio captured and tried him (incidentally misidentifying him as "Portuguese"). Scholars have proposed diverse theories to explain Enríquez' repatriation. See for example I. S. Révah, "Un pamphlet"; Rose; Amiel. McGaha, sheds new light on the matter. See also Wilke, *Jüdisch-christliches*. These authors' theories merit greater attention than I can provide in the present work. My point here is that Enríquez's return, like that of Fernando Alvarez, precludes the assumption that all Castilian refugees wished to become permanently absorbed into "Portuguese" communities.

119. On the perpetuation of conversos' cultural ties to the Iberian Peninsula, see for example Cecil Roth, "The Role of Spanish in the Marrano Diaspora," *Hispanic Studies in Honor of I. Fonzález Llubera*, ed. Frank Pierce (Oxford: The Dolphin Book Co., 1959), 299–308.

120. AHN, Inquisición de Toledo, leg. 177, exp. 11 (1641–78), fols. 33r–34v. See also AHN, Inquisición de Toledo, leg. 177, exp. 1 (1664–70), fol. 16r.

121. AHN, Inquisición de Toledo, leg. 152, exp. 6 (1663–65), fol. 8v–9r.

122. AHN, Inquisición de Toledo, leg. 166, exp. 6 (1622–25), not foliated.

123. Ibid.

124. At the time of Nunes' deposition the Amsterdam *kehillah* was in a relatively early stage of its development, although its growth during that stage was dramatic (from five hundred individuals in 1612 to one thousand in 1620). See Kaplan, *Judíos nuevos*, 15.

125. AHN, Inquisición de Toledo, leg. 177, exp. 2 (1650–53), fols. 49v–50r, 51r. The cited testimony is that of Francisco Cardoso Ortiz (1641).

126. AHN, Inquisición de Toledo, leg. 177, exp. 11 (1641–78), 214v. Here Manuel Machuca's testimony derives from a separate trial commenced in Valencia in on August 14, 1662.

127. Kaplan, "Familia, matrimonio y sociedad: Los casamientos clandestinos en la diáspora sefardí occidental," in *Judíos nuevos*, 112.

128. C. Roth, "Immanuel Aboab," 131, 150.

129. Ibid., 130–31, 146.

130. Ibid., 145–47.

131. For instance, in 1613 Nuno D'Oliveira testified that he had initially intended to return to Portugal from the Netherlands because "he did not find any means of life there" (*nam ach[ou] ahy algú modo de vida*). ANTT, Inquisição de Evora, proc. no. 2305 (1612–14), not foliated.

Chapter 4

1. Perhaps the most exhaustive recent work on the functioning of inquisitorial tribunals in Spain is Joaquín Pérez Villanueva and Bartolomé Escandell Bonet, eds., *Historia de la Inquisición en España y América*, 2 vols. (Madrid: Biblioteca de Autores Cristianos, 1984–93) (hereafter cited as *España y América*). See also Joaquín Pérez Villanueva, ed., *La Inquisición española: Nueva visión, nuevos horizontes* (Mexico City: Siglo XXI, 1980) (hereafter cited as *Inquisición española*).

2. As Amos Funkenstein has suggested, "[F]acts are not atomic entities out there which declare their own importance. . . . Facts gain their meaning and even their very factuality from the context in which they are embedded, a context reconstructed solely by the historian." Id., "History, Counterhistory, and Narrative," *Perceptions of Jewish History* (Berkeley: University of California Press, 1993), 34. In our case, "context" consisted of the environment(s) in which the renegades moved. Here the renegades were the "historians" of their own lives.

3. Ibid., 35.

4. ANTT, Inquisição de Lisboa, proc. no. 3080 (1619), not foliated. The testimony cited is that of Pantaleón da Silva.

5. See for example Saraiva, *Inquisição e cristãos-novos*.

6. Ferro Tavares, *Los judíos en Portugal*, 354–56.

7. For discussions of inquisitorial finances see Kamen, *The Spanish Inquisition*, 149, 151, 154–56. See also José Martínez Millán, "Structures of Inquisitorial Finance," *The Spanish Inquisition and the Inquisitorial Mind*, ed. Angel Alcalá (New York: Co-

lumbia University Press, 1987), 159–76; id. *La hacienda de la inquisición (1478–1700)* (Madrid: Instituto Enrique Flórez, 1984). For information regarding the Portugal tribunals see Saraiva, 167–74.

8. Saraiva, 121.

9. AHN, Inquisición de Toledo, leg. 159, exp. 9 (1625), fols. 6v–7v. The declarant in question was Diego de Lima.

10. AHN, Inquisición de Toledo, leg. 138, exp. 12 (1668–70), fols. 64r, 149r.

11. Henry Charles Lea, *A History of the Inquisition of Spain*, 4 vols. (New York: Macmillan Company, 1906), 2:3.

12. Cf. López Belinchón, 312–15, 320. López explains that the Count-Duke Olivares mobilized the Inquisition to attempt to disrupt the smuggling networks through which Luso-conversos side-stepped Habsburg authorities and fed the economies of France and the Netherlands, especially during the Spanish embargo against the Dutch provinces. However, "the effectiveness of [Olivares's] measures was very scant." Furthermore, "at no time was [the policy of disruption] intended to finish off [Luso-converso businessmen], neither socially nor economically." Id., 315, 327. An exception to the relative ineffectiveness of the Inquisition in this regard is the episode concerning the inquisitorial functionary Juan Bautista de Villadiego. Sent by the Holy Office to investigate Judaizing in France, Villadiego denounced several conversos in Rouen. In the ensuing scandal, some sixty-six converso families whose members claimed to identify with Catholicism returned to Spain from France. Id., 321–23.

13. AHN, Inquisición de Toledo, leg. 136, exp. 5 (1654–57), fol. 44v.

14. Kamen, *The Spanish Inquisition*, 194–195. Efficient overviews of the standard procedures that inquisitorial tribunals followed in the conduct of trials include id., 174–213, and Beinart, *Conversos on Trial*, 105–93. A more extensive discussion is Pérez Villanueva and Escandell Bonet, *España y América*, 1:334–474.

15. See Lea, 3:13–16. In theory the tribunals did not prosecute anyone who had not reached "the age of reason" (twelve for girls and fourteen for boys). In practice inquisitors violated this restriction, even while they routinely assigned a *curador* (guardian) to defendants who were under twenty-five years of age, and hence "minors." Id., 2:3–4.

16. Kamen, *The Spanish Inquisition*, 188.

17. AHN, Inquisición de Toledo, leg. 150, exp. 17 (1669–70), fol. 78r. On the similarly lenient manner in which Portuguese tribunals approached ultra-delators such as Gil see Herman P. Salomon, "The Case of Luis Vaz Pimentel: Revelations of Early Jewish Life in Rotterdam from the Portuguese Inquisition Archives," *Studia Rosenthaliana* 31 (1997): 7–30. See also C. Roth, "Hector Mendes Bravo."

18. Contrition and its manifestation were (and are) central elements of the experience of sacramental confession, ideally conceived. For a discussion of high medieval and early modern theological approaches to contrition as a Christian religious imperative see Thomas N. Tentler, *Sin and Confession on the Eve of the Reformation* (Princeton, N.J.: Princeton University Press, 1977), 104–33, 250–300, 353–54.

19. For instance, Felipe Diaz Gutiérrez "showed signs of contrition and remorse in his confessions [by] asking God for His . . . pardon for his crimes and us for merciful penitence." AHN, Inquisición de Toledo, leg. 142, exp. 2 (1636), not foliated. So

too, during his confession the suspected Judaizer Enrique Gómez de Fonseca "knelt and and asked God our Lord for pardon . . . which he did with many tears." AHN, Inquisición de Toledo, leg. 189, exp. 10 (1657), fol. 8v.

20. Here I merely provide a summary of the inquisitorial protocol. Complete versions of standard *nterogatorios* have been published elsewhere. Cf. Pilar Huerga Criado's reproduction of a 1661 protocol developed by the Suprema (the Spanish Inquisition's chief tribunal). Id., 239.

21. A host of recent studies have focused on the pedagogical and political nature of inquisitorial functions while treating the *procesos* themselves as sources of sociological and anthropological data. These works include Jaime Contreras and Gustav Henningsen, "Forty-Four Thousand Cases of the Spanish Inquisition (1540–1700): Analysis of a Historical Data Bank," *The Inquisition in Early Modern Europe: Studies on Sources and Methods,* ed. Gustav Henningsen and John Tedeschi (Dekalb: Northern Illinois University Press, 1986), and Dedieu. The socio-political ground of denunciations has been explored by Jaime Contreras Conteras in the microhistorical study *Sotos contra Riquelmes.* For a discussion of the inquisitorial enterprise as a cultural phenomenon and means of social control see Bartolomé Benassar, ed., *L'Inquisition espagnole: Xve–XIXe siècle* (Verviers: Marabout, 1979) (hereafter cited as *L'Inquisition espagnole*). For a meticulous examination of the representational strategies of the Spanish Inquisition and the aesthetic culture of the Spanish Baroque as these were deployed against conversos during the seventeenth century, see especially sections 5–8 of Pulido Serrano.

22. On the medieval conception of heresy as an illness see R. I. Moore, "Heresy as Disease," *The Concept of Heresy in the Middle Ages (11th–13th Centuries): Proceedings of the International Conference, Louvain, May* 13–16, 1973, ed. W. Lourdaux and D. Verhelst (Louvain: Leuven University Press, 1976), 1–11.

23. Del Olmo, 180.

24. See for example the sermon published in ibid., 145–99.

25. Several of Spain's Visigothic rulers devised and applied discriminatory legislation against the Christian descendants of converted Jews. A recent treatment of this phenomenon is Biagio Saitta, *L'Antisemitismo nella Spagna Visogotica* (Rome: "L'Erma" di Bretschneider, 1995). For a summary of Visigothic regulations against former Jews and their descendants see also Norman Roth, *Jews, Visigoths, and Muslims in Medieval Spain: Cooperation and Conflict* (Leiden: E. J. Brill, 1994), 31–38.

26. None of this is to say that Old Christians were alone in harboring Judeophobic attitudes. New Christians internalized such attitudes as well. For instance, before his inquisitorial trial and subsequent transformation into a "New Jew" in the Sephardi Diaspora, Fernão Alvares Melo alleged that he had once called an enemy a "Jew, dog, returned refugee from France!" Alvares Melo also alleged that he had expelled a fellow member of the Lisbon Brotherhood of Our Lady of the Peace of the Hospital, specifically because the man was a *cristão-novo.* Salomon, *Portrait,* 99, 103.

27. For instance, Antonio de Acosta de Paz, a merchant returnee and inquisitorial informer, "testified regarding many Portuguese who reside in France and other places of *judíos judaizantes.*" AHN, Inquisición de Toledo, leg. 180, exp. 6 (1635–50), fol. 14r.

28. During the first decade of the seventeenth century the Castilian lexicographer

Sebastián de Covarrubias Orozco defined *judíos* as "those who today do not believe in the coming of the Savior Messiah . . . and continue to *profess* the Law of Moses. . . . In Spain there inhabited Jews for many centuries, until at the time of our grandparents, the Catholic Kings . . . when they were thrown out of Spain" (emphasis added). For Covarrubias, however, *judaizar* meant merely "to *perform* ceremonies of [the] Jews" (emphasis added). Id., *Tesoro de la lengua castellana o española*, ed. Felipe C. R. Maldonado (1611; reprint, revised by Manuel Camarero, Madrid: Editorial Castalia, 1995), 688 (hereafter cited as *Tesoro*). From these definitions it follows that, while there were no actual *judíos* left in Spain, anyone in the country (and in Spain, "anyone" necessarily meant a Christian) could conceivably be a *judaizante*.

29. The following observation of the *cristão-novo* Duarte Gomes Solís (ca. 1620), intended to criticize the Old Christian nobility, might have easily applied to the lower classes as well: "If some sustain a hatred for Jews, others sustain it for rich and powerful merchants, thus the two causes of hatred combine. . . . So the [Jew-haters] placate themselves by holding all [conversos] to be sham Christians (in which the populace, hearing the arguments of the preachers, is less restrained)." Id., *Discorsos sobre los commercios de las dos Indias*, ed. M. B. Amzalak (Lisbon, 1943), 20, quoted in Samuel, "The Trade" 2:101.

30. Diego Serrano de Silva, a member of the Suprema and a former Inquisitor General of Cuenca, quoted in Henry Kamen, "A Crisis of Conscience," 15.

31. Del Olmo, 291.

32. If the defendant was engaged in an occupation that required him or her to maintain written records, feigning illiteracy was not a realistic option. Inquisitors habitually reproached declarants whose statements they considered *inverosímiles* (lacking verisimilitude). See note 83 below.

33. By "*la Biblia en castellano*" or "*la Biblia en romance*," defendants probably meant an edition of the 1553 Ferrara Bible or a version based on it. Yerushalmi, "The Re-education of Marranos," 7.

34. For example, Francisco Díaz Méndez indicated that all his relatives were New Christians and "*de la nación hebrea de Portugal*." AHN, Inquisición de Toledo, leg. 142, exp. 4 (1609–10), not foliated. Likewise Felipe Díaz Gutiérrez said that the members of his family "*son de la nación hebrea*." AHN, Inquisición de Toledo, leg. 142, exp. 2 (1636), not foliated.

35. AHN, Inquisición de Toledo, leg. 141, exp. 7 (1632–33), not foliated. In a similar vein, twenty-year-old Beatris Marcos testified in 1583 that "she did not know if her father and mother were New Christians or Old Christians, and she did not understand that, and it would never have occurred to her [*nuqua lhe viera pela imaginaca*] to ask her mother whether she was a New Christian or an Old Christian, and in this she persisted despite being repeatedly warned." ANTT, Inquisição de Coimbra, proc. no. 2376 (1583), quoted in Salomon, *Portrait*, 4. See also my slightly different translation of the testimony on p. 128, above.

36. The claim of Old Christian status was not entirely uncommon among putative New Christians. In AHN, Inquisición de Toledo, leg. 138, exp. 10 (1671–74), Antonio de Borjas testified that he was a Portuguese immigrant from Mogodouro, a pharmacist, fifty years of age, who lived by petty commerce as the owner of a tobacco stand. He also admitted that he was a crypto-Jew. In other words, the declarant

painted himself as a stereotypical Portuguese New Christian. However, he claimed to be of Old Christian stock.

37. AHN, Inquisición de Toledo, leg. 138, exp. 12 (1668–70), fol. 65v.

38. AHN, Inquisición de Toledo, leg. 166, exp. 6 (1622–25), not foliated.

39. AHN, Inquisición de Toledo, leg. 165, exp. 12 (1661–71), fol. 59r.

40. The same was true of Ana Díaz's mother and aunt. As Díaz put it, *after* her religious initiation, "she never communicated concerning the Law of Moses with her mother and aunt, although this declarant saw that they did the same as she did [in observance of the Law of Moses], and they saw what she did, without openly acknowledging it to each other. As for her father, Antonio, she did not see him do anything [of the Law of Moses] except that one Friday, at night, he dressed in a clean shirt that she gave to him." AHN, Inquisición de Toledo, leg. 141, exp. 7 (1632–33), not foliated.

41. Ibid.

42. I am not saying that the image of women as secluded and exclusively domestic was always true. See Magdalena Sánchez and Alain Saint-Saens, eds., *Spanish Women in the Golden Age: Images and Realities* (Westport, Conn.: Greenwood Press, 1996). As Marcelin Defourneaux suggests, the image of respectable women's total seclusion and political exclusion is as exaggerated as the black image of wantonness that Golden Age satirists and pious moralists painted of less respectable women. All the same, "confinement . . . especially in the towns and in 'polite society,' was imposed upon Spanish women. They seldom left their homes, and then only to pursue their religious duties." Id., 146.

43. AHN, Inquisición de Toledo, leg. 147, exp. 1 (1663–65), fol. 29v.

44. Ibid., fol. 14r.

45. Ibid.

46. Ibid., fol. 14v.

47. Ibid.

48. Ibid., 15r.

49. Defourneaux, 145–48.

50. AHN, Inquisición de Toledo, leg. 147, exp. 1 (1663–65), fol. 20v.

51. AHN, Inquisición de Toledo, leg. 131, exp. 10 (1652–54), fols. 19r–20r.

52. Ibid., fol. 32r. Along the same lines, another declarant recalled that "Juan López Díaz, his stepfather . . . taught him and advised him to keep the Law of Moses . . . because if he did not do so, his stepfather would not give him a single *real* from the property of his [the defendant's] parents that he [the stepfather] possessed, and [the defendant], led by these exhortations and wishing to collect his assets [began to] keep the Law of Moses. . . ." AHN, Inquisición de Toledo, leg. 131, exp. 10 (1652–54), fol. 32v.

53. AHN, Inquisición de Toledo, leg. 167, exp. 9 (1670), fols. 37v–38r.

54. Ibid., fol. 45r.

55. My impression is that Portuguese tribunals classified defendants' racial identities much more specifically than did their Spanish counterparts. Lusitanian functionaries used designations such as: "*parte de xpao novo*" (part New Christian), ANTT, Inquisição de Coimbra, proc. no. 4228 (1625–26); "*hum outavo de xptao novo*" (one-eighth of a New Christian), ANTT, Inquisiçao de Evora, proc. no. 1495

(1639–40); and even "*me[i]o oitavo de christão novo*" (half an eighth New Christian), ANTT, Inquisição de Lisboa, proc. no. 7938 (1650). I have found very few specific designations such as these in Spanish dossiers.

56. Incidentally, the same appears to have been true of French authorities. As late as 1698 they designated Iberian immigrants in Saint Esprit as a "communauté de *la Nation judaique ou portugaise* du port Saint-Esprit de Bayonne" (emphasis added). Nahon, "La 'nation juive,'" 8.

57. ANTT, Inquisição de Coimbra, proc. no. 2376 (1583), quoted in Salomon, *Portrait*, 4.

58. AHN, Inquisición de Toledo, leg. 141, exp. 15 (1629), not foliated. Information regarding the identity of the assailant is in the above-cited case of Ana Díaz, Paz's sister: AHN, Inquisición de Toledo, leg. 141, exp. 7 (1632–33), not foliated. López Belinchón, 343, cites the *proceso* of another young Luso-converso who, according to one witness, "goes out to the street yelling when he is angry that his father and his grandmother are Jews and he would have them burned."

59. AHN, Inquisición de Toledo, leg. 152, exp. 1 (1621–22), not foliated.

60. Paz also testified that his family had had contact with Jews from Oran who resided temporarily in Madrid. He added that the latter had given the family a book of Jewish content. Ibid.

61. Ibid.

62. Ibid.

63. Ibid.

64. AHN, Inquisición de Toledo, leg. 141, exp. 15 (1629), not foliated.

65. Ibid. Similarly, the defendant Manuel Fernández y Márquez accused his relatives of bringing him to a small room and advising him to keep the Law of Moses by fasting, yet "without saying what fasts, and in what manner [he should observe the fasts]. . . . And they did not say in particular anything that one should do to observe [the law]." AHN, Inquisición de Toledo, leg. 147, exp. 5 (1651–52), fol. 74r–74v.

66. AHN, Inquisición de Toledo, leg. 142, exp. 2 (1636), not foliated. Here Felipe Díaz Gutiérrez attributed to his religious initiator the opinion that "now He does not favor us [the Jewish people] because we are sinner-idolaters."

67. Huerga Criado, 240.

68. AHN, Inquisición de Toledo, leg. 177, exp. 11 (1641–78), fol. 192r. The witness furnished his testimony in Granada in 1662.

69. AHN, Inquisición de Toledo, leg. 169, exp. 10 (1663–68), fol. 49r.

70. ANTT, Inquisição de Lisboa, proc. no. 12493 (1618), fol. 16r.

71. AHN, Inquisición de Toledo, leg. 177, exp. 2 (1650–53), fol. 52r.

72. Ibid., fols. 49v–50r. It is telling of the quotidian nature of return that even the allegedly zealous Judaizers in question were in contact with returnees: "Twelve days ago one of the [daughters] arrived [?] in Bidache, which is next to Peyrehorade, already fixed up to marry so-and-so Arias, who deals in silk in Pastrana [New Castile]."

73. The only exceptions to this comparative mildness were the infrequent threat of forced circumcision and the even less common threat of death. Allegations of forced circumcision appear, for example, in AHN, Inquisición de Toledo, leg. 166, exp.

6 (1622–25), not foliated. Here the defendant Manuel Méndez Cardoso also stated that the Jews of Amsterdam "told him that if he did not become a Jew . . . they would divulge to the Magistracy the dealings in which he was involved on behalf of the [Spanish] king against the rebel provinces. . . . He feared [the Jews'] furor and the bad intentions with which they had [previously] led [the Dutch police] to arrest him . . . and he considered that this [situation] could result in his being killed . . . [so] he responded to them that . . . he would do all they ordered." I have found only one additional instance in which a defendant claimed he had been threatened with death: AHN, Inquisición de Toledo, leg. 177, exp. 11 (1641–78), fol. 192v. Here the witness Pedro Henríquez Peteño, testifying in Granada in October of 1662, alleged that "sometimes the Jews [of Bayonne] told him that if he did not [become a Jew], they would give him death [*le abian de dar la muerte*]."

74. Again, this excludes the testimony of arch-delators such as João de Aguila, whom I discussed in the previous chapter.

75. AHN, Inquisición de Toledo, leg. 177, exp. 1 (1664–70), fol. 16v.

76. *Diccionario*, s.v. "reducir." Covarrubias Orozco, 854, opined that *reducirse* meant *convencerse*—a reflexive verb translatable as "to convince oneself." Significantly, *convencerse* also conveys "to be convinced (by others)."

77. AHN, Inquisición de Toledo, leg. 165, exp. 12 (1661–71), fol. 43r.

78. AHN, Inquisición de Toledo, leg. 159, exp. 9 (1625), not foliated. The statement cited is that of Diego de Lima, a twenty-six-year-old converso and self-described pilgrim from Moncorvo, Portugal. He appeared unexpectedly in Madrid in June of 1625 to depose before the Toledan Inquisition.

79. AHN, Inquisición de Toledo, leg. 147, exp., 1 (1663–65), not foliated. In a confession reminiscent of that of Jorge Fernández de Castro, a converso declarant stated that he had returned to Catholicism because he had noticed that those who followed the Law of Moses were "the lowest people in the world." Here the phrase "*la gente mas abatida del mundo*" conveys that Jews were downhearted and unfortunate, not merely that they were despised. Quoted in López Belinchón, 351.

80. AHN, Inquisición de Toledo, leg. 165, exp. 12 (1661–71), fol. 63v.

81. AHN, Inquisición de Toledo, leg. 177, exp. 11 (1641–78), fol. 43v.

82.AHN, Inquisición de Toledo, leg. 150, exp. 6 (1669–70), fol. 30r.

83. For instance, during a fairly typical interrogation of 1655 (recorded, as was customary, as a third-person narrative), an inquisitor admonished a defendant repeatedly, as follows: "he did not satisfy the question"; "he should beware that he is contradicting himself; he should concur with the truth and unload his conscience completely"; "it is not possible that he believed the consecrated Host to be the body of our Lord at the time that he followed the Law of Moses, as he [the defendant] has confessed . . . and that he is contradicting himself and is admonished to assent in the truth, because his contradiction is manifest, and it cannot be that anyone should have, follow, and believe in two laws and still think that he can be saved following both." AHN, Inquisición de Toledo, leg. 189, exp. 10 (1657), fols. 8r, 11r–11v.

84. AHN, Inquisición de Toledo, leg. 177, exp. 2 (1650–53), fol. 48r. Cardoso's reference to *judíos antiguos* reminds us of the fact that he regarded himself, his expatriated relatives, and their fellow Iberian exiles as "New Jews," that is to say, recently Judaicized conversos.

85. AHN, Inquisición de Toledo, leg. 147, exp. 1 (1663–65), fols. 54r, 65r. The defendant reported that in the year 1656 alone he and others had traveled with merchandise from southern France to Spain, and from Spain to France, more than thirty times.

86. Huerga Criado, 252.

Chapter 5

1. AHN, Inquisición de Toledo, leg. 177, exp. 1 (1664–70), fols. 10r, 17r. The witnesses in question were the returnees Fernando Henríquez de la Vega and Rafael Méndez.

2. Ibid. The defendant claimed that he did not know what types of merchandise she and Rodríguez Mota sold there.

3. Ibid. Martín Rodríguez was a *golillero*, an artisan who made ornaments of cloth. Hence it is not surprising that the defendant, who dealt in fabrics, engaged in business with him.

4. See Pedro de Teixeira, *Topographia de la Villa de Madrid* (1656; Madrid: Ayuntamiento de Madrid, 1995).

5. The *hakham* was perhaps Isaac Israel de Avila, who performed the first halakhic marriage in Bayonne in 1673. Gérard Nahon, "Les 'conversos' en France" in *Métropoles*, 238, 241. Rodríguez summoned the possibility that Avila was of converso origin when he recalled, "the doctor's sons, as they were students and young men, learned [to read Hebrew] quickly." Ibid., fol. 32v.

6. Ibid., fol. 23v. The cited testimony is that of Juan Fernández de Acuña (1659).

7. Ibid., fol. 63r. It is not clear from Rodríguez's account whether by "the Martyrs of Santa Engracia" the pope was referring only to the fourth-century Christians (including St. Engracia) whose remains are supposedly preserved in the crypt of the eponymous church in question, or whether the pontiff also meant confraternal flagellants who marched from the shrine of the cross to their church, splattering their blood on the unpaved street. On Zaragozan monuments, see for example Guillermo Fatás, coord., *Guia histórico-artística de Zaragoza* (Zaragoza: Delegación de Patrimonio Histórico-Artístico, Ayuntamiento de Zaragoza, 1982).

8. Bernhard Blumenkranz, *Histoire des Juifs en France* (Tolouse: Privat, 1972), 226. On the common practice of charity among members of the "Nation" within Iberian realms, see López Belinchon, 275–78.

9. Needless to say, unqualified belief or disbelief are not helpful approaches to the evaluation of any testimony, especially that produced under the pressure of interrogation. In presenting the two interpretive extremes I realize that I have painted an exaggerated dichotomy. My purpose has not been to set up these extremes as "straw men," but to highlight the inadequacy of applying an overly rigid positivistic epistemology to the study of inquisitorial cases such as Rodríguez's. Ultimately my quarrel is with the ostensibly unproblematic categories of "truth" and "untruth" as applied to the reconstruction of a person's situationally determined perception of herself or himself.

10. Richard Sennet, *Authority* (New York: W. W. Norton, 1980), 126.

11. Ibid.

12. AHN, Inquisición de Toledo, leg. 177, exp. 1 (1664–70), fol. 74v.

13. See Bartolomé Benassar, "Patterns of the Inquisitorial Mind as the Basis for a Pedagogy of Fear," The Spanish Inquisition and the Inquisitorial Mind, ed. Angel Alcalá, (New York: Columbia University Press, 1987). See also Benassar, *L'Inquisition espagnole.* To suppose that Rodríguez was not at least somewhat intimidated by the power of his interrogators would be to attribute to him an exceptional stoicism or valor.

14. AHN, Inquisición de Toledo, leg. 177, exp. 1 (1664 –1700), fol 82r.

15. On Alvares Melo and his work see Salomon, *Portrait.* As for Enríquez Gómez, see for example Dille; Nechama Kramer-Hellinx, "El Aspecto de la Inquisición en la Obra de Antonio Enríquez Gómez (1600–1663)," *The Heritage of the Jews of Spain,* ed. Aviva Doron, (n.p.: Levinsky College of Education, 1994), 174, 178; more generally, see id., *Gómez.* On the self-representation of New Jews see Karsten Lorenz Wilke, "Conversion our retour? La métamorphose du nuveau chrétien en juif portugais dans l'imaginaire sépharade du XVIIe siècle," *Memoires juives d'Espagne et du Portugal,* ed. Esther Benbassa (Paris: PUBLISUD, 1996), 53–90. Wilke shows, among other aspects, that much New Jewish literature of the seventeenth century did not portray converso émigrés as returnees to an ancestral faith, rather as religious pilgrims, as converts to Judaism, thus betraying a sense that the Christianity these conversos had professed in Iberia had been genuine.

16. Arguably, in the religious ferment of the Early Modern Period in Europe this wisdom was successfully challenged (though not necessarily overthrown) only by radically egalitarian Protestant groups.

17. A curious (if somewhat distant) parallel is the sixteenth-century farmer Sanxi Daguerre, who moved his household from the French Basque country to a village in the county of Foix. In the latter county he and his family adapted to the culture of their new milieu, which encompassed a host of Gascon and Occitan elements. Among other things, the immigrants changed their names, some of their ways, and married into local families. Thus they became respectable. In a more extreme example of self-transformation, Arnaud du Tilh usurped that respectability as the infamous impersonator of Sanxi's son, Martin Guerre. Natalie Zemon Davis, *The Return of Martin Guerre* (Cambridge, Mass.: Harvard University Press, 1983), 6–12.

18. Peter L. Berger, *The Sacred Canopy: Elements of a Sociological Theory of Religion* (New York: Anchor Books, 1967), 31–32.

19. Ibid., 26.

20. AHN, Inquisición de Toledo, leg. 177, exp. 1 (1664–70), fol. 55v. In fol. 81v, Rodríguez alludes to the 613 halakhic commandments by explaining that the Law of Grace had come to lighten the load of those commandments. Under Christ's law, he argued, one had to keep only the ten commandments delivered to Moses at Sinai.

21. I borrow this formulation from Berger, 26.

22. Ibid., 34, 37.

23. The Spanish Inquisition prosecuted scores of "illuminists" during the sixteenth and seventeenth centuries. Bataillon, *Erasmo y España* is a fundamental work on *alumbrados.* Recent surveys of the phenomenon of illuminism include Antonio Márquez, *Los Alumbrados: Origenes y Filosofía (1525–1559),* 2nd ed. (Madrid: Taurus, 1980); Alastair Hamilton, *Heresy and Mysticism in Sixteenth-Century Spain: The*

Alumbrados (Toronto: University of Toronto Press, 1992). For a discussion of conversos as illuminists see Selke.

24. Archivo Diocesano de Cuenca, Inquisición, leg. 239, exp. 3092 (1568), quoted in Sara T. Nalle, *God in La Mancha: Religious Reform and the People of Cuenca, 1500-1650* (Baltimore: Johns Hopkins University Press, 1992), 182.

25. Yovel, 11. Cryptic bibliographical notations (e.g., "the Soria records") do not permit a specific citation of the quoted material. Deponents' confessions dating from the seventeenth century convey the same pragmatic reading of personal fortunes as Rodríguez did in his own deposition. For instance, a converso deposed that he and his family "had resolved to abandon the [Jewish] Law because they found themselves lost [*andaban perdidos*] and they did not prosper in terms of property [*en la hacienda*] whereby they knew it was for being outside the Law of God." Quoted in López Belinchón, 351. (The primary source in question is either Archivo Diocesano de Cuenca, Inquisición, leg. 415, exp. 5831, or leg. 462, exp. 6350. López's notation does not indicate the years of these records.) For his part, a certain converso and *lencero* from Cieza testified that he had "fasted [in accordance with the Law of Moses] before buying [merchandise] that God would give him good luck" in his *negocios*. Archivo Diocesano de Cuenca, Inquisición, Leg. 417, ex. 5861 (folio not cited), quoted in id., 355.

26. AHN, Inquisición de Toledo, leg., 177, exp. 12 (1661–62), fol. 67r.

27. Ibid., not foliated.

28. See note 25, above.

Chapter 6

1. See for example Perez Zagorin's otherwise admirable essay, "The Marranos and Crypto-Judaism," *Ways of Lying: Dissimulation, Persecution and Conformity in Early Modern Europe* (Cambridge, Mass.: Harvard University Press, 1990), 38–62.

2. I am referring to Révah, "Les Marranes," 55.

3. Yovel, 2.

4. AHN, Inquisición de Toledo, leg. 177, exp. 12 (1661–62), fol. 74r. The statement is that of the defendant Diego Rodríguez de Leon.

5. AHN, Inquisición de Toledo, leg. 152, exp. 6 (1663–65), fols. 8v–9r.

6. AHN, Inquisición de Toledo, leg. 147, exp. 1 (1663–65), not foliated.

7. I am borrowing this formulation from R. Po-Chia Hsia, *Social Discipline in the Reformation: Central Europe, 1550–1750* (London: Routledge, 1989), 5.

8. Benjamin Beit-Hallahmi, *Prolegomena to the Psychological Study of Religion* (London: Associated University Presses, 1989), 98.

9. See Contreras and Henningsen, "Forty-Four Thousand Cases," 100–129.

10. Yosef Kaplan, "La comunidad sefardí de Amsterdam en el siglo XVII: Entre la tradición y el cambio," *Judíos Nuevos*, 33–34.

Glossary

Castilian Nouns

arbitrista(s)	A writer of politicoeconomic critiques and proposals of reform known as *arbitrios*.
arrendador	A tax farmer; the holder of a contract to farm taxes (*arrendamiento*).
audiencia	An inquisitorial hearing.
camino(s)	Road(s).
casta y generación	Stock and origin.
cristiano(s) nuevo(s)	New Christian(s). Equivalent of the Portuguese term *cristão(s)-novo(s)*.
comerciante	Merchant; storekeeper; someone who engages in commerce.
consanguíneos	Consanguineous relatives.
converso	Literally, a "convert." More narrowly, a convert from Judaism to Christianity. This term applied to his or her descendants as well.
familiar(es)	Lay assistants(s) of the Holy Office.
fiscal	An inquisitorial prosecutor.
hidalgo	A nobleman.
interrogatorio	An interrogatory. For our purposes, the standard inquisitorial interrogatory.
judería	A designated Jewish neighborhood.
malsín	An informer. From Heb. *malshin*.
madrileño/a(s)	A permanent resident and/or native of Madrid.
mercader(es)	Merchant(s).
moriscos	Iberian Muslims who converted to Christianity and their descendants.
negocios	Business, business deals.
pícaro	A cynical, dishonorable person, usually of low social origin and economic status, who mocks and subverts respectable society through mischief.
posada	An inn.
proceso	An inquisitorial trial.
reducción	Subjugation, persuasion.
Santo Oficio	Holy Office.
tocino	Pig fat, a main ingredient in Ibero-Christian cuisine.
tratante(s)	Dealer(s), trader(s).
vecino(s)	Neighbor(s), tax paying citizen(s) of a locality.

Hebrew Nouns

brit milah	The procedure and covenant of circumcision.
Halakhah	Jewish law.
hakham(im)	Rabbi(s), sage(s).
kahal	The governing body of a *kehillah* (see below); often used, in my view incorrectly, instead of *kehillah*.
kehillah	An organized, autonomous Jewish community.
kehillot	The plural form of *kehillah*.
parnass(im)	Lay magistrate(s) of a *kehillah*.
Sepharad	A biblical term that in the Middle Ages came to denote (and still denotes) "Spain," including all Iberian lands, principally Castile and Aragon.
Sephardi(m)	Jew(s) of Iberian origin.

Selected Bibliography

Listed here are only the writings that have been of use in the making of this book. This bibliography is not a complete record of all the primary sources and secondary works that were consulted.

Archival Documents

Archivo Histórico Nacional, Madrid

Inquisición de Toledo, leg. 131, exp. 10 (1652–54)
Inquisición de Toledo, leg. 134, exp. 18 (1624–25)
Inquisición de Toledo, leg. 136, exp. 5 (1654–57)
Inquisición de Toledo, leg. 136, exp. 6 (1659–61)
Inquisición de Toledo, leg. 138, exp. 10 (1671–74)
Inquisición de Toledo, leg. 138, exp. 12 (1668–70)
Inquisición de Toledo, leg. 141, exp. 7 (1632–63)
Inquisición de Toledo, leg. 141, exp. 15 (1629)
Inquisición de Toledo, leg. 142, exp. 2 (1636)
Inquisición de Toledo, leg. 142, exp. 3 (1609–10)
Inquisición de Toledo, leg. 142, exp. 4 (1609–10)
Inquisición de Toledo, leg. 145, exp. 9 (1634)
Inquisición de Toledo, leg. 147, exp. 1 (1663–65)
Inquisición de Toledo, leg. 147, exp. 5 (1651–52)
Inquisición de Toledo, leg. 150, exp. 6 (1669–70)
Inquisición de Toledo, leg. 150, exp. 17 (1669–70)
Inquisición de Toledo, leg. 152, exp. 1 (1621–22)
Inquisición de Toledo, leg. 152, exp. 6 (1663–65)
Inquisición de Toledo, leg. 159, exp. 9 (1625)
Inquisición de Toledo, leg. 161, exp. 5 (1653–55)
Inquisición de Toledo, leg. 165, exp. 12 (1661–71)
Inquisición de Toledo, leg. 166, exp. 6 (1622–25)
Inquisición de Toledo, leg. 166, exp. 8 (1664)
Inquisición de Toledo, leg. 167, exp. 9 (1670)
Inquisición de Toledo, leg. 169, exp. 10 (1663–68)
Inquisición de Toledo, leg. 174, exp. 17 (1661)

Inquisición de Toledo, leg. 177, exp. 1 (1664–70)
Inquisición de Toledo, leg. 177, exp. 2 (1650–53)
Inquisición de Toledo, leg. 177, exp. 11 (1641–78)
Inquisición de Toledo, leg. 177, exp. 12 (1661–62)
Inquisición de Toledo, leg. 180, exp. 6 (1635–50)
Inquisición de Toledo, leg. 184, exp. 12 (1651–53)
Inquisición de Toledo, leg. 184, exp. 13 (1636–39)
Inquisición de Toledo, leg. 187, exp. 4. (1687–88)
Inquisición de Toledo, leg. 189, exp. 10 (1657)

Arquivos Nacionais, Torre do Tombo, Lisboa.

Inquisição de Coimbra, proc. no. 2376 (1583)
Inquisição de Coimbra, proc. no. 4228 (1625–26)
Inquisição de Evora, proc. no. 1495 (1639–40)
Inquisição de Evora, proc. no. 2305 (1612–14)
Inquisição de Lisboa, proc. no. 3080 (1619)
Inquisição de Lisboa, proc. no. 7938 (1650)
Inquisição de Lisboa, proc. no. 12493 (1618)

Printed Primary Sources

Acosta, Uriel. *A Specimen of Human Life.* N. trans. 1687. New York: Bergman Publishers, 1967.
de Covarrubias Orozco, Sebastián. *Tesoro de la lengua castellana o española.* Ed. Felipe C. R. Maldonado. 1611. Reprint, revised by Manuel Camarero. Madrid: Editorial Castalia, 1995.
Dulaurens, E. *Inventaire sommaire des Archives communales antérieures à 1790, ville de Bayonne.* Archives de Bayonne, GG, 229. Paris, 1894–97.
Méchoulan, Henry. *Hispanidad y judaísmo en tiempos de Espinoza: Edición de La certeza del camino de Abraham Pereyra.* Salamanca: Ediciones Universidad de Salamanca, 1987.
Nahon, Gérard, ed. *Les "Nations" juives portuguaises du sud-ouest de la France (1684–1791): Documents.* Paris: Fundaçâo Calouste Gulbenkian, 1981.
del Olmo, Joseph Vicente. *Relación histórica del auto general de fe que se celebró en Madrid este año de 1680 con asistencia del rey.* Madrid, 1680.
de Rivadeneira, Pedro. *Tratado de la religión y virtudes que debe tener un príncipe cristiano. 1601. Antología de escritores políticos del siglo de oro.* Ed. Pedro de Vega. Madrid: Taurus, 1966.
Romero de Castilla, Manuel, ed. *Singular suceso en el reinado de los reyes católicos.* Madrid: Ediciones Rubí, 1946.

Schwartzfuchs, Simón. *Le registre des déliberations de la Nation juive portugaise de Bordeaux (1711–1787)*. Paris: Fundaçâo Calouste Gulbenkian, 1981.

de Teixeira, Pedro. *Topographia de la Villa de Madrid*. 1656. Madrid: Ayuntamiento de Madrid, 1995.

de Vega, Pedro, ed. *Antología de escritores políticos del siglo de oro*. Madrid: Taurus, 1966.

Willemse, David. *Un portugués entre los castellanos: El primer proceso inquisitorial contra Gonzalo Báez de Paiba, 1654–1657*. Paris: Fundaçâo Calouste Gulbenkian, 1974.

Secondary Sources

Alcalá, Angel, ed. *The Spanish Inquisition and the Inquisitorial Mind*. New York: Columbia Univerity Press, 1987.

Amiel, Charles. Introduction. *El siglo pitagórico y vida de don Gregorio Guadaña,* By Antonio Enríquez Gómez. Paris: Ediciones Hispanoamericanas, 1977.

Araújo, Maria Benedita. "Família e grupo social no criptojudaísmo português (século XVII)." *Oceanos 29* (January–March 1997): 49–66.

Assaf, Simha. *Be'Oholey Ya'akov*. Jerusalem: Mosad ha-Rav Kuk, 1943.

Avilés Fernández, Miguel, Siro Villas Tinoco, and Carmen García Cremades. *La crisis del siglo XVII bajo los últimos austrias (1598–1700)*. Madrid: Gredos, 1988.

Baer, Yitzhak. *A History of the Jews in Christian Spain*. Trans. Louis Schoffman. 2 vols. 1959–61. Reprint, with an introduction by Benjamin R. Gampel, Philadelphia: Jewish Publication Society, 1992.

Barros, Carlos, ed. *Xudeus e conversos na historia, actas do Congreso Internacional Ribadavia, 14–17 de outubro de 1991*. Santiago de Compostela: La Editorial de la Historia, 1994.

Bartlett, Robert. "Medieval and Modern Concepts of Race and Ethnicity." *Journal of Medieval and Early Modern Studies* 31.1 (2001): 39–56.

Bataillon, Marcel. *Erasmo y España: Estudios sobre la historia spiritual del siglo XVI*. Trans. Antonio Alatorre. Mexico City: Fondo de Cultura Económica, 1950.

Beinart, Haim. "The Converso Community in 16th and 17th Century Spain." In *The Sephardi Heritage*. Ed. R. D. Barnett. 2 vols. London: Valentine, Mitchell, 1971.

———. *Conversos on Trial: The Inquisition in Ciudad Real*. Trans. by Yael Guiladi. Jerusalem: Magnes Press, 1981.

———, ed. *Moreshet Sepharad: The Sephardi Legacy*. 2 vols. Jerusalem: The Magnes Press, 1992.

——— "The Travel of Jews from Morocco to Spain in the Early Seventeenth Century" (in Hebrew). *The Jubilee Volume in Honor of Salo W. Baron on the Occasion of His Eightieth Birthday*. Jerusalem: American Academy for Jewish Research, 1974.

Beit-Hallahmi, Benjamin. *Prolegomena to the Psychological Study of Religion*. London: Associated University Presses, 1989.

Benassar, Bartolomé, ed. *L'Inquisition espagnole: Xve–XIXe siècle.* Verviers: Marabout, 1979.

———. "Patterns of the Inquisitorial Mind as the Basis for a Pedagogy of Fear." *The Spanish Inquisition and the Inquisitorial Mind.* Ed. Angel Alcalá. New York: Columbia University Press, 1987.

———. *Valladolid en el Siglo de Oro: Una ciudad de Castilla y su entorno agrario en el siglo XVI.* 2d ed. Valladolid: Ambito, 1989.

Benassar, Bartolomé, and Lucille Benassar. *Los cristianos de Alá: La fascinante aventura de los renegados.* Tran. José Luis Gil Aristu. Madrid: Nerea, 1989.

Berger, Peter L. *The Sacred Canopy: Elements of a Sociological Theory of Religion.* New York: Anchor Books, 1967.

Blasco Martínez, Asunción. "Los malsines del reino de Aragón: Una aproximación." *Proceedings of the Eleventh World Congress of Jewish Studies, Jerusalem, June 22–29, 1993.* Jerusalem: World Union of Jewish Studies, 1994.

Blázquez Miguel, Juan. *Inquisición y criptojudaísmo.* Madrid: Kaydeda, 1988.

Blumenkranz, Bernhard. *Histoire des juifs en France.* Tolouse: Privat, 1972.

Bodian, Miriam. "'Men of the Nation': The Shaping of *Converso* Identity in Early Modern Europe." *Past and Present* 143 (1994): 49–76.

———. *Hebrews of the Portuguese Nation: Conversos and Community in Early Modern Amsterdam.* Bloomington: Indiana University Press, 1997.

de Bofarull, Francisco. "Los judíos malsines." *Boletín de la Real Academia de Buenas Letras de Barcelona* 11.41 (1911): 207–16.

Boyajian, James C. *Portuguese Bankers at the Court of Spain, 1626–1650.* New Brunswick, N.J.: Rutgers University Press, 1983.

Brown, Jonathan. *Images and Ideas in Seventeenth-Century Spanish Painting.* Princeton, N.J.: Princeton University Press, 1978.

Carlebach, Elisheva. *Divided Souls: Converts from Judaism in Germany, 1570–1750.* New Haven, Conn.: Yale University Press, 2001.

Caro Baroja, Julio. *La sociedad criptojudía en la corte de Felipe IV.* Madrid: Real Academia de la Historia, 1963.

———. *Los judíos en la España Moderna y Contemporánea.* 3rd ed. 3 vols. Madrid: Ediciones Istmo, 1986.

Carrete Parrondo, Carlos. "Nostalgia for the Past (and for the Future?) among Castilian *Judeoconversos.*" *Jews, Christians and Muslims in the Mediterranean World after 1492.* Ed. Alisa Meyuhas Ginio. London: Frank Cass and Co., 1992.

Casey, James. *Early Modern Spain: A Social History.* London: Routledge, 1999.

———. "Spain: A Failed Transition." *The European Crisis of the 1590s.* Ed. Peter Clark. Boston: Allen and Unwin, 1985.

Castro, Américo. *España en su historia: Cristianos, moros, y judíos.* Buenos Aires: Editorial Losada, 1948.

———. *La realidad histórica de España.* Mexico City: Editorial Porrúa, 1954.

———. *The Structure of Spanish History.* Trans. Edmund L. King. Princeton, N.J.: Princeton University Press, 1954.

———. Prologue. *El Ingenioso Hidalgo Don Quixote de la Mancha.* By Miguel de Cervantes. Mexico City: Editorial Porrúa, 1979.

Cavillac, Michel. *Pícaros y mercaderes en el Guzmán de Alfarache: Reformismo burgués y mentalidad aristocrática en la España del siglo de oro.* Trans. Juan M. Azpitarte Almagro. Granada: Universidad de Granada, 1994.

Contreras Contreras, Jaime. "Criptojudaísmo en la España moderna: Clientelismo y linaje." *Inquisição: Ensaios sobre mentalidade, heresias, e arte.* Comp. Anita Novinsky and Maria Luiza Tucci Carneiro. Sao Paulo: EdUSP, 1992.

———. "Estructuras familiares y linajes en el mundo judeoconverso." *Solidarités et sociabilités en Espagne.* Ed. Raphael Carrasco. Paris: Les Belles Lettres, 1991.

———. *Sotos contra Riquelmes.* Madrid: Anaya y M. Muchnik, 1992.

Contreras, Jaime, and Gustav Henningsen. "Forty-Four Thousand Cases of the Spanish Inquisition (1540–1700): Analysis of a Historical Data Bank." *The Inquisition in Early Modern Europe: Studies on Sources and Methods.* Ed. Gustav Henningsen and John Tedeschi. Dekalb: Northern Illinois University Press, 1986.

Crossan, John Dominic. *Who Killed Jesus? Exposing the Roots of Anti-Semitism in the Gospel Story of the Death of Jesus.* San Francisco: HarperSanFrancsico, 1996.

Davis, Natalie Zemon. *The Return of Martin Guerre.* Cambridge, Mass.: Harvard University Press, 1983.

Dedieu, Jean-Pierre. *L'Administration de la foi: L'Inquisition de Tolède, XVIe–XVIIIe siècle.* Madrid: Casa de Velázquez, 1989.

Defourneaux, Marcelin. *Daily Life in Spain in the Golden Age.* Trans. Newton Branch. Stanford, Calif.: Stanford University Press, 1970.

Deleito y Piñuela, José. *Solo Madrid es corte: La capital de dos mundos bajo Felipe IV.* Madrid: Espasa-Calpe, 1942.

Dever, William G. *What Did the Biblical Writers Know and When Did They Know It? What Archeology Can Tell Us about the Reality of Ancient Israel.* Grand Rapids, Mich.: William B. Eerdmans Publishing Company, 2001.

Dille, Glen F. *Antonio Enríquez Gómez.* Boston: Twayne, 1988.

Domínguez Ortiz, Antonio. *Crisis y decadencia de la España de los Austrias.* Barcelona: Ariel, 1984.

———. *Los extranjeros en la vida española durante el siglo XVII y otros artículos.* Sevilla: Diputación de Sevilla, 1996.

Domínguez Ortiz, Antonio. *The Golden Age of Spain, 1516–1659.* Trans. James Casey. New York: Basic Books, 1971.

———. *Los judeoconversos en España y América.* Madrid: Ediciones Istmo, 1971.

———. *La sociedad española en el siglo XVII.* 2 vols. Madrid: Instituto Balmes de Sociología, 1963.

Domínguez Ortiz, Antonio, and Bernard Vincent. *Historia de los moriscos.* Madrid: Revista de Occidente, 1979.

Faingold, Reuven. "Searching for Identity: The Trial of the Portuguese Converso Vicente Furtado, 1600–1615" (in Hebrew). *Pe'amim* 46–7 (1991): 235–59.

Fatás, Guillermo, coord. *Guía histórico-artística de Zaragoza.* Zaragoza: Delegación de Patrimonio Histórico-Artístico, Ayuntamiento de Zaragoza, 1982.

Ferro Tavares, Maria José. "Judeus de sinal em Portugal no século XVI." *Revista Cultura, História, e Filosofia* 5 (1986): 339–63.

Ferro Tavares, María José Pimenta. *Los judíos en Portugal.* Madrid: Editorial MAPFRE, 1992.

Funkenstein, Amos. "History, Counterhistory, and Narrative." *Perceptions of Jewish History.* Berkeley: University of California Press, 1993.

Ginzburg, Carlo. *The Cheese and the Worms: The Cosmos of a Sixteenth-Century Miller.* Trans. John Tedeschi and Anne C. Tedeschi. New York: Penguin Books, 1982.

———. "The Inquisitor as Anthropologist." *Clues, Myths, and the Historical Method.* Trans. John Tedeschi and Anne C. Tedeschi. Baltimore: Johns Hopkins University Press, 1986.

Gitlitz, David M. *Secrecy and Deceit: The Religion of the Crypto-Jews.* Philadelphia: Jewish Publication Society, 1996.

Glick, Thomas F. "On Converso and Marrano Ethnicity." *Crisis and Creativity in the Sephardic World, 1391–1648.* Ed. Benjamin R. Gampel. New York: Columbia University Press, 1997.

Glaser, Edward. "Referencias antisemitas en la literatura peninsular de la edad de oro." *Nueva Revista de Filología Hispánica* 8 (1954): 39–62.

Goldish, Matt. "Jews, Christians and Conversos: Rabbi Solomon Aailion's Struggles in the Portuguese Community of London." Journal of Jewish Studies 45 (1994): 227–57.

Gómez-Ibáñez, Daniel Alexander. *The Western Pyrenees: Differential Evolution of the French and Spanish Borderlands.* Oxford: Clarendon Press, 1975.

Hamilton, Alastair. *Heresy and Mysticism in Sixteenth-Century Spain: The Alumbrados.* Toronto: University of Toronto Press, 1992.

Hamilton, Earl J. "The Decline of Spain." *Economic History Review* 8.2 (1938): 168–79.

Hanson, Carl A. *Economy and Society in Baroque Portugal, 1668–1703.* Minneapolis: University of Minnesota Press, 1981.

Henningsen, Gustav, and John Tedeschi, eds. *The Inquisition in Early Modern Europe: Studies on Sources and Methods.* Dekalb: Northern Illinois University Press, 1986.

Herculano, Alexandre. *Da origem e establecimiento da Inquisição em Portugal.* Lisbon, 1854–59.

Hernández Franco, Juan. *Cultura y limpieza de sangre en la España moderna: Puritate sanguinis.* Murcia: Servicio de Publicaciones, Universidad de Murcia, 1996.

Hsia, R. Po-Chia. *Social Discipline in the Reformation: Central Europe, 1550–1750.* London: Routledge, 1989.

Huerga Criado, Pilar. *En la Raya de Portugal: Solidaridad y tensiones en la comunidad judeoconversa.* Salamanca: Ediciones Universidad de Salamanca, 1993.

Israel, Jonathan I. *Diasporas within a Diaspora: Jews, Crypto-Jews and the World Maritime Empires (1540–1740).* Leiden: Brill, 2002.

———. *Empires and Entrepots: The Dutch, the Spanish Monarchy, and the Jews, 1585–1713.* London: Hambledon Press, 1990.

———. *European Jewry in the Age of Mercantilism, 1550–1750.* 2d ed. Oxford: Clarendon Press, 1989.

———. "The Sephardi Contribution to Economic Life and Colonization in Europe and the New World (Sixteenth–Eighteenth Centuries)." *Moreshet Sepharad: The Sephardi Legacy.* Ed. Haim Beinart. 2 vols. Jerusalem: Magnes Press, 1992.

———. "Some Further Data on the Amsterdam Sephardim and Their Trade with Spain During the 1650s." *Studia Rosenthaliana* 14.1 (1980): 7–19.

Jastrow, Marcus, comp. *A Dictionary of the Targumim, the Talmud Babli and Yerushalmi, and the Midrashic Literature.* New York: Judaica Press, 1992.

Kamen, Henry. *Crisis and Change in Early Modern Spain.* Brookfield: Variorum, 1993.

———. *Inquisition and Society in Spain in the Sixteenth and Seventeenth Centuries.* London: Weidenfeld and Nicolson, 1985.

——— "Public Authority and Popular Crime: Banditry in Valencia, 1660–1714." *Journal of Modern History* 49 (1977): 210–30.

———. *Spain, 1469–1714: A Society of Conflict.* London: Longman, 1991.

———. *Spain in the Later Seventeenth Century, 1665–1700.* London: Longman, 1980.

———. *The Spanish Inquisition: A Historical Revision.* London: Weidenfeld and Nicolson, 1997.

Kaplan, Yosef. *An Alternative Path to Modernity: The Sephardi Diaspora in Western Europe.* Leiden: Brill, 2000.

———. *From Christianity to Judaism: The Story of Isaac Orobio de Castro.* Trans. Raphael Loewe. Oxford: Oxford University Press, 1989.

———. "The Jewish Profile of the Spanish and Portuguese Community of London in the Seventeenth Century." *Judaism* 41.3 (1992): 229–40.

———. "Jews and Judaism in the Political and Social Thought of Spain in the Sixteenth and Seventeenth Centuries." *Antisemitism Through the Ages.* Ed. Shmuel Almog. New York: Pergamon Press, 1988.

———. *Judíos nuevos en Amsterdam: Estudios sobre la historia social e intelectual del judaísmo sefardí en el siglo XVII.* Barcelona: Gedisa, 1996.

———. "The Role of Rabbi Moshe D'Aguilar in His Contacts with Refugees from Spain and Portugal in the Seventeenth Century" (in Hebrew). *Proceedings of the Sixth World Congress of Jewish Studies, Hebrew University of Jerusalem, August 13–19 1973.* Jerusalem: World Union of Jewish Studies, 1975.

———. "The Self-definition of the Sephardic Jews of Western Europe and Their Relation to the Alien and the Stranger." *Crisis and Creativity in the Sephardic World, 1391–1648.* Ed. Benjamin R. Gampel. New York: Columbia University Press, 1997.

———. "The Struggle against Travelers to Spain and Portugal in the Western Sephardi Diaspora" (in Hebrew). *Zion* 64.1 (1999): 65–100.

———. "The Travels of Portuguese Jews from Amsterdam to the 'Lands of Idolatry' (1644–1724)." *Jews and Conversos: Studies in Society and the Inquisition.* Ed. Yosef Kaplan. Jerusalem: Magnes Press, 1981.

———. "Wayward New Christians and Stubborn New Jews: The Shaping of a Jewish Identity." *Jewish History* 8.1–2 (1994): 27–41.

Kaufman, David. "Jewish Informers in the Middle Ages." *Jewish Quarterly Review* 7 (1895–1896): 217–38.

Kramer-Hellinx, Nechama. *Antonio Enríquez Gómez: Literatura y sociedad en* El siglo pitagórico y vida de Don Gregorio Guadaña. New York: Peter Lang, 1992.

———. "El aspecto de la Inquisición en la obra de Antonio Enríquez Gómez (1600–1663)." *The Heritage of the Jews in Spain.* Ed. Aviva Doron. N.p.: Levinsky College of Education, 1994.

Kriegel, Maurice. "The 'Modern' Antisemitism of the Inquisition" (in Hebrew). *Zemanim* 41 (1992): 23–33.

Ladurie, Emmanuel Le Roy. *The Beggar and the Professor: A Sixteenth-Century Family Saga*. Trans. Arthur Goldhammer. Chicago: University of Chicago Press, 1997.

Lapeyre, Henri. *Une famille des marchands, les Ruiz: Contribution à l'etude du commerce entre la France et l'Espagne au temps de Philippe II*. Paris: Colin, 1955.

Le Flem, Jean Paul, et al. *La frustración de un imperio, 1476–1714*. Barcelona: Editorial Labor, 1982.

Lea, Henry Charles. *A History of the Inquisition of Spain*. 4 vols. New York: Macmillan Company, 1906.

Lipiner, Elias. *Izaque de Castro: O mancebo que veio preso do Brasil*. Recife: Fundação Joaquim Nabuco, 1992.

López Belinchón, Bernardo. *Honra, libertad y hacienda: Hombres de negocios y judíos sefardíes*. Alcalá de Henares: Instituto Internacional de Estudios Sefardíes y Andalusíes, Universidad de Alcalá, 2001.

Lorence, Bruce A. "Professions Held by New Christians in Northern and Southern Portugal During the First Half of the Seventeenth Century." *History and Creativity in the Sephardi and Oriental Jewish Communities*. Ed. Tamar Alexander et al. Jerusalem: Misgav Yerushalayim, 1994.

Lourie, Elena. "Mafiosi and Malsines: Violence, Fear and Faction in the Jewish Aljamas of Valencia in the Fourteenth Century." *Crusade and Colonisation: Muslims, Christians, and Jews in Medieval Aragon*. Hampshire, England: Variorum, 1990.

Lynch, John. *Spain Under the Habsburgs*. 2 vols. New York: Oxford University Press, 1969.

Mackenney, Richard. *Sixteenth-Century Europe: Expansion and Conflict*. New York: St. Martin's Press, 1993.

Madrazo, Santos. *El sistema de comunicaciones en España, 1750–1850*. 2 vols. Madrid: Ediciones Turner, 1984.

Márquez, Antonio. *Los Alumbrados: Origenes y filosofía (1525–1559)*. 2nd ed. Madrid: Taurus, 1980.

Martínez Millán, José. *La hacienda de la Inquisición (1478–1700)*. Madrid: Instituto Enrique Flórez, 1984.

———. "Structures of Inquisitorial Finance." *The Spanish Inquisition and the Inquisitorial Mind*. Ed. Angel Alcalá. New York: Columbia University Press, 1987.

Mathorez, Jules. "Notes sur le la colonie portugaise de Nantes." *Bulletin Hispanique* 15 (1913): 316–30.

Matilla Montáñez, María. *El correo en la España de los Austrias*. Madrid: Consejo Superior de Investigaciónes Científicas, Escuela de Historia Moderna, 1953.

McGaha, Michael. "Biographical Data on Antonio Enríquez Gómez in the Archives of the Inquisition." *Bulletin of Hispanic Studies* 69.2 (1992): 127–39.

Méchoulan, Henry. Introduction. *Hispanidad y judaísmo en tiempos de Espinoza: Edición de* La Certeza del Camino *de Abraham Pereyra*. Salamanca: Ediciones Universidad de Salamanca, 1987.

Mitchell, Timothy. *Violence and Piety in Spanish Folklore*. Philadelphia: University of Pennsylvania Press, 1988.

Moore, R. I. "Heresy as Disease." *The Concept of Heresy in the Middle Ages (11th–13th Centuries); Proceedings of the International Conference, Louvain, May 13–16,* 197. Ed. W. Lourdaux and D. Verhelst. Louvain: Leuven University Press, 1976.

Myers, David N. *Re-Inventing the Jewish Past: European Jewish Intellectuals and the Zionist Return to History.* New York: Oxford University Press, 1995.

Nader, Helen. *Liberty in Absolutist Spain: The Habsburg Sale of Towns, 1516–1700.* Baltimore: Johns Hopkins University Press, 1990.

Nahon, Gérard. "Une délibération de la 'nation portugaise de Saint-Esprit' relative aux synagogues (1776)." *Revue des Etudes Juives* 124 (1965): 422-27.

———. "From New Christians to the Portuguese Jewish Nation in France." *Moreshet Sepharad: The Sephardi Legacy.* 2 vols. Ed. Haim Beinart. Jerusalem: Magnes Press, 1992.

———. *Métropoles et périphéries Sepharades d'occident: Kairouan, Amsterdam, Bayonne, Bordeaux, Jérusalem.* Paris: Les éditions du Cerf, 1993.

———. "La nation juive portugaise en France, XVIeme–XVIIIème siecle: Espaces et pouvoirs." *Revue des Etudes Juives* 153 (1994): 353–82.

———. "La 'nation juive' de Saint-Esprit-Les-Bayonne du XVIe au XVIIIe Siécle: Escale ou havre de Grace?" *L'Exode des juifs d'Espagne vers Bayonne: Des Rives de l'Ebre et du Tage à celles de l'Adour.* Comp. Maïte Lafourcade. Bayonne: Faculté pluridisciplinaire de Bayonne-Anglet-Biarritz, 1993.

———. "Les séfarades dans la France moderne (XVIe–XVIIIe siecles)." *Nouveaux Cahiers* 62 (1980): 16–25.

———. "The Sephardim of France." *The Sephardi Heritage.* Ed. R. D. Barnett and W. M. Schwab. 2 vols. Grendon: Gibraltar Books, 1989.

Nalle, Sara T. *God in La Mancha: Religious Reform and the People of Cuenca, 1500–1650.* Baltimore: Johns Hopkins University Press, 1992.

Netanyahu, Benzion. *The Marranos of Spain: From the Late 14th Century to the Early 16th Century, According to Contemporary Hebrew Sources.* 3rd ed. Rev. and exp. Ithaca, N.Y.: Cornell University Press, 1999.

———. "Sánchez-Albornoz' View of Jewish History in Spain." *Toward the Inquisition: Essays on Jewish and Converso History in Late Medieval Spain.* Ithaca, N.Y.: Cornell University Press, 1997.

Novinsky, Anita, and Maria Luiza Tucci Carneiro, comps. *Inquisição: Ensaios sobre mentalidade, heresias, e arte.* Sao Paulo: EdUSP, 1992.

O'Callaghan, Joseph F. *A History of Medieval Spain.* Ithaca, N. Y.: Cornell University Press, 1975.

Oliel Grausz, Evelyne. "Relations et reseaux intercommunautaires dans la diaspora sefarade d'occident au XVIIIe siecle." Ph.D. diss., University of Paris, 1999.

Pelorson, Jean-Marc. "¿Cómo se representaba a sí misma la 'sociedad española' del 'siglo de oro'?" *La frustración de un imperio (1476–1714).* By Jean-Paul Le Flem et al. Barcelona: Editorial Labor, 1982.

Peña, Aniano. *Américo Castro y su visión de España y de Cervantes.* Madrid: Gredos, 1975.

Perceval, José María. *Todos son uno: Arquetipos, xenophobia, y racismo: La imagen del morisco en la monarquía española durante los siglos XVI y XVII.* Almería: Instituto de Estudios Almerienses, 1997.

Pérez Villanueva, Joaquín, ed. *La Inquisición española: Nueva visión, nuevos horizontes.* Mexico City: Siglo XXI, 1980.

Pérez Villanueva, Joaquín, and Bartolomé Escandell Bonet, eds. *Historia de la Inquisición en España y América.* 2 vols. Madrid: Biblioteca de Autores Cristianos, 1984–93.

Pulido Serrano, Juan Ignacio. *Injurias a Cristo: Religión, política y antijudaísmo en el siglo XVII: Análisis de las corrientes antijudías durante la edad moderna.* Alcalá de Henares: Insituto Internacional de Estudios Sefardíes y Andalusíes, Universidad de Alcalá, 2002.

Pullan, Brian. "The Inquisition and the Jews of Venice: The Case of Gaspare Ribeiro, 1580–1581." *Bulletin of the John Rylands University Library* 62 *(1979–80): 207–31.*

———. *The Jews of Europe and the Inquisition of Venice, 1550-1670.* Oxford: Blackwell, 1983.

———. "'A Ship with Two Rudders': Righetto Marrano and the Inquisition in Venice." *The Historical Journal,* 20.1 (1977): 25–58.

Real Academia Española. *Diccionario de la lengua española.* 21st ed. Madrid: Real Academia Española, 1992.

Révah, I. S. "Autobiographie d'un Marrane. édition Partielle d'un Manuscrit de João (Moseh) Pinto Delgado." *Revue des Etudes Juives* 119 (1961): 41-130.

———. "Les Marranes." *Revue des Etudes Juives* 118 (1959–60): 29–77.

———. "Un pamphlet contre l'Inquisition d'Antonio Enríquez Gómez: La Seconde Partie de la 'Politica Angélica' (Rouen, 1647)." *Revue des Etudes Juives,* n.s., 4.1 (1962): 83–168.

Ringrose, David. *Madrid and the Spanish Economy, 1560–1850.* Berkeley: University of California Press, 1983.

———. *Transportation and Economic Stagnation in Spain, 1750–1850.* Durham, N.C.: Duke University Press, 1970.

Rose, Constance H. "The Marranos of the Seventeenth Century and the Case of the Merchant Writer Antonio Enríquez Gómez." *The Spanish Inquisition and the Inquisitorial Mind.* Ed. Angel Alcalá. New York: Columbia University Press, 1987.

Roth, Cecil. *A History of the Marranos.* Philadelphia: Jewish Publication Society, 1932.

———. "Immanuel Aboab's Proselytization of the Marranos." *Jewish Quarterly Review,* n.s., 23 (1932–33): 121-62.

———. "Les Marranes à Rouen: Un chapitre ignoré de l'histoire des juifs de France." *Revue des Etudes Juives* 88(1929): 113-55.

———. "The Role of Spanish in the Marrano Diaspora." *Hispanic Studies in Honor of I. Fonzález Llubera.* Ed. Frank Pierce. Oxford: The Dolphin Book Co., 1959.

———. "The Strange Case of Hector Mendes Bravo." *Hebrew Union College Annual* 18 (1943–44): 221–45.

Roth, Norman. *Conversos, Inquisition, and the Expulsion of the Jews from Spain.* Madison: University of Wisconsin Press, 2002.

———. *Jews, Visigoths and Muslims in Medieval Spain: Cooperation and Conflict.* Leiden: E. J. Brill, 1994.

Saitta, Biagio. *L'Antisemitismo nella Spagna Visogotica.* Rome: "L'Erma" di Bretschneider, 1995.

Salomon, H. P. "The Case of Luis Vaz Pimentel: Revelations of Early Jewish Life in

Rotterdam from the Portuguese Inquisition Archives." *Studia Rosenthaliana* 31 (1997): 7–30.

———. *Portrait of a New Christian: Fernão Alvares Melo (1569–1632)*. Paris: Fundação Calouste Gulbenkian, Centro Cultural Portugues,1982.

——— . *Le Procès de l'inquisition Portugaise comme documents littéraires, ou du bon usage du fonds inquisitorial de la Torre do Tombo*. Lisbon: Torre do Tombo and Estudos Portugueses-Homenagem a António José Saraiva, 1990.

Samuel, Edgar R. "The Trade of the New Christians of Portugal in the Seventeenth Century." *The Sephardi Heritage*. Ed. by R. D. Barnett and W. M. Schwab. Vol. 2. Grendon: Gibraltar Books, 1989.

Sánchez Albornoz, Claudio. *España, un enigma histórico*. 2 vols. Buenos Aires: Editorial Sudamericana, 1962.

Sánchez, Magdalena, and Alain Saint-Saens, eds. *Spanish Women in the Golden Age: Images and Realities*. Westport, Conn.: Greenwood Press, 1996.

Saraiva, António José. *Inquisição e cristãos-novos*. 5th ed. Lisbon: Editorial Estampa, 1994.

Schreiber, Markus. "Cristianos Nuevos de Madrid." *Historia de la Inquisicíon en España y América*. Madrid: Biblioteca de Autores Cristianos, 2000.

Schwartzfuchs, Simón. "Le Retour des Marranes au Judaisme dans la littérature rabbinique." *Xudeus e Conversos na Historia, Actas do Congreso Internacional Ribadavia, 14–17 de outubro de 1991*. Ed. Carlos Barros. Santiago de Compostela: La Editorial de la Historia, 1994.

Selke, Elke. "El iluminismo de los conversos y la Inquisición: Cristianismo interior de los Alumbrados: Resentimiento y Sublimación." *La Inquisición española: Nueva visión, Nuevos horizontes*. Ed. Joaquín Pérez Villanueva. Mexico City: Siglo XXI, 1980.

Sennet, Richard. *Authority*. New York: W. W. Norton, 1980.

Sicroff, Albert A. *Los Estatutos de Limpieza de Sangre: Controversias entre los siglos XV y XVII*. Trans. Mauro Armiño. Madrid: Taurus, 1985.

Sieber, Claudia W. "The Invention of a Capital: Philip II and the First Reform of Madrid." Ph.D. diss., Johns Hopkins University, 1985.

Simon, Marcel. "Christian Anti-Semitism." *Essential Papers on Judaism and Christianity in Conflict: From Late Antiquity to the Reformation*. Ed. Jeremy Cohen. New York: New York University Press, 1991.

Stuczynski, Claude B. "Libros y técnicas de lectura entre los cristianos nuevos portugueses: El caso de Bragança, siglo XVI." Working Paper, A Literatura Judaico-Portuguesa, Cursos da Arrábida, Arrábida, Portugal, July 22, 1997.

Surtz, Ronald E., Jaime Ferrán, and Daniel P. Testa, eds. *Américo Castro: The Impact of His Thought: Essays to Mark the Centenary of His Birth*. Madison, Wis.: Hispanic Seminary of Medieval Studies, 1988.

Swetchinski, Daniel. "Kinship and Commerce: The Foundation of Portuguese Jewish Life in Seventeenth-Century Holland." *Studia Rosenthaliana* 12 (1978): 55–87.

Szajkowski, Zosa. "An Autodafé against the Jews of Tolouse in 1685." *Jewish Quarterly Review*, n.s., 49 (1958–59): 278–81.

———. "The Marranos and Sephardim of France." *Abraham Weiss Jubilee Volume*. New York: n.p., 1964.

————. "Population Problems of Marranos and Sephardim in France, from the 16th to the 20th Centuries." *Proceedings of the American Academy for Jewish Research* 27 (1958): 83–105.

————. "Trade Relations of Marranos in France with the Iberian Peninsula in the Sixteenth and Seventeenth Centuries." *Jewish Quarterly Review* 50.1 (1959): 69–78.

Tentler, Thomas N. *Sin and Confession on the Eve of the Reformation.* Princeton, N.J.: Princeton University Press, 1977.

Thompson, I. A. A., and Bartolomé Yun Casalilla, eds. *The Castilian Crisis of the Seventeenth Century: New Perspectives on the Economic and Social History of Seventeenth-Century Spain.* Cambridge: Cambridge University Press, 1994.

Tishby, Isaiah. "New Information about the Community of Conversos in London According to the Letters of Sasportas of 1665" (in Hebrew). *Galut Ahar Golah: Studies in Jewish History Presented to Professor Haim Beinart in Honor of his Seventieth Year.* Ed. Aaron Mirsky, Avraham Grossman, and Yosef Kaplan. Jerusalem: Mehkon Ben-Tsevi le-heker kehilot Yisra'el ba-Mizrah, 1988.

Trachtenberg, Joshua. *The Devil and the Jews: The Medieval Conception of the Jew and Its Relation to Modern Antisemitism.* 2nd ed. New York: Meridian, 1943.

Van Praag, J. A. "Almas en Litigio." *Clavileño* 1 (1950): 14–26.

Vassberg, David. *The Village and the Outside World in Golden Age Castile: Mobility and Migration in Everyday Rural Life.* Cambridge: Cambridge University Press, 1996.

Wilke, Carsten Lorenz. "Conversion our retour? La métamorphose du nuveau chrétien en juif portugais dans l'imaginaire sépharade du XVIIe siècle." *Memoires juives d'Espagne et du Portugal,* ed. Esther Benbassa. Paris: PUBLISUD, 1996.

————. *Jüdisch-christliches Doppelleben im Barock: Zur Biographie des Kaufmanns und Dichters Antonio Enríquez Gómez.* New York: Peter Lang, 1994.

Willemse, David. Introduction. *Un portugués entre los castellanos: El primer proceso inquisitorial contra Gonzalo Báez de Paiba, 1654–1657.* Paris: Fundação Calouste Gulbenkian, 1974.

Yerushalmi, Yosef Hayim. "Conversos Returning to Judaism in the Seventeenth Century: Their Jewish Knowledge and Psychological Readiness" (in Hebrew). *Proceedings of the Fifth World Congress of Jewish Studies.* 4 vols. Jerusalem: World Union of Jewish Studies, 1972.

————. *From Spanish Court to Italian Ghetto: Isaac Cardoso: A Study in Seventeenth-Century Marranism and Jewish Apologetics.* New York: Columbia University. Press, 1971.

————. *The Lisbon Massacre of 1506 and the Royal Image in the Shebet Yehudah.* Hebrew Union College Annual Supplements 1. Cincinnati: Hebrew Union College, 1976.

————. "Professing Jews in Post-Expulsion Spain and Portugal." *Salo Wittmayer Baron Jubilee Volume.* New York: Columbia University Press, 1974.

————. "The Re-education of Marranos in the Seventeenth Century." *The Third Annual Rabbi Louis Feinberg Memorial Lecture in Judaic Studies, March 26, 1980.* Cincinnati: University of Cincinnati, 1980.

Yovel, Yirmiyahu. "The New Otherness: Marrano Dualities in the First Generation."

The 1999 *Swig Lecture, September 13, 1999.* San Francisco: The Swig Judaic Studies Program at the University of San Francisco, 1999.

Yuval, Israel Jacob. "Yitzhak Baer and the Search for Authentic Judaism." *The Jewish Past Revisited: Reflections on Modern Jewish Historians.* Ed. David N. Myers and David B. Ruderman. New Haven, Conn.: Yale University Press, 1998.

Zagorin, Perez. *Ways of Lying: Dissimulation, Persecution, and Conformity in Early Modern Europe.* Cambridge, Mass.: Harvard University Press, 1990.

Zink, Anne. "Bayonne arrives et departs au XVIIe siècle." *1492: L'expulsion des juifs d'Espagne.* Ed. Roland Goetschel. Paris: Maisonneuve et Larosse, 1996.

———. "La Comunidad judía de Bayona y su contexto." *El Olivo* 49 (1999): 55–64.

———. "L'Activité des juifs de Bayonne dans la seconde moitié du XVIIe siecle." *L'exode des juifs d'Espagne vers Bayonne: Des rives de l'Ebre et du Tage à celles de l'Adour.* Comp. Maïté Lafourcade. Bayonne: Faculté pluridisciplinaire de Bayonne-Anglet-Biarritz, 1993.

———. "Une Niche juridique: L'installation des juifs à Saint-Esprit-lès-Bayonne au XVIIe siècle." *Annales, Histoire, Science Sociales* 49.3 (1994): 639–69.

Index

Aboab, Rabbi Immanuel, 103, 216 n.22
Acosta, Luis de, 130
Aguila, João de, 91–92
Aguilar, Francisco de, 125
"Although he sins he is a Jew," 2, 191 n.4
Alvares Melo, Fernão, 163, 191 n.5, 227 n.27
Alvarez, Catalina de, 94, 123
Alvarez, Fernando, 92–99, 123
Alvarez, Pedro, 92, 94
Amidah ("Amidad"), 147. *See also*
    Crypto-Judaism
Amsterdam: converso returnees from
    France contrasted with those from,
    79; as a destination for converso
    exiles, 68; growth of Jewish
    community (1612–20), 225 n.124;
    Jewish authorities' outlook and
    regulations against return to Iberia,
    72–73; official Sephardi opposition to
    the immigration of Jewish paupers,
    216 n.21; return to Iberia from, 77–78,
    84; and Sephardi economic networks,
    78; Sephardi *ma'amad* and the
    problem of religious indiscipline, 221
    n.70
Andalusia, 84–87
Antequera, 144–46
Anti-converso sentiment and behavior:
    allegation that conversos subverted
    the Iberian class system, 44;
    ascription of materialism to
    conversos, 44; associated with
    prejudice against merchants and
    commerce, 44, 221 n.74, 228 n.29;
    blood libels and desecration libels,

59, 212 n.149; and conversos'
ethnicity, 50; conversos reputed to
want to escape to France, 64; directed
against "Portuguese of the Nation,"
48; economic dimension and
attendant stereotypes, 48–49;
essentialist and Judeophobic
character, 48; expressed as anti-
Portuguese prejudice in Spain, 21, 50;
euphemisms and related anti-
converso terminology, 206 n.99;
generalized suspicions against
conversos, 191 n.5; impact upon social
atmosphere in Spain, 1–3, 50, 66;
internalization of anti-converso
sentiment by New Christians,
227 n.27; Judeophobic folklore
and "learned" treatises, 61–62, 211–12
n.141; low reputation of converso
émigrés to France, 227 n.27; mob
violence against conversos, 209
nn.111–12; in Portugal, 44; as a
product of conditions in
seventeenth-century Iberia, 60;
racialization of, 49, 53; rhetorical
peculiarities (e.g., "semantic
slippage"), 48, 53, 209 n.106. *See also*
Purity of blood
Antwerp, 77
Apostates, 5, 8
Aragon, 22, 67, 199 n.1
Atlantic Pyrennees. *See* Basque country;
    Bayonne; Saint Esprit-lès-Bayonne;
    Southwestern France
Avila, Isaac de, 151, 232 n.7

Baer, Yitzhak, 8–10, 193 n.19, 194 n.21

Báez de Paiba, Gonzalo, 85–87

Bankruptcy: as impetus for moving to and from Iberia, 85. *See also* Economic profile and activities of conversos

Baptism, 93. *See also* Circumcision

Basque country, 66–67, 199 n.1. *See also* Southwestern France

Bay of Biscay, 69 (Map 2), 70

Bayonne, 69 (Map 2), 124; access and spatial relation to borderland routes, 67–68; as place of settlement for Iberian exiles, 66; relative scale and importance of its mercantile economy, 79; return to Iberia from, 77, 88, 92, 141. *See also* Basque country; Saint Esprit-les-Bayonne; Southwestern France

Beinart, Haim, 11, 64, 194 nn. 30, 34, 197 n.41

Ben Israel, Abraham, 151

Bernal de Caño family, 56

Bertaut, François, 36, 204 n.48

Biarritz, 66–67, 69 (Map 2)

Bidache, 66

Bilbao, 33, 69 (Map 2)

Blázquez Miguel, Juan, 96

Bordeaux: economic status of Portuguese converso population, 68; return to Iberia from, 77–78

Boyajian, James, 11, 194 n.30, 201 n.15

Braganza, 22

Brazil, 77

Breve discurso contra a heretica perfidia do Iudaismo. See Costa Mattos, Vicente de

Brunel, Antoine de, 32

Burgos, 69 (Map 2)

Burguete, 67, 69 (Map 2)

Businessmen. *See* Economic profile and activities of conversos

Cádiz, 33, 42–43, 49, 84

Cañizáres, José de, 59

Cardoso de Velasco, Aldonza, 15, 121

Cardoso Ortiz, Francisco, 134, 140–41

Caro Baroja, Julio, 10, 193 n.13, 222 n.87

Carpentras, 66

Casta y Generación, 121, 126

Castile, 20–22, 199 n.1; access to French southwestern borderlands from, 67

Castilian, use of the language among conversos, 98, 121

Castilla, Don Diego Manuel de, 41

Castro, Américo, 8–9, 11, 193 n.18, 194 n.19

Catalonia, 67, 199 n.1

Catholicism. *See* Ideology of Iberian Inquisitions

Cebada, Francisco Esteban de, 38

Centinela contra judíos. See Torejoncillo, Francisco de

Cervantes Saavedra, Miguel de, 60

Charles V (Holy Roman Emperor; Charles I of Castile), 20

Chocolate trade, 57, 88, 153

Christianization, 105. *See also* Judaicization; Renegades

Chronic returnees. *See* Renegades

Circumcision, 101, 148–49; conversos' "sacramental" understanding of, 93, 223 n.107

Coimbra, 22

Coloquio de los perros, El. See Cervantes Saavedra, Miguel de

Compra, Juan, 149, 152–54

Confession: depicted as spiritual "enlightenment," 116; adherence to and departure from narrative formulas of, 136; triggered by and interpreted in light of incarceration, 137–39. *See also* Ideology of Iberian Inquisitions; Structure and Procedures of Iberian Inquisitions

Confessionalization, 172. *See also* Judaicization

Contraband. *See* Economic profile and activities of conversos

Contreras Contreras, Jaime, 12, 195 nn.33–37

Contrition, 81, 157–58

Cordova, 88

Correa, Gonzalo, 124

Costa, Uriel da, 5, 97

Costa Mattos, Vicente de, 59, 62

Cotton trade, 88

Counter-Reformation, 24

Credo, the Christian, 39, 43

Cristo de la Paciencia Affair, 59. *See also* Anti-converso sentiment and behavior

Crypto-Judaism: allegations of bizarre "Jewish" rituals, 223 n.112; alleged fasting in observance of, 94, 223 n.108; anchored in ethnic community, not in religious ideation, 135–36; conversos' use of deception assessed, 46–47; denunciations as weapons in familial power struggles, 129, 131; initiations, 129, 131–33, 135, 146, 169–70, 229 n.40; modeled by proselytizers, 134–35; obscured by inquisitorial questioning, 133; opacity of the "Law of Moses" allegedly taught to conversos, 132, 230 n.65; possibility of its survival among Portuguese conversos, 50; religious interiorism and negation, 95, 148; "residual," 96, 132, 224 n.13; "sacramental" view of circumcision, 93, 223 n.107

Cuenca, 88, 92

Cultural history, 13

Cultural profile of conversos: called "of the Nation," 43–44; conversos as chroniclers of their own lives, 225 n.2.; conversos in the clergy, 54; cultural liminality, 2–4, 106, 171; deceit attributed to them, 171; diversity of rabbinical opinions on their Jewishness, 217 n.28; endogamy, 52; ethnic ties and solidarity, 52, 75–76, 101; general contrast between history of Castilian and Portuguese conversos,

50–53, 224 n.118; and geographic mobility, 127, 139, 216 n.22; heterodoxy among, 3, 192 nn.7–8; historical use(s) of the term "converso," 191 n.3; historiography depicting conversos as inherently "Jewish," 64; Ibericization and Hispanicity, 57, 98; intellectuals, 11, 193 n.15; and ironic skepticism, 174; martyrdom, 217 n.29; Portuguese as diasporic *lingua franca*, 98; responses to coercion, 106; social and religious indiscipline, 76; social pressure to conform, 90, 93, 96–97, 99–101, 104; sociological study of their ethnic ties, 210 n.117. *See also* Anti-converso sentiment and behavior; Crypto-Judaism; Economic profile and activities of conversos; Exile; Judaicization; Judeophobia

Curaçao, 4

D'Aguilar, Moses Raphael, 73, 103

Dax, 66–67

"Decline" of Spain. *See* Habsburg Spain

Día Grande, 148. *See also* Crypto-Judaism; Rodríguez de Amézquita, Antonio

Diaspora. *See* Amsterdam; Exile; Judaicization; Southwestern France

Díaz, Ana, 121, 123

Díaz Gutiérrez, Felipe, 72

Díaz Méndez, Francisco, 85, 87, 217 n.27

Discurso de su vida, 112. See also *Discursos*; Protocol of Iberian Inquisitions

Discursos: equivocal responses regarding "stock and origin," 126–28; reflective of generational estrangement and familial strife among conversos, 128; relative credibility of portrayal of Judaizers, 135. *See also* Protocol of Iberian Inquisitions

Domínguez Ortiz, Antonio, 10, 12, 55, 201 n.20

Duke of Pastrana, 153–54
Dutch-French-Spanish trading network, 87. *See also* Economic profile and activities of conversos; Southwestern France
Dutch Provinces, 26, 199 n.2

Ecija, 88
Economic profile and activities of conversos: bankers and financiers, 11; collective wealth of Portuguese conversos, 22; continuation of Portuguese Jews' economic roles by Portuguese conversos, 52; crucial role of Portuguese conversos in Habsburg economy, 58; economic coordination among Portuguese conversos, 52; integration into Iberian economy, 55; merchants, contractors, and "businessmen" (*hombres de negocios* or *homens de negocios*), 22, 36, 54–56, 125; range of occupations, 4; Sephardi communal charity and assistance for resettlement in the Diaspora, 68, 156; smuggling networks, 70, 220 n.56, 226 n.12; trading activities as historical matrix of religious equivocation, 70. *See also* Anti-converso sentiment and behavior
Enríquez, Manuel, 84
Enríquez Gómez, Antonio, 163, 196 n.40, 198 n.51, 224 n.118
Erasmianism, 3
Escobar de Corro, Juan, 60
Espina, Alonso de, 5
Exile of conversos within and from Iberia: conversos' search for familiar cultures and community in exile, 99–100; logistical and other obstacles to emigration from Iberian realms, 66; migrations from Portugal to Spain, 21–23; property lost and/or expropriated by Inquisition, 68, 80–81. *See also* Cultural profile of

conversos; France; Judaicization; Saint Esprit-les-Bayonne; Southwestern France
Extremadura, 199 n.1

Faingold, Reuven, 13
Ferdinand I of Aragon, 34
Fernández, Simon, 56–57
Fernández de Castro, Jorge, 81, 137, 141
France, 6, 13, 23; as an attractive destination for conversos, 65; civil wars, 199 n.2; conditions of converso settlement in the southwest, 67; emigration by "Portuguese of the Nation," 65; war with Spain, 68. *See also* Basque country; Bayonne; Saint Esprit-les-Bayonne; Southwestern France
Furtado, Vicente, 13

Galicia, 143, 199 n.1
García, Román, 81–82
Gil de Espinosa, Fernando, 84, 87, 113, 138–39
Golden Age. *See* Golden Century of Spain
Golden Century of Spain, 7–8, 24, 201 n.19
Goldish, Matt, 12, 195 n.34, 197 n.48
Gómez, Diego, 149
Gómez, Jerónimo, 141
Gómez, Leonor, 87, 145–46, 150
Gómez Núñez, Domingo, 129
Gómez Tejadillos, Fernando, 94, 99
Graetz, Heinrich, 8
Guadalajara, 6
Guadalupe, 6

Habsburg Spain: conquest of Portugal, 21; "decline" and structural deficiencies, 27–29, 63, 202 n.28, 204 n.64, 205 nn. 66, 85; economy and geopolitical hegemony, 19–20, 24; famine, poor urban infrastructure, and demographic loss, 28; fiscal crisis,

203 n.41; overall and local economic resiliency, 33, 202 n.29; reports of rural lawlessness, 206 n.89; views of its religious character, supposed mission and destiny, 25–26; views of status of women, 229 n.42. *See also* Madrid; Road networks of Spain

Halakhah, 102. *See also* Identity construction among conversos; Judaicization

Hamburg, 68, 73

Henríquez Peteño, Pedro, 133

Herder, Johann Gottfried von, 9

Hernández, Gabriel, 101

Hidalgo, 42–43

Hispania, 20, 200 n.3

Historiography on conversos: approach pursued here to inquisitorial testimonies, 14–16; focusing on Franco-Sephardim, 13–14; since the 1960s, 9–12; to the 1960s, 8–9. *See also* Cultural history; Jerusalem School; Social history

Hombres (*Homens de negocios*). *See* Economic profile and activities of conversos

Huerta, Friar Anselmo de la, 38, 45

Huete, 88

Identity construction among conversos: compulsory socialization to suppress cultural duality, 172; conversos as "potential Jews" and "potential Christians," 171–72; doubt as an alleged cause of religious equivocation, 137; flight from Iberia interpreted as a sign of "intense Jewish commitment," 213 n.2; Hispanicity as a factor in, 98; the imposture case of Martin Guerre, 233 n.17; the question of conversos' "Jewishness," 2–3, 12–13, 15; as self-subjugation, 136, 173–74; social liminality sustainable through travel, 172. *See also* Cultural profile of

conversos; Judaicization

Ideology of Iberian Inquisitions: and coerced testimony, 116; and concepts of lineage, 116–17; and the imprint of colloquial misconceptions, 118; institutionalized bias against conversos, 119; logical inconsistency and attempts to harmonize ideals of purity of blood and purity of faith, 118–19; quest for thorough subjugation of the souls of sinners, 120; religious bases and assumptions, 115–18; and the spiritual transformation of convicts, 115

Indies, 144

Informers, medieval, 193 n.12. *See also* Renegades

Inquisition: Spanish and Portuguese Tribunals contrasted, 23, 108–9, 200 n.6. *See also* Ideology of Iberian Inquisitions; Inquisitorial Tribunals of Portugal; Inquisitorial Tribunal of Toledo; Protocol of Iberian Inquisitions; Structure and Procedures of Iberian Inquisitions

Inquisitorial Tribunals of Portugal, 21; assessing the reliability of the testimony collected by, 107–9; Coimbra, 128; Goa, 100; Lisbon, 91; Porto, 200 n.6; relative prosecutorial harshness of, 23, 200 n.6. *See also* Protocol of Iberian Inquisitions

Inquisitorial Tribunal of Toledo: investigations of petty "Portuguese" businessmen, 57; peaks of activity against "Judaizers," 200 n.6; spying in Rouen, 226 n.12

Irún, 69 (Map 2), 87

Isabel I of Castile, 34

Israel, Jonathan I., 11, 70, 195, n.36

Jerusalem School, 9

Jews: conversion to Christianity among Portuguese and Spanish, 51–52;

Jews (*cont.*)
  sixteenth-century Spanish definition,
    228 n.28
João III of Portugal, 52
Joly, Barthélemy, 32, 205 n.85
Judaicization: alleged threats of forced
    circumcision, 231 n.73; anchored in
    the existence of ethnic community
    and on circumstance, not on religious
    ideation, 135–36; confusion and
    ignorance of normative Judaism
    among conversos, 219 n.44; contrast
    between inquisitorial coercion and
    Jewish social pressure, 219 n.43;
    converso renegades and the option of
    conformity, 173; conversos' social
    liminality as a challenge to the ideal
    of integral identity, 173; double
    meaning of *reducción* as a key to
    understanding, 136; educational role
    of Jewish emissaries and self-styled
    missionaries to conversos, 75, 217 n.29;
    ethnic and communal bases of, 135;
    familial pressure as means of
    enforcing discipline, 133–35; fear of
    "renegades" among Judaicized
    conversos, 101; liturgy taught to
    conversos in Spanish, 222 n.75;
    materialism, pragmatism, and
    religiosity as factors in, 234 n.25; as
    natural outcome of conversos'
    supposedly inherent Jewishness,
    64–65, 76; reeducation in Judaism, 74;
    reflected in *discursos*, 128; and the self-
    perception of newly Judaicized
    converso émigrés in Amsterdam, 233
    n.15; social discipline through
    marriage, 134–35; and societal
    expectations and local convention in
    exiles' decision to conform, 133, 173;
    threat of sanctions as means to social
    discipline, 101, 126, 230–31 n.73; use of
    the term in this study, 198 n.50
Judaizing, sixteenth-century Spanish

  definition of, 228 n.28. *See also*
    Crypto-Judaism
Judeophobia: accusation and literary
    motif of whipping Christ's effigy, 59.
    See also Anti-converso sentiment and
    activity
Juderías, 8
Judíos antiguos ("Old Jews"), 141

Kamen, Henry, 62
Kaplan, Yosef, 5, 10, 12, 13, 72, 78, 193 n.13,
    217 n.28

La Coruña, 33
La Rochelle, 67, 141
Labastide-Clairence, 66
Lands of Apostasy. *See* Lands of Idolatry
Lands of Idolatry, 12, 76, 103
Law of Moses: contrasted with Law of
    Grace, 233 n.20; observed in greater
    Bayonne, 75, 91–92. *See also*
    Judaicization
Leghorn. *See* Livorno
Leon, 199 n.1
Leon, Manuel de, 91
Lerma, Duke of, 22
Les Landes, 66. *See also* Southwestern
    France
Lima, Diego de, 137
Limpieza de sangre. See Purity of blood
Linens trade, 88. *See also* Economic
    profile and activities of conversos
Lisbon, 12, 22, 33, 42
Livorno, 73, 140, 151
Logroño, 67, 69 (Map 2)
London, 12, 73
López, Ana, 143
López, Francisco, 92, 94
López, Simon, 149–50
López Capadocia, Francisco, 80, 83
Lorca, 12

Machuca, Manuel, 101
Madrid, 29; areas of Portuguese

settlement, 211 n.135; centrality to Iberian trade networks, 33; condition of roads leading to, 34; as consumption-oriented magnet for imports, 32; converso merchants in, 56–57; critiques by *arbitristas*, 32; demographic growth and limitations of urban infrastructure, 29–31; dependence on external supplies, 30–32; economic opportunities it offered to conversos, 32; in inquisitorial jurisdiction, 6; physical condition, 30–31; returnees arrested in, 6; in the travels of various inquisitorial suspects, 87, 123, 140, 145, 169 (*see also individual names of suspects*); ultimate economic resiliency and dynamism, 32; underdevelopment of export markets, 30; urban underclass and crime, 31–32

Málaga, 33, 80, 88, 146

Malsín(es), 17, 128, 131, 198–99 n.51. *See also* Renegades

Manuel Gómez, 76

Martínez, Magdalena, 41

Mártir, Pedro, 38–41, 206 n.92

Medina del Campo, 35 (Map 1), 80

Méndez, Rafael, 99, 135

Méndez Cardoso, Manuel, 121, 216 n.22

Méndez Silveira, Cristobal, 1, 122, 136, 138–39

Merchants. *See* Economic profile and activities of conversos; Renegades

Meshummad, 199 n.51

Methodology, 14–15, 197–98 n.49, 232 n.9

Millones, 44, 206 n.100

Mogadouro, 144

Monte, Antonio del, 126

Montesinos, Duarte, 129–31

Moriscos, 28, 191 n.3, 203 n.45

Morteira, Saul Levi, 91–92

Murcia, 12, 199 n.1

Nahon, Gerard, 13–14, 196 n.41, 214 nn. 10, 14

Nantes, 66–67, 215 n.16

Naples, 27

Navarre, 22, 69 (Map 2), 199 n.1

Netanyahu, Benzion, 9, 194 n.22

Netherlands: economic history of the, 8. *See also* Amsterdam; Economic profile and activities of conversos; Renegades

New Jews. *See* Judaicization; Renegades

Núñez Redondo, Francisco, 83, 87, 133

Olivares, Count-Duque of, 118, 226 n.12

Order of Christ, 42, 45

Order of Santiago, 41

Páez de Santi, Antonio, 45, 207–8 n.104

Paiba, Catalina de, 86

Pamplona, 67, 69 (Map 2), 91

Paniagua, Joseph, 42

Pan y Agua, Mathias, 40

Paraíba, 141. *See also* Brazil

Pardons, of Portuguese conversos, 22

Pasaña, Josepha María de, 124

Pasaña, Manuel, 123

Pastrana, 152–54

Paz, Cristobal de, 169

Paz, Enrique de, 129–31

Perceval, José Maria, 61, 203 n.45

Pereira de Castro y Moscoso, Diego: assailed as a "Portuguese Jew" by his traveling companions, 38–42; assessment of his credibility, 45–48, 207–9 n.103; claims noble lineage and "clean" blood, 42–43; relates and justifies his own abuse of merchants "of the Nation," 43–44. *See also* Anti-converso sentiment and behavior

Pereyra, Enríquez, 84

Pérez, Barbol, 125

Permanent returnees. *See* Renegades

Pernambuco, 141

Perpignan, 68

Persuasiones, 124, 147. *See also* Judaicization

Peyrehorade, 66, 91, 101, 141. *See also* Exile; Southwestern France

Philip II of Spain, 20–21, 25, 29

Philip IV of Spain, 11, 22–23, 27, 55, 58, 168, 201 n.18

Pícaros, 19, 30–32, 43–44, 162–63

Piñero family, 56

Porto, 33, 144

Portugal, history: conquest and partial administration by Spain, 20–21; and Portuguese conversos to 1536, 50–51; war of secession from Spain, 42. See also Inquisitorial Tribunals of Portugal

"Portuguese of the Nation," 53, 58

Procesos, 14. See also Protocol of Iberian Inquisitions; Structure and Procedures of Iberian Inquisitions

Protestantism, 24, 112

Protocol of Iberian Inquisitions, 107; admonitions, 113; with regard to auricular confession, 114; assessment of the credibility of typical discursos, 122–23, 126; collection of genealogical data, 110; discurso de su vida, 112; familial ties described in discursos, 122–23; informants' possible confusion and/or ignorance regarding questions of "stock and origin," 121, 128; instrumentality of "declaração" in Portuguese trials, 108; and jurisdiction over suspects, 111; nature and purposes of audiencias, 110; Portuguese and Spanish interrogations contrasted, 109, 111; protocol following confessions, 114; relative (dis)interest in the commercial transactions of informants, 112; survey of suspects' contacts outside the Iberian Peninsula, 111; survey of suspects' religious education, 111; with regard to suspects' motivations, 114; typical responses to standard questions and variety apparent in discursos, 120–22

Pruebas de Limpieza, 4, 42, 46. See also Anti-converso sentiment and behavior; Purity of blood

Pullan, Brian, 11, 195 n.31

Pureza de fe. See Purity of faith

Pureza de sangre. See Purity of blood

Purity of blood, 2–4, 42, 46, 60, 62, 117–18, 127–28. See also Anti-converso sentiment and behavior; Ideology of Iberian Inquisitions; Protocol of Iberian Inquisitions

Purity of faith, 115, 117–18. See also Ideology of Iberian Inquisitions

Pyrénées-Atlantiques, 66–68, 172, 215–16 n.20. See also Bayonne; Saint Esprit-les-Bayonne; Southwestern France

Quiñones, Juan de, 59, 64

Reconquista, 20, 24

Reducción, 124. See also Judaicization

Religion: anthropological views of, 168; defined, 97

Renegades: approach to religious "truth," 174; approach to their own religious equivocation, 102; and bankruptcy while traveling in Iberia, 140; challenge to Jewish communal ideals, 76; chief behavioral patterns, 171; chronic (or habitual) and permanent returnees defined and contrasted, 77; condemned by rabbinic authorities, 103; contingency of their social and religious identities, 176; correspondence with Amsterdam's Sephardi trade network, 78; credibility of chronic returnees evaluated, 81–83, 87; cultural flexibility relative to that of non-conversos, 175; the difficulty of quantifying incidence of, 220 n.52; dimensions of the phenomenon of renegade behavior, as surveyed here, 77; economic motives, 76, 78, 80; general sociological profile, 77; geographic mobility and cultural transience, 139–40; indigent and wealthier returnees compared and contrasted, 89; and inquisitorial surveillance, 80; and ironic skepticism of modern outlooks, 174; mass denunciation by, 82; merchandise handled and geographic scope of commercial activities, 79–80; motivations of permanent returnees, 89–91, 92, 97–100, 102–4; not "exotic," 177; the paradox of their economic integration and acculturation coupled with their social marginalization, 176; perceived affronts to orthodox Catholicism and normative Judaism, 71–72; places of origin in the Sephardi Diaspora, 77, 81, 84; possible testimonial strategies of, 82–83; quotidian nature of return, 102, 230 n.72; relative demographic weight in greater Bayonne (mid-1600s), 78; reliability of their claims assessed, 91–92, 95–104; returnees as economic refugees, 103, 123; returnees from southwestern France and Amsterdam contrasted, 79; returnees viewed as overly idealistic and disillusioned Jews, 64–65; self-denunciation, 90; self-subjugation as pragmatic acculturation, 174, 177; their place in history of social disciplining and confessionalization, 175; their rationalization of conformity, 173–74; types of traders among chronic returnees, 79; viewed as "strange," 213 n.6; women among returnees, 90. See also *Malsín(es)*

Returnees. *See* Renegades

Révah, Israel Salvator, 10, 12; position on crypto-Judaism among conversos, 194 n.27, 197 n.48; view of the "Jewishness" of conversos and his debt to Carl Gebhardt, 213 n.3

Rioseco, 80

Rivadeneria, Pedro de, 24–25

Road networks of Spain: in the Basque country, 33; caravan traffic, 34; commercial roads, 23, 29; condition of roads leading to Madrid, 34; convergence of major routes in Madrid, 33; customs and other costs of commercial travel, 36; danger and social disorder in the, 36–37, 41; desolation, 37; first builders of the, 34; Habsburgs' expenditures on, 204 n.54; insufficiency of upkeep in rural areas, 34; Madrid-Bayonne axis, 70; major trade routes depicted, 33, 35 (Map 1); marginal nature and attraction to the socially marginalized, 140; poor quality of lodging and food for travelers, 36; and rural xenophobia and protectionism, 37; seasonal use, 34

Rodríguez, Beatriz, 144, 146

Rodríguez, Francisco, 146–47

Rodríguez, Martin, 144, 146

Rodríguez Cardoso, Diego, 10, 88

Rodríguez de Amézquita, Antonio, 139–41; and abstract theology, 161; assessment of his testimony, 159–60, 162–63, 167; bankruptcy and Christian "enlightenment" in Zaragoza, 154–55; commercial activities and methods, 88, 141–42; and communities of faith, 164; compared to other renegades, 169; crypto-Judaic initiation, 146–47; crypto-Judaic practices in Spain, 146, 148; description of his physique and speech, 143; emigration to France, 88, 149; factors conducive to his conformity, 165; final confession and renunciation of Judaism, 157–58; genealogy and immediate family, 87–89, 143–46; his understanding of God's immanence and judgment, 166–67; initial failure to explicitly renounce Jewish belief, 156; inquisitorial sentence and its completion, 158; interpreted his fate in religious terms, 163–66, 168;

Rodríguez de Amézquita, Antonio (*cont.*) Judaicization in Saint Esprit, 149–51; knowledge of anti-Jewish, Christological exegesis, 157; materialism, pragmatism, and religious mindset combined, 168, 175; narrative construction of his identity, 160; option for conformity in Saint Esprit and Zaragoza, 163–64; prestige among New Jews, 88, 152; and the psychology of imprisonment, 166–67; receptiveness to predominant religious tastes, 163; reflection on his own transience, 167; religious behavior while self-depiction as an unlearned man and imputation of authority to religious experts, 148, 161–63; and religious cynicism, 162; traveling in Iberia, 88, 149; travels in Iberia after emigration to France, 152–53; travels in the peninsula before emigration to France, 88

Rodríguez de Leon, Diego, 169
Rodríguez Lopes, Balthasar, 143, 145
Rome, 77
Rosh ha-Shanah (Rosaná), 169. *See also* Crypto-Judaism
Roth, Cecil, 12, 192 n.6, 195 n.32, 197 n.48
Rouen, 12, 68, 77–78, 85, 226 n.12
Roussillon, 68

Sabbath, 149
Saffron trade, 88
Saint Esprit-les-Bayonne, 66, 86, 91, 140; dating the social and religious cohesiveness of its New Jewish enclave, 224 n.114; economic status of converso population, 68; evidence of religious laxity among Iberian émigrés, 151–52; poverty of converso population assessed, 214 n.14; as reputed refuge for Iberian Judaizers, 121, 125; rituals and religious practices

of Judeo-Portuguese community, 151; role of emissaries in Judaicization, 151. *See also* Bayonne; Exile; Renegades; Rodríguez de Amézquita, Antonio; Southwestern France

Salazar, Juan de, 25
Salomon, Herman Prins, 10, 191 n.5, 194 n.25, 201 nn. 11, 14
Sánchez Albornoz, Claudio, 8–9, 193 n.20
Sánchez, Joseph, 80
San Sebastián, 85
Santa Fe, Gerónimo de, 8
Santa María, Pablo de, 8
Sao João de Pesqueria, 145
Saraiva, José António, 109, 192 n.9, 194 n.27
Scholem, Gershom, 10
Sebastian I of Portugal, 20
Seville, 33, 40, 43, 49, 84, 92, 144, 147
Shema Israel ("semá"), 75, 146, 148. *See also* Crypto-Judaism; Judaicization
Sicily, 27
Sierra, María de, 59
Silva, Violante da, 146
Simon de Solís, 81
Simon Fernández, 63
Social history, 11
Soria, 152
Southwestern France, 27; contiguity with Spanish road networks, 68; converso demography and settlement patterns, 66–67; the cultural liminality of local converso colonies, 73; economic hardship among converso settlers, 73, 216 n.22; evidence surveyed of return by local conversos to Iberia, 77; and historiography on Franco-Sephardim, 13–14; importance to Dutch and Dutch Sephardi trade with Spain, 70; Judeophobic persecution of "Portuguese" immigrants in Biarritz, 214–15 n.15; paucity of documentation attesting to Jewish communal life, 218 n.40; points of entry and routes into

Spain used by returnees, 217 n.27; and
   smuggling networks during Spanish
   embargoes, 70; socioeconomic origins
   of converso immigrants to, 68; as a
   "transit point" for conversos fleeing
   the Iberian Peninsula, 66
Spain, component kingdoms and
   territories, 199 n.1
Spinoza, Benedict, 5, 193 n.15
St. Jean de Luz, 66–67, 69 (Map 2); return
   to Iberia from, 78. *See also* Exile;
   Renegades; Southwestern France
St. Peter Martyr, confraternity of, 105
Structure and Procedures of Iberian
   Inquisitions: approach to confessants'
   contrition, 113–14; *audiencias*, 113;
   composition and personnel, 110;
   evaluation of "complete" and
   "incomplete" confessions, 114;
   familiars, 112; issuance of formal
   charges, 113; interrogators' skepticism,
   231 n.83; judicial torture and approach
   to testimony extracted, 113; light
   punishment of arch-denunciators, 113,
   226 n.17; "negative" or "denying"
   suspects, 113; presumption of guilt of
   suspect, 112; prosecution of minors,
   226 n.15; punishment and execution
   of convicts, 115; ratification of
   testimony, 113; recording of "stock and
   origin" of deponents, 229–30 n.55;
   surveillance of prisoners, 207–8 n.103;
   suspects' access to defense counsel
   and accusing witnesses, 113. *See also*
   Ideology of Iberian Inquisitions;
   Protocol of Iberian Inquisitions
Sugar trade, 87. *See also* Economic profile
   and activities of conversos
Szajkowski, Zosa, 13–14, 195 n.36

Tetouan, 141

Textiles trade, 57, 87. *See also* Economic
   profile and activities of conversos
Tishby, Isaiah, 13
Tobacco trade, 57, 123–24, 141. *See also*
   Economic profile and activities of
   conversos
Tocino, 39, 149
Toledo, 6, 40, 144. *See also* Inquisitorial
   Tribunal of Toledo
Tolosa, 69 (Map 2)
Tolouse, 67, 126
Torre, Fernando de la, 41
Torrejoncillo, Francisco de, 59, 63
Tridentine Catholicism, 172. *See also*
   Ideology of the Iberian Inquisitions
Trinitarian doctrine, 39, 161

Valencia, 199 n.1
Valladolid 34, 87, 143
Van Praag, Jakob, 10–11
Vassberg, David, 34, 37
Vega, Lope de, 59
Venice, 11; as destination of better-off
   converso exiles, 68; as place of origin
   of Jewish emissaries to conversos in
   France, 74; as place of origin of
   returnees, 77
Virgin Mary, 110, 133, 169
Visigothic heritage, 20
Vitoria, 67, 69 (Map 2)

Wool trade, 87

Yerushalmi, Yosef H., 10–11, 28–29, 201
   n.17, 213 n.2
Yovel, Yirmiyahu, 9

Zaragoza, 154–56
Zink, Anne, 13–14, 214 n.14

Acknowledgments

I am indebted to several people for their helpful review of early versions of the manuscript on which this book is based. Todd Endelman, Miriam Bodian, Tom Tentler, Diane Owen Hughes, Elliot Ginsburg, and Gabriele Boccaccini evaluated the work at its early stages. Stephanie Siegmund and Hillel Kieval read two early versions of chapters and provided encouraging comments. José Schraibman offered encouragement and invaluable procedural help. Dorothy Marschke provided such help in the administrative realm. Much later, Yosef Kaplan and Thomas Glick reviewed the manuscript for the University of Pennsylvania Press and provided incisive suggestions. I am very thankful for their enthusiastic approval of the work. Here and there I gathered additional encouragement from various individuals, although they probably do not realize it as most of them did not read the work and our interaction was very brief. They include Matt Goldish, Norman Stillman, and Joseph Abraham Levi. At the archives in Madrid I appreciated the camaraderie of Kathy Camp and Bethany Aram, and of Leo Cohen and Claude (Dov) Stuczynski at the Torre do Tombo, Lisbon. Martha Castleberry provided crucial help with the formatting of the appendix. My colleagues at the Committee on Judaic Studies at the University of Arizona, chief among them the committee's director, Ed Wright, fostered a nurturing and collegial environment in which to complete the project. Michelle Michelson gave me helpful comments and encouragement throughout the writing stages. I am responsible, though, for any errors found in this work.